INTERNATIONAL ECONOMIC LAW SERIES

General Editor: JOHN H. JACKSON

Development at the World Trade Organization

GW00385450

Development at the World Trade Organization

SONIA E. ROLLAND

OXFORD
UNIVERSITY PRESS

OXFORD
UNIVERSITY PRESS

Great Clarendon Street, Oxford OX2 6DP
United Kingdom

Oxford University Press is a department of the University of Oxford.
It furthers the University's objective of excellence in research, scholarship,
and education by publishing worldwide. Oxford is a registered trade mark of
Oxford University Press in the UK and in certain other countries

Published in the United States of America by Oxford University Press
198 Madison Avenue, New York, NY 10016, United States of America

British Library Cataloguing in Publication Data
Data available

Library of Congress Cataloguing in Publication Data
Data available

ISBN 978–0–19–960088–5
ISBN 978–0–19–968227–0 (pbk)

Typeset by Newgen Imaging Systems (P) Ltd, Chennai, India
Printed in Great Britain on acid-free paper by
CPI Group (UK) Ltd, Croydon, CR0 4YY

Preface to the Paperback Edition

In recent years, commentators and policy-makers alike have heralded the advent of a different era of international economic governance characterized by a post-Washington consensus ethos, the growing role of some emerging economies, and the proliferation of trade and investment agreements outside of the World Trade Organization (WTO). Indeed, the World Bank and other international agencies are embracing more holistic approaches to development. The BRICS countries and others have gained more weight in international economic relations, Russia has become a WTO member and most recently, a Brazilian national was chosen as the new Director General of the WTO. The number of bilateral and regional trade agreements has boomed at the same time that the WTO negotiations have stalled. China is challenging the traditional bilateral investment framework in proposing alternative models of trade and investment relations to many of its partners. Meanwhile, the Millennium Development Goals' target date of 2015 is looming large but achievements have fallen well short of the objectives. Income inequality has increased overall even as extreme poverty has receded. In some ways, then, the realities and policies of international economic governance and development have evolved, but in many ways, the issues and concerns offer a depressing continuity.

If we are at the dawn of a new era, albeit one with that comes with much baggage, what role might the WTO play in it? The new blueprint launched in May 2013 under the aegis of the United Nations dubbed "A New Global Partnership: Eradicate Poverty and Transform Economies through Sustainable Development" clearly posits the post-2015 development agenda in relation to trade and economic governance. The WTO, as the only global trade organization, is showing no sign of imminent dissolution. Its main disciplines, such as national treatment, the reduction of tariffs, most-favored nation treatment, and the current emphasis in trade facilitation rules are mirrored in the rules and agenda of most other trade agreements. Its dispute settlement system also gives it a unique standing in international economic law and even in international law more generally. As such, examining the trade and development relationship at the WTO remains an important part of the broader enquiry into the future of global economic governance and development policy.

One major issue must be raised at this juncture. The WTO has a weak explicit mandate regarding development. Some will therefore question whether the WTO is an appropriate forum for raising development questions, arguing that free trade in itself fosters development but that other impacts or shortcomings of trade liberalization for development should be considered elsewhere. Undeniably, the WTO was not created as a development agency, nor does it have the capacity to be one. The preamble to its founding document does, however, situate its purpose in relation to sustainable development. In practice, WTO rules unavoidably have an impact on development. The organization comprises over 75 percent developing members for which trade and development are inseparable in a much broader sense than simply an increase of overall economic wealth. Considering the trade and development relationship in the WTO legal framework, then, is not an ill-conceived attempt at turning the WTO into a development agency, but rather proceeds from a more fundamental query about the purpose of trade liberalization. As the preamble to the Marrakesh Agreement clearly establishes, the WTO is not pursuing trade liberalization for its own sake, but rather for the purpose of increasing the economic opportunities of its members in a way that is cognizant of sustainable development.

One contribution to this objective, then, is to better understand how the WTO legal framework affects development dynamics and opportunities for its members. Are there gaps between intended and actual effects of trade liberalization? Could WTO rules and institutions be realigned to better respond to the needs and demands of the various segments of the organization's membership? This book explores these critical issues with a view to providing concrete options for negotiators, tools for litigators and adjudicators, and a more coherent understanding of the trade and development relationship at the WTO in the longer term.

WTO rules affect developing members in three significant ways:

- Organizational and institutional rules govern how the WTO functions as a law-making institution and an adjudicatory body. These rules apply to all members (with some exceptions). Together with political processes, decision-making rules shape trade disciplines. WTO institutions govern how these rules are applied and enforced. Developing members' participation and access to the institution and processes are of fundamental importance if they are to influence the regulatory work-product. This book devotes significant analysis to the systemic impact of the WTO as an institution on developing members. The analysis will be of interest particularly to developing country policy-makers and representatives, to the WTO Secretariat, and to trade law and international relations scholars interested in institutional dynamics at the WTO.

- General trade rules and commitments (such as the most-favored nation rule, the national treatment obligation, general rules limiting subsidies, tariff reductions, etc.) affect developing members' trade relations with other members and constrain their domestic policies. These obligations apply uniformly to all members, though they sometimes affect developing members disproportionately. The WTO enshrines a preference for trade-led development. History suggests that overall, trade-oriented strategies have been more successful in terms of macro-economic growth. However, the specific effects of particular trade disciplines, such as tariff reductions, constraints on subsidies and other industrial policies, have much more complex development impacts that are not captured by national macroeconomic indicators. Some specific effects of the general rules will be discussed, but are not the main focus of this book. A fairly extensive literature already exists in the economics field but a more comprehensive study of the development impact of general trade liberalization rules would require interdisciplinary collaborations involving social sciences and economics analyses alongside the legal analysis.

- Specific development-oriented rules, known as special and differential treatment (SDT), apply only to developing members and Least Developed Country (LDC) members. They are exceptions from the general disciplines. This book presents a coherent and systematic analysis of the legal meaning, the implementation, and the adjudication of these rules. These aspects will be most useful to delegates, practitioners, administrators and adjudicators involved with WTO law and policy. Here again, the economics literature provides some complementary readings on the effect of preferences, exemptions from tariff reductions, etc. The approach in this book is to focus on the qualitative, regulatory content of the rules, rather than on their quantitative economic impact.

The interaction between these three components is key to understanding the place and challenges of developing countries in the multilateral trading system historically as well as today. This book argues that institutional processes and substantive regulatory outcomes are inseparable at the WTO, as in any legal system, so that a consideration of the development dimension at the WTO must examine both jointly. It shows that the shortcomings of the Doha Development Round are in part due to the failure to assess the rules not only for themselves, but also as part of the legal processes and institutions that produced them.

At the conceptual level, this book presents two theoretical paradigms to assess the normative, institutional and regulatory aspects of a development dimension at the WTO. In one model, the trade and development relationship is managed by *ad hoc* instruments deployed when the need arises. The relationship is not principled, but rather depends on the specifics of each case. By contrast, the second model posits trade and development as normative co-constituents, as inseparable pillars of the trading system. The model explores how that would impact the WTO's law and institutions.

At the pragmatic level, the book provides a menu of options towards a more functional relationship between the trade liberalization process and the development imperatives of many WTO members.

Acknowledgments

Sincere thanks are owed to the many individuals and institutions that have supported this research and contributed to its original publication in 2012 and to the present release in paperback.

I am particularly grateful to the diplomatic trade representatives from around the world and the WTO officials who have taken the time to discuss my questions and to comment on my writing. Their insights and reactions were crucial to the evolution of my thinking about trade and development. Equally, I have benefitted from the thoughtful reflections of academic colleagues on all continents, particularly James Crawford, Joel Trachtman, Gary N. Horlick, Guglielmo Verdirame, and the anonymous book manuscript reviewers commissioned by Oxford University Press.

The financial support of a number of institutions was key to the making of this book. The United Kingdom's Arts and Humanities Research Council, Cambridge University, and Pembroke College funded the initial research; Northeastern University School of Law, my home institution, continues to support my work.

A special mention must go to my research assistants at Northeastern University School of Law, although that is hardly repayment for their diligent work. Christopher Wurster's contribution was truly invaluable; others are acknowledged in specific chapters.

Lastly, I owe a debt of gratitude to Frank J. Garcia, who patiently read the whole manuscript and whose encouragement has been an immense source of support.

La majestueuse égalité des lois, qui interdit au riche comme au pauvre de coucher sous les ponts, de mendier dans les rues et de voler du pain.
Anatole France, *Le Lys Rouge [The Red Lily] (1894), ch. 7*

The law, in its majestic equality, forbids the rich as well as the poor to sleep under bridges, to beg in the streets, and to steal bread.

Contents

Annexes at <http://ukcatalogue.oup.com/product/9780199600885.do>:

- Annex 1 SDT Provisions by Agreement and Decision
- Annex 2 Notified Recourse to Balance of Payments Restrictions
- Annex 3 Subsidies Notifications
- Annex 4 Development Arguments in GATT and WTO Disputes
- Annex 5 Time Periods Granted in Article 21.3(c) Arbitrations

List of Tables and Figures

Table of Cases

OTHER JURISDICTIONS

International Courts/Arbitral Bodies

Permanent Court of International Justice

International Court of Justice

International Tribunal for the Law of the Sea

List of Cited GATT Panel and Working Party Reports and their Common Abbreviations

Australia Waiver	GATT Working Party Report, *Report of the Working Party on the Australian Request to Grant Tariff Preferences to Less-Developed Countries,* adopted 23 December 1965, L/2527
Brazil–EEC Milk	GATT Panel Report, *Imposition of Provisional and Definitive Countervailing Duties on Milk Powder and Certain Types of Milk from the European Economic Community*, SCM/179, Report of the Panel adopted by the Committee on Subsidies and Countervailing Measures on 28 April 1994, BISD 41S/467
Canada–FIRA	GATT Panel Report, *Canada—Administration of the Foreign Investment Review Act*, L/5504, adopted 7 February 1984, BISD 30S/140
EC–Sugar Exports (Australia)	GATT Panel Report, *European Communities—Refunds on Exports of Sugar*, L/4833, adopted 6 November 1979, BISD 26S/290
EC–Sugar Exports (Brazil)	GATT Panel Report, *European Communities—Refunds on Exports of Sugar—Complaint by Brazil*, L/5011, adopted 10 November 1980, BISD 27S/69
EEC–Apples I (Chile)	GATT Panel Report, *EEC Restrictions on Imports of Apples from Chile*, L/5047, adopted 10 November 1980, BISD 27S/98
EEC–Cotton Yarn	GATT Panel Report, *European Economic Community—Imposition of Anti-Dumping Duties on Imports of Cotton Yarn from Brazil*, ADP/137, adopted 30 October 1995, BISD 42S/17
EEC–Dessert Apples	GATT Panel Report, *European Economic Community—Restrictions on Imports of Dessert Apples—Complaint by Chile (II)*, L/6491, adopted 22 June 1989, BISD 36S/93
India–Import Restrictions on Almonds	Unadopted GATT Panel Report, *India–Import Restrictions on Almonds—Recourse to Article XXIII:2 by the United States*, 15 November 1987, L/6197
Italy–Agricultural Machinery	GATT Panel Report, *Italian Discrimination Against Imported Agricultural Machinery*, L/833, adopted 23 October 1958, BISD 7S/60
Japan–Leather II (US)	GATT Panel Report, *Panel on Japanese Measures on Imports of Leather*, L/5623, adopted 15 May 1984, BISD 31S/94

List of Cited WTO Panel and Appellate Body Reports, Other Initiated WTO Disputes, and their Common Abbreviations

Argentina–Hides and Leather	Panel Report, *Argentina—Measures Affecting the Export of Bovine Hides and Import of Finished Leather*, WT/DS155/R and Corr.1, adopted 16 February 2001, DSR 2001:V, 1779
Argentina–Hides and Leather (Article 21.3(c))	Award of the Arbitrator, *Argentina—Measures Affecting the Export of Bovine Hides and Import of Finished Leather—Arbitration under Article 21.3(c) of the DSU*, WT/DS155/10, 31 August 2001, DSR 2001:XII, 6013
Brazil–Aircraft	Appellate Body Report, *Brazil—Export Financing Programme for Aircraft*, WT/DS46/AB/R, adopted 20 August 1999, DSR 1999:III, 1161
Brazil–Aircraft	Panel Report, *Brazil—Export Financing Programme for Aircraft*, WT/DS46/R, adopted 20 August 1999, as modified by Appellate Body Report WT/DS46/AB/R, DSR 1999:III, 1221
Chile–Alcoholic Beverages (Article 21.3(c))	Award of the Arbitrator, *Chile—Taxes on Alcoholic Beverages—Arbitration under Article 21.3(c) of the DSU*, WT/DS87/15, WT/DS110/14, 23 May 2000, DSR 2000:V, 2583
Chile–Price Band System	Panel Report, *Chile—Price Band System and Safeguard Measures Relating to Certain Agricultural Products*, WT/DS207/R, adopted 23 October 2002, as modified by Appellate Body Report WT/DS207AB/R, DSR 2002:VIII, 3127
Chile–Price Band System	Appellate Body Report, *Chile—Price Band System and Safeguard Measures Relating to Certain Agricultural Products*, WT/DS207/AB/R, adopted 23 October 2002, DSR 2002:VIII, 3045 (Corr.1, DSR 2006:XII, 5473)
Chile–Price Band System (Article 21.3(c))	Award of the Arbitrator, *Chile—Price Band System and Safeguard Measures Relating to Certain Agricultural Products—Arbitration under Article 21.3(c) of the DSU*, WT/DS207/13, 17 March 2003, DSR 2003:III, 1237
China–Raw Materials	Panel Reports, China—*Measures Related to the Exportation of Various Raw Materials*, WT/DS394/R, WT/DS395/R, WT/DS398/R, circulated 5 July 2011

US–Steel Safeguards	Panel Reports, *United States—Definitive Safeguard Measures on Imports of Certain Steel Products*, WT/DS248/R / WT/DS249/R / WT/DS251/R / WT/DS252/R / WT/DS253/R / WT/DS254/R / WT/DS258/R / WT/DS259/R, and Corr.1, adopted 10 December 2003, as modified by Appellate Body Report WT/DS248/AB/R, WT/DS249/AB/R, WT/DS251/AB/R, WT/DS252/AB/R, WT/DS253/AB/R, WT/DS254/AB/R, WT/DS258/AB/R, WT/DS259/AB/R, DSR 2003:VIII, 3273
US–Upland Cotton	Appellate Body Report, *United States—Subsidies on Upland Cotton*, WT/DS267/AB/R, adopted 21 March 2005
US–Upland Cotton (Article 22.6–US I)	Decision by the Arbitrator, *United States—Subsidies on Upland Cotton—Recourse to Arbitration by the United States under Article 22.6 of the DSU and Article 4.11 of the SCM Agreement*, WT/DS267/ARB/1, 31 August 2009
US–Upland Cotton (Article 22.6–US II)	Decision by the Arbitrator, *United States—Subsidies on Upland Cotton—Recourse to Arbitration by the United States under Article 22.6 of the DSU and Article 7.10 of the SCM Agreement*, WT/DS267/ARB/2 and Corr.1, 31 August 2009
US–Upland Cotton (Article 21.5–Brazil)	Appellate Body Report, *United States—Subsidies on Upland Cotton—Recourse to Article 21.5 of the DSU by Brazil*, WT/DS267/AB/RW, adopted 20 June 2008, DSR 2008:III, 809
US–Upland Cotton (Article 21.5–Brazil)	Panel Report, *United States—Subsidies on Upland Cotton—Recourse to Article 21.5 of the DSU by Brazil*, WT/DS267/RW and Corr.1, adopted 20 June 2008, as modified by Appellate Body Report WT/DS267/AB/RW, DSR 2008:III, 997 to DSR 2008:VI, 2013
US–Wool Shirts and Blouses	Appellate Body Report, *US—Measures Affecting Imports of Woven Wool Shirts and Blouses from India*, WT/DS33/AB/R and WT/DS33/AB/R/Corr.1, adopted 23 May 1997
US–Zeroing (Japan)	Appellate Body Report, *United States—Measures Relating to Zeroing and Sunset Reviews (Complainant: Japan)*, WT/DS322/AB/R, adopted 23 January 2007

Table of Conventions and Treaties

List of Abbreviations

AB	Appellate Body
ACP	African, Caribbean, and Pacific
ACTA	Anti-Counterfeiting Trade Agreement
AGOA	African Growth and Opportunity Act
ASEAN	Association of Southeast Asian Nations
BITs	bilateral investment treaties
CARICOM	Caribbean Community
COMESA	Common Market for Eastern and Southern Africa
DSB	Dispute Settlement Body
DSU	Dispute Settlement Understanding
EC	European Community
ECJ	European Court of Justice
ECLAC	Economic Commission for Latin America (CEPAL in Spanish)
ECOSOC	Economic and Social Council (United Nations)
ECOWAS	Economic Community of West African States
EIF	Enhanced Integrated Framework
EPA	Economic Partnership Agreement
EU	European Union[1]
FDI	foreign direct investment
FTA	Free Trade Agreement
GATS	General Agreement on Trade in Services
GATT	General Agreement on Tariffs and Trade
GDP	gross domestic product
GSP	Generalized System of Preferences
GSTP	Global System of Trade Preferences
HDI	Human Development Index
IBRD	International Bank for Reconstruction and Development
ICC	International Commercial Court
ICJ	International Court of Justice
ICSID	International Centre for Settlement of Investment Disputes
IMF	International Monetary Fund

---

[1] "European Economic Community," "European Community," and "EC" are used to reflect the technical legal terminology used historically. The EC has now officially changed its name at the WTO to European Union (EU). EU is used in the book to reflect recent positions and proceedings involving the EU.

ITLOS	International Tribunal for the Law of the Sea
ITO	International Trade Organization
LDC	Least-Developed Country
MERCOSUR	Southern Common Market
MFA	Multifiber Agreement
MFN	most-favored nation
NAFTA	North American Free Trade Agreement
NAMA	non-agricultural market access
NIEO	New International Economic Order
OECD	Organisation for Economic Co-operation and Development
OPEC	Organization of Petroleum Exporting Countries
RTA	regional trade agreement
SACU	Southern Africa Customs Union
SCM Agreement	Agreement on Subsidies and Countervailing Measures
SDT	special and differential treatment
SPS	sanitary and phytosanitary
TBT	technical barriers to trade
TIFA	Trade and Investment Framework Agreement
TPR	Trade Policy Reviews
TRIMS Agreement	Agreement on Trade Related Investment Measures
TRIPS Agreement	Agreement on Trade-Related Aspects of Intellectual Property Rights
UN	United Nations
UNCTAD	United Nations Conference on Trade and Development
UNDP	United Nations Development Programme
WTO	World Trade Organization

Introduction

The Marrakesh Agreement establishing the World Trade Organization (WTO) recognizes the "need for positive efforts designed to ensure that developing countries, and especially the least developed amongst them, secure a share of growth in international trade commensurate with the needs of their economic development." While some 75 percent of WTO members currently are developing countries, the promises of welfare gains from trade liberalization have not materialized for many of them or have been much more modest than anticipated in the 1990s. More recently, the failure of the last several WTO ministerial meetings and the limited progress made in the ongoing Doha Development Round have brought into the limelight the complexity of the relationship between trade liberalization and development in the multilateral system.

To date, there has been no systematic legal framework to accommodate developing countries' needs in the WTO legal regime. Instead, exceptions to the general rules and disciplines provide some measure of flexibility for developing countries. This piecemeal and *ad hoc* approach is now clearly showing its limits. Multilateral negotiations over the past decade have been unsuccessful, with the WTO increasingly becoming associated with public protest rather than with the fruitful steerage of international trade. The regime established by the Uruguay Round is still very much unfinished business. Developing members have now gained a blocking power, in political terms, at the WTO. Yet members still shy away from the broader issue of the relationship between development and trade liberalization, preferring instead technical fixes. Today, a reconsideration of the legal implications of development issues within the organization is all the more pressing to ensure the continuity of the multilateral trading regime.

Developing members' rights and obligations at the WTO encompass both general rules binding on all members and specific rules intended for developing members (dubbed "special and differential treatment," SDT). Both create opportunities and constraints for socio-economic, human and political development. However, the former (general rules) was not devised with development in mind, while the latter (SDT) ostensibly aimed to cater to development needs. The very structure of WTO disciplines, then, places development at the margins of the trade regime, circumscribing it to exceptions and carve-outs from the mainstream rules. Development is seen as distinct from the primary endeavor of trade liberalization. Is the trade liberalization objective then supported by some other normative principle? Or is it devoid of normativity, and pursued for its own sake? While this book does not seek to answer these questions in general terms, it explores their implications with respect to the trade and development relationship. Ultimately, it asks whether development-oriented trade rules could evolve from their current status as exceptions to a more coherent system of rules fully integrated in the WTO legal regime and that would more effectively address developing countries' demands. Normatively, it argues that a conceptual framework for the trade and development relationship at the WTO needs to emerge if the multilateral regime is to stay relevant for its constituents.

The Current Practice: What Informs the Development Dimension at the WTO?

Originally, development at the WTO reflected the traditional focus of the General Agreement on Tariffs and Trade (GATT) on macro-economic growth. More recently, WTO regulation shifted away from quantitative benchmarks (such as tariff reductions) and moved towards qualitative regulation (SPS standards, various technical standards, intellectual property protection, etc.). However, development considerations at the WTO largely remained hinged on traditional macro-economic policy factors such as tariffs, preferences, and balance of payments. A first question, then, is why the diversification of the WTO's regulatory universe has not translated into a broader understanding of development?

In some areas, developing members themselves have been resistant. The rejection of any substantive negotiation on labor standards and environmental issues are two examples. Both have bearings on the human aspects of development alongside its economic aspects. As the Brundtland Commission Report aptly put it twenty years ago: "Poverty reduces people's capacity to use resources in a sustainable manner; it intensifies pressure on the environment." Viewed in the extreme, environmental plunder provides subsistence today and impoverishment tomorrow.[1] In many instances, the development debate at the WTO has consisted mostly in an effort by developing countries to maintain the possibility of protecting their domestic markets against unfettered liberalization. Beyond the protectionist versus openness debate, the issue goes to development policies and what has been called "policy space" (describing the range of domestic economic and industrial policies, in particular, that would be compatible with WTO disciplines). The more trade disciplines restrict policy choices, the less "policy space" a country has to shape its socio-economic and development trajectory.

The diversification of WTO regulation suggests that if members want a development dimension to be incorporated at the core of the WTO regime, all of the organization's activities should be evaluated for their development impact. For example, a human development approach to development is incompatible with the present method for setting the negotiation agenda, which excludes important trade-related development issues such as labor standards. It is also incompatible

---

[1] Although there is no framework agreement on environmental protection and labor standards, a number of legal instruments at the WTO already allow members to take some regulatory action. For example, the increase of technical standards regulation indirectly affects those areas and recourse to broad provisions such as GATT Article XX has allowed some health and environmental regulation in the trade context.

with considering the human impact of trade disciplines as an afterthought, as exemplified by the TRIPS amendment on public health. The current distinction between trade and trade-related issues would need to be reconsidered so that the development impact of a proposed discipline would be part of the assessment whether to regulate the trade-related issue at the WTO.

Another aspect of considering a development dimension at the WTO relates to the relevant geopolitical and economic scale for regulatory intervention. Is the state the appropriate unit of reference? Should it be the only one? The traditional Westphalian assumption of public international law is reflected quite strongly in the nature and form of WTO rules and processes. The reluctance to fully open the dispute settlement to submissions by non-state actors is but one illustration. Should infra-state units be considered (such as provinces or communities)? At the other end of the spectrum, is the supranational, regional level the best to deal with trade and development issues? Should it be a combination of state, infra-state and supra-national levels? The recent proliferation of regional trade agreements (RTA), including amongst emerging economies, has resulted in a set of experiments on the trade and development relationship that may hold valuable lessons for the WTO. Or should it depend on the economic sector at stake? For instance some sectors of Brazil's economy are severely underdeveloped and the population serving these sectors lives in abject poverty but other sectors are amongst the most competitive in the world. In reality, domestic dynamics and actors shape WTO members' positions as much as inter-state relations. Increasingly, RTAs create a multiplicity of overlapping, complementary and conflicting trade agendas that influence the multilateral negotiations. They also offer real-life "laboratories" to explore alternatives to the WTO model of trade liberalization, including novel approaches with respect to asymmetric commitments and other forms of development support.

Yet another issue in framing the trade and development relationship at the WTO is the question of sovereign autonomy. The more WTO regulation focuses on specific segments of its members' economy and regulation, the more sovereign states' political decisions are up for multilateral bargaining, and even subject to international adjudication. This in turn affects members' autonomy in shaping their development policies. For example, WTO rules on sanitary standards and efforts to harmonize administrative procedures will necessarily take away from members some of their autonomy. Although the Agreement on the Application of Sanitary and Phytosanitary Measures (SPS) states that members are free to choose the level of protection they see fit, a number of high-profile cases have shown that, in combination with other WTO disciplines, that freedom is now subject to review, if not outright limited in practice. This trend is described in the discourse on the loss of "policy space." "Mainstreaming development" is often presented as an antidote that would empower developing members to re-capture the lost "policy space." Yet incorporating development at the WTO is also fraught with difficulties. It might mean shaping development-related rules applicable to a wide range of developing countries with different needs. That too may be seen as a loss of "policy space" in the choice of development strategies. Members pushing for incorporating development at the core of the WTO's architecture should consider the possible trade-off in terms of loss of individual domestic autonomy in setting development policies. At present, groups of developing members wishing to leverage their collective bargaining power already find it difficult to balance their priorities within the group. For instance, Brazil's shifting position from the Cairns Group to the G-20[2] in 2003 in relation to agriculture negotiations reflected its concern that Australia and Canada favored meeting some of the United States and Europe's demands prior to getting any concession of interest to the developing members of the Cairns Group.

Clearly then, a multiplicity of factors, including economic, strategic, political social and legal, contribute to the shaping of the trade and development relationship at the WTO. As a theoretical matter, this study posits two paradigms for evaluating how development is or can be integrated in the WTO's legal architecture. These paradigms are meant purely as theoretical constructs, not as descriptive or predictive models. Nor is this book about the fairness of one model or another. An extensive literature deals with issues of fairness in international trade, ranging from Rawlsian approaches to theological interpretations.[3] Rather the two paradigms are presented as conceptual benchmarks to assist in situating the legal and institutional nature of current WTO rights and obligations for developing countries, the proposals that have been submitted in the Doha Round, and thoughts for reform presented in the last chapter of this book.

The two paradigms represent two legal frameworks corresponding to opposing conceptions of the relationship between WTO disciplines and the constraints experienced by most developing members. They center on a normative query regarding the place that development could occupy at the WTO. Depending how the costs and benefits of trade liberalization and their impact on the development of its poorer members are balanced in the WTO's mandate, two different directions may be outlined. First, the primary normative focus can be on trade liberalization, with development issues addressed on a case-by-case basis, as they arise, with little or no overarching normative reference. This first paradigm, then, embodies

---

[2] G-20 in this book refers to the coalition that formed during the GATT and WTO years amongst a number of developing countries. It is distinct from the eponymous Group of Twenty (G-20) Finance Ministers and Central Bank Governors established in 1999 as an extension of the G-8 and that focuses mostly on financial and monetary matters.

[3] See e.g., R. Bhala, 'Theological Categories for Special and Differential Treatment' 2002 *Kansas Law Review* 50(4) 635; B.S. Chimni, 'Alternative Visions of Just World Order: Six Tales from India' 2005 *Harvard International Law Journal* 46(2) 389; B.S. Chimni, 'The World Trade Organization, Democracy and Development: A View from the South' 2006 *Journal of World Trade* 40(1) 5; J.L. Dunoff, 'Is the World Trade Organization Fair to Developing States?' 2003 *American Society of International Law Proceedings* 97 153; G. Feuer, 'Libéralisme, mondialisation et développement: à propos de quelques réalités ambiguës' 1999 *Annuaire Français du Droit International* 148; F.J. Garcia, *Trade, Inequality, and Justice: Toward a Liberal Theory of Just Trade* (Ardsley: Transnational Publishers, 2003); F.J. Garcia, *Global Justice and International Economic Law: Three Takes* (Cambridge University Press, 2013) J.T. Gathii, 'Institutional Concerns of an Expanded Trade Regime: Where Should Global Social and Regulatory Policy Be Made?: Re-characterizing the Social in the Constitutionalization of the WTO: A Preliminary Analysis' 2001 *Widener Law Symposium Journal* 7 137; F. Ismail, 'Mainstreaming Development in the World Trade Organization' 2005 *Journal of World Trade* 39(1) 11; J.P. Trachtman, 'Legal Aspects of a Poverty Agenda at the WTO: Trade Law and "Global Apartheid"' 2003 *Journal of International Economic Law* 6(1) 3.

an *idiosyncratic, ad hoc approach* to development at the WTO. In practice, it resembles more closely the current practice. Second, development-oriented obligations can be conceptualized at the core of the WTO's legal framework, with development considered as normatively on par with the objective of trade liberalization. In this second paradigm, development and trade liberalization are *normative co-constituents* of the WTO legal framework.

First Paradigm: Development on an *Ad Hoc* Basis

The first paradigm treats development as a second-order consideration that does not fundamentally displace the objective of trade liberalization as the primary mandate of the WTO. In this framework, the needs of developing members arising out of their economic, social and political constraints are dealt with on a case-by-case basis rather than at a systemic level. Exceptions and carve-outs dealing with development issues, whether in general agreements or in individual members' schedules of commitments and accession protocols are idiosyncratic – *ad hoc* solutions rather than instantiations of an overarching normative principle.

The key feature of the idiosyncratic paradigm is the absence of a principled approach to incorporating development at the WTO. Of course, that does not mean that development considerations will not be included in WTO rules, but simply that there will be no systematic or coherent approach, no overarching legal obligation or, at best, only a very loose and soft one such as the statements in the preamble to the Marrakesh Agreement.

Absent an overarching legal obligation to take into account development factors, the scope and nature of development-related rules are mostly left to members to negotiate on a case-by-case basis when a country encounters or foresees a particular difficulty. Members could undertake such negotiations as part of the accession package of a new developing member, or in the course of multilateral rounds of negotiations as part of new individual or collective commitments.

An important advantage of this framework is that it allows a dynamic understanding of members' development needs: As their needs evolve, they can, in principle, negotiate appropriate exceptions or derogations without having to comply with the constraints of a pre-defined notion of development. The open-endedness of this framework apparently gives members the maximum legal flexibility. In practice, in this model, the incorporation of development-oriented provisions in WTO rules would be primarily a political bargaining exercise. Because developing members are not constrained by a common legal framework, those that do not wish to avail themselves of development provisions would not have to pay the political price currently associated with SDT, in terms of negotiations and credibility of their concessions.

In theory, the absence of a pervasive or overarching legal framework for development at the WTO means that there is no principle limiting the adoption of rules that favor developing countries, in addition to specific *ad hoc* provisions. If, for instance, newly powerful middle-income developing countries have the political clout to impose a general discipline that caters primarily to their interests, there is no legal impediment to such a "mainstreaming" of development.

The idiosyncratic model relies more heavily on the procedural framework for considering and addressing the development constraints of WTO members. Because there is no overarching norm regarding development, there is no guarantee that substantive rules will take into account development specificities. In that sense, this *ad hoc* model may be at its most powerful as a procedural model to determine how and when development-oriented rules can be produced and implemented. While apparently neutral because it does not favor particular development objectives or rules, this *ad hoc* paradigm might still assume some sort of normative consensus on the nature of the trade and development relationship. Absent such an assumption, the treatment of development issues would be purely arbitrary and governed by power plays, rather than by anything recognizable as the rule of law.

Second Paradigm: Development as a Normative Co-constituent

In this paradigm, development is considered as part of the trade liberalization objective of the WTO. As a result, the need for recourse to derogations, safeguards and escape clauses should be reduced because the mainstream rules are built to account for development constraints. The issue is how the WTO legal architecture would be redrawn if development considerations were understood to be part of the trade liberalization process.

The normative co-constituent paradigm fundamentally displaces the mercantilist ethos of the WTO, where liberalization results from the exchange of equally valuable concessions. But perhaps, the GATT and WTO's mercantilist strategy is not the only way to bring about trade liberalization, and other approaches might be more adequate to current challenges.

This model accounts for the development needs of the WTO membership because rules are tailored to members' different objectives as a matter of principle, rather than as a matter of derogations as is the case with the *ad hoc* model. In this model, mechanisms can allow members to continue participating in the system while not undertaking commitments that are too burdensome or exacting to them. Conversely, it provides members wishing a higher level of commitments to undertake such deepened liberalization. Such a variable geometry of obligations and commitments can take various forms:

- allowing each member to opt in or out of each agreement, or
- integrating all members in all agreements but differentiating each member's obligations under the agreements.

The first option conjures up ghosts of the Tokyo Round where the lack of a single undertaking resulted in a patchwork of agreements with varying (and generally low) membership. Additionally, non-reciprocity in the Tokyo Round prevented developing members from obtaining valuable concessions if they elected not to opt in to the agreements. The last part of this book suggests ways in which this could be reconsidered. In particular, a revised opt-out approach may ensure a more meaningful participation by a large number of members.

The second option evokes the controversial formulation of the Appellate Body (AB) in the *EC–Tariff Preferences* case[4] on "differentiation." In that case, the AB found that it could be permissible, under the Enabling Clause, for the preference grantor to differentiate among beneficiaries based on their trade, financial and development needs. A number of developing countries took exception to this formulation, perceiving it as an attempt to do away with the legal category of "developing members." However, there is a major conceptual difference between differentiation in the *EC–Tariff Preferences* case and differentiation in the normative co-constituent paradigm. Differentiation as envisioned in *EC–Tariff Preferences* erodes developing members' ability to exercise collective political leverage through the common legal identification of "developing member." By contrast, the basic proposition of the normative co-constituent paradigm is that development becomes a core normative pillar of the WTO supported by a legal mandate for addressing development considerations throughout the organization' activities in exchange for developing countries accepting a general differentiation of their commitments.

General differentiation relies perhaps even more heavily on the overarching codification of development as a norm of the first order than the opt-out system. As discussed above, general differentiation entails a credible *quid pro quo* between giving up the blanket "developing country" designation and offering a real opportunity for development to be considered as a core part of the WTO mandate. The dispute settlement system would have a heavy burden in ensuring that the *quid pro quo* is upheld and that the differentiated obligations are truly cognizant of members' needs and vulnerabilities.

General differentiation also entails a radical change in the understanding of what constitutes reciprocity and non-discrimination. So far, with the exception of SDT, WTO members are treated as formally equal and hence subject to formally equal obligations. Formal equality and formal reciprocity reflect the Talion-like underpinnings of public international law (an eye for an eye). Although proportionality in countermeasures was perceived as a major progress in international relations, notably in the area of the regulation of the use of force, it may be that the international legal community should now consider how the legal culture of formal equality might itself be a source of inequity. Should the WTO system become one where the unequal situation of members are recognized through formally unequal obligations, it could become an inspiration for the development of legal philosophy. Some areas of public international law, such as environmental law, have already opened new pathways in this direction.

---

[4] AB Report, *EC–Tariffs Preferences*. India unsuccessfully argued that the different treatment was in violation of the non-discrimination requirement of the Enabling Clause.

Methodology and organization of the book

The pragmatic and empirical concerns that infuse the present work are constrained by the difficulty of accessing non-public sources within the WTO. This research relies mostly on public documents and publicly documented practices. Some WTO experts argue that the practice often bears little resemblance to the mandated procedures and that the public face of the organization (including its legal work-product) widely differs from its actual operation. Nonetheless, an analysis based on publicly available information is warranted for a number of reasons.

First and foremost, political science has long demonstrated that formal rules and procedures affect actors' behavior even when they do not abide by the rules. Linguistics philosophy also has demonstrated the operational power of language and discourse. Here, language encompasses legal rules, WTO members' declarations and proposal tabled during negotiations, WTO Secretariat statements, and other statements by members' spokespersons, many of which are publicly available. Even when the practice circumvents or ignores the rules, it is still shaped in relation to the rules and to the public discourse. Second, if the legal rules and procedures are not followed, it is important to understand why. The present study devotes considerable attention to understanding how and why given rules came about, what they strive to achieve, whether they are successful in that endeavor, and if not, what is being done in response. Virtually all the information needed to conduct this analysis may be found in publicly available sources, directly or by deduction. Third, doctrinal analysis, which constitutes an important contribution of this book, relies on treaties and case law, which are publicly available. Fourth, WTO members' efforts to change the rules prospectively (which constitutes much of the work undertaken in the current Round of negotiations) serve to document what some problems with the current rules may be. In other words, proposals for amendments to the rules offer clues as to how the rules have actually been used or ignored. Fifth, even if practice eventually disproves some of the present analysis, the latter will have shed some light on the possible effects of the law and as such, may offer some alternative ways of thinking to WTO insiders. There is value in an external analysis that is relatively immune from the perspective of those concerned with immediate decision-making. Indeed, a number of WTO delegates interviewed for this research have expressed an avid interest in the findings of independent academic research. Last, a certain amount of non-public information does filter outside of the organization and has been used as a check in the present research. Personal interviews conducted with a number of WTO Secretariat members and WTO delegates from member states have been used to support this research.

As a result, the methodological problems arising from non-public and informal practices within the WTO have been mitigated to an extent sufficient to validate the balance between empirical and pragmatic concerns, and theoretical research.

This book is divided into four parts. Part I asks who decides what development means. It proposes a theoretical and historical construct of development in international law, showing how development has been progressively captured by international economic law and its institutions to the detriment of general public international law. This shift is critical because it constrains the substance and type of development-oriented provisions that eventually emerged at the GATT and WTO. Part II frames development at the GATT and WTO, surveying the emergence of development-oriented provisions in GATT and WTO law but also considering developing countries' position within the WTO as an institution. In particular, the evolution of developing country participation in negotiations and their accession process informs this analysis. Part III focuses on the doctrinal analysis of development provisions in the WTO agreements and their interpretation in dispute settlement. It also considers how general development arguments separate from SDT provisions have been received in disputes. This Part proposes a dynamic interpretation of SDT provisions that could help members implement their commitments in a way that is mindful of development policies. A comparative perspective on special and differential treatment in other trade and non-trade treaties provides further perspectives. Similarly the adjudication of development in dispute settlement at the WTO is compared to the treatment of development arguments in other international fora. Leaving aside development-specific provisions, this Part then assesses the impact on developing members of procedural and decision-making rules that govern the WTO as an institution. Part IV offers a forward-looking perspective on the trade and development relationship at the WTO. It takes stock of the limited advances of the Doha Development Round and assesses the legal and institutional challenges for addressing development at the WTO. It ultimately proposes a menu of options for addressing the needs and concerns of developing members more effectively, with a view to improving the WTO's relevance, legitimacy, and practical ability to deliver the benefits of free trade to its members.

I

DEVELOPMENT AND ITS INSTITUTIONS IN INTERNATIONAL ECONOMIC LAW: WHO DECIDES WHAT DEVELOPMENT MEANS?

The debate surrounding the trade and development relationship at the WTO has been deeply rooted in the evolution of international regulation since the nineteenth century. This Part proposes a theoretical and historical construct of development in international law, showing how development concerns have been progressively captured by international economic law and its institutions to the detriment of general public international law. This shift in turn affects the substance of international trade regulation and its relationship with development. The development dimension at the GATT—and later the WTO—is a product of this displacement.

Developing countries very early on raised their concerns regarding the unequal distribution of international trade, and continually sought remedies for these imbalances through the framework of traditional public international law, international organizations, and intergovernmental negotiations. By contrast, developed states quickly moved away from the post-war project of a collective regulation of international economic relations through a network of organizations comprising the United Nations (UN), the International Trade Organisation, and the Bretton Woods institutions. Instead, they developed a network of rules by-passing the veil of state sovereignty in many ways, using international organizations such as the IMF, the World Bank, and the GATT as conduits to disseminate industrial country norms and standards within the domestic legal orders of developing states.

One caveat must be mentioned at this time. Although it is now endorsed by many thinkers from developing countries[1] the concept of development was, and

---

[1] Various terms have been used to designate and categorize countries. "Third World," "developed," "underdeveloped," "developing," "South," and "North" come with much historical and political baggage. The terms will be used here without reference to their arguably moral undertones, but rather as historical artifacts, depending on the time period discussed. See also B. Rajagopal, *International Law from Below: Development, Social Movements and Third World Resistance* (Cambridge: Cambridge University Press, 2003).

still largely remains, a Western idea resulting in part from the colonial enterprise. Much Western scholarship on development now emphasizes social justice
and fairness in international trade relations. By contrast, there is little scholarship
from developing countries on moral, political, and ideological theories of development. Chimni is an exception but his theory of international law is entrenched
in a Marxist perspective, which is also a product of Western culture. While recognizing the political, moral, cultural ambivalence of the concept of development[2] the lack of alternative terminology makes it difficult to find a more neutral
term. Nonetheless, this book hopes to do justice to the dialogue between so-called
"developed" and "developing" countries.

By way of background, the first chapter introduces the theoretical literature on
the concept of development. The purpose of this brief survey is to understand the
influences that have driven normative, regulatory, and institutional evolutions
in the trade and development relationship. At one end of the spectrum, development has been largely equated with gross domestic product (GDP) growth; this
macroeconomic perspective has fuelled much of the Washington Consensus[3] and
the international organizations associated with it. At the other end of the spectrum, development has been seen primarily as a human rights issue; its components are education, and access to basic necessities, gender issues, access to health
care, and associated mortality issues. The Human Development Index created by
the UN is one of the measures of such human development. In theoretical terms,
that conception of development is then associated with a discourse of rights, entitlements, and a linkage between development and political and social rights, rather
than being limited to a technical economic issue. To a large extent, the WTO has
inherited a perspective of development close to a purely macroeconomic-centered
approach.

Chapter 2 then examines the influence of international organizations on
development policy-making, tracing each contribution to the theoretical perspectives outlined in Chapter 1. The legal framework for development has drifted
from its initial formulation in the 1950s, emphasizing sovereignty over natural
resources and self-determination to include a complex set of economic, political,
and cultural components. Correlatively the institutional home for formulating

---

[2] Much of the political and moral justification for the colonial enterprise, both in France and in
Great Britain, was premised on European colonial powers' "duty to civilize" (in the words of French
Minister Jules Ferry in a speech to the National Assembly, 28 March 1884), understood to include
education, cultural, political, and economic development.

[3] The term "Washington Consensus" was coined in 1989 by John Williamson to describe a
set of ten specific economic policy prescriptions for developing countries facing economic crises
and that were promoted and implemented by Washington, DC-based institutions such as the
International Monetary Fund (IMF), the World Bank, and the US Treasury Department. The
policy recommendations include fiscal policy discipline, broadening the tax base and adopting
moderate marginal tax rates, interest rates that are market-determined and positive (but moderate) in real terms, competitive exchange rates, trade liberalization, liberalization of foreign
direct investment, privatization of state enterprises, deregulation, and legal security for property
rights.

development norms (whether soft law or binding obligations) has moved from the UN to a variety of economic organizations with various decision-making processes and different balances of power between developed and developing countries. These legal and institutional metamorphoses shape the contemporary framework for development considerations in international trade law. More broadly, Chapter 2 serves to identify the roots of developing countries' current concerns and demands at the WTO.

1

The Multiple Meanings of Development

While inequalities between countries and regions have existed throughout history, only relatively recently have the particular processes of economic growth, industrialization, and the expansion of social and political opportunities become encapsulated in the term "development." Yet despite its ubiquitous use in the international legal discourse, the precise meaning of "development" is elusive and has evolved over time. This chapter provides an overview of development theories as a foundation to understanding the role of international law and its institutions with respect to development discussed in Chapter 2.

From colonial times to the "Washington Consensus" policies promoted by the World Bank and the IMF in the 1980s and 1990s, political economy has fueled a number of institutional perspectives on development. As a counter-narrative, legal and social approaches have conceptualized development as a human right, supported by notions such as "sustainable development" or the "right to development." These, too, have influenced the policies and decision-making processes in multilateral development agencies, the UN, in particular.

In practice, the evolving blend of development economics and rights-based approaches has changed what we understand to be the substance of development. While GDP per capita has long been used as a proxy for measuring a country's development, the United Nations' Human Development Index (HDI) now includes factors measuring the degree to which a country's basic needs are met, such as to the accessibility of water or the weight of children by age, as additional critical components of development. Even more sophisticated understandings of development encompass elements such as economic opportunity and gender empowerment. The Gini coefficient measuring national income inequalities is also a relevant development measure. The variety of ways to measure development reflects both its continual evolution as an economic, social, and political construct, as well as the increasing difficulties of defining its conceptual boundaries. Some scholars choose to restrict the meaning of development to its economic dimension; others recognize its broader reach and shy away from adopting a closed, enumerative definition.

This chapter presents an overview of the major trends in development economics in Section 1. Then, it examines integrated perspectives on development that go beyond the purely economic dimension, including human development and rights-based approaches, and the notion of sustainable development (Section 2).

Finally, Section 3 presents the emerging "new developmental state" movement proposing a radically different approach to development.

1. Development Economics Theories:
From Political Economy to Microeconomy

The notion of development is rooted in the industrialization of Western European countries, beginning in the eighteenth century. In the 1750s, the gross national product per capita in countries just beginning their industrialization and in other countries were almost identical. Over the next two centuries, these figures remained close to constant for what became known as the Third World, while they increased tenfold for industrialized countries. Economic, scientific, and technical discrepancies became even more staggering during the second half of the twentieth century. This evolution reinforced the Western notion that it was a more advanced civilization and that other regions were—at least economically—"underdeveloped."

1.1 Classical development theories

At one end of the spectrum, classical development economists followed the teachings of Adam Smith, sharing his preference for laissez-faire economics and minimal government intervention. They argued that such policies would permit individuals to pursue their self-interest and subsequently foster economic growth and prosperity. David Ricardo emphasized the importance of capital accumulation and the law of comparative advantage. Ricardo explained that "[w]ith a population pressing against the means of subsistence, the only remedies are either a reduction of people, or a more rapid accumulation of capital."[1] Ricardo's law of comparative advantage was (and still is) the premise used by advocates of trade liberalization and division of labor.

W.W. Rostow also explained economic underdevelopment from a liberal perspective. He identified five stages of economic growth that every developed national economy has gone through.[2] The first stage was the "traditional society," in which people lived at the mercy of external forces of nature, and the production of technology was static. The second stage, the precondition stage, was marked by key historical events such as the evolution of modern science and modern scientific attitude, and colonialism. These changes widened the market, brought trade, increased specialization of production and dependency between regions and nations, bolstered financial institutions, and also enhanced inclinations of markets to create production functions. The third stage, the "take-off stage," was the most

---

[1] D. Ricardo, "Ricardo on Population" 1988 *Population and Development Review* 14(2) 339, at 343.
[2] W.W. Rostow, "The Stages of Economic Growth" 1959 *The Economic History Review* 12(1) 1, at 1–13.

crucial, consisting in "the achievement of rapid growth in a limited group of sectors, where modern industrial techniques are applied."[3] Rostow observed that the structure of the economy changed drastically in only a ten- to twenty-year span. In this stage, countries invested heavily in their secondary/manufacturing sectors. The fourth stage—the "drive to maturity"—was defined as "the period when a society ha[d] effectively applied the range of then modern technology to the bulk of its resources . . . [T]he industrial process [was] differentiated, with new leading sectors gathering momentum to supplant the older leading sectors of the take-off."[4] Rostow's final stage, "the age of high mass consumption," characterized "economic maturity." Rostow pointed to patterns such as migration to suburbia, the extension of the automobile industry, and the dissemination of consumer household products as significant signs of high mass consumption.

Both Ricardo's and Rostow's theories can be understood as "catching up theories" because they place underdeveloped nations on the same sequential chain as those nations that are considered economically mature, with the underdeveloped countries lagging a few steps behind. From such a perspective, the role of development institutions and the law would be to enable and accompany the transformation of a country's economy from what is perceived as a primitive socioeconomic structure, into a modern structure akin to industrial societies. Inevitably, these perspectives posit industrial countries as experts on development, and attempt to distill the economic histories of developed countries into a single model that developing countries could use to achieve a similar "success." As a result, policy-makers and thinkers from the "advanced" industrial countries tend to hold the reigns of the institutional development channels.

However, earlier classical economists had also highlighted the negative impacts of free trade on developing economies. For example, German economist Friedrich List observed that only the dominant powers profit from free trade, and that developing economies are hindered by competition from existing industrialized powers. Based on these observations, List coined the "infant industry argument," positing that "production costs for newly established industries within a country are likely to be initially higher than for well-established foreign producers of the same line, who have greater experience and higher skill levels."[5] Government intervention would therefore be necessary, according to List, to support the transformation from an agrarian society to an industrial economy.

Each of these development economics theories featured a single model, which could be applied universally to jump-start development in any country. Relatively little attention was paid to the circumstances of individual countries. In their twentieth-century incarnations, classical theories emphasized the accumulation of capital, with the prediction that the amassed wealth would in due course "trickle down" to the most impoverished populations. Thus, the key to development was simply getting the process started; from there, it would occur organically. Until the

---

[3] Ibid at 7.   [4] Ibid at 8.

[5] R. Baldwin, "The Case against Infant-Industry Tariff Protection" 1969 *The Journal of Political Economy* 77(3) 295.

1990s, the decision-making structure of the Bretton Woods institutions, as well as the motivation behind and implementation of their decisions, manifested a belief in "catching up" development models that could be applied universally.

1.2 Leftist classical theories

List laid the foundation for more left-leaning approaches to development economics. Along those lines, Marx originally argued that a country must phase through earlier stages of primitive original communism, slavery, feudalism, and capitalism, before succeeding to the ultimate stage of economic development, socialism. However, neo-Marxists rejected Marx's classical notion that indigenous and underdeveloped societies must first develop capitalist economies before they could immerse themselves in the global market. The crux of the neo-Marxist argument was that capitalism did not function efficiently in underdeveloped post-colonial nations.

Immanuel Wallerstein pioneered the "world-system" theory, which characterized the new world economy as an international division of labor between "core," "semi-periphery," and "periphery" nations. He argued that "[t]hird World countries [were] not 'underdeveloped' nations but 'peripheral capitalist' nations."[6] Wallerstein referred to Moïses Ikonicoff's claim that such economies "operate[d] by economic laws and growth factors [that were] clearly different from those of the economies one might call the model of classic capitalism."[7] In Wallerstein's world-system, the core nations were characterized by concentrated, high-profit, high-technology, high-wage, and diversified production, whereas peripheral countries displayed the opposite characteristics. The remarkable divergence between the dysfunctional systems of the periphery and the prosperous systems of the core demonstrated that the model of classic capitalism was inherently flawed. "[T]he core and the periphery of the world economy were not two separate 'economies' with two separate 'laws' but one capitalist economic system with different sectors performing different functions"[8] (emphasis omitted).

Meanwhile, Andre Gunder Frank viewed market liberals as falsely claiming that underdeveloped countries had simply failed to draw themselves up from their dire conditions in disregard of the global economic history of trade and development. Frank felt that the term "underdeveloped" implied that a country, region, or people had been actively dispossessed, deskilled, denied access to capital and employment opportunities, and culturally and linguistically dominated by particular outside entities. In contrast, Frank favored the term "undeveloped" because it more neutrally defined a region or population that had not expanded its technological knowledge to exploit its natural resources and grow economically.

---

[6] I. Wallerstein, "Dependence in an Interdependent World: The Limited Possibilities of Transformation within the Capitalist World Economy" 1974 *African Studies Review* 17(1) 1, at 2.

[7] M. Ikonicoff, "Sous-Développement, tiers monde ou capitalisme périphérique" 1972 *Revue Tiers-Monde* 13(52) 691, at 692.   [8] Wallerstein, above fn 6, at 2.

Frank also debunked development models premised on stages of growth. He argued instead that the currently developed nations reached their state of prosperity through destruction of the socioeconomic infrastructure of societies in Asia, Africa, and Latin America.[9] Frank perceived as sheer fallacy the assertions by Rostow and Manning Nash that the underdeveloped parts of the world were being self-constrained. Rather, Frank countered that although capital and labor were typically domestically produced and native to the periphery countries, the ownership of such resources was ultimately ceded upwards into the hands of the colonial or quasi-colonial powers, which developed good relations with a minority bourgeoisie comprador class, and who were in fact the ones who constrained developing economies. Using the example of Brazil, he showed that Bretton Woods' institutional loans granted to developing countries in fact had economic and political strings attached, coercing the recipient countries to forfeit their critical economic sectors to foreign interests. Once capital and wealth had been consolidated into the hands of a minute group of entrepreneurs, central countries became less concerned about the welfare of the peasant population, primarily because peasants no longer had the means, via education and communication, to voice their qualms. Ultimately, "the extent of the market, in turn, depend[ed] less on its territorial extension than on the income of its consumers."[10]

Unlike classical and liberal development economists, who viewed underdevelopment as a gap in socioeconomic conditions that could be bridged over time by the application of specific policies, left-leaning development economists and structuralists viewed the divide as a feature of a single global political-economic system. Left-leaning economists see developing societies as a very important piece of developed countries' industrialization process and a conduit for their wealth: Developed and developing countries play different roles in a single socioeconomic system. Development could therefore only be achieved by a transformation of the entire global economic system; it could not be taught to—or mimicked by—developing countries. The call for a New International Economic Order (NIEO) in the 1970s is a natural extension of left-leaning perspectives on development.

1.3 Non-Marxist structuralists and the New International Economic Order

Although they subscribed to a lesser degree of radicalism, structuralists, like neo-Marxists, promoted policies that would liberate developing countries from their dependency on international trade.[11] Structuralists argued, for example, that independence from international trade could be achieved through import substitution industrialization, a process by which a country's imports are replaced by locally

---

[9] A. Frank, *Capitalism and Underdevelopment in Latin America: Historical Studies of Chile and Brazil* (New York: Monthly Review Press, 1967).
[10] Ibid at 175.   [11] Ibid.

produced goods wherever possible in order to promote domestic industries and to reduce balance of payment deficits.[12]

Dr. Raúl Prebisch, a leading structuralist, criticized the notion that one could transpose economic theories and policies that had proven effective in Northern economies by direct application to the distinct situations of developing countries in the 1970s. Instead, Prebisch pointed out the need to engage in "internal structural reform within developing countries so as to achieve more dynamic and equitable economic and social development."[13] He saw regional economic cooperation among developing countries, with the crucial benefit of expanding their market access, as an essential component of this economic reconfiguration. Prebisch had the opportunity to implement these theories while serving as Executive Secretary of the Economic Commission for Latin America (now ECLAC or CEPAL in Spanish) and first Secretary-General to the United Nations Conference on Trade and Development (UNCTAD) created in 1964.

In addition to Prebisch's efforts, the work of Caribbean economist Arthur Lewis also helped shape the contemporary approach to development. Lewis noted "growth poles," which he characterized as "huge concentrations, holding many millions of people, far beyond economies of scale into diseconomies of congestion."[14] Lewis credited the externalities of such growth poles with the "destruction of growth potential elsewhere . . . [and] smaller production for the same total of resources than one would have if the resources were distributed over more growth centers."[15] He observed that developing countries sought to attain wealth by exporting goods to industrialized countries, but developing countries' failure to diversify their exports undermined their access to industrialized country markets:

All underdeveloped countries want to export the same narrow lines of goods . . . If they exported some of everything, their arrival on the market would hardly be noticed, but since they concentrate on a few lines, they hurt some sectors of the industrial countries very hard, and provoke enormous resistance.[16]

Rather, he advocated for trade *amongst* developing countries: "In agriculture [developing countries] are perfectly capable of feeding themselves, through exchange with each other, and do not have to beg the United States to buy more tea and coffee so that they can pay for American grain, when they could produce more grain for themselves."[17]

In the 1970s, Arthur Lewis, along with other structuralists, called on the international community to regulate international trade in keeping with these theories, and moved to implement the NIEO. They argued that the NIEO would allow developing countries to evolve from dualistic agricultural-commercial systems to

---

[12] See the works of Raúl Prebisch, Hans Singer, and Celso Furtado on import substitution industrialization.

[13] Third World Foundation Selection Committee, "Third World Prize 1980" 1981 *Third World Quarterly* 3(1) vi, at vii.

[14] W.A. Lewis, "The State of Development Theory" 1984 *American Economic Review* 74(1) 1, at 2.   [15] Ibid.

[16] W.A. Lewis, "World Trade Since the War" 1968 *Proceedings of the American Philosophical Society* 112(6) 363, at 365.   [17] Ibid at 366.

fully commercialized economies, which in turn would offer them a better chance to participate in the international free market.

Economist H.W. Singer was at the forefront of the NIEO movement. Singer noted that the Bretton Woods system, which modeled the old international economic order, had become obsolete, and attributed three key events to its ultimate demise: the end of the US dollar as the world's main reserve currency in 1971, the world food crisis in 1972, and the Organization of the Petroleum Exporting Countries (OPEC) oil embargo of 1973.[18] He claimed that

the creation of a new international economic order in place of the present disorder represents a broad overall mutual interest... [T]he development of the poorer nations, and the reduction of world poverty, could be the "engine of growth" for the world as a whole.[19]

While the NIEO embodied yet another attempt by economists to conceive of a single model that could be applied on a global scale to create economic prosperity in developing countries, some economists tried to scale down the NIEO concept and tailor it to specific continents. Arnold thought that the NIEO in Africa would entail the dispersal of resources to rural parts of the continent in order to meet the fundamental needs of the majority of the population.[20] Economist and former President of the Caribbean Development Bank, William G. Demas also advocated tailoring the NIEO for the Caribbean.[21]

Whether classical, Marxist-inspired, or structuralist, most development economics since the eighteenth century have sought to discern patterns in international economic relations (focusing on trade, labor, capital, and investment flows) which could be distilled into a universal formula for development. While the quest for such a formula has certainly unveiled the complex dynamics of international economic relations, it has failed in its prescriptive dimension. The inadequacy of one-size-fits-all development theories continued to be demonstrated in the late twentieth century, with the failure of the IMF's structural adjustment model in the late 1980s,[22] and the doubts cast over the World Bank's export-driven development policy after the Asian crises of the mid-1990s. It is perhaps because of these realities that the most recent trend of development economics is more focused

---

[18] H.W. Singer, "The New International Economic Order: An Overview" 1978 *The Journal of Modern African Studies* 16(4) 539, at 541. [19] Ibid at 542–3.

[20] H. Arnold, "Africa and the New International Economic Order" 1980 *Third World Quarterly* 2(2) 295, at 301 (citing extensively D.P. Ghai, "Perspectives on Future Economic Prospects and Problems in Africa," in J.N. Bhagwati (ed), *Economics and World Order* (New York: Macmillan, 1972)).

[21] W. Demas, "The Caribbean and the New International Economic Order" 1978 *Journal of Interamerican Studies and World Affairs* 20(3) 229, at 245–6.

[22] Structural adjustment describes a set of government expenditure reduction, privatization and market-oriented deregulation policies that have been imposed by the World Bank and the IMF as pre-requisites to granting loans to developing countries (conditionality). For a critical evaluation of structural adjustment programs, see, eg, D. Rodrik, "How Should Structural Adjustment Programs Be Designed?" 1990 *World Development* 18(7) 933; D. Dollar and J. Svensson, "What Explains the Success or Failure of Structural Adjustment Programmes?" 2000 *The Economic Journal* 110(446) 894.

on development at the microeconomic level and on promoting initiatives for socio-economic empowerment from the ground up.

1.4 Beyond top-down theories: The privatization of development?

More recent approaches to development economics focus not only on the role of the state with respect to the promotion of domestic industries and the redistribution of public resources, but also on the intervention of private actors as arbitrageurs and primary forces of development. This new approach arose largely out of studies on globalization conducted in the late 1990s. Those critical of the amount of power that globalization has created for private actors point out that the latter are ill-equipped to deal with social policies and the broader socioeconomic impact of development. On the other hand, a number of economists believe that globalization has transformed the private sector into a possible frontline for achieving socio-economic development. Whether they focus on multinational corporations, the economic empowerment of women in rural and urban Africa, or microfinancing, development theories have migrated from the sphere of the political economy to the realm of private microeconomics.

Jeffrey Sachs depicts globalization as a beneficial phenomenon for both rich and poor countries: "[T]he developed countries [reach] a larger market for new innovations, and the developing economies [enjoy] the fruits of those innovations while sharing in global production via multinational enterprises."[23]

Sachs argues that developing countries can become active players in the global market by shortening the technological gap between themselves and developed nations. He explains that developing countries can foster technological growth by facilitating knowledge transfer by the "importation of capital goods from the [technological] leaders, and through the process of [foreign direct investment], joint ventures, strategic alliances, and original equipment manufacturing."[24] Sachs cites Korea, Taiwan, Israel, Mexico, Ireland, China, and Singapore as examples of countries that have utilized such techniques to learn from technological leaders. Sachs' recommendations have found resonance in a number of international organizations. From 2002 to 2006, Sachs was the Director of the UN Millennium Project and Special Advisor to then Secretary-General Kofi Annan on the Millennium Development Goals project; he also served as advisor to the World Bank.

The exponential rise in foreign direct investment (FDI) and its legal avatar, bilateral investment treaties (BITs) over the past two decades[25] testify to the popularity of the type of development strategies advocated by Sachs and other proponents

---

[23] J. Sachs, "International Economics: Unlocking the Mysteries of Globalization" 1998 *Foreign Policy* 110 (Spring) 97, at 101.

[24] J. Sachs, "The Global Innovation Divide," in *Innovation Policy and the Economy, Vol. 3* (Chicago: University of Chicago Press, 2003), at 131–41.

[25] Z. Elkins, A. Guzman, and B. Simmons, "Competing for Capital: The Diffusion of Bilateral Investment Treaties, 1960–2000" 2008 *University of Illinois Law Review* 2008(1) 265, 269–71; J. Tobin and S. Rose-Ackerman, "Foreign Direct Investment and the Business Environment in Developing Countries: The Impact of Bilateral Investment Treaties," Research Paper No 293, Yale Law School, Center for Law, Economics and Public Policy, 2005.

of private-sector microeconomic-led development. However, the critique has not lagged far behind, questioning whether FDI and the increased presence of multinational corporations in developing countries have in fact delivered the expected developmental benefits. For example, such critics point to the fact that the capacity of the local workforce does not increase when the investing foreign corporation uses domestic workers in low-skilled positions only. They also argue that investors and the host state have not always delivered on promises of infrastructure development. The activities of Shell in the Niger Delta, for example, remain a searing example of problematic development implications for the host country of foreign corporations' operations.

Joseph Stiglitz also examines the relationship between capital market liberalization and developing economies. He observes that large externalities are created by capital flows, which affect other market players besides the borrower and lender.[26] In particular, he found that the poorer countries throughout the world bear the brunt of volatility and risk created from capital market liberalization.[27] He concludes that one of the most effective, yet difficult, ways of cultivating economic growth through intervention is to prevent massive amounts of capital outflow. Stiglitz cites China as a prime example of a country where "if most people keep their money in the economy, it grows, and it becomes attractive for others to do so... The restrictions on capital outflows can 'force' the economy to the 'good' equilibrium, and once there, it is self-sustaining."[28] His focus on microeconomics and financing was reflected in his work as Senior Vice President and Chief Economist of the World Bank between 1997 and 2000, and in his vocal critique of the stringent monetary policies advocated by the IMF in the 1980s and 1990s.

Development concerns also find their way in the microeconomic decisions of individuals in developed countries. For example, the recent proliferation of "fair trade" labels, signaling that the producer obtained more remunerative wages, and the promotion of products certified as "fairly traded" is an attempt to promote development through consumerism in developed countries. The desired aggregate effect of such measures is to improve the terms of trade for the exporting country, a long-standing concern for many developing countries reliant on undiversified primary commodity exports. The notion of "sustainably produced" goods also allows consumers of a finished product to influence the conditions of production at the source, often in a developing country. Goods labeled as sustainably produced typically assure that certain environmental protections are implemented to prevent depletion of local resources and promote sustainable development.

Just as macroeconomic development models were promoted as universal cure-alls, some microeconomic strategies that were successful in certain regions have been promoted as transposable across the globe, sometimes without much concern for the local socioeconomic situations. This was the case, for example, with the microlending model. Generally considered to have originated in Bangladesh with

---

[26] J. Stiglitz, "Capital Market Liberalization and Exchange Rate Regimes: Risk without Reward" 2002 *Annals of the American Academy of Political and Social Science* 579, 219. [27] Ibid at 222.
[28] Ibid at 234–5.

the Grameen Bank, the microlending model was then exported to other Southern Asian countries, Africa, and even impoverished regions of the United States. However, when applied to different cultures and economic conditions, the model has not been equally successful, nor has it served all populations equally. In some places, the exclusion of certain groups and the continued marginalization of the poorest sectors of society indicated the limitations of microfinancing as a development policy.[29] Critics also raise concerns about the potential for upsetting dynamics between state and private development initiatives. For example, with respect to microlending, critics emphasize the risk that private financial institutions will take over the state's role in providing a basic socioeconomic safety net.

More generally, critics of the microeconomic approach to development caution that the privatization of development should not obfuscate the need to coordinate national or even regional development policies. Indeed, it is perhaps the focus on either macro- or microeconomic-led development policies that has had deleterious effects over the past few decades, as coordination between state-level policies and private initiatives has been weak. Studies of the Chilean macroeconomic reform and its impact at the microeconomic level on the banking sector illustrate some of these dynamics.[30]

Doubts cast on both state-led development policies and privately run initiatives make it clear that no single model will be universally accepted, or—more importantly—successful. This is particularly true as developing countries increasingly recognize that they do not actually share a common perspective on the meaning of development. An understanding of development that relies primarily on economic indicators and benchmarks, while it has strongly influenced the law and institutions of international development over the past century, is now recognized as too limited, both in its descriptive and prescriptive dimensions.

2. Integrated Perspectives on Human Development: Rights-based Approaches

The late 1980s and early 1990s saw the emergence of a new vocabulary for development reflective of several trends. First, it showed a renewed interest in development as a theoretical concept, rather than as a series of economic and technological problems affecting developing countries. Correlatively, those who view development as a holistic concept tended to require a comprehensive set of policies that included not only economic, but also social and cultural elements. Second, the new development lexicon was precipitated by a variety of agendas, often coming from different constituencies with markedly different goals. For example, the concept of

---

[29] R. Dyal-Chand, "Reflection in a Distant Mirror: Why the West has Misperceived the Grameen Bank's Vision of Microcredit" 2005 *Stanford Journal of International Law* 41(2) 217, at 217.

[30] F. Gallego and N. Loayza, "Financial Structure in Chile: Macroeconomic Developments and Microeconomic Effects," *Econometric Society* (December 1999) <http://www.econometricsociety.org/meetings/wc00/pdf/1115.pdf>.

the "right to development" originated from a Senegalese scholar, whereas the term "sustainable development" was coined by the United Nations World Commission on Environment and Development (Brundtland Commission). While the right to development is promoted by advocates seeking to help developing countries, the concept of sustainable development was originally used by industrialized countries to promote environmental regulation, which developing countries often view as a hindrance to their comparative advantage. Thus, far from being a mere quarrel of words, the debate over development terminology underscores very real divergences regarding the trade and development relationship.

2.1 Defining development through human rights

The goals of development rights are often largely coextensive with those of human rights, simply because development focuses on providing for certain basic needs, the fulfillment of which, in turn, is viewed as a right inherent to every human being. Food, clean water, and shelter are necessities commonly understood as basic socioeconomic human rights.[31] Those viewing development through the human rights lens may also consider other items such as personal security, education, controlling child labor, and providing health services as essential to development. As the 1966 International Covenant on Economic, Social and Cultural Rights puts it, all human beings have a right to "freely pursue their economic, social and cultural development."[32] Similarly, the African Charter on Human and Peoples' Rights proclaims that "All peoples shall have the right to their economic, social and cultural development with due regard to their freedom and identity and in the equal enjoyment of the common heritage of mankind."[33]

More recently, Amartya Sen's influential writings have contributed to a reconsideration of development as a concept comprising more than just aggregate economic benchmarks such as GDP per capita. Sen defines development in relation to freedom. Whereas "unfreedom" is marked by famine, malnutrition, unnecessary morbidity, and a lack of access to health care, education, sanitation, and clean water, development is characterized as freedom from these obstacles.[34] In yet another rights-based approach, Martha Nussbaum defines development in terms of "capabilities." Her studies focus in particular on women's human development.[35]

Development as a set of human rights tends to focus on the achievement of minimum standards. The result is a very dynamic concept of development: As the subject matter of human rights expands, thus adding to the minimum standards, so

---

[31] On development as a human right, and on human rights as the means of development, see generally, P. Alston and M. Robinson (eds), *Human Rights and Development Towards Mutual Reinforcement* (Oxford: Oxford University Press, 2005).

[32] International Covenant on Economic, Social and Cultural Rights, Art 1(1) (Geneva, 16 December 1966; 993 UNTS 3 (1976)).

[33] African Charter on Human and Peoples' Rights (Banjul Charter), Art 22(1) (Nairobi, July 1981; 21 ILM 59 (1982)).

[34] A.K. Sen, *Development as Freedom* (New York: First Anchor Books Edition, 2000), at 15.

[35] M.C. Nussbaum, *Women and Human Development: The Capabilities Approach* (Cambridge: Cambridge University Press, 2000), at 70–96.

does the meaning of development. For example, while the development as human rights approach once contemplated only physical necessities (such as the rights to life, food, and shelter), it now encompasses broad (and more abstract) benchmarks, such as gender empowerment and socioeconomic opportunity.[36] However, critics fear that the rights-based discourse might lead to a dilution of the notion of development because of the aspirational or "soft law" nature of many more advanced human rights instruments.[37]

Through external pressure and internal reform, in the late 1990s the World Bank began accepting that human rights are inherent to development.[38] Whether this reorientation of its activities translated into a more positive result on the ground has been the subject of significant criticism.[39]

2.2 The right to development

Rather than conceptualizing development as a collection of human rights, the notion of the "right to development" asserts the existence of a separate, autonomous human right.[40] Unlike the multiple human rights comprised in the rights-based approach to development, which are individual or group rights, the right to development is usually understood to belong to the state, as a right to pursue the development policies of its choice.[41]

The first assertion of a right to development is credited to Senegalese scholar and judge M'Baye.[42] In 1977, the Commission on Human Rights called for a study on the right to development as a human right, which presumes the existence of a right

---

[36] UN Development Programme, *Human Development Report 2009*.

[37] A.M. Jerve, "Social Consequences of Development in a Human Rights Perspective: Lessons from the World Bank," in H. Stokke and A. Toslensen (eds), *Human Rights in Development Yearbook 1998: Global Perspectives and Local Issues* (The Hague, Netherlands: Kluwer Law International, 1998), at 39.

[38] See K. Tomasevski, "The World Bank and Human Rights," in N. Swineheart and T. Swineheart (eds), *Human Rights in Developing Countries: Yearbook 1989* (The Hague: Kluwer Law International, 1990), at 79–82; I.F.I. Shihata, "Human Rights, Development, and International Financial Institutions" 1992 *American University Journal of International Law and Policy* 8(1) 27, at 33.

[39] See, eg, J. Oloka-Onyango, "Beyond the Rhetoric: Reinvigorating the Struggle for Economic and Social Rights in Africa" 1995 *California Western International Law Journal* 26(1) 1, at 21–9; Jerve, above fn 37.

[40] See, eg, B. Andreassen and S. Marks (eds), "Development As a Human Right: Legal, Political, and Economic Dimensions," in *Harvard Series on Health and Human Rights* (London: Harvard University Press, 2006).   [41] See, eg, African Charter, Art 22(2), above fn 33.

[42] K. M'Baye, "Le Droit au Développement comme un Droit de L'Homme," 1972 *Revue Des Droits de L'Homme* 5, 503–34, at 503. A large body of literature addresses the "right to development." See, eg, on the emergence of development as a human right, O. Schachter, *International Law in Theory and Practice* (The Hague, Netherlands: Kluwer Academic Publishers, 1991), at 348–52; see also H.G. Espiell, "The Right of Development as a Human Right" 1981 *Texas International Law Journal* 16(2) 189, at 189–205; R. Rich, "The Right to Development as an Emerging Human Right" 1983 *Virginia Journal of International Law* 23(2) 287, at 287–328; R. Rich, "The Right to Development: A Right of Peoples?" in J. Crawford and H.G. Espiell (eds), *The Rights of Peoples* (Oxford, Oxford University Press, 1988); R.N. Kiwanuka, "Developing Rights: The UN Declaration on the Right to Development" 1988 *Netherlands International Law Review* 35(3) 257; L.B. Sohn, "The New International Law: Protection of the Rights of Individuals Rather than States" 1982 *American University Law Review* 32(1) 1, at 52–6.

to development.[43] The United Nations General Assembly proclaimed the right to development in several instruments, advocating an integration of social, political, civil, and cultural rights and development.[44]

From a legal perspective, the "right to development" raises numerous issues, not least of which is the task of defining development and determining the nature and content of development rights and obligations. According to the UN General Assembly's *Declaration on the Right to Development*, states have a duty to create "national and international conditions favourable to the realization of the right to development."[45] Somewhat along those lines, Matsushita has argued that the right to development is best understood as a "right to a process" of development.[46] Despite the difficulty of pinpointing the exact form and content of the right to development, it has found some legal and practical grounding in international institutions, in particular the United Nations Development Programme. The right to development perspective must be recognized as a powerful counter-narrative to the Washington Consensus approach to development.

While the concept of a "right to development" originates from a developing country scholar and may well reflect concerns of developing countries, the implementation of such a right (if it gains that legal status over time) may be viewed quite differently by developed and developing countries, in the context of international trade. For example, the ostensibly development-oriented effort beginning in the mid-1990s to include a so-called "social clause" setting minimum standards on labor conditions in trade agreements, has been received with much skepticism by developing countries, which argued that it was really a protectionist ploy by industrialized members to limit poor countries' comparative advantage in cheap labor. The call for a "right to development" also reveals policy conflicts within developing countries: On the one hand governments want to improve the living conditions of their population, and on the other hand they want to benefit from the comparative advantages they have in international trade, even if it comes at the price of social development and environmental safety.

The legal and political impacts of the "right to development" on the conduct of international trade relations seem quite uncertain. In part, the failure of rights-based approaches to development as an operative principle for trade relations can be explained by the cultural dominance of development economics theories. For instance, the rights-based approach to development often clashes with

[43] Commission on Human Rights, "Report of the UN Secretary-General on the International Dimensions of the Right to Development as a Human Right," Res 4 (XXXIII), UN Doc E/CN.4/1334 (1979).

[44] UN General Assembly Resolution 34/46, A/RES/34/46 (23 November 1979); UN General Assembly Resolution 35/174, A/RES/35/174 (15 December 1980), UN General Assembly Resolution 36/133, A/RES/36/133 (14 December 1981), UN General Assembly Resolution 37/199, A/RES/37/199 (18 December 1982); UN General Assembly Resolution 37/200, A/RES/37/200 (18 December 1982).

[45] UN General Assembly Resolution 41/128, A/RES/41/128 (4 December 1986).

[46] M. Matsushita, T.J. Schoenbaum and P.C. Mavroidis, *The World Trade Organization: Law, Practice, and Policy* (New York: Oxford University Press, 2003), at 389–90; see also I.D. Bunn, "The Right to Development: Implications for International Economic Law" 2000 *American University International Law Review* 15(6) 1425, at 1442–3.

the Ricardian idea that development can occur through trade in sectors in which a country has a comparative advantage. The idea of reframing development as a human issue inseparable from the increasingly complex network of human rights generally has not percolated to the WTO.

2.3 Sustainable development

Sustainable development is based on the notion that economic growth and the use of natural resources should not hamper future generations' opportunities. At its core is a time dimension to distribution and allocation of resources, and a belief that present development is not really development if it is pursued inequitably or at the expense of future generations. In other words, development cannot be a transfer from one geographic region to another or be an advance on future generations' environmental patrimony.

During the late 1980s, the concept of sustainable development gained traction in large part thanks to the Brundtland Commission. In its 1987 report, the Commission found that the components of development it deemed to be essential (peace and security, economic development, social development, and governance) were positively correlated to the quality and preservation of the environment. Later still, in the midst of an increasing number of reports by UN agencies and other groups, sustainable development found its paramount expression in the 1992 Rio Declaration on Environment and Development.

Sustainable development joins other rights-based approaches to development[47] because it considers the environment as a global good to which all persons, individually and collectively, present and future, have a right of access. However, some developing countries have argued that the principle of sustainable development, while laudable, is tantamount to a restriction on crucial means and resources required for their development, in particular energy resources. They further argue that developed countries exercised no such restraint or consideration toward future generations when they industrialized in the eighteenth and nineteenth centuries, and that it would thus be unfair to impose such restrictions on countries still in the process of developing. The position of China with respect to international climate change negotiations, in particular, illustrates this divide.[48] Some developing countries have suggested that if environmentally friendly economic growth and industrialization policies are foisted upon them, the rich countries should bear the cost. Others have advocated direct monetary transfers to developing countries as compensation for not polluting—a novel form of rent payment. Still others have campaigned for improved technology sharing and technology transfers so that more sustainable technologies would be shared at lower costs with developing countries.

---

[47] On the relationship between human rights and "environmental rights," see generally, A. Boyle, "Human Rights or Environmental Rights? A Reassessment" 2007 *Fordham Environmental Law Review* 18(3) 471, at 471–511.

[48] On China's positions regarding energy, the environment, and development, see generally, D. Zang, "From Environment to Energy: China's Reconceptualization of Climate Change" 2009 *Wisconsin International Law Journal* 27(3) 543.

Eventually, middle-income developing countries developed their own "green"—or at least "greener"—technologies and in some cases have taken the lead over members of the Organisation for Economic Co-operation and Development (OECD). China's use of coal to fuel rapid economic growth was for a long time in total disregard of environmental implications, but "clean coal" technology is now more widespread in China than it is in the United States.[49] Moreover, the push towards sustainable development has at times been embraced by developed and developing countries alike, for example with respect to the increased use of environmental impact assessments as a preliminary step to development projects.[50]

The purported conflict between sustainable development and economic growth has been the topic of much debate at the GATT and later at the WTO. Under the multilateral trade regime, members can use domestic environmental norms to derogate from their WTO obligations. In some instances, developing countries have argued that such environmental claims were mere pretense to protect developed countries' industries against competition from developing countries. The founding instrument of the WTO, the Marrakesh Agreement Establishing the World Trade Organization, although it refers to "sustainable development," does not clearly define the term or its implications on the adoption of trade-restrictive development policies.

3. "Law and Development" Perspectives

Thus far, we have looked at economic and human rights-based models of development. Starting in the 1960s, American legal academia has tried to conceptualize the relationship between law and development by demonstrating the impact of the rule of law (or lack thereof) on development. In its prescriptive dimension, what has become known as the "Law and Development" movement has promoted several generations of legal reform projects funded by public and private donors to attempt to tackle development and poverty challenges through the diffusion of the rule of law. After its initial success in the late 1960s, law reform efforts faltered in the 1970s, reemerged in the 1990s, and now seek a reincarnation as the "New Developmental State" school, with ongoing experiments in Latin America.

3.1 Modernization through legal reform and legal education

At its inception in the 1960s, the "Law and Development" movement was a response to calls from government funding bodies and foundations to propose and staff development assistance projects as part of the first "Development Decade"

---

[49] J.B. Eisen, "China's Renewable Energy Law: a platform for green leadership?" 2010 *William and Mary Law and Policy Review* 35(1) 1, at 1–2; E. Osnos, "Green Giant: Beijing's crash program for green energy," *The New Yorker* (21 December 2009), 54.
[50] S. Atapattu, "Sustainable Development, Myth or Reality?: A Survey of Sustainable Development Under International Law and Sri Lankan Law" 2001 *Georgetown International Environmental Law Review* 14(2) 265, at 290–2.

launched by the UN.[51] As with earlier iterations of development theory, some even expected that academia would "create a science of development to guide the effort to 'modernize' Third World nations," in the wake of decolonization.[52] As it slowly crystallized, the Law and Development movement came to see legal reform as a driving force of socioeconomic development, with a modernization agenda. David Trubek, one of the leading figures of the Law and Development movement, describes it as a "liberal legalism paradigm:"

> Development was assumed to involve an increase in man's rational capacity to control the world, and thus in his ability to improve his material well-being...
>
> "Law" was seen as both a necessary element in "development," and a useful instrument to achieve it. "Law" was thus "potent," and because legal development would foster social development and improve human welfare it was also "good." Law implied impersonal governance through universal rules, and governance through law would lead to more inclusive and more equal treatment of all citizens. (citations omitted)[53]

Embedded in this approach was the assumption that changes in the law and institutions of developing countries would change behaviors and would do so in a way that would represent and benefit the public interest. In practice, proponents of this vision adopted the fairly ethnocentric view that development would be achieved by modeling the developing country's regulatory framework after those of industrialized states, often supplying the country with "legal transplants" from the North. The first wave of projects focused on reforming and promoting legal education in developing countries in order to fast-track developing states' regulatory modernization. The strengthening or creation of legal institutions then became the target of "Law and Development" reforms.

At the same time, the movement attempted (ultimately unsuccessfully) to organize itself as a distinct academic field, which would give it more weight as an arbitrageur of developmental reform.

When the theoretical and pragmatic limits of this strategy became apparent[54] and neoliberalism became prevalent in the 1980s, a new approach to development through legal reform took root, in large part resulting from loan conditionality imposed by the IMF and the World Bank. During this period, legal reform focused on the deregulation of state macroeconomic policies and increased regulation of microeconomic actors in the private sectors. International financial institutions

---

[51] D. Trubek and M. Galanter, "Scholars in Self-Estrangement: Some Reflections on the Crisis in Law and Development Studies" 1974 *Wisconsin Law Review* 1974(4) 1062, at 1065.

[52] C.L. Merillat, "Law and Developing Countries" 1966 *American Journal of International Law* 60(1) 71, at 76–9; see also, D. Apter, *Rethinking Development: Modernization, Dependency and Post-Modern Politics* (Thousand Oaks, CA: Sage Publications, Inc, 1987).

[53] Trubek and Galanter, above fn 51, at 1073.

[54] A. Seidman and R.B. Seidman, *State and Law in the Development Process* (New York: St Martin's Press, 1994), at 44–51 (documenting the "almost universal failure" of legal "imports" from developed to developing countries). There were also ontological causes for the collapse of the first wave of the "Law and Development" movement. See Trubek and Galanter, above fn 51. Finally, the mixed socioeconomic evidence in developing countries, the lack of dissemination of liberal democratic regimes, and the rise of military dictatorship cast as many doubts as to the ability of the modernist progressive agenda to deliver results. Eventually, funding by major international donors, public and private, to support the modernization project dried up.

believed that development could be achieved by improving the regulatory frame-work for corporations, investors, and the financial sector in general. The focus of the relationship between law and development had shifted from an emphasis on public institutions and regulation to private law.

Interestingly, the collapse of the Soviet Union in the early 1990s gave a new, if short-lived, breath to wholesale exports of North American and Western European legal models. As Eastern and Central European countries became autonomous, they faced sudden pressure to quickly adopt constitutions and codes to prevent a collapse of the rule of law in the vacuum left by the former Soviet Union. With lit-tle connection to the traditional "Law and Development" movement, lawyers and legal scholars from the Western hemisphere were quick to offer their services to cre-ate new laws, in most cases reproducing frameworks from their home countries.[55]

3.2 "Comprehensive" approaches to the rule of law

The "Law and Development" movement did not generally subscribe to Washington Consensus-style deregulation, but instead proposed an alternative approach of "comprehensive" legal reform that would integrate the social and the economic. An early advocate of the move away from the American ethnocentric approach to "Law and Development" can be found with Trubek, a self-critique of the move-ment he was instrumental in launching.[56] More generally, the backlash against the Western-inspired modernization project framed itself at times as an anti-imperialist critique, an anti-(economic) liberalism critique, and a proponent of recognizing and respecting the cultural specificities of indigenous peoples in developing coun-tries.[57] The inherent contradictions and continued ethnocentricity of the second movement of "Law and Development" may account in part for its ultimate eclipse. For instance, the embrace of socialism as an anti-imperialist move at times clashed with traditional societal organizations in some developing countries.

Rittich provides a more recent perspective on the second generation of the move-ment, situating it as a post-Washington Consensus moment, where international financial institutions became aware of the indispensible consideration of social impacts of economic policies.[58] Rittich views the World Bank's Comprehensive Development Framework, announced by Wolfenson in 1999, and the glo-bal endorsement of the Millenium Development Goals as examples of the shift towards a more holistic approach to development policy-making in international organizations. Economists have also joined the call for this more comprehensive

---

[55] See eg, J.C. Reitz, "Symposium: Export of the Rule of Law" 2003 *Transnational Law & Contemporary Problems* 13(2) 429, at 429.

[56] D.M. Trubek, "Toward a Social Theory of Law: An Essay on the Study of Law and Development" 1972 *Yale Law Journal* 82(1) 1, at 2.

[57] For a succinct account, see eg, B.Z. Tamanaha, "Review: The Lessons of Law-and-Development Studies" 1995 *American Journal of International Law* 89(2) 470, at 481.

[58] K. Rittich, "The Future of Law and Development: Second Generation Reforms and the Incorporation of the Social" 2004 *Michigan Journal of International Law* 26(1) 199, at 199.

approach, and some, such as Dani Rodrik, have become influential policy-makers in international organizations.

Conceptually, the second generation "Law and Development" project is still premised on the instrumental role of the law in bringing about and supporting development. Perhaps even more strongly, it asserts law and the rule of law as "definitional to development."[59] At the same time, the second generation recognizes that "because legal rules and institutions constitute an important means of allocating power and resources to different social groups, the form and content of legal reforms can be crucially important to the question of who benefits and who loses in the course of reforms."[60] Abandoning the assumption that legal reform will necessarily and automatically result in Western-style liberal democracy, it recognizes the more complex relationship between development, markets and democracy.[61]

Rather than attempt to transplant legal frameworks from industrialized countries into developing countries, the second generation "Law and Development" movement looks at a number of sources before recommending a "model" for reform, including best practices, governance practices, and international human rights instruments. Unlike the state-centric approach of the first generation, the second generation seeks to involve a number of actors in the reform agenda, including market and non-market actors, civil society organizations, religious groups, ethnic groups, etc. The empowerment of these groups is then strengthened by judicial reform and training and the development of non-judicial dispute fora to sensitize adjudicators to social realities. The recognition of local specificities and diverse inputs into the developmental reality is key to second generation prescriptions. Meanwhile, the state is seen as an "enabler" rather than a driver.[62]

While respect for human rights is announced as an important normative objective of the second generation law reform agenda, the economic orthodoxy of the 1980s has also left its mark: Rule of law projects are largely aimed at promoting market-oriented economic development, with a belief that social development will also follow from the emergence of a grass-root private sector.

3.3 Towards a "New Developmental State?"

In the past decade, the "Law and Development" movement has again drawn lessons from its mixed achievements and is re-emerging under the label of "New Developmental State."[63] A product of its time, the "New Developmental State" concept is imbued with the post-modern belief that "there is no sure fire formula for development—the best that can be done is to proceed with a contextual

---

[59] Ibid at 204.   [60] Ibid at 211.

[61] See, eg, A. Chua, "Markets, Democracy, and Ethnicity: Toward a New Paradigm for Law and Development" 1998 *Yale Law Journal* 108(1) 1, at 1.

[62] Rittich, above fn 58, at 233–4.

[63] D.M. Trubek, "The Political Economy of the Rule of Law: The Challenge of the New Developmental State" 2009 *Hague Journal on the Rule of Law* 1(1) 28, at 28–32; D.M. Trubek, "Developmental States and the Legal Order: Towards a New Political Economy of Development and Law," Legal Studies Research Paper No 1075, University of Wisconsin Law School, Madison, 2009.

and detailed analysis" specific to one particular country, or perhaps even to one particular region or community within a country.[64] Hence, unlike most of the development economics theories presented earlier in this chapter, or even the first generation "Law and Development" thinking, the "New Developmental State" explicitly rejects the single model approach to development. While the "New Developmental State" project is still in its infancy, some work has been conducted in Brazil[65] and in Asia.[66]

Perhaps the best hope for the "New Developmental State" approach is that it will foster the emergence of complex and diverse viewpoints from developing countries themselves about the meaning of development. Some economists from developing countries have generated original theories and have even had a landmark influence on policy-making in international institutions, as was the case for Dr. Prebisch. Other scholars, like Chimni, posit themselves as representing a view from "the South," but their thinking is largely influenced by Western ideas, such as Marxism.[67] Because traditionally the notion of development has been inextricably tied to the industrial North as a socioeconomic and cultural model, it is quite understandable that there has been comparatively little scholarship on development by intellectuals from the South. With its highly localized and contextualized ethos, and its partnership with researchers in the target area, the "New Developmental State" movement may give an unprecedented platform to new thinking on development and that may yet be its most important contribution.

4. Conclusion

This necessarily brief overview of trends in development theory hardly does justice to the wealth of literature available on the subject. The purpose of this chapter is simply to introduce the concepts and schools of thoughts on development that have shaped international economic law over the past century and a half and to relate them to the institutions they have most influenced.

Many of the intellectual movements presented here have intersected over time and have meshed with political considerations and power-plays in international institutions dealing with development. As such, there is no historical moment in which a single theory of development has presided over the implementation of

[64] B. Hauserman, "Review Essay—Exploring the New Frontiers of Law & Development: Reflections on Trubek/Santos eds., The New Law and Economic Development (2006)" 2007 *German Law Journal* 8(6) 533, at 547.

[65] D.R. Coutinho and P. Mattos, *LANDS—Law and the New Developmental State (Brazilian pilot project)* (Madison, University of Wisconsin Law School, 2008) at <http://www.law.wisc.edu/gls/lands.html>.

[66] See, eg, J.K.M. Ohnesorge, "Developing Development Theory: Law and Development Orthodoxies and the Northeast Asian Experience" 2007 *University of Pennsylvania Journal of International Economic Law* 28(2) 219, at 308; Y. Kaneko, "Symposium: The Future of Law and Development, Part III—An Asian Perspective on Law and Development" 2009 *Northwestern University Law Review Colloquy* 104 (November) 186, at 195.

[67] See, eg, B.S. Chimni, "A Just World under Law: A View from the South" 2006 *American Society of International Law Proceedings* 100(1) 17, at 17.

development projects. However, it is useful to recognize the theoretical assumptions and conceptual genesis of different development ideas as we turn to the legal instruments and institutions of development in the next chapter. For example, import substitution theories and endogenous approaches to development translate into vastly different trade policy instruments than are required for export-led development. Similarly, prioritizing private economic regulation over public law and institutions can drive trade negotiations in a different direction than it would otherwise have taken. Perhaps most importantly, the substantive and institutional design of international economic law is highly dependent on whether development is reduced to its macro- or microeconomic component, or whether it is conceived more broadly as a multifaceted social, political, and economic endeavor.

2

The Contribution of International Organizations to Development Policy-Making

At the close of the Second World War, states devised a network of international organizations to regulate various segments of international relations, and in particular economic relations. This chapter tracks how a range of international institutions shaped the concept of development. Building on Chapter 1, it also explores how development economics theories have percolated to these international organizations and determined their approach to development. In line with the overall approach of this book, it focuses on the interplay between regulatory and decision-making processes regarding development.

While development policy-making could have become primarily the province of newly independent states during the decolonization process, it was instead taken over by international organizations, particularly the UN, the IMF, and the World Bank. Developing countries themselves soon voiced their development concerns within international organizations, even those not endowed with a development mandate. Today, the ubiquitous discourse of trade and development at the WTO is a testimonial to this enduring trend of the capture of the development agenda by international organizations.

The original thrust for international development policy-making centered on developing countries' right to self-determination and sovereignty over their natural resources The UN was the leading forum for addressing that concern. With the rise of liberal economic orthodoxy at the IMF and the World Bank, the scope of development policies shifted to a narrower microeconomic focus. Ultimately, the Bretton Woods organizations reshaped the legal systems and internal affairs of the targeted states by instituting technical and administrative reforms. In these financial institutions, the development agenda was no longer formulated and advanced within the traditional international law framework relying on states' sovereign prerogatives, such as the control of their natural resources. Rather, a new type of development governance emerged that bypassed state sovereignty in many ways, reached within states' borders, and subjugated sovereign prerogatives to institutional consensus and decision-making weighted in favor of developed countries. Shifting the institutional home for addressing development from the sovereignty-based UN to the economically weighted World Bank, IMF, and—in practice—GATT transformed the understanding of development.

Starting with the influence of the colonial heritage on economic development tools (mandates, trade preferences, and commodities agreements) (Section 1), this chapter proceeds with the contribution of the UN (Section 2) and the Bretton Woods institutions (Section 3) in framing and implementing development strategies. It concludes with a comparative examination of development objectives in regional trade organizations involving developing countries (Section 4). Most of the development policies and legal tools created or promoted by international organizations over the past century or so are still fundamental to the current debates on trade and development. Tracing their history serves to show the deep roots of current developing country demands at the WTO.

1. The Colonial Heritage for Development Instruments

In the nineteenth and twentieth centuries the colonial policies of a handful of European countries controlled (or attempted to control) the political and economic organization of much of the world.[1] Although there was no uniform formula by which these empires exercised economic and political control over their colonies, a common trend, particularly for France and Great Britain, was to "export" their economic, political, and legal systems to their colonies and dominions, especially in the later part of their colonial enterprises. Much of the political and moral justification for the colonial enterprise, both in France and in Great Britain, was premised on European colonial powers' "duty to civilize," understood as an obligation to foster educational, cultural, political, and economic development.[2] As such, colonialism carried with it, in theory, a development agenda.

The purpose of this section is not to assess the normative value of these colonial projects, nor is it to provide a critique of colonialism, both of which have been thoroughly explored elsewhere. Rather, the objective is to identify some of the vestigial legal institutions inherited from colonialism that continued to be used, purportedly to foster development, in newly independent states. Three institutions are particularly significant in this regard: the mandates system, trade preferences, and commodities agreements. Section 1.1 discusses how the mandates system continued to disseminate the industrialized North's progressive notion of development. Section 1.2 presents the role that trade preferences played in perpetuating codependent economic relationships between the former colonial powers and their former colonies or dominions. Trade preferences eventually became embedded in the multilateral trading system that seems organic to us today. Finally, Section 1.3

---

[1] By the end of the nineteenth century, the British Empire accounted for nearly one-quarter of the world's land surface and more than one-quarter of its total population. From the nineteenth to the early twentieth century, the French Empire was the second largest in size, encompassing about 12.3 million square kilometers at its apogee. The Netherlands, Portugal, Germany, and a few other states also held colonies during this time period.

[2] See C. François and J. Ferry, "Speech Before the French Chamber of Deputies, March 28, 1884" in P. Robiquet (ed), *Discours et Opinions de Jules Ferry* (Paris: Armand Colin & Cie, 1897). Trans. by Ruth Kleinman in Brooklyn College Core Four Sourcebook.

discusses commodities agreements. Although commodities agreements have also largely followed from the economic patterns of the colonial years (particularly the undiversified exportation of agricultural and raw commodities from the colonies), they constitute an attempt by former colonies to leverage the power of their exports in international markets to achieve better control over their domestic economic development.

1.1 Mandates: Embedding a progressive notion of political development

The mandates system was originally intended as a bridge between the old colonial system and the new "concert of nations" orchestrated by the League of Nations.[3] The first targets for this project were the colonies of the former German, Russian, Austro-Hungarian, and Ottoman empires.

Administration of defeated territories after the First World War via a supranational authority, rather than simple annexation by the victors, was a historical turning point. However, the mandates project was also loaded with remnants of the "duty to civilize" sentiment of the colonial enterprise. As Antony Anghie describes the spirit of the time: "The essential purpose of the system was to protect the interests of backward people, to promote their welfare and development and to guide them toward self-government and, in certain cases, independence."[4] Article 22 of the Covenant of the League of Nations testifies to the political development project at the core of the mandate system:

To those colonies and territories which as a consequence of the late war have ceased to be under the sovereignty of the States which formerly governed them and which are inhabited by peoples not yet able to stand by themselves under the strenuous conditions of the modern world, there should be applied the principle that the well-being and development of such peoples form a sacred trust of civilisation and that securities for the performance of this trust should be embodied in this Covenant.

The best method of giving practical effect to this principle is that the tutelage of such peoples should be entrusted to advanced nations who by reason of their resources, their experience or their geographical position can best undertake this responsibility, and who are willing to accept it, and that this tutelage should be exercised by them as Mandatories on behalf of the League.

The character of the mandate must differ according to the stage of the development of the people, the geographical situation of the territory, its economic conditions and other similar circumstances.

The League of Nations—and behind it, the still-dominant European powers—intended to propagate the Western-style parliamentary democracy model of the nation-state to the territories administered by mandates. The dissemination of

---

[3] See generally A. Anghie "Colonialism and the Birth of International Institutions: Sovereignty, Economy, and the Mandate System of the League of Nations" 2002 *New York University Journal of International Law and Politics* 34(3) 513.

[4] A. Anghie, *Imperialism, Sovereignty and the Making of International Law* (Cambridge: Cambridge University Press, 2004), at 120.

this model was accompanied by the exportation of legal codes and legal systems inspired by the civil and common law traditions. In practice, the mandates system largely perpetuated an attenuated version of the former colonial scheme. Yet, it also arguably became a conduit for modern international law—with its trade agreements, institutions, and development project.

This narrative of the mandates system, however, takes a different shade once its specifics are further explored. Notably, Anghie has argued that the very concept of sovereignty was significantly distorted in the course of its exportation to non-European territories through the mandates system. Ultimately, according to the critics, international law, rather than institutionalizing sovereign equality, in fact created a system of juridical inequality, which in turn generated patterns of neo-colonialism, particularly in the form of economic dependence.[5]

1.2 Trade preferences: Multilaterizing "special" trade relationships

Apart from the political and cultural motives for colonialism, economic incentives such as trade, commercial relations, and access to resources were undoubtedly key drivers of the colonial enterprise. Regardless of whether trade preceded the flag or followed it, the trade relationship established between former colonies and their respective former empires often proved to be an enduring one even post-decolonization, particularly through preference programs.

Indigenous economies were structured by colonial powers to export only a limited number of primary commodities, and they typically continued to use this export-driven model after gaining political independence. In fact, trade preferences, which gave exports of the former colonies privileged access to the markets of their former occupiers, ensured that these trade patterns would endure. As former colonial territories gained their independence, they typically formalized their trade preferences in the form of bilateral or multilateral agreements. In reality, the existence of trade preferences depends on the self-interest or goodwill of the preference grantors. Behind the multilateral façade of preferential trade agreements lay the unilateral power of the preference-granting country to amend, deny, or expand tariff benefits to suit its domestic political priorities and economic needs. How the emerging Economic Partnership Agreements between the EU and a number of ACP countries will recast these dynamics will become clearer in the years to come.[6]

Imperial trade preferences can be traced back to 1912, but were not formalized until the 1932 Ottawa Accords, which provided for bilateral or unilateral non-reciprocal

---

[5] See, eg, M. Bedjaoui, *Towards a New International Economic Order* (New York: Holmes & Meier, 1979); B.S. Chimni, *International Law and World Order: A Critique of Contemporary Approaches* (New Delhi: Sage Publications, 1993); J. Gathii, "Alternative and Critical: the Contribution of Research and Scholarship on Developing Countries to International Legal Theory" 2000 *Harvard International Law Journal* 41(2) 263; see generally Harvard Law School, "Symposium: International Law and the Developing World: A Millennial Analysis—Symposium Panel Reports" 2000 *Harvard International Law Journal* 41(2) 595.

[6] See K. Serrano, "The Trade-Development Nexus in EU-Pacific Relations: Realism, Dependence or Interdependence?" 2011 *Global Change, Peace & Security* 23(1) 89.

tariff agreements between the United Kingdom, Canada, Australia, New Zealand, the countries of the West Indies region, most African Commonwealth countries, India, and Pakistan.[7] The protectionist wave of the 1930s, with the Smoot-Hawley Tariff Act in the United States and comparable legislation in European countries, often made exceptions for trade from dominions and colonies. Because of the European Communities (EC)'s external tariff structure, the post-colonial relations between EC states and their respective former colonies were managed through preference programs.[8] France's extensive commercial interests in Africa, for example, came under the aegis of the EC's preference programs when France's former African colonies gained their independence in the 1960s. Preferences were formalized in a number of agreements providing a multilateral framework for unilateral non-reciprocal preferences, as well as a number of other development-related issues, such as public aid. In 2000, the Cotonou Agreement superseded these agreements between the European Union (EU)'s twenty-seven member states and seventy-nine African, Caribbean, and Pacific (ACP) countries. An official preference program was introduced in the EC in 1971 for a ten-year period, with the option of subsequent renewals and modifications every decade.[9]

A number of other countries responded to the UNCTAD's call for Generalized System of Preferences (GSP). For example, Australia instituted its first official trade preference program for developing countries in 1966, offering non-reciprocal preferential tariffs on certain manufactured and semi-manufactured goods.[10] Canada's General Preferential Tariff came into effect in 1974 and was most recently extended until 2004; it presently provides that certain imports, including textile and agricultural processed products, from forty-eight specified Least-Developed Countries (LDCs) are duty-free and quota-free.[11] Japan was another early proponent of trade preferences, having instituted a program dating back to 1971.[12] Similarly, New Zealand[13] and Switzerland[14] both instituted trade preference programs in 1972. A more recent trade preference program enacted in the United States in 2000, the African Growth and Opportunity Act (AGOA), is focused on sub-Saharan African countries. The program expands on the benefits already established by the

---

[7] G. Denis, "Un régime de préférences tarifaires généralisées pour le tiers monde" 1971 *Etudes Internationales* 2(2) 231.

[8] See generally K. Anderson and H. Norheim, "From Imperial to Regional Trade Preferences: Its Effect on Europe's Intra- and Extra-Regional Trade" 1993 *Review of World Economics* 129(1) 78.

[9] See UNCTAD, *Generalized System of Preferences Handbook on the Scheme of the European Community 2008*, UNCTAD/ITCD/TSB/Misc.25/Rev.3 (3 January 2009).

[10] For an overview of the current version of Australia's trade preference scheme, see UNCTAD, *Handbook on the Scheme of Australia 2000*, UNCTAD/ITCD/TSB/Misc.56 (6 January 2000).

[11] See UNCTAD, *Handbook on the Scheme of Canada 2002*, UNCTAD/ITCD/TSB/Misc.66 (12 January 2002).

[12] See UNCTAD, *Handbook on the Scheme of Japan 2006*, UNCTAD/ITCD/TSB/Misc.42/Rev.3 (8 January 2006).

[13] See UNCTAD, *Handbook on the Scheme of New Zealand 1999*, UNCTAD/ITCD/TSB/Misc.48 (4 January 1999).

[14] See UNCTAD, *Handbook on the Scheme of Switzerland 1999*, UNCTAD/ITCD/TSB/Misc.28/Rev.1 (10 January 1999).

GSP by allowing certain goods (in particular, textiles) from forty-one specified countries to have quota-free and duty-free entry into the United States.[15]

Despite UNCTAD's insistence on "generalized" and non-discriminatory preferences, most GSP schemes are neither. Far from being purely legalistic, the conditions and scope of trade preferences continue to shape the economic development of many developing countries by creating incentives for the recipient countries to focus on narrow categories exports, and thus to forgo more comprehensive industrialization or socio-economic development policies. An extensive literature also discusses the erosion of trade preferences as across-the-board decreases of tariffs on primary goods have decreased the relative value of the preferences.[16] This issue, along with the legal compatibility of trade preferences with the WTO legal regime, will be revisited in later chapters.

1.3 Commodities agreements: Primary resources to fund development?

In many developing countries, colonialism left a legacy of primary commodity extraction and exportation, which together became the foundation of the newly independent countries' economic growth. International law proclaiming the sovereignty of developing countries over their own natural resources provided legal backing for reliance on extraction of primary materials as the means to control economic development. However, exports of raw materials are only able to jump-start an economy, as prescribed by many of the "catching up" development economics theories and endorsed by several UN Resolutions,[17] if the export price of these commodities remains high, or at least high enough to allow the country to afford its imports. Since the early 1960s a high priority of many developing countries has been to improve their terms of trade (defined as the relative price of a country's exports compared to its imports) in the face of the declining price of primary commodities.

Later in the decade, developing countries forcefully advocated the creation of mechanisms to stabilize and manage the trade of primary commodities in an attempt to forestall the declining value of such exports and to lessen the volatility

---

[15] For an overview, see UNCTAD, *Handbook on the Scheme of the United States of America 2003*, UNCTAD/ITCD/TSB/Misc.58/Rev.1 (8 October 2003), which includes features of the African Growth and Opportunities Act (AGOA) Program.

[16] See, eg, UNCTAD Secretariat, *Quantifying the Benefits Obtained by Developing Countries From The Generalized System of Preferences*, UNCTAD/ITCD/TSB/Misc.52 (7 October 1999); B.M. Hoekman, W. Martin, and C. Braga (eds), *Trade Preference Erosion: Measurement and Policy Response* (United Kingdom: Palgrave Macmillan, 2009); D.K. Brown, "Trade Preferences for Developing Countries: A Survey of Results" 1988 *Journal of Development Studies* 24(3) 335.

[17] See UN General Assembly Resolution 1707(XVI), A/RES/1707(XVI) (19 December 1961) (urging developing countries to ensure "an increase in their foreign exchange income as a result of growth in the volume and value of their exports"); UN General Assembly Resolution 1710(XVI), A/RES/1710(XVI) (19 December 1961) (calling on member states and UN specialized agencies to ensure price stabilization of primary commodities at remunerative prices).

of earnings due to fluctuations in market prices.[18] A series of commodities agreements were formed in the late 1960s and throughout the 1970s to regulate the world prices and supply of sugar, timber, various metals, and other agricultural commodities. A few agreements were renegotiated or extended throughout the 1990s but most disintegrated in the 1980s due to insufficient funds for the management of buffer stocks.[19] From 1980 to 1991, the average annual decline in the terms of trade was equivalent to nearly 25 percent of the value of commodity exports in 1980; by 1989–1991, the corresponding relative loss had doubled.[20]

The OPEC stands out as a uniquely enduring mechanism to control prices of a primary commodity. Since 1965, the OPEC has managed to successfully contain the volatility of the price of oil, a key primary commodity, and has prevented the erosion of its value by allocating production quotas amongst its members.

Another example is the STABEX, a stabilization fund for primary commodities exported by ACP countries to the EC.[21] The STABEX was grounded in firmer financial grounds than most commodities agreements, but even it was no match for the commodities crisis of the mid-1980s and early 1990s. The ACP countries' share of the EC market, which was intended to be protected by the agreement, increased from 6.7 percent in 1976 to 7.2 percent in 1980, but then decreased to 3.7 percent by 1992.[22] Even despite the limitations of its product and country coverage, the STABEX has been the most comprehensive commodities agreement to date. It also resulted in a direct linkage between the EC market and the exports and domestic incomes of the participating ACP countries. The availability and consistency of the aid provided by the STABEX was essential to the success of domestic economic development programs and to the political stability of participating ACP countries. The STABEX is a salient illustration of developed countries' and the international community's involvement in the domestic economic affairs of developing countries through aid or assistance programs. As such, the STABEX is very different from other types of commodity agreements that are managed by a consortium of developing countries.

Although it was not a stabilization mechanism for primary commodities like those discussed above, the 1973 Multifiber Agreement (MFA)[23] was also a major instrument dealing with primary commodities exported from developing countries to developed countries. One of the MFA's objectives was "to further the economic

---

[18] See, eg, Islamic Conference of Foreign Ministers, *Cairo Declaration on Human Rights in Islam*, at para 32; Charter of Algiers, preamble, Part 2 (A); UN General Assembly Resolution 2626(XXV), A/RES/2626(XXV) (24 October 1970), at para 21.

[19] G. Koehler, "The Future of STABEX," Issues Paper Prepared for the Summit of ACP Heads of State and Government (November 1997) <http://www.acpsec.org/summits/gabon/koehler.htm>.

[20] A. Maizels, "The Continuing Commodity Crisis of Developing Countries" 1994 *World Development* 22(11) 1685.

[21] From the phrase "stabilization of export earnings;" the STABEX was established by the EC in 1976 alongside the first Lomé Convention.   [22] Koehler, above fn 19.

[23] Arrangement Regarding International Trade in Textiles (Multifiber Agreement or MFA) (Geneva, 20 December 1973; 25 UST 1001); see also its predecessors: Interim Arrangement Regarding International Trade in Cotton Textiles (Geneva, 21 July 1961; 12 UST 1674) and the Long-Term Arrangement Regarding International Trade in Cotton Textiles (Geneva, 9 February 1962; 13 UST 2672).

and social development of developing countries and secure a substantial increase in their export earnings from textile products and to provide scope for a greater share for them in world trade in these products,"[24] while also liberalizing trade in this sector. Under the MFA, developing countries negotiated bilaterally with developed countries for quotas on imports of products covered by the agreement (cotton, wool, etc). These quotas were to be progressively increased (and ultimately phased out) but remained much more restrictive than initially anticipated until the entire scheme expired in January 2005. By contrast, no restriction existed on textile imports between developed countries. The MFA was negotiated and implemented outside of the GATT but was replaced in 1995 by an agreement within the WTO, the Agreement on Textile and Clothing.

The colonial contribution to development policies and instruments still shapes international economic law today. Trade preferences and commodities agreements in particular have become features of trade law. Their underlying political projects, be it securing access to certain resources by industrialized countries through trade preferences or the attempt by developing countries to organize themselves with commodities agreements, are still relevant. Their economic impact, both on developing countries and on international trade relations, also persists to date.

2. The United Nations:
Public International Law Approaches to Development

The UN both contributed to substantive norms regarding development and promoted an institutional framework to address development issues.[25] The basis for the UN's role as a coordinator of development efforts is found in Article 1 of the Charter and further expounded in Chapter IX on international economic and social cooperation. When the International Trade Organization (ITO) was abandoned in 1948 (see Chapter 3), the UN came to assume an even broader role, as some macroeconomic issues assigned to the ITO (employment, in particular) fell upon the UN by default.[26]

At the institutional level, development policies are to be framed primarily by the General Assembly, with the advice of the Economic and Social Council. In the decades following World War II, a number of technical bodies were created to address specific aspects of development,[27] culminating with the creation of UNCTAD in 1964. Regional economic development and planning institutes were also created

---

[24] Art 1(3) MFA.

[25] UN Charter, Preamble (the French version of the Charter is even more explicit regarding the central place of international institutions).

[26] See, eg, J.M. Clark, *National and International Measures for Full Employment* (New York: United Nations Department of Economic Affairs, 1950).

[27] UN General Assembly Resolution 1712(XVI), A/RES/1712(XVI) (19 December 1961) (creating a Center for Industrial Development, later to become the UN Industrial Development Organization (UNIDO)). See also UN General Assembly Resolution 1715(XVI), A/RES/1715(XVI) (19 December 1961) (creating the Expanded Program for Technical Assistance and the Special Fund).

for Africa, Latin America, and Asia to provide training on economic planning and to help members devise development plans tailored to their needs.

Developing countries pursued the public international law strategy they had inaugurated at the close of World War II in an attempt to steer international economic law toward a development objective. As a result, the UN's development activities focused on national sovereignty, self-determination, and the right of states and peoples to freely exploit national resources.[28] This approach garnered momentum in the 1960s when many former colonies became independent states and joined international organizations, but it plummeted in the mid-1970s after the Charter for Economic Rights and Duties of States[29] and the New International Economic Order[30] both failed.

2.1 A comprehensive approach to development

The 1961 United Nations' Programme for a Development Decade, in conjunction with a series of General Assembly resolutions, set the stage for a broad regulatory overhaul of economic development. The UN identified international trade as a "primary instrument for economic development,"[31] but the Development Decade program included wide-ranging macroeconomic tools: industrial policy (and the social implications of industrialization), technical assistance and access to capital, and technology transfer.[32] Although it acknowledged concerns regarding the imbalances of the international trading system, the General Assembly passed a resolution specifically identifying the GATT as an appropriate forum for trade negotiations. Agriculture was identified as an issue of concern and indeed remains salient to this day. This is not to say that the UN was advocating unfettered, market-run economic relations; to the contrary, it underlined the need for economic planning—a term more reminiscent of state-planned economies—in a number of resolutions.

When the UN launched a second Development Decade in 1968–1971, the context was not a congratulatory one: The results of the first Development Decade and

---

[28] UN General Assembly Resolution 626(VII), A/RES/626(VII) (21 December 1952); UN General Assembly Resolution 1720(XVI), A/RES/1720(XVI) (19 December 1961); UN General Assembly Resolution 1803(XVII), A/RES/1803(XVII) (14 December 1962); UN General Assembly Resolution 2692(XXV), A/RES/2692(XXV) (11 December 1970); UN General Assembly Resolution 3201(S-VI), A/RES/3201(S-VI) (1 May 1974), at para 4(e).

[29] UN General Assembly Resolution 3281(XXIX), A/RES/3281(XXIV) (12 December 1974).

[30] The NIEO consisted of a set of proposals that were largely promoted by developing countries through the UNCTAD, and which resulted in a number of UN resolutions. See generally, R.L. Rothstein, *Global Bargaining: UNCTAD and the Quest for a New International Economic Order* (Princeton: Princeton University Press, 1979), at 280. The principles articulated in those resolutions reflect a post-colonial critique of sovereignty over natural resources and the role of multinational corporations in developing countries. Another major area of focus was the pricing of raw commodities exported by developing countries. With respect to trade, the NIEO called for non-reciprocal and non-discriminatory tariff preferences, unconditional aid, technical assistance, and technology transfer.   [31] UN General Assembly Resolution 1707(XVI), above fn 17.

[32] UN General Assembly Resolution 1712(XVI), above fn 27; UN General Assembly Resolution 1711(XVI), A/RES/1711(XVI) (19 December 1961); UN General Assembly Resolution 1713(XVI), A/RES/1713(XVI) (19 December 1961).

of the first UNCTAD conference had fallen short of expectations.[33] Although the plan for the second Development Decade emphasized economic growth and set many quantitative targets, it also identified a more extensive list of social factors to be improved, reflecting the UN's new multifaceted approach to development. In contrast with the first Development Decade, the plan for the second Development Decade mapped out ways to achieve these social goals, with recommendations regarding schooling, reducing illiteracy, improving nutrition, along with other programs pertaining to health and housing.[34] The UN had become increasingly willing to formulate specific recommendations in matters of development previously left to the discretion of domestic policy-makers. The shift is notable as it testifies to the increasing power of international organizations to define, implement, and evaluate development needs and priorities.

With respect to trade, UN recommendations for the second Development Decade replicated earlier calls for industrialized countries to offer duty-free treatment (or at least to freeze duties) on products imported from developing countries,[35] and for developing countries to increase and diversify their exports, especially in light of the new competition created by synthetic substitutes. A more original feature was the explicit linkage between aid and trade, where international aid was promised for the purpose of supporting trade promotion efforts by developing countries.[36] Assistance in support of trade was previously considered "technical assistance," but the plan for the second Decade inaugurated a *quid pro quo* of aid for trade that endures to date.

2.2 Transforming international economic relations?

Although a decade separated them, the program of the first Development Decade resembled a blueprint for the NIEO. The Declaration and Program on the Establishment of a New International Economic Order of 1974 proposed a comprehensive reconfiguration of international economic relations under the aegis of the UN (UNCTAD in particular). It was a progeny of left-leaning approaches to development economics, which viewed a radical reordering of global economic relations as the necessary precondition to true development. In fact, the NIEO was in many ways part of a continuum for concerns expressed by developing countries since World War II. For example, the Declaration's preamble reaffirmed the fundamental principles of sovereignty, equality, and independence as the basis for any reconsideration of international economic law. Moreover, the Program's focus on terms of trade and the valuation of raw materials manifested the resurgence of concerns that developing countries first voiced when they gained independence.

The renewed emphasis on legal, political, and economic sovereignty conveyed a profound discomfort with an international system that failed to protect the most

---

[33] UN General Assembly Resolution 2571(XXIV), A/RES/2571(XXIV) (13 December 1969). See also, Charter of Algiers (noting the deterioration of many economic indicia as to the progress of developing countries and the failure to achieve the goals set by the first UNCTAD conference in 1964).   [34] UN General Assembly Resolution 2626(XXV), above fn 18.   [35] Ibid at paras 25–8, 33–4.   [36] Ibid at para 36.

vulnerable states, despite unprecedented amounts of regulation in the area of economic policy. The Declaration acknowledged that some progress had been made since decolonization, but insisted that the "vestiges of alien and colonial domination, foreign occupation, racial discrimination, apartheid and neo-colonialism in all its forms continue[d] to be among the greatest obstacles to the full emancipation and process of developing countries." It therefore required that the new order should be premised on "non-interference in the internal affairs of other states," "the right of every country to adopt the economic and social system that it deems most appropriate for its own development," the "rights of states or peoples under foreign occupation, colonial domination or apartheid to full compensation and restitution," assistance to these states and their "liberation," and "assistance to developing countries without military or political conditions."[37] Although the UN was committed to maintaining the economic sovereignty of developing countries, it occasionally ventured into the realm of domestic policy choices, even going so far as to recommend an export-driven model for development.

Regarding trade measures, the Declaration for an NIEO insisted on "preferential and non-reciprocal treatment for developing countries in all fields of international economic co-operation." It identified trade as having the potential both for cooperation (in the form of South–South trade between developing countries)[38] and competition (developing countries competing for preferences from developed countries).[39] These issues remain highly relevant today.

The legacy of the NIEO for the GATT is further explored in Chapter 3 but should be summarized here. The 1971 Temporary Waiver permitting preferences in favor of developing countries at the GATT was a landmark gain for developing GATT members. The hopes raised by the discussions of a NIEO had played a key role in leading developing members of the GATT to support the Tokyo Round of trade negotiations (1973–1979). The NIEO movement can also be credited in part for the adoption at the GATT of a permanent "Enabling Clause" at the close of the Tokyo Round, allowing non-reciprocal preferences both amongst developing countries and between developed and developing countries.[40] Institutionally and procedurally as well, the NIEO had an impact on the position of developing countries at the GATT. First, the format of the Tokyo Round resulted in a number of plurilateral agreements to which parties could selectively agree, as opposed to a single one-size-fits-all agreement. Second, the principle of non-reciprocity (the notion that developing countries should not have to make concessions in exchange for the benefits of trade liberalization granted by others) became a cornerstone of developing countries' approach to multilateral trade negotiations and perhaps the most successful element of the NIEO. It was the conceptual forefather of the broader

[37] UN General Assembly Resolution 3201(S-VI), above fn 28; UN General Assembly Resolution 3202(S-VI), A/RES/3202(S-VI) (1 May 1974).
[38] UN General Assembly Resolution 3201(S-VI), above fn 28, at para 4(s).
[39] UN General Assembly Resolution 3202(S-VI), above fn 37, at para I.3(x).
[40] GATT Contracting Parties, *Decision on Differential and More Favourable Treatment, Reciprocity and Fuller Participation of Developing Countries*, GATT Doc.L/4903, adopted 28 November 1979 (hereinafter Enabling Clause).

notion of special and differential treatment of developing countries at the GATT and later at the WTO.

2.3 Promoting coherence in development planning

UNCTAD's 2004 Trade and Development Report argued that a feasible development agenda has to be based on the concept of "coherence." The report points to the growing interdependence of countries (when internal performance is closely contingent on external factors) and the need to craft development agendas that will meet both internal and external needs. Coherence requires finding a balance between the competing goals of openness, integration, and national policy space. It also entails coordination between the myriad domestic and international agencies involved in development policy-making.

Multiple international accords recognize the need to integrate the various facets of development policies: the Sao Paulo Consensus (final declaration of UNCTAD XI in 2004), the Millennium Development Goals, the Monterrey Consensus, the Program of Action for the LDCs, the Almaty Program of Action, the Barbados Programme of Action, the Johannesburg Declaration on Sustainable Development, the Plan of Implementation from the World Summit on Sustainable Development, and the Declaration of Principles and the Plan of Action of the World Summit on the Information Society. The Sao Paulo Consensus offers a synthesis of the multiple elements of an integrated development policy: eradicating poverty and hunger by creating jobs, paying special attention to LDCs, accelerating multilateral trade negotiations under the Doha Work Program, facilitating accession of LDCs to the WTO, improving coherence between national and international efforts and organizations, achieving positive integration, increasing participation of all social and political forces in the creation of effective national policies, and assisting with regional and interregional initiatives.

A number of UN agencies have created specific tools to support integrated development policies and projects. One example is UNCTAD's Trade and Development Index, comprised of thirty-four indicators (including human capital, environmental sustainability, physical infrastructure, macroeconomic stability, etc) to assist countries in formulating sound trade and development policies.[41] The United Nations Development Programme (UNDP) largely through the work of Amartya Sen, has promoted "human development" understood as greater access to knowledge, better nutrition, and health services; economic growth as a means to reduce inequality and improve levels of human development; efficient and equitable use of production resources to benefit the poor, women, and other marginalized groups; empowerment, democratic governance, gender equality, civil and political

---

[41] UNCTAD, *Developing Countries in International Trade 2007: Trade and Development Index,* UNCTAD/DITC/TAB/2007/2 (10 January 2007), at 4, Fig. 1 and Appendix 3. The Trade and Development Index was developed with the assistance of Lawrence R. Klein, Nobel Economics Prize winner in 1980.

rights, and cultural liberty, particularly for marginalized groups defined by urban-rural, sex, age, religion, ethnicity, physical/mental parameters, etc; sustainability in ecological, economic, and social terms; and security in daily life against such chronic threats as hunger and abrupt disruptions including joblessness, famine, conflict, etc. Since its first Human Development Report in 1990,[42] the UNDP has developed three other composite indices for development: the Gender-Related Development Index, the Gender Empowerment Measure, and the Human Poverty Index. All these measures require a coherent and coordinated approach to development policy-making.

The UN Economic and Social Council (ECOSOC) focuses on identifying and sharing the best practices of development policies throughout the world. For example, ECOSOC maintains a website called "Development Strategies that Work," and also hosts the Development Cooperation Forum. Additionally, the ECOSOC tracks the progress of the Millennium Development Goals[43] with the help of an independent advisory body headed by Jeffrey Sachs.[44]

A number of other UN agencies play a role in international development, usually as part of their specialized focus. For example, it is difficult to discuss development without taking into consideration migration and population displacement issues within the purview of the UN High Commissioner for Refugees (UNHCR). Human rights are the focus of the Human Rights Council, which has a broader objective than just development. The UN Industrial Development Organization (UNIDO) has long played an important part in contributing to development policy. It currently focuses on capacity building and poverty reduction and is particularly attuned to issues of energy and environmental resources. Even more technical agencies such as the International Maritime Organization, responsible for improving maritime safety and preventing pollution from ships, can play a role with respect to development.

In sum, both sectoral agencies and broad-based multilateral fora at the UN reach into every conceivable aspect of development, however broadly understood. Unlike international financial institutions, which focus first and foremost on economic benchmarks, the UN's approach to development has long been more comprehensive, perhaps a result of the historical involvement of many scholars and policy-makers from developing countries in UN agencies, be it Dr. Prebish at the UNCTAD, or Mahbub ul Haq and Amartya Sen at the UNDP, for example. However, the UN and its agencies have been less effective in seeing their recommendations implemented in international trade law and policy.

---

[42] Mahbub ul Haq is the founder of the Human Development Report.

[43] The Declaration set forth specific objectives to be achieved by 2015: (1) the end of poverty and hunger; (2) universal education; (3) gender equality; (4) child heath; (5) maternal health; (6) a cure for HIV/AIDS; (7) environmental sustainability; and (8) global partnership.

[44] UN Millennium Project, *Investing in Development: A Practical Plan to Achieve the Millennium Development Goals* (New York: Earthscan, 2005).

3. The Bretton Woods Institutions:
From International Reconstruction to Domestic Restructuring

The post-World War II period inaugurated a turn away from the economic protectionism of the 1930s as countries embraced the notion of an open trading regime regulated by international institutions. The economic and political causes for this shift are debated by political scientists and economists,[45] but the resulting multilateral system was unprecedented from a legal perspective.[46] This new system, devised with the economic and political reconstruction of Europe in mind, outgrew its initial mandate and became increasingly focused on development. Whereas the UN, with its objective of guaranteeing international peace and "social progress,"[47] concerned itself with the social and political aspects of development, the Bretton Woods institutions (the IMF and the International Bank for Reconstruction and Development (IBRD)) and the ITO (with its gap-filler, the GATT) occupied the field of economic and monetary relations, with varying degrees of development mandates. The IMF was entrusted with the regulation of the international monetary system, with no particular development vocation. However, its statute was later reinterpreted to permit a development-oriented agenda; a close examination of the IMF's constitutive document reveals how this evolution was possible. The IBRD was created to lead post-war reconstruction. While it later expanded its activities to development-related loans, a sister institution, the International Development Association (IDA) was created in 1955 specifically to give loans to the poorest countries. The two eventually formed the World Bank. As with the IMF, an analysis of the founding document of the World Bank reveals how it came to occupy the development field beyond its initial mandate.

3.1 Institutional framework for the IMF and the World Bank's development activities

The IMF was established to facilitate international monetary relations at a time when the monetary crises and inflationary spikes of the 1930s were all-too-recent memories. Besides its role as a regulator of monetary policies, the Fund has the broader goals of "facilitat[ing] the expansion and balanced growth of international trade and [contributing] thereby to the promotion and maintenance of high levels of employment and real income and to the development of the productive resources of all members as primary objectives of economic policy."[48] Macroeconomic growth,

---

[45] See, eg, A.J. Crozier, *The Causes of the Second World War* (Oxford: Blackwell Publishers Ltd, 1997), at 320 (arguing that protectionism had been an important cause of the war).

[46] The prior era was characterized by bilateral trade agreements concluded on an ad hoc basis between countries. See S. Zamora, "Economic Relations and Development," in O. Schachter and C. Joyner (eds), *United Nations Legal Order* (Cambridge: Cambridge University Press, 1995), at 515.

[47] UN Charter, Preamble.

[48] Art I(ii) Articles of Agreement of the International Monetary Fund (IMF Agreement) (Bretton Woods, 22 July 1944; 2 UNTS 39).

defined by the expansion of employment, production, and income, is therefore at the core of the IMF's mission and provides a legitimate basis for development activities. However, the IMF's Articles of Agreement are silent on the implementation of this mandate: They fail to link the Fund's stated purpose of regulating monetary policy with the promotion of employment and income growth in developing countries. Similarly, Article VIII ("General Obligations of Members") only entails obligations regarding monetary policies, and does not create any right or obligation regarding employment and income policies.

In practice, decisions on loans and on the conditions for granting the loans are concentrated in the hands of OECD countries that largely control the Executive Board. While the IMF is formally led by the Board of Governors, on which each member state has one representative, the day-to-day management of the Fund is conducted by the twenty-four members of the Executive Board. Each member of the Executive Board possesses a number of votes proportional to the amount contributed to the Fund by the country or group of countries he or she represents. The United States currently holds the biggest voting block (16.75 percent), followed by Japan, Germany, France, and the United Kingdom. Saudi Arabia, China, and Russia also have individual representatives on the Executive Board with smaller shares. The remaining 180 member states are assigned by loose geographic regions, with one representative on the Executive Board holding each region's aggregated shares. After the 2010 reform (not yet in effect as of June 2013), "Emerging Market and developing Countries" will hold 44.8 percent of the votes, compared with 41.2 percent for the G7 countries. African countries will hold 5.7 percent of the votes, China will hold 6 percent, India 2.6 percent and Brazil 2.2 percent. A number of researchers show that the recipients of IMF loans tend to be countries that are politically allied with or otherwise useful to the United States.[49]

The IBRD and the IDA now jointly form the World Bank. The Bank's purposes (Article I) give little indication that the institution would find a role beyond postwar reconstruction. At most, it could be inferred that the Bank could be reactivated to facilitate reconstruction in what we now call post-conflict situations.

Although the Articles mainly provide for the rehabilitation of production facilities in war-torn territories, the possibility of lending aid to development projects is mentioned in broad terms in Article I(i) calling for the Bank to assist reconstruction and development through "the investment of capital for productive purposes, including the restoration of economies destroyed or disrupted by war, the conversion of productive facilities to peacetime needs and *the encouragement of the development of productive facilities and resources in less developed countries*" (emphasis added). Article I(iii) reinforces that mandate: The Bank must "promote the long-range balanced growth of international trade and the maintenance of

---

[49] See generally R.J. Barro and J. Lee, "IMF Programs: Who Is Chosen and What Are the Effects?" 2005 *Journal of Monetary Economics* 52(7) 1245. For specific cases, see A.O. Krueger, "Whither the World Bank and the IMF?" 1998 *Journal of Economic Literature* 36(4) 1983; M. Bordo and H. James, "The International Monetary Fund: Its Present Role in Historical Perspective," NBER Working Paper 7724, National Bureau of Economics, 2000; P. Blustein, *The Chastening: Inside the Crisis that Rocked the Global Financial System and Humbled the IMF* (New York: Public Affairs, 2001).

equilibrium in balances of payments by encouraging international investment for the development of the productive resources of members thereby assisting in raising productivity, the standard of living and conditions of labour in their territories." Interestingly, this provision contains language similar to Article I(ii) of the IMF's Articles of Agreement. Unlike the IMF's statute, the substantive provisions of the Bank's Articles of Agreement do provide details on the modalities of its development mission.[50] The World Bank began sending "economic missions" to developing countries in the 1960s to advise them on economic policy and infrastructure restructuring,[51] and the first structural adjustment loan (to Turkey) was signed in 1980.

The IDA was created as a counterpart to the IBRD to provide low- or no-interest long-term loans to the world's poorest countries which could not borrow under normal market terms, or even under the terms of the IBRD. The first IDA loans were approved in 1961 and granted to Chile, Honduras, India, and Sudan. Recently, the IDA has granted an average of USD14 billion per year in loans, most of which disbursed to sub-Saharan African countries. Seventy-nine countries currently are eligible for IDA lending, based on measures of poverty. IDA loans support a variety of projects including infrastructure, social projects, public law and administrative capacity building, agricultural development, industrial projects, and financial sector strengthening.[52]

Like the IMF, the World Bank is overseen by a Board of Governors and is managed by a Board of Directors with weighted votes similar to the IMF Directors. In sum, with respect to development, the IMF deals with general macroeconomic equilibrium and growth, while the World Bank facilitates the practical implementation of development projects by providing access to financing.

3.2 Development policies at the World Bank and the IMF

Although the IMF and the World Bank still formally operate according to their original statutes, their conception of development has evolved over time, somewhat in line with the theoretical scholarship discussed in Chapter 1. Both institutions have traditionally promoted a development paradigm stressing market-based economic policies designed to promote economic growth. The member states themselves, not the organizations, were primarily responsible for addressing issues of income equity. However, in the 1950s and 1960s, a "growth with equity" approach to development emerged at the World Bank and the IMF. It remains to be seen how successful it has been at addressing income equity issues,[53] but it testifies to an

---

[50] Art III Articles of Agreement of the International Bank for Reconstruction and Development (IBRD Agreement) (Washington, 27 December 1945; 16 UST 1942).

[51] See, eg, economic missions in Brazil (1964), Peru, Venezuela, Turkey, and Nigeria (1965).

[52] International Development Association, "What is IDA?" <http://go.worldbank.org/ZRAOR8IWW0>.

[53] See generally E.R. Carrasco and M.A. Kose, "Income Distribution and the Bretton Woods Institutions: Promoting an Enabling Environment for Social Development" 1996 *Transnational Law and Contemporary Problems* 6(1) 1.

effort to broaden the understanding of development beyond pure macroeconomic benchmarks.

With the profound transformation of the international monetary system in the early 1970s,[54] the role of the Bretton Woods institutions evolved significantly. The increasing debt of developing countries[55] and their precarious dependency on a handful of exported commodities that were subject to fluctuating market prices caused them to require more assistance from the IMF and the World Bank. By its own count, the World Bank supported foreign exchange policy reforms and trade reforms through over 200 loans between 1981 and 1994.[56]

In the early 1980s the IMF and the World Bank, where the US and the United Kingdom had a dominant voice, promulgated the strong market-oriented policies advocated by their leaders. Other "clubs" formed by industrialized countries, such as the G8, also grew in influence and reinforced the trend. Because regulation of the international economy had been entirely captured by these organizations, free trade in its neo-liberal version became the prevailing (perhaps even exclusive) model. It consisted of assorted privatization, trade and investment liberalization, and tight fiscal and monetary disciplines.[57] The term "Washington Consensus" was coined to describe how the Bretton Woods institutions followed the US Treasury in formulating these policies.[58]

Both the IMF and the World Bank played a growing role in all-encompassing "structural adjustment" programs designed to support (and often promote) fundamental reforms of public management structures in developing countries alongside reshaping their macroeconomic and monetary policies. Structural adjustment policies were often implemented when developing countries turned away from import-substitution strategies, particularly in Latin America. The IMF responded to the debt crises of the 1980s by extending its structural adjustment programs in the form of providing assistance over longer periods and in larger amounts. Ultimately,

---

[54] In 1971, the United States informed the IMF that it would no longer freely buy and sell gold to settle international transactions. Thus, par values and convertibility of the dollar—the two main features of the Bretton Woods system—ceased to exist, and gold lost the status it had enjoyed as a benchmark of the international monetary system.

[55] As early as 1965, the OECD's Development Assistance Committee and UNCTAD commissioned a study on the problem of external debt, which found that the debt of thirty-seven developing countries had increased from USD7 million in 1955 to over USD18 million in 1962. D. Avramovic, *Economic Growth and External Debt* (Washington: Johns Hopkins University Press, 1965). See also D. Horowitz, *The Horowitz Proposal: A Plan for Financing the Economic Development of Developing Countries* (Washington: IBRD, 1965).

[56] World Bank, *World Bank Support for Developing Countries on International Trade Issues*, DC/99-19 (14 September 1999), at para 3.

[57] T. Lothian, "The Democratized Market Economy in Latin America (and Elsewhere): An Exercise in Institutional Thinking within Law and Political Economy" 1995 *Cornell International Law Journal* 28(169) 176.

[58] See generally J. Williamson, "What Washington Means by Policy Reform," in J. Williamson (ed), *Latin American Adjustment: How Much Has Happened?* (Washington: Institute for International Economics, 1990), at 445; J. Williamson, "The Washington Consensus Revisited," in L. Emmerij (ed), *Economic and Social Development into the XXI Century* (Washington: Johns Hopkins University Press, 1997), at 579.

the IMF's Structural Adjustment Facility provided balance of payments assistance on concessional terms to low-income developing countries.

Although structural adjustment programs were formally authorized by the recipient state, in apparent respect for state sovereignty, the lack of alternative funding available to developing countries gave the IMF and the World Bank significant clout to push forward their agenda and impose their market economy orthodoxy within states' borders. As Hudec noted, the shift of many developing countries from a planned or semi-planned economy to a market-oriented economy in the 1980s was often "more a leap of faith than a fully-considered judgment" in the face of stalling economies and overwhelming public debt.[59]

Social and environmental policies emerged as a new area of focus at the Bank in the late 1990s, concomitant with the emergence of human rights approaches to development. The importance of social safety nets and long-term investment in human capital (such as health and education) to countries undergoing structural adjustment became more prominent on the IMF and World Bank agendas, particularly after the formulation of the "Comprehensive Development Framework" at the World Bank in 1998. In response to worldwide criticism regarding the impact of the Bank's policies on developing countries, the Framework called for a "holistic approach to development." It emphasized cooperation among development actors, providing governments, civil society, and the private sector alike a place at the policy-making table.[60] The conceptual realignment of the World Bank's approach to development came with a commitment to two fundamental principles: "do no harm" and ensuring that vulnerable groups have a share in project benefits.[61]

Ultimately, both the Bank and the IMF modified their understanding of development to incorporate human rights, more successfully so at the Bank. Indeed, the Bank now promotes economic, social, and cultural rights, such as the rights to health, education, social welfare, jobs, and property, and has expanded the range of stakeholders in its decision-making processes. It appears to have embraced the notion of sustainable development. The IMF has also engaged in discussions regarding health care, the environment, welfare, housing, unemployment, labor markets, and military expenditures.[62] These trends mirror, to some extent, the evolution of the theoretical understanding of development over the past three decades, discussed in Chapter 1.

---

[59] R.E. Hudec, "GATT and the Developing Countries" 1992 *Columbia Business Law Review* 67(1) 74.

[60] R.C. Blake, "The World Bank's Draft Comprehensive Development Framework and the Micro Paradigm of Law and Development" 2000 *Yale Human Rights and Development Law Journal* 3(1) 158. See also, D.L. Clark, "The World Bank and Human Rights: The Need for Greater Accountability" 2002 *Harvard Human Rights Journal* 15(1) 205.   [61] Jerve, above Ch 1 fn 37, at 45.

[62] D.D. Bradlow, "The World Bank, the IMF, and Human Rights" 1996 *Transnational Law & Contemporary Problems* 6(1) 47.

4. Institutional Arrangements and Development Ethos in South–South Economic Organizations

Although large multilateral institutions largely took the helm of development policy-making, a number of regional organizations are also active in the field. Their existence is often premised on a desire to tailor development models that prevail in the multilateral institutions to the specific region or constituency that they serve. For instance, regional development banks focus on particular geographic zones and seek to promote local culture and expertise. Perhaps even more so, regional human rights treaties and regional trade agreements have sought to distinguish themselves from the market-oriented liberal democracy ethos promoted by large multilateral organizations. This section considers the development ethos of regional development banks and South–South regional trade agreements in contrast to their multilateral counterparts. It offers clues to a dichotomy between the legal and institutional tools for addressing developments that have emerged in the regional fora and at the WTO. The specifics of those legal instruments will be further discussed in Chapter 8.

4.1 Regional development banks

In Asia, Latin America, and Africa, regional development banks have been established to provide better access to capital for countries to finance their development. Perhaps because they are managed more directly by the beneficiary countries, their objectives differ from the IMF and World Bank.

The Organization of American States established the Inter-American Development Bank in 1959 as an initiative by President Juscelino Kubitschek of Brazil. Forty-eight states are parties, including twenty-six Latin American and Caribbean borrowing members, which have a majority ownership of the Bank. Through project financing, technical assistance, and knowledge generation, the Inter-American Development Bank aims to reduce poverty and social inequalities, paying particular attention to small and vulnerable countries. The Bank's core objectives also include addressing climate change, developing renewable energies, and fostering regional cooperation and integration. Regionalism and socioeconomic development are sometimes combined for projects such as the Initiative for the Promotion of Regional Public Goods, which offers public goods on a regional basis to countries with similar needs in order to harness economies of scale and other collective benefits.

Although the UN had called for a regional development bank for Africa,[63] such a bank was created independently by twenty-three African governments in 1964. Headquartered in Abidjian, Tunisia, the African Development Bank now serves fifty-three African states and twenty-four non-African states. The African

---

[63] UN General Assembly Resolution 1718(XVI), A/RES/1718(XVI) (19 December 1961).

Development Institute, a sister institution, was created more recently to provide training activities for Bank staff and member countries. Since 2001, the Institute has focused on generating and sharing knowledge amongst the workers and policy-makers of the Bank's African member states. The African Development Bank seeks to mobilize the resources of the African continent to provide sustainable economic and social development for its member states; these goals have been incorporated by reference into the Millennium Development Goals. Recognizing the size and diversity of the continent, the Bank implements its local focus by delegating as many of its operations as possible to its twenty-three field offices.

The Economic and Social Council's Economic Commission for Asia and the Far East (later to become the Economic Commission for Asia and the Pacific) created the Asian Development Bank in 1966. The Bank's "Strategy 2020" describes its development objective as supporting "inclusive growth, environmentally sustainable growth, and regional integration." It expressed particular concern about the growing disparities and socio-economic inequalities amongst its members, viewing these imbalances as a threat to the welfare of the entire region. The Bank hopes to reach its goals by mobilizing regional resources, in particular savings and inbound capital flows, and by "maximiz[ing] returns on its unique regional experience and comparative strengths within the evolving aid architecture." The Bank plans to focus on "(i) private sector development and private sector operations, (ii) good governance and capacity development, (iii) gender equity, (iv) knowledge solutions, and (v) partnerships."[64] It is not yet clear how the economic crisis of 2008 will affect the Bank's priorities.

Institutionally, the banks differ markedly. The Inter-American Development Bank is largely modeled after the World Bank and the IMF, with a board of governors and an executive board, where votes are allocated proportionally to shareholdership. The preponderance of the US share in the Bank (about 30 percent) perhaps explains this influence. By contrast, the Asian Development Bank's Board of Directors (the organization's managerial and executive entity) has a system of indirect representation where each of the twelve Directors represents between one and eleven member states of various sizes. Executives Directors at the African Development Bank combine group representation and weighted voting rights associated with each country they represent.

4.2 Development objectives in South–South trade agreements

Development is a stated objective in several dozens of regional trade agreements (RTAs) spanning Africa, South and Central America, Asia, and the Pacific.[65]

---

[64] Asian Development Bank, *Strategy 2020—The Long-Term Strategic Framework of the Asian Development Bank 2008–2020* (April 2008) <http://www.adb.org/documents/policies/strategy2020/Strategy2020-print.pdf>.

[65] Treaty Establishing a Common Market between the Argentine Republic, the Federative Republic of Brazil, the Republic of Paraguay, and the Eastern Republic of Uruguay (MERCOSUR) (Asuncion, 26 March 1991; 30 ILM 1041); Agreement on South Asian Trade Area (SAFTA) (Islamabad, 6 January 2004).

Even bilateral agreements between developed and developing countries, such as the United States–Morocco free trade agreement, understood to closely serve the US trade agenda, mention a development objective.[66] Development goals in South–South RTAs are varied, including sustainable development, self-reliance, equitable development, development disparities (including regional disparities), and the differential development impact of trade liberalization.

That said, the balance between economic and broader development concerns varies significantly. For example, the Common Market for Eastern and Southern Africa associates—and even seems to equate—sustainable growth and development with "a more balanced and harmonious development of its production and marketing structures."[67] The East African Community, too, speaks of "a fast and balanced regional development" and "balanced and sustainable development."[68] By contrast, some agreements associate sustainable development more closely with environmental sustainability.[69]

The notion of self-reliance also appears in several treaties and could be seen as both a means to, and product of development, particularly industrial development. Most African RTAs include language referring to self-reliance as a goal of industrial policy.[70] A number of Asian RTAs, although not explicitly framed in

[66] See, eg, Preamble, United States–Morocco Free Trade Agreement (US–Morocco FTA) (Washington, 15 June 2004; Hein's No KAV 7206). Other agreements between developed and developing partners with a clear development objective include the Agreement on the Common Effective Preferential Tariff Scheme for the ASEAN Free Trade Area, (Singapore, 28 January 1992; 31 ILM 513) and the Framework Agreement on Enhancing ASEAN Economic Cooperation (Singapore, 28 January 1992; 31 ILM 506).

[67] Treaty Establishing the Common Market for Eastern and Southern Africa (COMESA) (Kampala, 5 November 1993; 2314 UNTS 265).

[68] Preamble, Treaty for the Establishment of the East African Community (EAC Treaty) (Arusha, 30 November 1999; 2144 UNTS 255); see also Art 38 Southern African Customs Union Agreement (SACU) (Gaborone, 21 October 2002) (recognizing the importance of "balanced industrial development"); Preamble and Art 1, Decision 563: Official Codified Text of the Andean Subregional Integration Agreement (Cartagena Agreement) (Quirama Recinto, 25 June 2003).

[69] Preamble, Trans-Pacific Strategic Economic Partnership Agreement (TPP) (Wellington, 18 July 2005) ("economic development, social development and environmental protection are interdependent and mutually reinforcing components of sustainable development"); see also Art 15.2(h) Revised Treaty of Chaguaramas Establishing the Caribbean Community Including the CARICOM Single Market and Economy (CARICOM) (Nassau, 5 July 2001; 2259 UNTS 293) (creating a council for trade and development to, *inter alia,* "promote and develop policies for the protection of and preservation of the environment and for sustainable development"); Art 51.2(g) CARICOM (industrial policy objectives include "enhanced industrial production on an environmentally sustainable basis"); Art 56.1(f) CARICOM (community agricultural policy objectives include "the efficient management and sustainable exploitation of the Region's natural resources"); Art 1.9, Charter of the Association of Southeast Asian Nations (ASEAN Charter) (Singapore, 20 November 2007) (purposes include "to promote sustainable development, so as to ensure the protection of the region's environment, the sustainability of its natural resources").

[70] Art 99(a) COMESA (objectives of cooperation in industrial development include the promotion of "self-sustained and balanced growth"); Art 79 EAC (members shall take steps in industrial development to "promote self-sustaining and balanced growth"); Art 26.2(a) Treaty of the Economic Community of West African States (ECOWAS) (Cotonou, 24 July 1993; 2373 UNTS 233) (to promote industrial developments, members shall "foster self-sustained and self-reliant development"); Art 5.1(d) Treaty of the Southern African Development Community, as Amended (SADC) (Windhoek, 17 August 1992; 32 ILM 116) (objectives include promoting "self-sustaining development on the basis of collective self-reliance, and the interdependence of Member States"); Preamble,

terms of self-reliance, posit the regional economy as a priority, clearly adopting an endogenous focus for development.

Many RTAs also speak of equitable development (development in which benefits are shared by all participants).[71] Generally, the requirement for an equitable share of the benefits of trade liberalization seems aimed at the several states participating in the agreement. In some cases equitable development is linked to the promotion of democratic and transparent institutions, suggesting that the concern is for the *domestic* equitable sharing of the benefits of development. Sustainable and equitable growth is sometimes also tied to the objective of raising the standard of living of the member states' population.

Some RTAs approach development concerns in the negative, focusing on reducing "development disparities" and "adverse impacts" of trade on development. As stated in CARICOM, "some Member States, particularly the Less Developed Countries, are entering the [single market] at a disadvantage by reason of the size, structure, and vulnerability of their economies."[72] RTAs stemming from ASEAN also typically recognize the disparities between their members; the agreements feature asymmetric provisions to address intra-regional developmental gaps.[73] Many

Charter of the South Asian Association for Regional Cooperation (SAARC Charter) (Dhaka, 8 December 1985) (noting that cooperation "would contribute significantly to national and collective self-reliance").

[71] Art 6(d) COMESA; Art 5.2 EAC (objectives include "accelerated, harmonious and balanced development and sustained expansion of economic activities, the benefit of which shall be equitably shared"); Art 7.1(f) EAC (principles include the "equitable distribution of benefits" of operation); ECOWAS Preamble ("Accepting the need to share the benefits of economic cooperation and integration among Member States in a just and equitable manner . . . "); Art 2(b) SACU (objectives include creating "effective, transparent and democratic institutions which will ensure equitable trade benefits to Member States"); Art 2(g) SACU (objectives include facilitating "the equitable sharing of revenue arising from customs, excise and additional duties levied by Member States"); Cartagena Agreement Preamble (community will "lead to the balanced, harmonious, and shared economic development of their countries"); Art 1 Cartagena Agreement (objectives are to "promote the balanced and harmonious development of the Member Countries under equitable conditions"); Art 60(f) Cartagena Agreement (objectives of industrial development include "equitable distribution of benefits"); Art 3.1(b) SAARC Charter ("ensuring equitable benefits to all Contracting States, taking into account their respective levels and pattern of economic development").

[72] CARICOM Preamble; see also SACU Preamble ("Mindful of the different levels of economic development of the Member States and the need for their integration into the global economy"); Preamble, Agreement Establishing the ASEAN–Australia–New Zealand Free Trade Area (Cha-am, Phetchaburi, 27 February 2009) ("Considering the different levels of development among ASEAN Member States and between ASEAN Member States, Australia and New Zealand and the need for flexibility, including special and differential treatment"); Preamble, South Pacific Regional Trade and Economic Cooperation Agreement (Tarawa, 14 July 1981; 1240 UNTS 66) ("Mindful of the differing economic potential of Forum Island countries and the special development problems of the Smaller Island countries"); Art 144 COMESA; Art 1 Cartagena Agreement (the agreement also seeks "to reduce existing differences in levels of development"); CARICOM Preamble ("the persistence of disadvantage, however arising, may impact adversely on the economic and social cohesion in the Community"); Art 1.6 ASEAN Charter (purposes include narrowing the development gap within ASEAN).

[73] See eg, Preamble para 9 and Art 1(d) Framework Agreement on Comprehensive Economic Cooperation among the Governments of the Republic of Korea and the Member Countries of the Association of Southeast Asian Nations (ASEAN–Korea) (Jeju-do, 2 June 2009); Preamble paras 2 and 7, Arts. 1(d) and 2(d)–(e) Framework Agreement on Comprehensive Economic Cooperation between ASEAN and the People's Republic of China (ASEAN–China) (Phnom Penh, 4 November

RTAs acknowledge what an increasing number of economists identify as the price of trade liberalization: Freer trade and economic integration can in fact have detrimental effects on less developed countries, at least initially. Unlike the WTO, a number of RTAs explicitly seek to address these tensions.[74] Some agreements even have specific monitoring mechanisms to assess the possible adverse impact of the RTA, as well as the pre-existing development disparities. For instance, the Andean Community agreement calls for the periodic evaluation of the process in light of the growth of each country's exports, each country's balance of trade with the region, GDP, creation of new jobs, and capital formation.

Several agreements include the concept of an "enabling environment," recognizing that certain conditions must exist in member states to achieve development objectives, including facilitative policies and physical infrastructure and also legal infrastructure. Some agreements specify that the environment must be enabling for private sector activities, in particular investment.[75] States have also recognized political stability as part of an "enabling environment."[76]

A different language and a distinct perspective on the intersection between trade regulation and development emerges from South–South agreements (trade agreements and regional development banks). First, development is conceived as a multi-level endeavor: intra-state locally, nationally, and internationally with the regional partners. Development policy implications for all three levels seem to be a driving force for entering into trade agreements and translate explicitly into the objective and purpose of the agreements. In many cases, operative provisions to substantiate this multilevel concern with development are included in the treaties (a further examination of substantive development-oriented and special and differential treatment provisions will be provided in Chapter 8). Suffice it to note here that although most of the trade agreements examined were between developing countries, many still included asymmetric commitments and mechanisms to support the weaker

2002); Preamble para 6 Framework Agreement on Comprehensive Economic Cooperation between the Republic of India and the ASEAN (ASEAN–India) (Bali, 8 October 2003).

[74] Art 6(d) COMESA (obligating members to "look into all possible economic problems that Member States may face during the implementation of this Treaty and propose ways and means of redressing such problems in a manner that will satisfy the conditions of equitable and balanced development"); Art 7.1(f) EAC (principles include "the equitable distribution of benefits accruing or to be derived from the operations of the Community and measures to address economic imbalances that may arise from such operations"); Art 143.2 CARICOM (measures necessary to "address economic dislocation arising from the operation of the [single market]...[and] to ameliorate or arrest adverse economic and social impact arising from the operation of the [single market]...[and to assist] economic enterprises disadvantaged by the removal of intraregional barriers"); Art 11(e) SAARC Charter (LDCs "may face loss of customs revenue due to the implementation of the Trade Liberalisation Programme under this Agreement.").

[75] Art 8.1(a) EAC (policies and resources should be directed "with a view to creating conditions favourable for the development and achievement of the objectives" of the treaty). See more specifically Art 3(c) COMESA (objectives include "creation of an enabling environment" for investment); Art 4.3(b) COMESA (members undertake to "provide an appropriate enabling environment" for private sector participation in development); EAC Preamble (members "are resolved to creating an enabling environment...").

[76] Art 4(f) ECOWAS (fundamental principles include the "promotion of a peaceful environment as a prerequisite for economic development").

members or regions. Second, development is seen as a comprehensive, multifaceted project that ranges from peace and security considerations to very concrete policy coordination on key infrastructure and strategic sectors including energy, transportation, and investment. Macroeconomic benchmarks such as GDP, economic growth, and employment are contextualized within broader industrial policies, government and administrative reform to foster the private sector, and virtually every aspect of the participating countries' socioeconomic make-up.

Unlike the IMF, the World Bank, or even the WTO, which ostensibly justify their restrictive view of development based on the narrow relationship between development and their financial, monetary, or trade missions, South–South RTAs boldly recognize the deep and complex relationship between trade liberalization and development, not limited to economic development. Undoubtedly, when developing countries are free to define the trade and development relationship, the result differs from the predominant approaches at the WTO, the World Bank, and the IMF, and even the UN.

5. Conclusion

The purpose of this chapter was to provide some insights into the question raised in the first part of this book: Who decides what development means? By correlating institutional structures and specific visions of development, it suggests that the meaning of development is very much a product of each organization's culture, policy-makers, and decision-making process. Realists would likely say that relative economic power largely holds the key to identifying who decides what development means. While the IMF and the World Bank's understanding of development has taken center stage in recent times, this predominance appears to be only a moment in history, perhaps more related to their institutional power structure than to how successful their ethos has been at promoting development. At the same time, developing countries have consistently pursued more comprehensive—if not necessarily cohesive—approaches to development, be it at the UN or in regional trade organizations. The legal analysis of the mandate and authority allocation of these various organizations showed that the composition and decision-making structure within an organization influence the agenda and substantive consideration of development.

Thinking back to the two paradigms for the trade and development relationship presented in the introduction of this book, international organizations with a development mandate illustrate different visions. The UN mandate presents a "normative co-constituent" feature, with economic and social development at the core of the organization's mission and institutions. Indeed, the UN has been the *situs* for voicing and addressing development demands for several decades. Most regional trade organizations between developing countries also include development as a core normative underpinning of the institution. By contrast, the IMF and the World Bank, with a weaker development mandate and institutions where developing countries had less weight, have crafted their development activities more on an *ad hoc* basis.

II

FRAMING DEVELOPMENT AT THE GATT AND WTO

Having considered theoretical perspectives on the concept of development and the role of international organization in producing development norms in the preceding chapters, this Part focuses on the intersection between trade and development at the WTO. Here again, both the substantive and the institutional aspects are inseparable. The hypothesis is that some key institutional features, or their absence, play a critical role in the way that development considerations have been framed in the trade regime since the inception of the GATT. The main argument is that many of the current debates surrounding trade and development in the Doha Round are not new. While they have come into the limelight more recently, they find their roots in the missing trade and development link in the GATT 1947. From product coverage to tariff escalation clauses to problematic access to—and participation in—the negotiations, developing members have in fact continuously voiced eerily similar concerns for the past six decades. That is not to say that the dynamics are the same in 2012 as they were in the 1950s or the 1970s. Indeed, while many of the hurdles faced by developing countries are the same, their response has evolved considerably. In particular the level of their participation has undergone a monumental transformation since the late 1990s. Not surprisingly, these evolving dynamics have spurred a legitimacy crisis for the WTO and the recognition that some institutional readjustment must be undertaken.

This Part makes three claims. First, it shows that the institutional failure of the ITO and the normative limitations of the GATT 1947 largely account for the unprincipled trade and development relationship in the multilateral trade liberalization system. Chapter 3 explores the impact of the missing institutional framework for development during the GATT years. Second, this Part argues that despite there being little unity amongst developing countries, the use of a single label has been a politically useful device. Chapter 4 examines the theory and practice of the developing country designation under the GATT and WTO agreements, particularly through the lens of accessions. Lastly, this Part claims that the visibility of the debate on trade and development has increased over the past decade in large part because developing countries have seized institutional opportunities for leveraging their power at the WTO. Notably, they have successfully captured parts of the negotiation agenda, which is key to delineating the disciplines and commitments that might come out of a negotiation round. Chapter 5 explores the evolution of developing country participation and their positioning at critical institutional "moments": the inception of a new round of negotiations, the definition of the agenda for negotiations, and the tabling of substantive proposals. In part, developing members' increased leverage stems from their strategic alliances and coordination in coalitions.

3

The Trade and Development Relationship during the GATT Years and the Genesis of the WTO

The dichotomy explored in Chapter 2 between a public international law approach to development governance and technical, domestic interventions is also reflected at the GATT and WTO. The shift from interstate economic relations to increasingly domestically focused regulation influenced the evolution of the GATT and the creation of the WTO. Indeed, since the 1960s, trade regulation progressively moved from reducing barriers *at the border* to advancing the international trading agenda *within states' borders*, using some international organizations as a conduit. The Tokyo Round inaugurated an era of regulating areas traditionally considered to be domestic matters (such as government procurement, subsidies), but the à-la-carte formula for participating in the agreements limited their impact. At the same time, the emergence of newly industrialized countries in Eastern Asia, fueling their economic growth by an export strategy, and the withdrawal from import-substitution strategies in Latin America and elsewhere meant that an increasing number of developing countries had a political as well as an economic stake in the international trading system. The Uruguay Round continued to expand the ambit of international trade regulation, but made participation in all agreements mandatory for all members. Much of the debate regarding trade and development during and since the Uruguay Round is a product of this increased reach within borders, as well as the ultimate prevalence of a technical regulation model over a general public international law model for international economic law.

In broad terms, the public international law approach translates into attempts to incorporate development concerns at the core of the trade liberalization regime and to modulate states' obligations based on their developing status. The ITO reflected that philosophy, but it never came to fruition. The addition of Part IV of the GATT in 1964 was another effort to introduce development at the core of trade liberalization disciplines. The concept of non-reciprocity introduced during the Tokyo Round and later embodied in the Enabling Clause of 1979 and the general provisions on least developed countries also included in the Enabling Clause both sought to address capability differentials between developed and developing states through a general undertaking of trade liberalization obligations. More recently, the reference to sustainable development in the Marrakesh Agreement establishing the WTO also sought a normative balance between the trade and development aspects of liberalization. All these measures left individual states free to define domestic development policies as they wished. State sovereignty and autonomy were the operative principles.

By contrast, the technical approach to trade regulation and development translates into *ad hoc* or limited carve-outs from general disciplines. For example, the addition of Article XVIII to the GATT in 1955 allowed derogations to support the development of infant industries and to remedy balance of payment crises. The Decision on Safeguard Action during the Tokyo Round also provided limited derogations,[1] as do trade preferences in favor of developing countries or between developing countries. The Uruguay Round agreements, with their plethora of "special and differential treatment" clauses, are another example. More recently, the Doha Decision on Public Health and pending TRIPS amendment are additional *ad hoc* measures in an area that is complex and critical to many developing countries. Such instruments often predetermine and limit the ability of developing countries to devise their own development policies. It is in part in reaction to these intrusions on state sovereignty that the notion of "policy space" emerged as a rallying cry for those who wanted to reclaim more control over domestic economic policy.

Through a more detailed discussion of the trade and development relationship during the GATT years, this chapter traces the origins of many issues that shape today's trade negotiations. It also shows that the problematic outcomes of the Uruguay Round for developing members are not so much the result of the final package, but rather were built into the negotiations long before the Round even began.

Section 1 compares the trade and development relationship in the GATT 1947 and the aborted Charter for an ITO. Two fundamentally different visions of the multilateral trading system emerge, with the ultimate prevalence of the GATT stirring early misgivings from developing countries. Section 2 assesses the legacy of UNCTAD for the GATT. The story is largely one of a missed opportunity: Development considerations, even after the adoption of Part IV of the GATT and the Enabling Clause, remained subordinate to a narrow perspective on trade liberalization. The expansion of trade regulation to new matters with the Tokyo Round transformed the place of developing countries in the GATT system perhaps even more fundamentally. Rather than taking into account the continuing concerns of developing countries and allowing for diverse perspectives on trade liberalization, the expansion of trade regulation largely marginalized the developing parties to the GATT, at a time when they made up the overwhelming majority of the membership (Section 3). The Uruguay Round offered the first real reconsideration of trade and development, but unlike the ITO, which placed development-related issues at the core of the Charter, the Uruguay Round engrained a singular neoliberal understanding of trade, where allowances for development are considered

---

[1] GATT Contracting Parties, *Decision on Safeguard for Development*, L/4897 (28 November 1979).

anomalies to be eventually phased out. Rather than mainstreaming development into the trade regime, then, the Uruguay Round mainstreamed Western liberal economic orthodoxy (Section 4).

1. The Trade and Development Component of the ITO and the GATT's First Steps

1.1 The ITO and the GATT: Two fundamentally different visions of multilateral trading

Beyond the idealistic and political motivations for the multilateral administration of trade, economic theories played a fundamental role in shaping the contours of the ITO and the GATT. The reaction against protectionist policies, seen as responsible for the economic crisis of the 1930s,[2] is often cited as a major motivation for the establishment of a multilateral system premised on free trade. However true that may be, it should not obliterate the fact that free trade theorists in the 1940s and 1950s advocated for a system quite different from the now-prevalent neo-classical approach to free trade. Indeed, Ohlin, Haberler, and Nurske's notion of free trade took into account market failures regarding employment and factor price inflexibility.[3] This group of Geneva economists was instrumental in elaborating the ITO Charter, which accorded significant attention to employment and made allowances for government policies meant to remedy macroeconomic disequilibria. Keynes also linked macroeconomic trade with employment policies and took an active role in formulating the early drafts for an international trade organization; he was convinced that it was integral to the post-war system. Politicians seemed to concur: Harry Truman, then-president of the United States, declared to the UN that a trade agreement would "complete the post-war structure of peace."[4] Ultimately, the ITO was to take its place alongside the World Bank and the IMF under the umbrella of the UN.

The Havana Charter establishing the ITO[5] is striking, first of all, for its length and its tone. In effect, it reads more like the UN Charter than like the short, functional Articles of Agreement of the IMF and the IBRD. Both Charters seek to set the foundation for a different international order. The UN Charter's foremost contribution is the assertion of the principle of *collective security*. Arguably, the

---

[2] The US Smoot-Hawley tariff is often cited as the most prominent example of these policies. It resulted in tariff duties on manufactured and agricultural goods imported in the United States averaging 40 percent of the value of the goods.

[3] A.M. Endres and G.A. Fleming, *International Organizations and the Analysis of Economic Policy, 1919–1950* (Cambridge: Cambridge University Press, 2002), at 125–32.

[4] T.W. Zeiler, *Free Trade, Free World—The Advent of GATT* (Raleigh: University of North Carolina Press, 1999), at 269; see also, US Department of State, *Proposals for the Expansion of World Trade and Employment*, Commercial Policy Series 79, Publication 2411 (Washington, DC, 6 December 1945).

[5] United Nations Conference on Trade and Employment, *Final Acts and Related Documents,* UN Doc E/Conf. 2/78, 21 November 1947.

ITO Charter endeavors to establish a *collective economic system*. Many of the ITO Charter's provisions do not create strict legal obligations; rather, they formulate a collaborative approach to economic growth and prosperity. Just as the UN Charter takes the power of waging war out of the hands of states (except in limited circumstances), the ITO Charter abolishes the mercantilist logic of country-versus-country competition and presents economic growth through trade and employment as a collective policy. This feature is perhaps what makes the ITO Charter such an original instrument, even more than the substantive obligations enshrined in the agreement.

The draft Charter was pushed forward by the United States and initially found support from the Europeans, Canada, and Cuba, while the United Kingdom's response was lukewarm. Australia, India, Lebanon, Brazil, and other developing countries were critical and wanted to maintain more opportunities for protection and preferences.[6]

Alongside the ITO Charter, a shorter, simpler agreement was negotiated and quickly entered into force on a provisional basis, pending the approval of the ITO Charter. This agreement, the GATT, was in line with traditional reciprocal trade agreements such as those negotiated bilaterally by the United States.[7] By 1950, the United States Congress had lost interest in the ITO project,[8] prompting it to be abandoned, and the GATT remained as the sole trade agreement devoid of an umbrella institution. Some parties to the GATT then sought the introduction of employment provisions inspired by the ITO into the GATT during the Torquay Round (1951). These efforts were resisted by the United States, Canada, and the United Kingdom.[9]

Comparing the substantive provisions of the ITO Charter and the GATT provides interesting insights regarding the foundation of the multilateral trading system. Robert Hudec has argued that because there was little experience to draw from, countries followed their "habit of thought" and their self-interest.[10] Thus, the United States sought a non-discriminatory trading system that would allow their export-oriented economy to continue to grow. As Hudec pointed out, the give-and-take bargaining for tariff concessions, in which a country "pays" for a concession on one product by giving access to its market for another product, testifies to a mercantilist understanding of international trade relations: "[R]eciprocity was the political balm that allowed harmful trade barriers reduction by one country to be compensated by equivalent action on the part of trading partners."[11] European colonial powers intended to protect the preferential schemes they had in place in favor of their empires. Developing countries had several goals. They

---

    6 Zeiler, above fn 4, at 70.
    7 S. Aaronson, *Trade and the American Dream: A Social History of Postwar Trade Policy* (Lexington: University Press of Kentucky, 1996), at 262.
    8 For an extensive discussion of the shelving of the ITO and the creation of the GATT, in particular the dynamics between the US and the USSR, see B. Gosovic, *UNCTAD Conflict and Compromise—The Third World's Quest for an Equitable Economic Order through the United Nations* (Leiden: A.W. Sijthoff, 1972), at 3–27.   9 Zeiler, above fn 4, at 162.
    10 P. Low, "Developing Countries in the Multilateral Trading System: the Insights of Robert E. Hudec" 2003 *Journal of World Trade* 37(4) 719, at 801–11.   11 Ibid at 802.

wanted to ensure the availability of trade preferences, non-reciprocity, and exemptions from trade rules to protect their infant industries; they sought a framework that would foster transfer of real resources in their favor; they required guarantees that foreign investment would not be used for purposes of political interference by foreign powers in their internal affairs; and they wished more leeway to institute development policies as they saw fit.[12]

The mercantilist ethos of the GATT is significant for developing countries because it contributed to their marginalization after many of them joined in the 1960s without having to negotiate concessions, and later when they obtained non-reciprocity treatment on certain concessions. Because it was thought that they did not "pay" for the benefits they received from the trading system, they were considered as free-riders, and there was no incentive to grant concessions of interest and value to them.

Table 3.1 provides an overview of the differences between the ITO Charter and the GATT. Most provisions regarding commercial disciplines are virtually identical between the two instruments, with a few notable exceptions. However, the two differ substantially regarding the role of government assistance for economic development. While the ITO Charter included detailed provisions regarding this matter, it was not until 1955 that Article XVIII was added to the GATT, offering Contracting Parties the possibility of limited exceptions to support new industries and trade restrictive measures to address balance of payment crises. The ITO embodied a strong view in favor of governmental protection of infant industries (and industries undergoing post-war reconstruction). It provided a complex and comprehensive mechanism to derogate from the main disciplines subject to consultations with affected members and the organization, with the latter sometimes having a power of approval over proposed measures. The GATT counterpart to this system was a streamlined and more limited framework: By default, governmental assistance should not derogate from fundamental GATT disciplines. Other subject matters addressed by the ITO were left aside by the GATT, in particular competition and the establishment of a comprehensive dispute-settlement mechanism. The difference in perspective on subsidies and investment was also left unresolved. Only decades later would competition, subsidies, and investment become part of the GATT negotiations. Commodity agreements to stabilize and manage trade in primary commodities (a concern raised by Keynes in the initial discussions of the ITO) were virtually left out of the GATT only to be negotiated separately fifteen years later. Unlike the ITO Charter, the GATT did not provide for coordination with other multilateral organizations.

Although the GATT was only meant as a temporary gap-filler pending the approval of a more comprehensive multilateral trade agreement, it remained virtually unchanged (with the exception of the 1955 addition of Article XVIII and the 1964 addition of Part IV on Trade and Development discussed below) until it was incorporated as part of the WTO agreements in 1995. More critically, the

---

[12] T.N. Srinivasan, *Developing Countries and the Multilateral Trading System—From the GATT to the Uruguay Round and the Future* (Boulder: Westview Press, 1998), at 20.

Table 3.1 Comparison of the ITO Charter and GATT 1947 provisions

Type of provision	ITO Charter	GATT 1947	Comparative notes
Government assistance to development and reconstruction (protection of infant industries)	Art 13	Art XVIII	Different structure for deviating from obligations. GATT Art XVIII added in 1955
Preferential agreements for development and reconstruction	Art 15	–	–
General MFN treatment	Art 16	Art I	–
Tariff concessions negotiations	Art 17	–	–
National treatment	Art 18	Art III	–
Special provision for films	Art 19	Art IV	–
Elimination of quotas and exceptions	Arts 20–24	Arts XI–XV	–
Subsidies	Arts 25–28	Art XVI	Very different obligations, particularly on primary commodities
State trading	Arts 29–32	Art XVII	ITO much more detailed on state monopolies
Freedom of transit	Art 33	Art V	–
Anti-dumping and countervailing duties	Art 34	Art VI	–
Valuation for customs purposes	Art 35	Art VII	–
Import and export formalities and fees	Art 36	Art VIII	ITO to assist members in simplifying and standardizing customs procedures
Marks of origin	Art 37	Art IX	ITO to assist members to eliminate unnecessary marking requirements
Publication and administration of trade regulations	Art 38	Art X	–
Information, statistics, terminology	Art 39	–	–
Emergency action on certain imports	Art 40	Art XIX	–
Consultations	Art 41	Art XXII	GATT provides additional consultation mechanism
Territorial application, frontier traffic, customs unions and FTAs	Arts 42–44	Art XXIV	–

(Continued)

Table 3.1 *Continued*

General exceptions	Art 45	Art XX (security exception at Art XXI)	ITO provides two additional exceptions: 1. actions taken under treaties relating to fisheries and wild life; 2. orderly liquidation of surpluses of government-owned stocks. No security exception in ITO
Restrictive business practices	Ch V	–	–
Intergovernmental commodity agreements	Ch VI	Art XX(h)	GATT much more limited
International Trade Organization	Ch VII	–	No institutional support in GATT
Dispute settlement	Ch VIII	Art XXIII	ITO has comprehensive adjudication mechanism, GATT provides for consultations between members

comprehensive and supranational system for economic relations envisioned at the close of the Second World War had failed.

1.2 Early misgivings regarding trade and development at the GATT

At the conclusion of the first round of GATT negotiations in 1947, the United States, which had been the driving force, ended up granting more concessions than it received, perhaps not surprisingly given its economic predominance at the time. In many ways the American vision of multilateral free-trading had given way to the constraints of drained European economies, vanishing British currency reserves, and large colonial and dominion territories heavily dependent on these failing European economies for the marketing of their commodities. Disputes arose concerning products exported by developing countries and dominions to the United States market. For example, raw wool producers from the Commonwealth (Australia, in particular) were bitterly disappointed by the United States' refusal to cut tariffs on that product; the issue was of such magnitude that a separate agreement on prices and import levels had to be negotiated.[13]

Developing countries' early misgivings intensified in the following years. China withdrew from the GATT in 1950, Lebanon and Syria in 1951, and Liberia in 1953. Cuba left the Annecy Round (1949) after the United States announced that it would reduce its commitment on sugar. Colombia also left the negotiations and Uruguay was considering an increase in duties of about 20 percent. The United

[13] Zeiler, above fn 4, at 94–104.

States had not cut its tariffs as much as expected, and agricultural protectionism in developed countries became increasingly apparent.[14] Nonetheless the negotiations resulted in further tariff reductions, down 37 percent for commodities and 50 percent for manufactures compared to pre-GATT levels. The next Round in Torquay (1951) gathered 38 countries, but the two following Rounds (Geneva in 1956 and the Dillon Round in 1960–61) involved only 26 countries.[15]

This troubling evolution led members to conduct a "Review Session" in 1954–55 to amend Part II and to attempt to create an "Organization for Trade Cooperation" to oversee GATT activities.[16] Although this attempt at institutionalization failed, a GATT executive committee was established, a sign that the provisional tariff agreement was now regarded as a permanent feature. Members also commissioned a report on trade negotiations from a group of experts (the Haberler Report), which concluded that trade barriers in developed countries on imports from developing countries significantly contributed to economic problems in the latter. In response, the GATT set up Committee III to review trade measures affecting developing countries. High tariffs on tropical products, tariff escalation, quotas, and certain taxes were identified by the committee as problematic, but no substantial reduction in these barriers ensued. The Haberler Report and the Committee's work form the first formal and explicit institutional consideration of the relationship between the GATT and development concerns.

The main result of the Review Session, with respect to development, was the addition of Article XVIII on Governmental Assistance to Economic Development. Although there is no formal restriction on which GATT parties can avail themselves of the provisions of Article XVIII, paragraph 1 cites "economies…which can only support low standards of living and are in the early state of development," understood by Note Ad Article XVIII to include both countries that are starting their economic development and those that are starting their industrialization.

In 1961, GATT parties acting jointly adopted a Declaration on the Promotion of Trade of LDCs, which reiterated many of the points brought to light by the Haberler Report. The Declaration focused on the shortcomings of trade liberalization in areas of interest to developing countries, particularly agriculture, and the growing discrepancy with the faster paced liberalization on industrial goods.[17] In 1963–64, a group of developing countries introduced a resolution at the GATT calling for the removal of barriers on trade in tropical products within two

---

[14] Ibid at 170–7.
[15] WTO, "Understanding the WTO—The GATT Years: From Havana to Marrakesh" <http://www.wto.org/english/thewto_e/whatis_e/tif_e/fact4_e.htm>. For a summary of trade concessions during the rounds, see BBC News, "Timeline—World Trade Organization" <http://news.bbc.co.uk/2/hi/europe/country_profiles/2430089.stm>; A.V. Morrison, "GATT's Seven Rounds of Trade Talks Span More Than Thirty Years—General Agreement on Tariffs and Trade," *Business America* (7 July 1986).
[16] J.H. Jackson, *Restructuring the GATT System* (New York: Council on Foreign Relations Press, 1990), at 15–16.
[17] D.A. Irwin, P.C. Mavroidis and A.O. Sykes, *The Genesis of the GATT* (Cambridge: Cambridge University Press, 2008), at 124.

years and for substantial concessions on tariffs on manufactured products from developing countries.[18]

In sum, the lack of an institution to oversee the process of trade liberalization, discord regarding agriculture liberalization, and barriers to trade on tropical products emerged as serious issues virtually from the inception of the GATT. They remain eerily familiar themes to date.

2. The UNCTAD Legacy for the GATT

Eventually, in reaction to the GATT's persistent shortcomings on agricultural issues and tariff negotiation on developing country exports, developing members of the GATT sought an alternative forum more hospitable to their concerns. UNCTAD provided a venue for discussing GATT policies and for putting pressure on the GATT.[19] At the same time, membership in GATT increased remarkably as former colonial territories were able to join automatically upon gaining independence, without needing to negotiate a "ticket to entry" in the form of tariff concessions.[20] Many sub-Saharan countries joined at that time. This shift in the balance of membership, combined with the political organization of developing countries at UNCTAD, resulted in an offer for non-reciprocity by developed countries to developing countries as a negotiating principle for the Kennedy Round (1964–1967).[21] The foundations for the addition of Part IV of the GATT were laid.

However, developing countries' strategy of reorienting the GATT through UNCTAD could only have limited legal effect. First, UNCTAD resolutions or declarations, like UN General Assembly resolutions, are not legally binding. Second, the separate legal structures of the GATT, the UN, and UNCTAD prevent instruments negotiated within UNCTAD from being automatically binding on GATT members as such. GATT parties are bound by the GATT treaty, which may only be amended by the procedures laid therein. An additional issue was that not all UN members were GATT signatories.

2.1 The addition of Part IV on Trade and Development

Despite the legal limitations inherent in attempting to modify GATT disciplines through UNCTAD, the strategy achieved some measure of success inasmuch as

---

[18] GATT, *Programme for the Expansion of International Trade—Trade in Tropical Products*, 21 May 1963, GATT Doc MIN (63)7. [19] Hudec above Ch 2 fn 59, at 71–2.

[20] GATT Article XXVI:5 allows former colonies to become Contracting Parties automatically when such territories "possess[] or acquire[] full autonomy in the conduct of [their] external commercial relations and of other matters provided for in this Agreement…upon sponsorship through a declaration by the responsible contracting party [the former colonial power]." The new state, sponsored by the former colonial occupier, is then deemed to be a contracting party. Those procedures are separate from the accession procedures of Article XXXIII, which make accession conditional to negotiations between the candidate state and the existing GATT Contracting Parties acting as a group.

[21] Srinivasan, above fn 12, at 24.

GATT members agreed to incorporate a Part IV on "Trade and Development" in 1964 (entered into force in 1966).[22]

Article XXXVI, reading like a preambular provision, sets out the general need for improving the relationship between trade and development. The operative provisions are found in Article XXXVII, but the existence of specific substantive obligations remains uncertain because the provisions are drafted in the form of "best efforts." While language of endeavor has now been recognized to be legally operative in certain contexts, it was generally not given as much weight at the time when Part IV was drafted (Chapter 6 discusses the legal value of Part IV and other SDT provisions). The lack of criteria and benchmarks against which to evaluate the performance of GATT Contracting Parties with respect to Part IV was an additional hurdle to the enforcement of the provisions. Part IV effectively gave no additional opportunities for developing countries to derogate from GATT disciplines for purposes of development, nor did it obligate developed countries to make additional concessions to developing countries.

Part IV nonetheless formally included for the first time the principle of non-reciprocity in the GATT[23] with Article XXXVI:8 ("The developed contracting parties do not expect reciprocity for commitments made by them in trade negotiations to reduce or remove tariffs and other barriers to the trade of less-developed contracting parties."). The Note Ad Article XXXVI specifies the meaning of the phrase "do not expect reciprocity":

> the less-developed contracting parties should not be expected, in the course of trade negotiations, to make contributions which are inconsistent with their individual development, financial and trade needs, taking into consideration past trade developments.

Hence, a clause that was already fairly ill-defined was further weakened by the Note. Non-reciprocity nonetheless prevailed as a guiding principle in negotiations during the Tokyo Round. Moreover, the format of the Tokyo Codes, which would only bind GATT Contracting Parties that specifically opted into the agreements, afforded more flexibility for developing countries. As a result, very few of them subscribed to the Tokyo Rounds or made any tariff concessions. Conversely, developing countries also gained very few concessions of value to them. Non-reciprocity quickly showed its limitations.

Developing countries had hoped to include a permanent exception to the Most-Favored-Nation (MFN) clause for preferential agreements in Part IV,[24] but that only came a few years later with the Enabling Clause.

---

[22] Protocol amending the General Agreement on Tariffs and Trade to introduce a Part IV on Trade and Development and to amend Annex I (Geneva, 8 February 1965; 572 UNTS 320).

[23] For a more detailed account of the negotiations of Part IV, see Irwin, Mavroidis, and Sykes above fn 17, at 125–33.

[24] J. Whalley, "Non-Discriminatory Discrimination: Special and Differential Treatment under the GATT for Developing Countries" 1990 *Economic Journal* 100(403) 1318, at 1320.

2.2 The Generalized System of Trade Preferences and the Enabling Clause

The original GATT 1947 already contained some exceptions to the MFN clause to allow trade preferences between certain countries (GATT Art I:2–4). However, this limited derogation was effectively a grandfathering clause for the preferences already accorded by the United States to Cuba, by France to its "French Union" territories in Africa, Asia, and the Pacific, and by other colonial-type customs unions. It was not the comprehensive access to preferences that developing countries had envisioned.

The second UNCTAD Conference deserves credit for formulating the GSP in 1968, whereby developed countries could grant non-reciprocal market access (low tariff or duty-free) to products from developing countries, and developing countries could grant each other more preferential tariffs. Non-discrimination between developing countries was at the core of the scheme, so that preferences had to be offered on an equal basis to all developing countries.

According to Resolution 21 taken at the UNCTAD II Conference in New Delhi in 1968:

the objectives of the generalized, non-reciprocal, non-discriminatory system of preferences in favour of the developing countries, including special measures in favour of the least advanced among the developing countries, should be: (a) to increase their export earnings; (b) to promote their industrialization; and (c) to accelerate their rates of economic growth.

Under the GSP scheme, preference-giving countries grant reduced or zero tariff rates on selected products originating in developing countries. LDCs receive special and preferential treatment for a wider coverage of products and deeper tariff cuts.

The GSP system conflicted with the GATT obligation of MFN treatment. In fact, this technical obstacle largely accounted for the delay in agreeing to a waiver since the negotiation of Part IV. GATT members eventually approved a temporary waiver to GATT Article I in 1971, thereby allowing members to conclude preferential agreements under the GSP scheme.[25]

This *ad hoc* manipulation of the GATT regime illustrated the impossibility of automatically carrying over UNCTAD agreements into the GATT. The United States and the EC thereafter adopted preference schemes to provide (generally) duty-free treatment on industrial products and reduced tariffs on agricultural products from developing countries.[26]

Interestingly, the logic of GSP schemes runs counter to developing countries' claims for independent, autonomous, and discretionary determination of their own domestic development policies, as preferences are granted at the discretion of developed countries and are revocable at will. Still, preferences were supported by a number of development economists, including Singer and Prebisch. Experience to date has uncovered the substantial costs to developing countries of playing the GSP card, in terms of their bargaining power within GATT (and later the WTO) and the impact of these schemes on their domestic policies.

---

[25] GATT Contracting Parties, *Waiver Decision on the Generalized System of Preferences*, L/3545 (25 June 1971), BISD 18S/24.

[26] C. Michalopoulos, *Developing Countries in the WTO* (New York: Palgrave, 2001), at 29–33.

Although the Tokyo Round may have been motivated by the United States' concern over the expansion of the EC to strategic markets such as the United Kingdom,[27] the Round had a strong development orientation, with goals including more favorable trading conditions for developing countries.[28] Some authors have also argued that the NIEO movement bolstered developing countries' support for the Round.[29] Development landmarks during the Tokyo Round took the form of the Enabling Clause consolidating the concept of "differential and more favorable treatment" for developing countries, the principle of non-reciprocity in trade negotiations in derogation to the MFN clause, and trade preferences. The Enabling Clause also supported South–South preferential trading schemes. Finally, it specifically recognized the status of LDCs and their special needs.

However, with the recognition of "special and more favorable treatment" also came the concept of "graduation," whereby developing countries were expected to eventually cease to use preferences as their economy grew. The concept was a concession to developed countries and raises major political issues to date, as the United States in particular disfavors applying preferential treatment to a number of advanced developing countries. Preferences and their legal interpretation will be discussed in more detail in Chapters 6 and 7.

The 1950s and 1960s therefore saw the progressive emergence of a number of carve-outs from the main GATT disciplines to address the needs and circumstances of developing countries. While the specificity of economic development and its impact on trade relations were recognized as a matter of principle, little was done to integrate development into the GATT regime more systematically. In practice, the effectiveness of these new development-oriented provisions varied greatly: Preferences proliferated (but often on a unilateral and discriminatory basis), trade liberalization on agricultural and tropical products continued to lag behind, non-reciprocity did not offer any leverage to developing countries to gain valuable concessions, and the implementation of Article XVIII proved limited.

3. The Expansion of GATT Subject Matters

As discussed in Chapter 2, developed countries and newly empowered international organizations after 1945 fashioned an economic law system where the boundary between international and domestic regulation became increasingly blurred. Starting with the Tokyo Round, the GATT participated in the trend towards international regulation of matters traditionally within states' domestic province. The Tokyo Round involved negotiations between 102 countries on tariff bindings, non-tariff measures, and framework agreements; it was unprecedented in scope and number of participants, about a third of which were developing countries forming

---

[27] J. Stiglitz and A. Charlton, *Fair Trade For All: How Trade Can Promote Development* (Oxford: Oxford University Press, 2005), at 44.

[28] Herstein "Trade with the Second and Third Worlds," in P. Macrory and P. Suchman (eds), *Current Legal Aspects of International Trade Law* (Chicago: American Bar Association, 1982), at 117–30.   [29] Matsushita, Schoenbaum, and Mavroidis, above Ch 1 fn 46, at 389.

a relatively united front.[30] Such an active participation by developing countries, in contrast with previous rounds, is attributable in part to the relative failure of the UNCTAD strategy. The Tokyo Round was the first to introduce a wide range of obligations pertaining to non-tariff matters, many of which were purely domestic measures. Subsidies, technical regulations and standards, licensing and customs valuation rules, and government procurement regulations traditionally were the sole province of domestic regulators and policy-makers until the Tokyo Codes.

Harmonization of domestic technical standards requirements facilitates trade, but their inclusion in the realm of international negotiations gives other countries a more direct role and greater weight in the formulation of these essentially domestic measures. This shift in regulatory model fuels interdependency in international economic relations; it also illustrates the increased transfer of sovereign prerogatives to international organizations since the Second World War. However, developing countries' participation in the Round's plurilateral agreements remained very low even fifteen years after their conclusion (see Table 3.2).

Table 3.2 Level of participation in the Tokyo Codes at the time of the Uruguay Round

Tokyo Code	Participating developing countries in 1992[a]	Signatories in 1994
Subsidies and countervailing measures	Argentina, Brazil, Chile, Colombia, Egypt, India, Indonesia, Pakistan, Philippines, Turkey, Uruguay	25[b]
Technical barriers to trade (Standards Code)	Argentina, Brazil, Chile, Egypt, India, Indonesia, Mexico, Pakistan, the Philippines, Rwanda, Thailand, Tunisia	46[b]
Import licensing procedures	Argentina, Chile, Egypt, India, Mexico, Nigeria, Pakistan, Philippines, South Africa, Venezuela	30[b]
Government procurement		12[b]
Customs valuation	Argentina, Brazil, India, Lesotho, Malawi, Mexico, Morocco, Peru, South Africa, Turkey, Zimbabwe	35[b]
Anti-dumping	Argentina, Brazil, Egypt, India, Mexico, Pakistan	25[b]
Bovine Meat Arrangement	Argentina, Belize, Brazil, Colombia, Egypt, Guatemala, Nigeria, Paraguay, South Africa, Tunisia, Uruguay	28
International Dairy Arrangement	Argentina, Botswana, Egypt, South Africa, Uruguay	16
Trade in Civil Aircraft	Egypt	22[b]

Sources:

[a] GATT Secretariat, *GATT Activities 1992—An Annual Review of the World of the GATT* (Geneva: June 1993).

[b] GATT Council, Overview of Developments in International Trade and the Trading System, C/RM/OV/5 (5 December 1994), at 10–11 (European Communities are counted as one).

---

[30] Srinivasan, above fn 12, at 25. See also F. Ismail, "Rediscovering the Role of Developing Countries in GATT before the Doha Round" 2008 *Law and Development Review* 1(1) 13.

With the Tokyo Round, rules and regulations themselves became the outcome and the product of negotiations, leading some authors to talk about a "legalization of the trading system."[31] This evolution in the GATT as an institution required a very different type of negotiator and expertise from participating countries. While economists may have played a key role in helping shape tariff negotiations, lawyers and regulators became crucial actors in rules-oriented negotiations. Such a shift in the required skills would be a major issue for developing countries with limited resources.

4. Towards a Free Trade Consensus? The Context of the Uruguay Round

The Uruguay Round, occurring at the same time as the break-up of the USSR, spanned the years that witnessed the most radical transformation in international relations since the end of the Second World War. Beyond canny assertions that "the Cold War is over, Japan won,"[32] the demise of the centralized state-planned economic model (with the exception of a few countries and the special case of China) gave a new dimension to multilateral trade negotiations. However, the needs and claims of developing countries remained much the same.

4.1 Setting the stage for the Uruguay Round: Pre-negotiation turbulences

As industrialized countries' economies shifted from producing goods to providing services, their multilateral trade agenda also changed.

As early as the GATT Ministerial Meeting of 1982, the United States and other developed countries suggested opening negotiations on investment and on two other areas that were previously outside the ambit of the GATT: services and certain aspects of intellectual property. An unprecedented number of items were included for consideration by ministers in these areas.[33] A number of developing countries, led by Brazil and India, fiercely opposed such an expansion of trade negotiations, requiring instead that developed countries reduce measures inconsistent with GATT in the areas of agriculture and textiles ("roll back" demands) or at the very least refrain from implementing further measures in violation of GATT disciplines ("stand-still" demands). The EC was strongly opposed to making any new commitments on agriculture. The final text listed issues of interest to each

---

[31] S. Ostry, "Looking Back to Look Forward: The Multilateral Trading System after 50 Years," in WTO Secretariat (ed), *From GATT to the WTO: The Multilateral Trading System in the New Millennium* (The Hague: Kluwer Law International, 2000), at 101.

[32] United States Senator P. Tsongas, quoted in M. Dowd, "The 1992 Campaign: Campaign Memo; Voters Want Candidates To Take a Reality Check," *The New York Times* (17 February 1992).

[33] P. Low, *Trading Free: The GATT and the US Trade Policy* (New York: Twentieth Century Foundation, 1993), at 191.

group,[34] but there was no real consensus on the substance of the commitments to be negotiated or undertaken.

During the 1986 Punta del Este Ministerial Meeting, developing countries opposed the efforts of the United States to include new issues in the negotiations, but ultimately gave in after the United States threatened to withdraw from the meeting, leaving the GATT without a roadmap for the upcoming round of negotiations.[35] The fear that a failure to launch a new round would threaten the integrity of the GATT appeared to be a strong factor in the outcome of the negotiations.

4.2 The Punta del Este Declaration

The Punta del Este Declaration established the framework for the Uruguay Round negotiations. The subjects for negotiations included those promoted by developing countries (such as tropical products, natural resource-based products, textiles, and agriculture) as well as developed countries' agendas, most notably trade-related aspects of intellectual property, trade-related investment measures, and negotiations on services.

The Declaration reaffirmed the principle of differential and more favorable treatment for developing countries, although it did not translate into any concrete obligation for members. To the contrary, it seemed to have only an advisory value. Regarding standstill and rollback demands, "*particular care should be given to avoiding disruptive effects* on the trade of less-developed contracting parties" (emphasis added). The language was not obligatory and indeed was interpreted by the EC as simply requiring the exercise of best efforts. The principle of non-reciprocity was also included in the Declaration as an expectation that developing countries "shall not be required to make concessions that are inconsistent with [their] development, financial and trade needs."[36] However, while developed countries could not require reciprocity from developing countries, they could simply refrain from offering them concessions. Non-reciprocity therefore only meant that developing countries were not required to give anything beyond their means, but did not guarantee that they would get anything for free. Furthermore, "graduation" was included in the governing principles to limit the effect of non-reciprocity. In sum, developing countries entered the Round with assurances only with respect to non-reciprocity, which placed them in the position of being second-rate participants in the negotiations while not granting them any affirmative benefit.

Another element played a crucial role in the outcome of the negotiations for developing countries: the "single undertaking" approach. The Declaration provided

[34] Safeguards, rules relating to developing countries, tariff escalation, trade in agriculture and particularly tropical products, trade in particular natural resources, trade in textiles, structural adjustments and trade policy, trade effects of currency fluctuations, rules of origin, dispute settlement, operation of the Tokyo codes, certain intellectual property issues (export of counterfeit goods), exports of capital goods and services.

[35] G. Windham, "The Prenegotiation Phase of the Uruguay Round," in J. G. Stein (ed), *Getting to the Table* (Baltimore: Johns Hopkins University Press, 1989), at 44–67.

[36] Part I. B.(v), *Ministerial Declaration on the Uruguay Round*, GATT Doc. MIN.DEC (20 September 1986), BISD 33S/19.

that "the launching, the conduct and the implementation of the outcome of the negotiations shall be treated as part of a single undertaking." This undoubtedly was a reaction to the piecemeal results of the Tokyo Round and the subsequent difficulties in implementing the multilateral agreements. However, in the context of the Uruguay Round, it also meant that the outcome of the negotiations regarding matters of interest to developing countries was tied to the outcome of negotiations on services, to which developing countries were opposed.

With respect to the subject matter of the negotiations, developing countries faced the prospect of renegotiating the implementation of concessions that had already been made to them, as rollback and standstill demands only required the removal of policies that were already deemed inconsistent with the GATT. Thus, in mercantilist terms, they were going to have to "pay," through additional concessions, for benefits they already had as a matter of right but that had not been implemented.

Hindsight confirms that all the issues that surfaced since the inception of the GATT later became major roadblocks in WTO negotiations. However, it is interesting to note that they did not actually *result* from the Uruguay Round agreements. Rather they were *built* into the negotiations before the Round even began.

5. Conclusion

The trade system that crystallized after the abandonment of the ITO Charter was not designed to cater to or even to address developing countries' commercial interests, largely because they were not a part of the system at the time. It is therefore not surprising that the trade regime did not, in fact, serve their interests. Even if we are to see, with Ruggie, the GATT as part of the "embedded liberalism" of the post World War II economic institutions,[37] the decline of the welfare state has since unmoored the GATT from its original context. More importantly, developing countries never had the type of welfare state that is critical to Ruggie's account: The bargain was not tailored to their socioeconomic realities. When they joined the GATT *en masse* in the 1960s and as an ongoing process until the close of the Uruguay Round, their development needs and the specificities of their socioeconomic make-up were not accounted for in the core principles of the negotiations or in the process of trade liberalization.

From an institutional perspective, the embryonic nature of the GATT infrastructure did not allow developing countries to organize and to promote their interests in a systematic and coherent fashion. Their attempts to do so in other settings (such as the Group of 77) and institutions (the UN, UNCTAD, and Bretton Woods institutions) failed because the institutional linkage envisioned after the Second World War never materialized, thereby precluding effective coordination

---

[37] J.G. Ruggie, "International Regimes, Transactions, and Change: Embedded Liberalism and the Postwar Economic Order," in S.D. Krasner (ed), *International Regimes* (Ithaca: Cornell University Press, 1983).

and collaborative efforts across organizations. The GATT's imperviousness to the incorporation of rules of general international law also limited substantive legal imports from other regulatory frameworks such as UNCTAD, with the exception of the Enabling Clause referring to GSP.

The creation of the WTO appears to address the need for a formal institution allowing interest coalitions to emerge, but the issue of coordination amongst international organizations remains unresolved. The WTO, inasmuch as it inherits the dynamics of the GATT's history, carries with it the bargaining disequilibrium that has cost so much to developing countries. Moreover, the theoretical underpinnings of the WTO assume that there is no market failure absent government intervention.[38] This presumption against government intervention shapes a new approach to trade and development, where participation in the main liberalization disciplines is thought to be the engine for development. Government policies that run counter to this orientation are seen with suspicion and limited in time and scope. The number of transitional periods for implementation in the Uruguay Round agreements and the limited development-oriented exceptions or derogations are all illustrative of this new trade and development relationship that emerged during the Uruguay Round.

---

[38] Y.S. Lee, *Reclaiming Development in the World Trading System* (Cambridge: Cambridge University Press, 2006), at 50–4.

4

"Developing Member" and Least-Developed Country Status at the GATT and WTO: Self-Designation versus the Politics of Accession

Just as we lack a clear, uniform characterization of the concept of development, so we would look in vain for a legal description of "developing country." Neither general international law nor the WTO legal system have a set definition of "developing country." Yet, the designation in large part conditions developing members' ability to exercise their rights under SDT provisions, the Enabling Clause, and a myriad other WTO instruments. From an institutional perspective too, the ability of members to organize under the unifying labels of "developing" or "least developed" plays an important role.

There are no criteria, tests, or standards to be met for qualifying as "developing country." In most cases there is no notification requirement either. Members simply designate themselves as developing member for purposes of particular WTO provisions. By contrast, countries qualify as LDCs at the WTO only if they meet the composite criteria set by the UN. The practice, however, offers a more nuanced picture. GATT parties that simply transitioned to WTO membership in 1995 could, in theory at least, avail themselves of the benefits of SDT provisions as they saw fit. Not so for developing countries that acceded to the WTO since 1995: Developing country status has largely become an accession issue for incoming members.[1]

Because a large number of developing countries joined during the GATT years under a procedure that essentially by-passed the formal accession process, the issue whether and when they could avail themselves of the developing country designation never arose as such. However, with respect to countries that joined after 1995, the availability of SDT and the level of concessions required from incoming developing countries and LDCs became a crucial accession question. Some authors have even claimed that "accession is unfortunately becoming a development issue in

---

[1] H. Basra, "Caribbean States and the Politics of WTO Accession" 2008 Thesis, University of Manchester. On accession and developing countries, see also, B. Taxil, *L'OMC et les pays en développement* (Paris: Montchrestien, 1998); UNCTAD, *WTO Accessions and Development Policies* (2001). On accessions, see generally, WTO, *A Handbook on Accession to the WTO* (Cambridge: Cambridge University Press, 2008).

the WTO because only developing and transitional economies have yet to join."[2] The accession process, including the availability of SDT and other benefits and the level of concessions extracted from the acceding members, has effectively become a critical threshold issue for the thirty-one developing countries and transitional countries (Eastern and Central European countries) that acceded since 1995 and the two dozen others that joined the GATT in the final years of the Uruguay Round. This is true also for the twenty-one developing countries currently negotiating their accession. Russia, which has an ambiguous status, became a member in 2012. Developing status and benefits negotiated as part of the accession package have affected over a third of the current WTO membership and will have affected over half of the membership by the time the ongoing negotiations are finalized.

At the same time, these incoming members represent (with the exception of China) a relatively small portion of world trade. Combined with the conflict of interest between incumbent members and candidate countries, this explains in part why the issue has not gained a very high profile within the institution and little has been proposed by the way of reform.

Because the question of accessions could warrant an entire volume in itself, only the most salient features and trends will be presented here to demonstrate what "rights" or special treatment developing countries have been granted as part of their accession package. Accessions are examined through the lens of special and differential treatment and developing country status. Section 1 presents the traditional practice regarding developing country and LDC status and access to SDT; section 2 considers how such status is affected by the accession process.

1. The Traditional Practice: "Developing Country" Self-Designation and LDC Status

Although there is no provision that creates a separate status for developing and LDC members, the practice is to read these categories into the WTO agreements in order to give meaning to the provisions addressed specifically to developing countries and LDCs. For instance, Article XI.2 of the Marrakesh Agreement stating that "[t]he least-developed countries recognized as such by the United Nations will only be required to undertake commitments and concessions to the extent consistent with their individual development, financial and trade needs or their administrative and institutional capabilities," implicitly recognizes the LDC status granted by the UN to certain countries.

---

[2] M. Bosworth and R. Duncan, "Current Status of the WTO Accession Process and the Experience of ESCAP Acceding Countries," in United Nations Economic and Social Commission for Asia and the Pacific, *Facilitating the Accession of ESCAP Countries to the WTO Through Regional Cooperation*, Studies in Trade and Investment No 49, ST/ESCAP/2215 (2002).

1.1 Developing and LDC status under the GATT

The notion of developing contracting parties can be traced to GATT Article XVIII stating:

[t]he contracting parties recognize that the attainment of the objectives of this Agreement will be facilitated by the progressive development of their economies, particularly of those *contracting parties the economies of which can only support low standards of living and are in the early stages of development* (emphasis added).

Annex I to the GATT further qualifies this broad statement by urging members to consider the "normal position of that economy" rather than the "exceptional circumstances such as those which may result from the temporary existence of exceptionally favourable conditions" to determine whether a country qualifies as "developing." The Annex also specifies:

the phrase "in the early stages of development" is not meant to apply only to contracting parties which have just started their economic development, but also to contracting parties the economies of which are undergoing a process of industrialisation to correct an excessive dependence on primary production.[3]

Still, no specific criteria or procedures for determining whether a country qualified as "developing" ever emerged.

The LDC category was created in 1971 at the UN, and Yugoslavia then proposed building into the GATT trade negotiations elements that would benefit "the least developed among the developing countries." Later that year, the Informal Group of Developing Countries, comprising Argentina, Brazil, Egypt, India, Yugoslavia, Chile, Pakistan, and Uruguay, and other GATT Contracting Parties formally proposed the creation of a special group for LDCs and the possibility of special provisions for them. Ultimately, the Enabling Clause established a permanent legal framework for special and more favorable treatment for LDCs in 1979. Currently, thirty-four of the forty-nine countries listed as LDCs by the UN are WTO members and a handful more are observers, some actively pursuing accession negotiations.

Accepted wisdom tells us that GATT Contracting Parties essentially self-designated as "developing Contracting Parties" in order to avail themselves of the benefits of Article XVIII and other provisions in their favor. A closer examination of the practice somewhat belies this proposition. While it was indeed up to individual countries to initiate a claim for qualification as "developing," the self-designation was not always free from scrutiny by other GATT Contracting Parties.[4] Overall, no consistent treatment of the developing country category emerged from the decades of GATT practice. The case law indicates that countries as varied as Chile, Brazil, India, and Korea have been treated as developing countries. Guglielmo Verdirame infers that any GATT Contracting Party

---

[3] GATT, Annex I Notes and Supplementary Provisions, Ad *Article XVIII.*

[4] G. Verdirame, "The Definition of Developing Countries under GATT and Other International Law" 1996 *German Yearbook of International Law* 39 164.

with a lower GDP per capita than these countries would likely have qualified as "developing." The *Australia Waiver* case provided a list of developing countries that could benefit from certain tariff preferences; it excluded OECD and Eastern European countries.[5] However, GSP schemes at the time did extend to Eastern and Central Europe.

Overall, developing country qualification was a case-by-case matter and Article XVIII is so indeterminate that it can hardly be called a definition.

1.2 Accession to the GATT by developing countries

The first wave of developing countries acceded to the GATT in the 1960s and 1970s through Article XVI:5(c), which enabled a Contracting Party to "sponsor" the automatic accession of "customs territories" for which it previously had "international responsibility" under Article XVI:5(a). In practice, most former colonies became GATT members under this facility without having to negotiate their accession under the normal procedures of Article XXXIII. Overall, sixty-four newly independent countries benefited from the Article XVI:5 procedure, eventually raising objections from the United States and Japan. Even countries in the process of accession under Article XVI:5(c) often benefited from provisional application of GATT treatment (including MFN) so long as they reciprocated.

The "normal" accession process, through Article XXXIII, also did not necessarily require the negotiation of a protocol of accession. In practice, a candidate country joined at the conclusion of a round simply by subscribing to the concessions and agreements negotiated during the round. Such was the case for fourteen new Contracting Parties, particularly during the early Annecy and Torquay Rounds. In subsequent years, it became customary for candidate countries to negotiate separate protocols of accession with a Working Party (a group of interested members typically comprising the EC and the US as well as other major trading partners), with ultimate membership being subject to a two-thirds approval vote by the existing membership, as required by Article XXXIII. This procedure was used for thirty-two countries between 1955 and 1994, almost half of which joined during the Uruguay Round.[6] Figure 4.1 shows the successive waves of new GATT and WTO members per year since 1947. Particularly for those joining in the 1990s, the cost of accession enshrined in the liberalization demands of the protocol of accession grew significantly. In part, the increased liberalization was required to bridge the gap between the high tariff barriers of the candidate country and the generally low tariff barriers of GATT members. Waivers were granted to ease the process, with no particular criteria, benchmarks, or consistency.

---

[5] GATT Working Party Report, *Report of the Working Party on the Australian Request to Grant Tariff Preferences to Less-Developed Countries*, GATT Doc L/2527 (23 December 1965), Annex B.

[6] Excellent data and analysis on accessions is provided in K. Jones, *The Doha Blues* (Oxford: Oxford University Press, 2010), at 50–83.

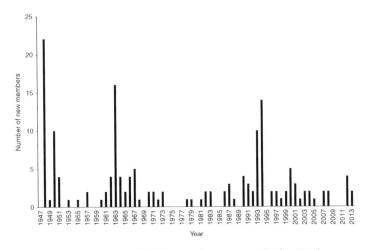

Figure 4.1 Number of new GATT/WTO members per year (1947–2013)

Sources: Country data collected from WTO, 'The 128 countries that had signed GATT by 1994.' <http://www.wto.org/english/thewto_e/gattmem_e.htm> and WTO, 'Understanding the WTO—Members and Observers.' <http://www.wto.org/english/thewto_e/whatis_e/tif_e/org6_e.htm>.

1.3 Developing country and LDC status under the WTO agreements: Business as usual?

The self-designating process for developing countries and the incorporation by reference of the UN's LDC category could have been challenged with the creation of the WTO; rather, they were implicitly ratified. The GATT 1994 simply noted in an Explanatory Note:

The references to "contracting party" in the provisions of GATT 1994 shall be deemed to read "Member". The references to "less-developed contracting party" and "developed contracting party" shall be deemed to read "developing country Member" and "developed country Member".

Additionally, the Marrakesh Agreement endorsed a wholesale adoption of earlier GATT practices in its Article XVI.1:

Except as otherwise provided under this Agreement or the Multilateral Trade Agreements, the WTO shall be guided by the decisions, procedures and customary practices followed by the CONTRACTING PARTIES to GATT 1947 and the bodies established in the framework of GATT 1947.

The only exception to this framework is provided by the Subsidies and Countervailing Measures Agreement (SCM). Annex VII excludes the application of the prohibition on export subsidies to LDCs designated as such by the UN and which are WTO members and appears to similarly exempt a number of countries until the time when their GNP per capita reaches USD1,000 per annum.[7] Other

---

[7] Bolivia, Cameroon, Congo, Côte d'Ivoire, Dominican Republic, Egypt, Ghana, Guatemala, Guyana, India, Indonesia, Kenya, Morocco, Nicaragua, Nigeria, Pakistan, Philippines, Senegal, Sri Lanka, and Zimbabwe.

developing countries (presumably under the self-designation scheme) benefit from an eight-year transitional period during which they are obligated to phase out their export subsidies. This tiered graduating scheme is unique within the WTO agreements. Some other provisions contain a soft graduation mechanism, but they are devoid of specific economic benchmarks.

The panels and the Appellate Body have specifically avoided resolving questions regarding a member's status as "developing." In a dispute with the United States, in which China claimed that Article 9.1 of the Agreement on Safeguards applied to it as a developing member, neither the panel nor the Appellate Body adjudicated the issue of China's status as a developing country.[8]

Is that to say that WTO developing members all benefit equally from self-declaring as developing or being classified as LDC? In fact, not only are developing countries subject to different obligations from their developed counterparts, but they also are in legally different situations vis-à-vis fellow developing members. Conversely, countries that would normally be considered as developed have invoked SDT provisions, as Israel recently showed.[9] The ultimate result remains a case-by-case approach, where the availability of specific SDT provisions differs for virtually each developing member.[10]

The recent Appellate Body Report in the *EC–Tariff Preferences* case (see Chapter 7) has been decried by some developing countries for institutionalizing differentiation among developing members. The reality is that differentiation through variable access to SDT has been endemic since the first development-oriented provision was adopted in 1955.

2. Restricting "Developing Country" and LDC Benefits through Accessions

In practice, the developing country designation is subject to *real politik* considerations and the landscape for "developing country" status has changed considerably through the practice of accessions since 1995. Unlike the discretion that members enjoyed in earlier times to avail themselves of the benefits of self-designation, candidates for accession are in a weak bargaining position to assert rights that have not yet vested in them, particularly against more powerful existing members which are intent on extracting the highest possible level of concession.

---

[8] Panel Report, *US—Steel Safeguards*, at para 10.714; Appellate Body Report, *US—Steel Safeguards*, at para 508.

[9] See, eg, WTO Trade Policy Review Body, *Trade Policy Review: Israel*, WT/TPR/S/58 (13 August 1999), at para 115 (Israel invoking developing country status in order to justify offset requirements in government procurement under Art XVI of the WTO's Government Procurement Agreement).

[10] T. Broude, "Essays on the World Trade Organization: The Rule(s) of Trade and the Rhetos of Development: Reflections on the Functional and Aspirational Legitimacy of the WTO" 2006 *Columbia Journal of Transnational Law* 45(1) 221, at 256–8; A.M. Ewart, "Small Developing States in the WTO: A Procedural Approach to Special and Differential Treatment Through Reforms to Dispute Settlement" 2007 *Syracuse Journal of International Law and Commerce* 35(1) 27.

2.1 Developing country and LDC status in accession negotiations

Developing country status, instead of being an overall entitlement to SDT pro-visions for new members, is in fact largely contingent upon individual accession negotiations: Whether a new member can avail itself of SDT provisions is negoti-ated for each agreement. The specific contours of an acceding member's "status," then, are contained in the Protocol of Accession and the accompanying Working Party report, the relevant paragraphs of which are referred to and incorporated into the Protocol.[11]

The accession process, specifically as it relates to developing country status, has been criticized for a lack of transparency.[12] The issue can be all the more salient when it comes to accession by countries that seem to defy "developed" or "devel-oping" labels. For example, both China and Russia boast economic power akin to developed countries, but the standard of living in both countries reflects that of developing countries, making their access to SDT (and more broadly their "devel-oping country" status) a hotly contested issue.[13]

Accession to the WTO is governed by Article XII of the Marrakesh Agreement stating that any country may accede "on terms to be agreed between it and the WTO." Unfortunately, unlike other international institutions such as the IMF and the World Bank, the WTO has not developed clear criteria—or a consist-ent practice—for dealing with the issue of developing status during accessions. Without an explicit standard, acceding countries may initially self-identify as

---

[11] See M. Bacchetta and Z. Drabek, "Effects of WTO Accession on Policy-Making in Sovereign States: Preliminary Lessons From the Recent Experience of Transition Countries," WTO Development and Economic Research Division, Paper No DERD-2002-02 (April 2002), at 5; see also Bosworth and Duncan, above fn 2, at 17. (The "specific commitments contained in the Protocol can cover:

   (a) Statements of fact rather than commitments and obligations to abide by existing WTO rules, sometimes specifying national measures to be amended to conform with WTO provisions;
   (b) Obligations not to make recourse to specific WTO provisions, and specific identification of transition periods available;
   (c) Authorization to depart temporarily from WTO rules or commitments;
   (d) Obligations to abide by rules created by the commitment paragraphs and not contained in the WTO Agreements.")

[12] A.D. Mitchell and J. Wallis, "Pacific Pause: The Rhetoric of Special & Differential Treatment, The Reality of WTO Accession" 2010 *Wisconsin International Law Journal* 27(4) 663, at 696.

[13] See eg, J.B. Rosen, "China, Emerging Economies, and the World Trade Order" 1997 *Duke Law Journal* 46(6) 1519, at 1552. Ultimately, China's accession protocol provides that it can use cer-tain SDT provisions but not others. M. Eglin, "China's Entry into the WTO with a Little Help from the EU" 1997 *International Affairs* 73(3) 489. See also L. Yongtu, Vice Minister and Head of the Chinese Delegation, Address at the Eleventh Session of the Working Party on China, 27 July 2000, <http://www.fmprc.gov.cn/ce/cegv/eng/gjhyfy/hy2000/t85629.htm>; R. Bhala, "Enter the Dragon: An Essay on China's WTO Accession Saga" 2000 *American University International Law Review* 15(6) 1469, at 1474–538; WTO Special Session of the Dispute Settlement Body, China—Responses to Questions on the Specific Input of China, TN/DS/W/57 (19 May 2003). Regarding Russia, see eg, C.B. Picker, "Neither Here Nor There—Countries that are Neither Developing nor Developed in the WTO: Geographic Differentiation as Applied to Russia and the WTO" 2004 *George Washington International Law Review* 36(1) 147, at 169–71.

"developing."[14] Existing WTO members can then challenge this status with respect to any of the WTO agreements.[15]

If the protocol of accession does not explicitly mention development status, the acceding member is free to designate itself as developing for purposes of taking advantage of favorable provisions in the WTO agreements. This self-designation, however, is largely irrelevant in practice because acceding countries typically make commitments during accession that restrict the scope of SDT available to them going forward. Hence, if a country commits during accession to restrict domestic agricultural support to "a level lower than what is allowed for developing countries, the commitment would be binding even if the country self-appoints itself to the developing country status or if it wanted to increase its agricultural support to the level allowed for 'developing countries' at a later stage."[16] The reverse situation is also possible; for instance where a transition period under a particular agreement has expired, a country may be able to negotiate an extension during accession negotiations, which could be considered as SDT.

2.2 The reality of developing country undertakings in accession packages

Trends in the specific commitments made by developing countries during accession negotiations show that they are asked to make far-reaching concessions and to disclaim access to existing SDT provisions[17]—at times undermining the notion that developing countries are receiving special treatment or that their development needs are accommodated. Typical commitments include binding tariffs at significantly lower levels than the overall WTO membership[18] and sometimes at applied levels, removing agricultural subsidies, making significant services commitments, joining plurilateral agreements, transitioning to a market economy, and complying with most or all WTO agreements upon entry without recourse to transitional periods.[19]

---

[14] R.J. Langhammer and M. Lücke, "WTO Accession Issues," Institut für Weltwirtschaft an der Universität Kiel, Kiel Working Paper No 905 (February 1999), at 23.

[15] United Nations Economic and Social Commission for Asia and the Pacific, *Accession to the WTO: Issues and Recommendations for Central Asian and Caucasian Economies in Transition*, Studies in Trade and Investment No 48, ST/ESCAP/2160(2001), at 23 (ESCAP Study).

[16] Bacchetta and Drabek, above fn 11, at 5–6.

[17] M. Tortora, "Special and Differential Treatment and Development Issues in the Multilateral Trade Negotiations: The Skeleton in the Closet," UNCTAD WEB/CDP/BKGD/16 (January 2003); C. Van Grasstek, "Why Demands on Acceding Countries Increase Over Time: A Three-Dimensional Analysis of Trade Diplomacy," in UNCTAD, *WTO Accessions and Development Policies* (Geneva: UNCTAD, 2001).

[18] Langhammer and Lücke, above fn 14 (comparing bound tariff rates of India and China).

[19] S.J. Everett, "Preparing for WTO Accessions: Insights from Developing Countries," IRDC Research Project (22 January 2005), at 14–15 <http://siteresources.worldbank.org/INTRANETTRADE/Resources/WBI-Training/PreparingforWTOAccessions.pdf>; ESCAP Study, above fn 15, at 47 ("the emerging common pattern includes the following set of requirements: (i) almost total binding of tariffs at considerably low levels; (ii) national treatment, including in the fiscal area, for goods and services; (iii) fair and transparent customs valuations; (iv) unbiased import licensing; (v) elimination of distorting export mechanisms: (vi) commitment to protection

Tonga, Vanuatu, and Samoa were all asked to make extensive concessions during the accession negotiations, in part leading to Vanuatu withdrawing its bid.[20] Cambodia and Nepal also were asked to make "WTO-plus" commitments as part of their accession packages.[21] Some have argued that Georgia and Kyrgyzstan, which both managed to accede in record time, may not have received a fair deal, giving up too much under the pressure of the negotiation process.[22] China's accession is a paradigmatic example of a package of commitments that went beyond the obligations of existing WTO members at the time.[23]

In the services area, acceding developing countries are often asked to make commitments that are more generous than even the most developed WTO members. Demands in the area of agriculture are particularly stringent and, in fact, some of the agreement's standard SDT provisions are negotiated away during accession. For example, the 10 percent agricultural support allowance for developing countries would be one of the easiest SDT provisions to extend to acceding members because it is clear-cut and measurable. However, even this exemption has not been granted to most acceding developing countries.[24] Some new members, including Estonia, Georgia, Kyrgyzstan, Latvia, and Mongolia, all committed to special *de minimis* levels of 5 percent—the default level for developed countries—rather than the 10 percent allowed for developing countries.[25] China, too, had to phase out all WTO-inconsistent subsidies, including

of intellectual property rights; (vii) negotiated market access in some specific sectors; (viii) transparent testing procedures for standards and certification; (ix) limitation of investment barriers; (x) to a lesser extent possible, the participation in plurilateral agreements, eg Government Procurement Agreement, and the acceptance of recent agreements, eg Information Technology Agreement"); Mitchell and Wallis, above fn 12, at 684–5 ("During these negotiations, demands will be made on Applicants which exceed those made on existing Members. These higher demands may include: binding all tariffs (normally at close to applied rates and often at relatively low rates) making significant services commitments, meeting all WTO commitments at entry without any transition period (China is a counter-example), committing to a timetable to join plurilateral agreements (eg the agreement on government procurement), and transitioning to a market economy (often while maintaining anti-dumping procedures that would maintain a 'non-market economy' designation of the Applicant)."); Bosworth and Duncan, above fn 2, at 20 ("It is also argued that...S&D treatment is not being granted to developing countries in the main areas of agricultural support commitments, export subsidy provisions, balance of payments consultations, and the Decision on Net Food Importing Countries.").

[20] Mitchell and Wallis, above fn 12, at 670. Vanuatu's second bid for accession has now been approved.

[21] P. Sauvé, "Economic Impact and Social Adjustment Costs of Accession to the World Trade Organization: Cambodia and Nepal" 2005 *Asia-Pacific Trade & Investment* 1(1) 27.

[22] ESCAP Study, above fn 15.

[23] K. Halverson, "China's WTO Accession: Economic, Legal, and Political Implications" 2004 *Boston College International and Comparative Law Review* 27(2) 319 ("[W]hen one takes into account the size of China's economy, its status as a developing country, and the degree to which China (until very recently) operated as a planned economy, the extent of China's commitments are unprecedented"); D.P. Harris, "The Honeymoon is Over: The US-China WTO Intellectual Property Complaint" 2008 *Fordham International Law Journal* 32(1) 96, at 108–13.

[24] Bosworth and Duncan, above fn 2, at 35. (The agricultural subsidies could "be made readily available to acceding countries, rather than members sometimes insisting that the lower agreed limits for developed countries apply.")   [25] Ibid at 42; ESCAP Study, above fn 15, at 85.

agricultural support, even before the transition period of the Agreement on Agriculture expired.[26]

Acceding developing countries are generally not afforded transitional periods to implement WTO commitments even in areas where such periods were provided to existing members. Implementation periods included in the WTO agreements are calculated from the entry into force of the WTO Agreement, not from the date of accession of a particular country. Some WTO members have in fact argued that the transition periods were only available to the original members and need not be extended to countries acceding under Article XII, regardless of their level of development.[27] This has at times been the case even where the original transitional provision contained in the agreement had not yet expired. Thus, Nepal, which acceded in April 2004, was allowed until December 2005 to implement the Trade-Related Aspects of Intellectual Property Rights Agreement (TRIPS), somewhat short of the implementation deadline for LDC of January 2006.[28] While the nominal time discrepancy may not have been relevant in practice, it demonstrates that there was little willingness on the part of the Working Parties to extend the benefit of transitional periods to countries that acceded during the intervening period, even as a token gesture. Similarly, Georgia, Kyrgyzstan, and Mongolia had to implement the Agreement on Trade Related Investment Measures (TRIMS) upon accession.[29] Bulgaria had to implement the WTO agreements either from the date of accession or, in some areas, with just a one-year transitional period.[30] Armenia, though it negotiated for transition periods, was forced to adhere to all WTO agreements upon accession because significant delays in the accession process erased the transition periods it had obtained.[31] China even had to show evidence of implementation *prior to* accession.[32]

Transition periods have not even been commonplace under TRIPS—an area where significant legal and regulatory change was often necessary for acceding countries to bring their domestic legislation into compliance with WTO commitments. For example, Georgia, Kyrgyzstan, and Mongolia had to implement TRIPS upon accession.[33] China also had to accept TRIPS upon accession and could not avail itself of SDT provisions available under that agreement.[34] Only in rare cases have some transitional periods been granted to acceding members under TRIPS. In addition to the few months given to Nepal as described above, Cambodia, which acceded in October 2004, was allowed until January 2007 to implement TRIPS.[35]

[26] Bhala, above fn 13, at 1495.
[27] ESCAP Study, above fn 15, at 24; see also Mitchell and Wallis, above fn 12, at 624.
[28] Sauvé, above fn 21.   [29] Bosworth and Duncan, above fn 2, at 42.
[30] Langhammer and Lücke, above fn 14, at 14.
[31] ESCAP Study, above fn 15, at 86.   [32] Langhammer and Lücke, above fn 14, at 14.
[33] Bosworth and Duncan, above fn 2, at 42.
[34] Bhala, above fn 13, at 1494.
[35] Sauvé, above fn 21.

3. Conclusion

With relatively few countries left outside of the WTO, the question of their status as developing countries during and after accession may seem mostly academic. Not so for LDCs, a number of which are still seeking accession. With candidate countries representing a very small percentage of the volume of world trade, the question may seem irrelevant from an economic standpoint as well. Yet, WTO membership is transformative for the economies of the countries seeking accession, and it is critical to them that it be done on feasible and equitable terms. Additionally, the impact on the organization's legitimacy and on the goodwill from all parts in future negotiations should not be ignored. To put it in game theory terms, accession negotiations by developing countries are largely treated by the Working Party as a single round game where the latter holds the cards and the power. The reality is that if the candidate country becomes a member, it is only the first step of an iterative game with no last round in sight, where cooperation should be the guiding principle.

Accession negotiation is an important point for assessing the status of an incoming member as developing or least developed, and the nature of the rights it can claim as such. Obliterating this discussion undermines the future of special and differential treatment for all members and preempts a serious consideration of development requirements in shaping trade policy at the WTO. Why lose this opportunity to tackle the question of the trade and development relationship for incoming members? Instead members are essentially pushing this inevitable debate to the even more complex moment of multilateral negotiation rounds. If members still believe in the global vocation of the WTO, why insist on the fiction of a one-size-fits-all approach to trade liberalization, with only limited carve-out governed by the lopsided power plays of the accession negotiations?

5

From the Uruguay Round to the Doha Round: Changing Dynamics in Developing Countries' Participation

After considering the substantive framing of development-oriented rights at the GATT and WTO (Chapter 3), we examined to the processes for developing countries' access to development-oriented provisions during accession negotiations (Chapter 4). This chapter now widens the enquiry to assess the framing of development in general negotiations amongst the full membership. The premise is that while developing country participation is a political and institutional question, it is in large part outcome-determinative with respect to the substance of the rules and disciplines. That is not to say that the presence of developing members in negotiations will necessarily result in regulatory outcomes favorable to them, but their marginalization, it has been proved in the past, certainly precludes a significant consideration of development constraints in the resulting trade rules.

Developing members' negotiation strategies have evolved considerably since the advent of the WTO; these transformations inform their approach to the Doha "Development" Round and their proposals throughout the Round. While developing countries were largely sidelined in the 1970s rounds and found themselves in a difficult position in the complex Uruguay Round negotiations, many of them have since worked hard to gain some measure of control over the negotiations. While this newfound voice has not yet translated into the actual ability to gain valuable concessions, it has been effective as a defensive mechanism to prevent negotiations on issues where developing countries felt they would be at a disadvantage. However, such a remarkable achievement should not obfuscate the very disparate positions of developing members: LDCs are still very marginalized in the negotiations and the implementation of the agreements (in particular, in dispute settlement), and the power of developing countries is mostly that of the middle-income countries including Brazil, India, South Africa, China, Mexico, Egypt, and a few others. These countries have in fact been more active participants throughout the life of the GATT (with the exception of China, which became a WTO member only in 2001).

The changing dynamic in developing country participation since the end of the Uruguay Round has taken several forms. First, developing members realized the critical aspect of agenda-setting in negotiations. Indeed, after decades of demands left unaddressed or sidelined, and the introduction of new topics during the Uruguay Round, they realized the strategic importance of gaining as much control as possible over the mandate for negotiation. A particularly striking illustration of developing country efforts in that respect is the rejection of the "new issues" at the 1996 Singapore Ministerial Meeting. Second, many developing countries made substantive contributions during the negotiations in an effort to shape the final package of agreements. The number of proposals emanating from developing countries has positively exploded during the Doha Round, especially in the early years of the round. While the proposals vary in scope and nature, their quantity and increasing sophistication is unprecedented in the history of the GATT and WTO.

Coalition-building between developing members plays a key role in placing on the agenda issues of interest to them and in putting pressure on the organization to reform its negotiation process. By acting in groups, developing countries are better able to harness and leverage their emerging power. Most proposals from developing countries tabled during the Doha Round have been submitted by groups; the WTO Secretariat even provided logistical support to particular groups to increase their voice. One of the major advances during the Hong Kong Ministerial meeting of 2005, the Cotton Four initiative, resulted from the coordinated stance of four West-African developing and least developed countries.

Coalition activity also signals the diversification of developing countries' priorities. The positioning of some countries as leaders and the pattern of regional or topical affinities testifies to the emergence of a complex mapping of developing country perspectives.

Steinberg analyzes WTO negotiations as:

three overlapping stages: (1) carefully advancing and developing initiatives that broadly conceptualize a new area or form of regulation; (2) drafting and fine-tuning proposals (namely, legal texts) that specify rules, principles and procedures; and (3) developing a package of proposals into a "final act" for approval upon closing of the round.[1]

He notes that this process is dominated by power-plays by the United States and the EU. By contrast, developing countries struggle to transform their demands into negotiating proposals, and from there, into operational legal claims and entitlements. The ubiquitous consensus decision-making, is, however, a significant hurdle in these efforts.

Nevertheless, ministerial meetings since 1995 show important transformations in the management of these three steps by developing members (agenda-setting, developing proposals during the negotiation stage, and finalizing the "package" for membership approval). This chapter reviews the WTO negotiations after the Uruguay Round, from the Singapore Ministerial Meeting to the ongoing Doha Round, through the lens of developing countries' participation. It emphasizes the role of developing country coalitions in shaping the negotiations.

---

[1] R.H. Steinberg, "In the Shadow of Law or Power? Consensus-Based Bargaining and Outcomes in the GATT/WTO" 2002 *International Organization* 56(2) 339, at 354.

1. The Singapore Ministerial Meeting: Understanding the Importance of Agenda-setting

While the initial mandate for negotiations traditionally tends to include most proposals and to be formulated in broad terms, developing countries have been increasingly cautious about agenda-setting both with respect to inclusion and to exclusion of topics.

In the early 1980s, Argentina, Brazil, Egypt, India, and Yugoslavia led the opposition to the launching of the Uruguay Round until some topics of interest to developing countries were included in the negotiation mandate, such as trade in tropical products and textiles, addressing Voluntary Restraints Agreements, and obtaining assurances that developed countries would not raise their tariff and non-tariff barriers (standstill agreement).[2] Similarly, the battle led by India over the new issues at the 1996 Singapore Ministerial Meeting was a remarkable example of the efforts by some developing members to exclude certain items from the negotiations. While a reluctant compromise was reached on investment and competition, the trade–labor linkage was more resolutely excluded.

The politics of Singapore inform the road to the Doha Round. The United States supported launching a narrow round at the Seattle Ministerial Meeting, while the EU wanted to include a large number of topics including the environment, labor, trade remedies, investment, and competition, all of which developing countries had already opposed at the Singapore Ministerial meeting. Developing countries wished to emphasize agriculture, trade in manufactures and tropical products, implementation issues relating to the Uruguay Round agreements, issues related to debt, technical assistance and capacity-building, and the reform of the decision-making procedures.

Ultimately, it was not before the 2001 Doha Ministerial meeting that some agreement was reached regarding the agenda for a new Round. Newly admitted China and the G-77 led the movement in favor of developing countries' agenda and threatened to block the consensus. The Ministerial resulted in a very broad "Doha Work Programme" that included virtually all the issues raised.

2. The Seattle Ministerial Meeting: Fighting for Participation

Traditionally, proposals relating to the substance of the negotiations are discussed and refined during the so-called "Green Room" process consisting of informal caucuses between a limited number of members (usually twenty to twenty-five). Green

---

[2] See *Ministerial Declaration Adopted on 29 November 1982*, L/5424 (29 November 1982), BISD 29S/9. The Ministerial Declaration includes several paragraphs on the trade interests of developing countries generally. It also requires negotiations to take into account interests of developing countries, including with respect to textiles, clothing, tropical products, and other tariff negotiations, with a special mention of the problem of escalation clauses.

Room meetings have always included the powerful members and some other members meant to represent the WTO membership at large. As such, the Green Room resembles an informal version of the UN Security Council, with quasi-permanent members and other members meant to represent the membership at large. One major difference between the WTO's Green Room process and the UN Security Council is that the non-permanent members of the Security Council are elected by the full UN membership based on several criteria, including geographic representation, whereas participation in the Green Room is by invitation from the main powers on political criteria.

Packages negotiated in the Green Room generally are adopted by the full membership by consensus with only minor amendments. Issues brought to the table by developing countries tend to be treated as negotiable side-issues. As a result, many members, particularly those with smaller delegations, feel excluded from the Green Room. They are marginalized by a powerful decision-making process that essentially bypasses formal mechanisms for consultations. Because packages finalized in the Green Room are presented to members essentially on a take-it-or-leave-it basis, with the deadline for closing the Ministerial meeting drawing near there is virtually no room for negotiation or amendments. Nor does this system allow delegates to examine in much detail the implications of the proposed deal for their economies.

Somewhat ironically, an alternative procedure to the Green Room was first used at the 1999 Seattle Ministerial Meeting with negotiations taking place in small open-ended working groups designed to be more inclusive. However, when deadlocks remained as the deadline for closing the meeting approached, the US Representative convened a Green Room meeting with the powerful members and some developing countries, including Egypt and Brazil, to set the agenda for a new round.[3] When some additional developing country delegations tried to access the Green Room, they were driven away, exposing the process as one undermining the WTO's legitimacy and preventing meaningful participation by many members.

In the aftermath of the Seattle events, the General Council examined the issue of internal transparency and effective participation during ministerial meetings.[4] Because not all issues can be discussed by all members at all times, most members recognize that smaller working groups may be inevitable, but they also require assurances regarding transparency and participation.[5] However, different views

---

[3] J. Burgess, "Green Room's Closed Doors Couldn't Hide Disagreements," *Washington Post* (5 December 1999); N. Pani, "Seattle Fails to Find Common Ground for Fresh Talks," *Economic Times of India* (5 December 1999) (noting that representatives from developing countries were forced away from the room by security forces); "African Countries Complained Friday," *Xinhua General News Service* (4 December 1999) (quoting the South African representative: "If African delegates are unable to make their positions known through the formal structures of the WTO, then they stand little chance of making sure that these real issues are addressed.").
[4] WTO General Council, *Minutes of the Meeting Held in the Centre William Rappard on 17 and 19 July 2000*, WT/GC/M/57 (14 September 2000).
[5] See S.E. Rolland, "Developing Country Coalitions at the WTO: In Search of Legal Support" 2007 *Harvard International Law Journal* 48(2) 483.

emerge regarding the modalities for managing the negotiation process. Some developing countries (including Barbados, Bolivia, Egypt, Pakistan, and Saint Lucia) are reluctant to agree to the principle of negotiations in working groups.[6] Others (for example, the African Group, the ASEAN group, Colombia, Jamaica, and Mexico) see it as a valid mechanism so long as the groups are open-ended, and all members are notified early and given an opportunity to participate. In addition, the group discussion should be disseminated to all WTO members and the work-product of the groups would be in no instance considered as formal consultations or be put up for adoption by consensus.[7]

The discussion on working groups is ongoing within the WTO. Forming open-ended working groups on specific issues with members free to participate in any group would shift the burden onto each member to manage its own participation. In theory, participation would be based on each member's priorities and interests. In practice it would largely be constrained by the member's institutional capacity and delegation size, and whether a particular issue is a negotiation priority at that point in time (as opposed to considering the long-term implications of issues that are not an immediate priority). Members' participation in this type of open-ended group may be limited to a relatively shallow participation, falling short of affording all members a genuine opportunity to participate. Additionally, the fluidity of membership in working groups could impede the continuity and consistency of the groups' work.

Some members already participate in negotiations through submissions by groups. Representatives from individual members regularly speak on behalf of groups such as the Paradisus Group, the African Group, and the ASEAN in working groups, committees, and even at the General Council. Members, including developing countries, recognize that consultations amongst groups of members are part of the negotiation process and should not be eliminated. At the same time, they insist that decision-making belongs to the membership as a whole, through the consensus procedure, and that the latter must take its full effect, instead of becoming a rubber stamp for decisions already made by a limited number of members. The question then is how to bridge the gap between discussions in open-ended, fluid, issue-based working groups and the finalization of a legitimate package of proposals for approval by the full membership. One option would be to combine individual member representation at the working group level with some form of legitimate formal group representation at the stage of putting together a package. Using a constitutional analogy, the idea would be to afford members both direct representation (through individual participation in deliberations and negotiations)

---

[6] WTO General Council, *Minutes of the Meeting Held in the Centre William Rappard on 17 and 19 July 2000*, above fn 4, at paras 138–42 (comments by Bulgaria), para 147 (comments by Saint Lucia), para 157 (comments by Bolivia), paras 159–60 (comments by Egypt explicitly referring to the Green Room process and to the Seattle failure), para 162 (comments by Barbados), para 165 (comments by Pakistan).

[7] Ibid at paras 149–53 (comments by Mexico, Singapore on behalf of the ASEAN group, Mauritius on behalf of the African Group, Colombia, and Jamaica).

and indirect representation through representative groups with a mandate and a reporting mechanism.

These questions remain very much unresolved at this time, with informal processes filling in the gaps. While informal mechanisms are helpful and even necessary, they do not guarantee a systematic or consistent representation of members, they are not transparent in terms of access and participation, and they raise issues regarding information-sharing and conflicts of interest between the group's spokesperson and its members. The political role of coalitions and groups is crucial and should be allowed to operate in a fluid environment but some degree of institutionalization would ensure more effective access and participation to members with serious capacity constraints. It would also enhance transparency, legitimacy, and accountability in what already amounts in practice to proxy participation by many members with limited resources.

3. The Doha Round: Shaping the Negotiations

The second stage in the negotiating process, which involves refining proposals to be submitted for approval by all members, is less law-based and more power-based.

After developing members put the issue of participation in full view and asserted their voices regarding agenda-setting, they proceeded to make good on the potentialities. Reflecting the broad agenda for the Doha "Development" Round, the 2001 Doha Work Programme includes the following topics for negotiations:

- Implementation issues (GATT, Agreement on Agriculture, Agreement on Sanitary and Phytosanitary Measures, Agreement on Textiles and Clothing)
- Technical barriers to trade
- Agriculture
- Services
- Market access for non-agricultural products
- TRIPS
- Trade and investment
- Trade and competition
- Transparency in government procurement
- Trade facilitation
- WTO rules
- Dispute Settlement Understanding
- Trade and the environment
- Electronic commerce
- Small economies
- Debt, trade, and finance

- Trade and technology transfer
- Technical cooperation and capacity-building
- Least-developed countries
- Special and differential treatment
- Cross-cutting issues
- Negotiation modalities.

Each item has a development impact and, in fact, constitutes a sensitive area for some or all developing members. This list can be divided in four broad categories: *agreement-specific issues* (such as agriculture, services, intellectual property, investment, competition, dispute settlement, TBT, government procurement, WTO rules, and the implementation issues pertaining to a number of Uruguay Round agreements), *subject-specific issues* (market access, trade facilitation, e-commerce, technology transfer, debt, and technical assistance), *issues common to all agreements* (the so-called cross-cutting issues and special and differential treatment), and *member-specific issues* (small economies, island-states, and LDCs).

The focus of developing member proposals and the likelihood of progress is very different for each category. In the months leading to the Doha Ministerial conference and in the first years of the Doha Round, developing members submitted an unprecedented number of proposals affecting virtually all domains of the agenda. Some proposals are framed by reference to existing provisions of the covered agreements, others introduce new provisions, and a few seek to create new legal tools distinct from the existing agreements. Most proposals focus on subject-specific issues, issues common to all the agreements, and member-specific issues.

Yet, little progress has been made and the opinion generally expressed both by negotiators and Secretariat staffers is that only agreement-specific proposals are likely to be given any weight. This is in large part due to the institutional structure of the negotiations, which have moved from the cross-cutting Trade Negotiations Committee to agreement-specific committees. The latter offer little opportunity for considering cross-cutting issues and they require sponsors of cross-cutting proposals to reframe the proposals on an agreement-specific basis, thereby defeating the very purpose of many such proposals. Moreover, agreement-focused negotiations essentially preclude the consideration of proposals outside of the existing agreements. Hence, the negotiation of new agreements, such as a development framework agreement proposed by some developing countries, is unlikely to gain momentum if only because of the negotiating structure. As a result, negotiations are unlikely to produce anything other than a marginal manipulation of the agreements that fails to address the more systemic issues. More than ten years into the Doha Round, this point has been amply proved by the facts.

Leaving aside the institutional features of the Doha negotiations, this Round also testifies to new dynamics in the positioning of developing members on substantive aspects. Generally, members showed a remarkable lack of convergence in the early years of the Doha Round, which may account for the protracted nature of the negotiations. Amongst developing countries, positions seem equally scattered.

An interesting study by Bjørnskov and Lind examines how members' positions correlate based on the proposals submitted in preparation to the Doha Ministerial and statements made during the Ministerial. It takes into account members' positions on tariffs (including tariff peaks and escalation), quotas, safeguard clauses, export credits and subsidies, domestic support (particularly on agriculture), and some non-trade concerns (position with respect to broad or narrow rounds, and inclusion of labor and environmental standards).[8] Using a variety of statistical methods, the study groups together members whose declarations and other official statements closely relate. All models show a high degree of divergence overall between the key members, particularly between the EU and the rest of the membership.[9] However, despite the variety of issues considered, the study reveals patterns loosely matching agricultural interests, probably in large part because a number of proposals submitted in 2000 and 2001 focused on agriculture. The repeated breakdowns in negotiations in past years, largely over agriculture, confirm these early trends.

Comparing the groups of converging interests identified by Bjørnskov and Lind's study and the active coalitions of members, it is notable that, to some extent, the groups defined by the study match the political groupings that have emerged in WTO negotiations, such as the African Group, the LDC group, the Cairns Group, and the G-20. However, another study shows that the correlation between the individual position of each group's leader and that group is not always a close one.[10] For instance, South Africa's interests mostly converge with, but sometimes strikingly differ from, those of much of the African Group it seeks to lead.[11] Canada's positions are also relatively far from the positions of other Cairns Group countries. As such, the study foreshadows the dissents in the Cairns Group that gave rise to the G-20.

The Bjørnskov and Lind study confirms the increasingly obvious fact that developing countries' interests are not aligned. It also confirms that developing members' insistence on maintaining the legally and politically unifying "developing country" category is belied by their actual positions on substantive issues. For example, the G-20's agenda runs counter to the extension of preferences advocated by the G-90 that includes the ACP, LDC, and African groups.

3.1 The Cancún Ministerial meeting: Substantive disagreements

Diverging positions and possibly irreconcilable claims quickly emerged in the Doha Round, crystallizing first at the failed 2003 Cancún Ministerial meeting

---

[8] C. Bjørnskov and K.M. Lind, "Where do Developing Countries Go After Doha? An Analysis of WTO Positions and Potential Alliances" 2002 *Journal of World Trade* 36(3) 543, at 544–5.
[9] Ibid at 549–50.
[10] P. Draper and R. Sally, "Developing-Country Coalitions in Multilateral Trade Negotiations," Paper, Jawaharlal Nehru University 2004 <http://www.ppl.nl/bibliographies/wto/files/3071.pdf>.
[11] Ibid at 44–5.

before a last-minute deal that started to bring parties together during the 2005 Hong Kong Ministerial gave new hope for the Round.

The Ministerial meeting at Cancún failed for several reasons. First, it became clear that the parties could not agree on modalities for negotiations on agriculture and non-agricultural products. In addition, differences remained irreconcilable regarding the so-called "Singapore issues," and implementation issues carried over from the Uruguay Round were left open along with the myriad of proposals on SDT (the latter in spite of the Chairman's attempt to categorize—and, some say, illegitimately prioritize—the proposals).[12]

Yet, one positive result emerged from the Cancún meeting in the form of a proposal by Benin, Burkina Faso, Chad, and Mali (the Cotton Four) to phase out export subsidies and other trade-distorting subsidies on cotton. The United States, the EU, and China were the primary targets for the reduction of these subsidies. The proposal garnered enough support to be taken up again at the following ministerial meeting in Hong Kong in December 2005, but has faltered since then. The only tangible accomplishment of the meeting was the Decision on Public Health under which the TRIPS will be amended to clarify the legality of parallel imports and compulsory licensing of drugs in developing countries in response to public health emergencies.

Nevertheless, trade talks stalled in November 2003[13] and the outlook at the beginning of the Hong Kong Ministerial was bleak.

3.2 The Hong Kong Ministerial meeting: Too late for convergence?

A day after the opening of the 2005 Ministerial, the Indian delegate stated on record that:

[t]rade commitments which throw hundreds of millions of people already on the edge of subsistence into a chasm of poverty and unemployment simply cannot be supported. The ambition of developed countries cannot and must not trample on the aspirations of four-fifths of humanity.[14]

With deadlines set in the original Work Programme passing with no substantive outcome (including the requirement for a comprehensive study on SDT in the covered agreements which was never fulfilled), the official line was still to conclude negotiations by the end of 2006 before the expiration of the United States' so-called "fast-track authority" and changes at the head of the EU.

---

[12] B. Hoekman, "Cancún: Crisis or Catharsis," Revised version of paper presented at Brookings-George Washington Roundtable on Trade and Investment Policy, Washington, DC, 23 September 2003 <http://siteresources.worldbank.org/INTRANETTRADE/Resources/Hoekman-Cancun Catharsis-092003.pdf>.

[13] WTO Press Release, *Supachai: Sluggish Trade Growth Calls for Urgent Pick Up of Stalled Trade Talks*, Press/363 (5 November 2003).

[14] *Statement by H.E. Mr. Kamal Nath, Minister of Commerce and Industry,* WT/MIN(05)/ST/17(14 December 2005).

Towards the end of the Hong Kong Ministerial, an agreement surfaced regarding the Cotton Four Initiative[15] as well as the duty-free and quota-free access for LDCs negotiated in response to the EU's Everything But Arms proposal.[16] Some important principles were also set forth regarding elimination of agricultural subsidies. However, agreements in those areas existed only on the surface, with much uncertainty and potential for discord regarding implementation.

The agreement on cotton as summarized in the final Hong Kong Ministerial Declaration provided that:

- All forms of export subsidies for cotton will be eliminated by developed countries in 2006.
- . . . developed countries will give duty and quota-free access for cotton exports from least-developed countries (LDCs) from the commencement of the implementation period.
- Members agree that the objective is that . . . trade-distorting domestic subsidies for cotton production be reduced more ambitiously than under whatever general formula is agreed and that it should be implemented over a shorter period of time than generally applicable.[17]

However, the 2006 deadline for phasing out export subsidies was not met and because the round has yet to be concluded, the second and third paragraphs have not been implemented either. In March 2005, the Appellate Body upheld panel findings against the United States on various cotton subsidies in response to a complaint by Brazil in which some of the Cotton Four and others joined as third parties.[18] A recent Congressional Research Service paper estimated that US subsidies on cotton averaged USD2.8 billion per year.[19] Brazil eventually obtained the authorization to suspend concessions against the United States to offset the continued US breaches of their obligations regarding cotton subsidies. When Brazil issued lists of goods that would be subject to higher tariffs on a rotating basis, the United States engaged in settlement negotiations.

The *US–Upland Cotton* case illustrates the interesting interplay between the negotiations and adjudication and between different types of developing countries. Undoubtedly, the complaint brought by Brazil in 2003 played a significant part in the agreement in principle won by the Cotton Four at the Hong Kong Ministerial. Yet only two of these countries joined the dispute as third parties. Differences in resources likely account for the fact that the case was spearheaded by Brazil, rather than the Cotton Four, and the structure of retaliatory rights means

---

[15] *Ministerial Declaration Adopted on 18 December 2005*, WT/MIN(05)/DEC (22 December 2005) (hereinafter Hong Kong Ministerial Declaration), at para 11. However, Annex A undermines some of the commitments and testifies to enduring disagreements on implementation.

[16] Ibid at Annex F, Decision on Measures in Favour of Least-Developed Countries.

[17] Ibid at para 11.

[18] Appellate Body Report, *US–Upland Cotton*. Argentina, Benin, Chad, China, India, Pakistan, Paraguay, Venezuela and Thailand, in particular, joined as third parties.

[19] R. Schnepf, "Brazil's WTO Case Against the US Cotton Program: A Brief Overview," Congressional Research Service Report for Congress No RS22187 (17 March 2009) <http://www.nationalaglawcenter.org/assets/crs/RS22187.pdf>.

that while Brazil may be able to offset the harm to it in the case of non-compliance, the Cotton Four will continue to bear the effects of the US subsidies pending either a reform of the US programs or an agreement in the Doha Round on the implementation of the agreement obtained at Hong Kong.

The duty-free/quota-free agreement, stemming from the EU's Everything But Arms initiative, raises different issues, but has been equally unsuccessful in practice. The agreement in principle provided that "developed-country Members, and developing-country Members declaring themselves in a position to do so, agree to implement duty-free and quota-free market access for products originating from LDCs"[20] by 2008 or no later than the start of the implementation period and would cover at least 97 percent of the tariff line items originating from LDCs. Since then, no implementation has taken place in part because no agreement was reached on the determination of the 3 percent of tariff lines that could be excluded from the preferential market access. Because exports from LDCs tend not to be diversified, large volumes of their exports can be excluded from the duty-free/quota-free access without exceeding the 3 percent of tariff lines allowance. The benefits of the initiative can therefore easily be eviscerated, particularly if the designation of the 3 percent of tariff lines is specific to each LDC, rather than applying across the board to all LDCs. The modalities for implementing the duty-free/quota-free initiative have, for the moment, defeated what had been a politically and—for LDCs—economically important concession in the Doha Round.

Headway on negotiations for the reduction of agricultural subsidies were heralded as a major area of progress at Hong Kong. Annex A of the Declaration, in the form of a "Report by the Chairman of the Special Session of the Committee on Agriculture to the TNC," belies this claim by reminding that "it was clear that, following the decision at the Heads of Delegation meeting that full modalities will not be achieved at Hong Kong. Members did not want anything that suggested implicit or explicit agreement where it did not exist." Unlike in the area of cotton subsidies and the duty-free/quota-free initiative, no agreement was reached, although members had devised a system of bands for capping and cutting various agricultural support as a working hypothesis for future negotiations.

The Hong Kong Ministerial breathed some life into the Doha negotiations and appeared to achieve more than earlier ministerials. However, the progress made on a number of issues of importance to developing members failed to materialize. The Declaration also mentions the lack of progress on special and differential treatment proposals. Already, the true agenda had narrowed down and many proposals or demands from developing countries were clearly sidelined.

3.3 Doha in the doldrums?

Since the Hong Kong Ministerial, several "mini-ministerials" have taken place in Geneva, alternating with suspensions of negotiations for significant periods, on the advice of the Director General. In July 2008, an attempt was made to re-launch the

---

[20] Hong Kong Ministerial Declaration, at para 47.

talks, with the objective of reaching an agreement on the modalities for agriculture and non-agricultural market access (NAMA) negotiations. Both agricultural subsidies and NAMA discussions focus on formulas to phase out or cut subsidies and to increase market access. Negotiations on trade in services and rules are also on the table. The wide range of other Doha agenda items are postponed, if not omitted altogether. The Chairs of the Agriculture and NAMA negotiating groups regularly produce revised drafts for modalities reflecting the state of play.

Although they put a positive note on the results overall, and the Director General claimed that "no one is throwing in the towel,"[21] a closer examination of the July 2008 reports reveals chasms between members in most critical areas. Since then, reports by chairs of the Committee on Agriculture, the NAMA group, the group on services and on rules have underlined lack of agreement, diverging views, and absence of consensus on virtually all critical issues.[22]

The change in administration in the United States in January 2009 opened the possibility of a renewed engagement in the negotiations, as Democratic administrations tend to favor a more trade-oriented agenda. However, climate change negotiations have taken the limelight and the rigid response from the United States to debates with developing countries at the Copenhagen and Barcelona Climate Change Conferences in 2009 have not sent encouraging signals on the likelihood of coming to terms with the currently entrenched positions on trade negotiations. While climate change talks and trade negotiations are different, some political dynamics are similar: In both fora, developing countries have argued that negotiations and developed countries' agenda run counter to the formers' development interests. An unfavorable response to developing countries' concerns in the climate change arena might foster skepticism regarding the willingness of the United States, Europe, and others to make concessions developing countries feel are necessary in the trade context.

A number of other elements contribute to the enduring stalemate at the WTO. First, the United States continues to demand improved offers from developing countries on services liberalization as a preliminary to further talks in this sector at least. Second, major fluctuations in world food prices and the increased price of staple foods (such as rice) disrupt agricultural negotiations. Finally, the financial crisis of 2008 has also led to a re-prioritization of international cooperation to deal with the collapse of the financial sector.

---

[21] WTO, "Statement by P. Lamy to the Trade Negotiations Committee" (24 July 2008) <http://www.wto.org/english/news_e/news09_e/tnc_dg_stat_24jul09_e.htm>.

[22] See eg, WTO Committee on Agriculture, Special Session, *Revised Draft Modalities for Agriculture*, TN/AG/W/4/Rev.4 (6 December 2008) (noting some progress since the July 2008 package, but no formal agreement on any issue and divergence in a number of areas); WTO Negotiating Group on Market Access, *Fourth Revision of Draft Modalities for Non-Agricultural Market Access*, TN/MA/W/103/Rev.3 (6 December 2008) (noting that "everything is conditional in the deepest sense"); WTO Negotiating Group on Rules, *New Draft Consolidated Chair Texts of the AD and SCM Agreements*, TN/RL/W/236 (19 December 2008) ("As I stated very clearly in July, and the situation has not changed since that time, it should not be expected that my new texts will offer any magic solutions in the many areas where Members' positions differ dramatically and where the alternatives remain as delegations originally tabled them, ie, very far apart.").

With the future of the Doha "Development" Round so uncertain, trade negotiations have moved to other fora, mostly regional trade agreements and some
smaller multilateral frameworks such as the Global System of Trade Preferences
(GSTP). Since 2004, the United States has entered into trade agreements with
thirteen countries, with another three pending.[23] It is currently engaged in negotiations with Singapore, Chile, New Zealand, Brunei, Australia, Peru, and Vietnam
for a Trans-Pacific Partnership Agreement. Thirty-one Trade and Investment
Framework Agreements (TIFA) have also been concluded with individual countries or regions since 2003.[24] These agreements are very short and typically create
a Council on Trade and Investment with a mandate close to the US's multilateral
trade agenda:

- To monitor trade and investment relations, to identify opportunities for expanding
  trade and investment, and to identify issues relevant to trade or investment, such as
  intellectual property, labor, or environmental issues that may be appropriate for negotiation in an appropriate forum.
- To hold consultations on trade and investment matters not arising under the relevant
  Bilateral Investment Treaties of interest to the Parties.
- To identify and work toward the removal of impediments to trade and investment
  flows amongst the Parties.

(language common to virtually all TIFAs).

The European Union has also developed trade relations on a bilateral or regional
basis in the sidelines of the WTO negotiations. With respect to ACP countries,
these agreements have taken the form of Economic Partnership Agreements (EPAs)
since 2005.[25] Although most EPAs are still only in provisional or interim form,

[23] Free trade agreements with Australia (2005), Bahrain (2006), Chile (2004), Costa Rica, El
Salvador, Guatemala, Honduras, Nicaragua, and the Dominican Republic (2004), Morocco (2006),
Oman (2009), Peru (2006), Singapore (2004), Colombia, Korea, and Panama (signed but not yet
ratified). See Office of the United States Trade Representative (USTR), "Free Trade Agreements"
<http://www.ustr.gov/trade-agreements/free-trade-agreements>.
[24] Angola (2009), the Common Market for Eastern and Southern Africa (2001), the East African
Community (2008), Liberia (2007), Mauritius (2006), Mozambique (2005), Rwanda (2006),
the West African Economic and Monetary Union, Uruguay (2007), Georgia (2007), Iraq (2005),
Kuwait (2004), Lebanon (2006), Libya (2010), Oman (2004), Qatar (2004), Saudi Arabia (2003),
Switzerland (2006), Ukraine (2008), United Arab Emirates (2004), Yemen (2004), Afghanistan
(2004), Kazakhstan, Kyrgyzstan, Tajikistan, Turkmenistan, and Uzbekistan (2004), Pakistan
(2003), the ASEAN (2006), Cambodia (2006), Malaysia (2004). A few TIFAs were signed before
2003 and TIFAs with several South East Asian countries pre-date the Doha Round. Office of the
USTR "Trade and Investment Framework Agreements" <http://www.ustr.gov/trade-agreements/
trade-investment-framework-agreements>.
[25] Provisional EPAs (also sometimes called "stepping stone EPAs") have been concluded with
the Ivory Coast, Ghana, Cameroon, Comoros, Madagascar, Mauritius, Seychelles, Zambia,
and Zimbabwe. Framework agreements for EPAs have been finalized with the members of the
Eastern African Community (Kenya, Uganda, Tanzania, Burundi, Rwanda). Botswana, Lesotho,
Namibia, Swaziland, and Mozambique have finalized EPAs with the EU through the South African
Development Community. All members of the CARICOM except Haiti have signed EPAs (Antigua
and Barbuda, The Bahamas, Barbados, Belize, Dominica, Grenada, Guyana, Haiti, Jamaica, Saint
Lucia, Saint Vincent and the Grenadines, Saint Kitts and Nevis, Surinam, Trinidad and Tobago).
Fiji and Papua New Guinea have also entered into an EPA. EPAs are being negotiated with Central
African countries including the Central African Republic, Chad, Congo, Democratic Republic of
Congo, Equatorial Guinea, Gabon, Sao Tome and Principe. Mauritius, Seychelles, Zimbabwe, and

the stated objectives are similar across agreements. For example, the Agreement between the European Community and the East African Community states in its Article II:

The objectives of the Economic Partnership Agreement are:

(a) Contributing to economic growth and development through the establishment of a strengthened and strategic trade and development partnership consistent with the objective of sustainable development;

(b) Promoting regional integration, economic cooperation and good governance in the EAC;

(c) Promoting the gradual integration of the EAC into the world economy, in conformity with its political choices and development priorities;

(d) Fostering the structural transformation of EAC economies, and their diversification and competitiveness by enhancing their production, supply and trading capacity;

(e) Improving EAC capacity in trade policy and trade-related issues;

(f) Establishing and implementing an effective, predictable and transparent regional regulatory framework for trade and investment in the EAC Partner States, thus supporting the conditions for increasing investment, and private sector initiative; and

(g) Strengthening the existing relations between the Parties on the basis of solidarity and mutual interest. To this end, consistent with WTO obligations, the Agreement shall enhance commercial and economic relations, support a new trading dynamic between the Parties by means of the progressive, asymmetrical liberalisation of trade between them and reinforce, broaden and deepen cooperation in all areas relevant to trade and investment.

EPAs are meant to be consistent with Article XXIV of the GATT. The framework agreements preliminary to the conclusion of EPAs plan negotiations on a number of topics, typically including trade in goods, rules of origin, trade defense instruments, customs cooperation and trade facilitation, sanitary and phytosanitary measures, technical barriers to trade, and agriculture. They also include trade in services, e-commerce, investments, intellectual property, competition, and government procurement. All of these topics are part of the Doha Work Programme.

A number of regional trade agreements (RTAs) also emerged in Asia, mostly in the form of bilateral trade agreements,[26] but also including some plurilateral agreements.[27] Unlike the US and EU agreements, they are much more diverse in scope.

Madagascar are also parties to the COMESA, a regional trade agreement. See European Commission, "Economic Partnerships—Negotiations and Agreements: The ACP Regions" <http://ec.europa.eu/trade/wider-agenda/development/economic-partnerships/negotiations-and-agreements>.

[26] Australia–Singapore (entered into force 2003), Australia–Thailand (in force 2005), China–Hong Kong SAR (in force 2004), China–Macao SAR (in force 2004), China–Thailand, (in force 2003), India–Sri Lanka (in force 2001), India–Thailand (in force 2004), Japan–Malaysia (in force 2006), Japan–Mexico (in force 2005), Japan–Singapore (in force 2002), Korea–Chile (in force 2004), Korea–Singapore (in force 2006), New Zealand–Singapore (in force 2001), New Zealand–Thailand (in force 2005), Singapore–Jordan (in force 2005), Sri Lanka–Pakistan (in force 2005). See generally P. Tumbarello, "Are Regional Trade Agreements in Asia Stumbling or Building Blocks? Implications for the Mekong-3 Countries," IMF Working Paper No WP/07/53 (March 2007), at 15 <http://www.imf.org/external/pubs/ft/wp/2007/wp0753.pdf>.

[27] ASEAN–China Free Trade Agreement (in force 2005), Pacific Island Countries Trade Agreement (PICTA) (in force 2003), South Asia Free Trade Agreement (SAFTA) (in force 2006),

Some are closer to the range of trade topics addressed at the WTO, while others are more limited agreements.

The ASEAN–China Free Trade Agreement illustrates the more comprehensive approach to regional trade negotiations which more closely mimics the WTO agenda:

The objectives of this Agreement are to:
- (a) strengthen and enhance economic, trade and investment cooperation between the Parties;
- (b) progressively liberalise and promote trade in goods and services as well as create a transparent, liberal and facilitative investment regime;
- (c) explore new areas and develop appropriate measures for closer economic cooperation between the Parties; and
- (d) facilitate the more effective economic integration of the newer ASEAN member States and bridge the development gap among the Parties.

Much like the European EPAs, the topics for negotiations include services, competition, and investment, but do not include intellectual property.[28] By contrast, the Pacific Island Countries Trade Agreement is solely concerned with trade in goods.[29] The agreement builds in differentiation at the core of its parties' obligations.

The shift from the multilateral forum for negotiations at the WTO to a plethora of regional and bilateral fora is again changing the dynamics of developing country participation in the making of trade rules. In part it may allow developing members to build a framework for development-oriented trade liberalization in settings that they control (such as RTAs between developing countries); in part, it may subject the weaker countries to pressure from more powerful trade partners in negotiations where they cannot use the power of numbers.[30]

4. Conclusion

The position of developing countries in trade negotiations has evolved considerably since the Uruguay Round. The agenda and priorities of many developing members have not changed greatly because of outstanding issues on "tropical products," tariff peaks and escalation, capacity-building, technical assistance, and others. However, some countries have changed tactics, sometimes in response to regional trade dynamics. For instance, Mexico, which used to support the more traditional developing country stance in favor of SDT, now positions itself as a mainstream

---

Trans-Pacific Strategic Economic Partnership Agreement (TPSEPA) (in force 2006). See generally Tumbarello, above fn 26, at 15.

[28] Framework Agreement on Comprehensive Economic Cooperation Between the Association of South East Asian Nations and the People's Republic of China (Phnom Penh, 4 November 2002), WT/COMTD/N/20 and WT/COMTD/51.

[29] Pacific Island Countries Trade Agreement (Nauru, 18 August 2001), WT/COMTD/N/29.

[30] For a discussion of this issue regarding American free trade agreements, see F.J. Garcia, "Is Free Trade 'Free?' Is it Even 'Trade?' Oppression and Consent in Hemispheric Trade Agreements" 2007 *Seattle Journal for Social Justice* 5(2) 505.

partner in negotiations with the biggest trading powers, in large part as a result of the NAFTA process.

The emergence of many political groupings of developing countries in negotiations, some of which are also mapped onto regional trade frameworks, now allow smaller countries and countries with trade interests in a limited number of sectors to gain leverage in the multilateral negotiations. The ability for developing countries to self-define as a group (or sub-group in the case of LDCs) is not only of political importance, but it has important bearings on the rights and opportunities that they might have as members of that group at the WTO. Chapter 6 discusses in greater detail the implications of the "developing country" and LDC designations in the WTO legal framework.

The qualitative and quantitative participation of developing countries in WTO negotiations has risen dramatically. However, the lackluster results from the ongoing Doha Round have eroded this momentum. The shift in forum from the WTO-based multilateral negotiations to bilateral, regional, or plurilateral frameworks also carries with it the risk that developing countries' newfound coalition-based bargaining power will be weakened and divided in individual negotiations with more powerful trading partners. The control that many developing countries gained in contributing to the agenda-setting exercise at the WTO could be largely lost if they are individually presented with bilateral free trade agreements that resemble adhesion contracts more than genuine negotiations between partners.

III

UNDERSTANDING AND CONTEXTUALIZING WTO DEVELOPMENT PROVISIONS

From a theoretical perspective, the Uruguay Round agreements reflect a move away from the view that development is a structural and systemic issue. Indeed, the dominant economic wisdom since the 1990s is that developing countries only need temporary adjustment strategies to come into the fold of free trade. Ironically, this is reminiscent of the early theories of development that viewed economic development as a "catching-up" process.

The GATT 1947 initially provided limited allowances for derogation in response to the prevalent economic development policies of the 1960s and 1970s (infant industry protection, balance-of-payment flexibility). Then, the à-la-carte plurilateral agreements in the late 1970s inaugurated a different way of dealing with the diverse economies of GATT members, also in line with dominant theories of development economics of the time. However, both the infant industry and balance-of-payment support of the GATT, and the opt-in approach of the Tokyo Codes, proved to be of limited effectiveness—if not outright failures. A third generation of development-oriented trade rules emerged in the Uruguay Round agreements, the so-called special and differential treatment. Although this new wave of SDT provisions presents itself as exceptions and carve-outs, the salient difference with earlier iterations is that most of these WTO provisions are temporary.

While SDT constitutes the principal tool for development at the WTO, much uncertainty remains regarding its interpretation and implementation. The objective of this part of the book is to provide a dynamic interpretation of the WTO agreements as they relate to development. It reads the WTO agreements in the context of international regulatory techniques and interpretations. For example, a "best efforts" provision, which would likely not have been given much weight in the 1950s, is now read in many areas of international law to entail at least a procedural obligation and most likely an affirmative obligation to at least refrain from doing anything that runs counter to the objective of the provision. Such evolutions create a new interpretative context for a broader view of the WTO agreements, and particularly SDT provisions, many of which were added in the Uruguay Round.

Chapter 6 examines the legal nature of SDT provisions in the WTO agreements. What do SDT provisions allow developing members to do? What rights and obligations do they create and for whom? While no systematic survey of the legal implications of SDT provisions has been undertaken to date, the Doha Ministerial Declaration mandated that "all special and differential treatment provisions shall be reviewed with a view to strengthening them and making them more precise, effective and operational."[1] Using the strict language of the provisions as well as developments in international law generally, Chapter 6 argues that many SDT provisions could be given more legal force than has been the case so far, and hence could become operational tools for developing members. Chapter 6 then surveys the implementation record of SDT provisions to assess whether developing members have in fact used them since the inception of the GATT. It demonstrates that only a handful of SDT provisions have been invoked consistently, and even some of those have fallen into disuse since the inception of the WTO. Annex 1 compiles the provisions by agreement and decision, with a note stating whether they are still in effect.[2]

Chapter 7 examines the recourse to and interpretation of SDT provisions in dispute settlement. Developing countries have been complainants in close to 150 disputes, respondents in close to 140 cases, and have participated as third parties in over 530 instances. They have made arguments relating to development or to SDT in over 60 cases since 1947. As a result there is a significant body of legal analysis that informs the WTO's understanding of trade and development, often in reference to SDT provisions. Much of the literature has focused on specific subject matters, such as subsidies, but no comprehensive analysis of the achievements and limits of development arguments in dispute settlement at the WTO has been undertaken to date. This study identifies trends in panels and AB analysis on SDT that will help developing country litigants to deploy more effective litigation strategies and better craft their arguments. It also will allow adjudicators (panelists, AB members, and arbitrators) to identify some recurrent blind angles and perhaps embrace some evolutions in their understanding of the provisions.

Taking a step away from the WTO agreements and disputes, Chapter 8 considers other international agreements for alternative ways to address development. Focusing primarily on regional trade agreements, but also on a few other treaties with provisions or regimes for developing country parties, Chapter 8 offers comparative perspectives for special and differential treatment in international and trade law beyond the WTO. It also analyzes the practice of adjudicators in dealing with development-related arguments in international fora. It bolsters the position taken throughout this book that the WTO can—and should—learn from the law and practice of other international institutions and legal regimes grappling with differential human development of their memberships.

---

[1] Doha Declaration, at para 44.
[2] Annex 1 at <http://ukcatalogue.oup.com/product/9780199600885.do>.

While the substantive rights and obligations relating to trade disciplines are quantitatively the most visible aspect of development at the WTO, institutional and decision-making aspects of the organization constitute the framework through which trade disciplines are devised. The opportunities of developing countries within that organizational framework are therefore of critical importance. Chapter 9 focuses on the institutional aspects of developing country participation at the WTO. While most organizational and decision-making rules are facially neutral, they tend to have a disparate impact for developed and developing members. Very few features of the WTO legal system do anything to remedy the institutional imbalance between members, and that institutional bias is reflected in the regulatory outcomes: The two are inextricably linked. The causes of this institutional imbalance are manifold: economic, political, and legal. This chapter considers the legal aspects only to assess the impact on developing members of the WTO's institutional rules and processes, with particular emphasis on the decision-making process.

6

Special and Differential Treatment in the WTO Agreements: A Legal Analysis

The Doha Round, particularly in the early years, has generated a huge amount of work on "operationalizing" SDT, both existing provisions and proposals for new provisions. Members' discontent with the current content and reading of SDT provisions spurred this unprecedented level of activity. Ten years later, it is equally clear that most of the proposals are unlikely to be adopted as no final package is in sight. With the way forward apparently foreclosed, the logical alternative would be to seek amendments to existing provisions, but if history is any guide, the prospect of speedy and widespread amendments to the agreements is just as forlorn. Members are then faced with two options: Either accept that SDT is essentially *lettre morte* and that flexibilities will have to be sought elsewhere, or find ways to reinforce these provisions (at least the ones that have not expired) through means other than formal treaty amendments. This chapter substantiates the latter option. By using treaty interpretation techniques and trends of contemporary international practice, it argues that a number of provisions could be read more effectively.

A revised and enhanced reading of SDT provisions would constitute a useful gap-filler for developing members pending the conclusion of the Doha Round and even beyond that. It could reshape members' practices, inform their arguments in dispute settlement, and strengthen their positions in negotiations. Revised interpretations could even be formalized as General Council Decisions, or as Understandings by the membership, both of which are much more flexible and effective processes than treaty amendments.

Section 1 presents an overview of the types of SDT provisions available in the WTO agreements. Rather than going through each provision, Section 2 identifies patterns and trends in their drafting. It also points out where the prevalent interpretation of SDT provisions falls short of the legal meaning they could have if WTO members and adjudicators wanted to give them more effective force. For example, a recurrent issue is the interpretation of provisions that seem hortatory and lacking in the sort of detailed implementation requirements normally associated with a legal obligation. This section develops a number of interpretative tools to give meaning to such provisions, drawing from traditional methods of international law interpretation as well as from the recent evolutions in the regulation of human rights and environmental law.

This chapter then presents the implementation record of SDT provisions. Section 3 analyzes which countries have used the derogations and exceptions. It demonstrates that a very small number of SDT provisions have been used with any degree of frequency, mostly by developing countries, but in some cases by industrialized members as well. Moreover, some of these facilities, in particular the balance-of-payment provisions, have been virtually phased out in the early years of the WTO even though they remain technically available. The role of committees is particularly relevant here to show how the institution can restrict the recourse to SDT provisions that may otherwise be available to developing members.

1. A Substantive Overview of SDT in the WTO Agreements

SDT as it currently exists theoretically serves three broad objectives of the development dimension at the WTO: Promoting North–South trade, enhancing South–South trade, and preserving domestic policy instruments that members may want to use in furtherance of development policies ("policy space").

In practice, SDT clauses in the WTO agreements have largely constrained "policy space" and have supported the other two objectives (promoting North–South trade and South–South trade) unevenly. The emphasis has shifted from creating opportunities for development, as envisioned at the time of the New International Economic Order, to bridging the gap between the trade liberalization expectations of the Uruguay Round agreements and the actual capabilities of developing country members.[1] Ultimately, SDT is largely designed to phase out allowances for WTO-incompatible policies.

Part IV of the GATT, Article XII (restrictions to safeguard the balance of payments), and arguably the proposed amendment to the TRIPS regarding public health allow for "policy space." The ability to opt-out of making additional commitments also affords some sort of policy space for developing countries, though at a price. The Enabling Clause paragraph 2(a) (developed country preferential agreements) pertains to the promotion of North–South trade and the Enabling Clause paragraph 2(c) (developing country preferences) can be used in support of South–South trade. Regional trade agreements, allowed under GATT Article XXIV, may also support both North–South and South–South trade. It is noteworthy that all these instruments (with the exception of the TRIPS amendment) pre-date the Uruguay round, and they remain the cornerstone of development provisions at the WTO.

SDT has been much less effective at dealing with potential structural issues specific to developing countries. Non-reciprocity is an example. It came about in response to developing countries' insistence that they were unable to make the same level of concessions as their developed counterparts. After its mixed success in the Tokyo Round, the mercantilist spirit of GATT negotiations prevailed over

---

[1] U. Ewelukwa, "Special and Differential Treatment in International Trade Law: A Concept in Search of Content" 2003 *North Dakota Law Review* 79(4) 831, at 855.

the demand by developing members that they gain concessions without having to make any in return (or making concessions of lesser value). Put plainly, getting something for nothing is not really an option, which strips non-reciprocity of its value as a flexibility instrument. There also are economic reasons why using SDT to address structural hindrances may not be effective. For instance, supply-side constraints caused by domestic factors will not be resolved by even generous preferential agreements or non-reciprocal concessions.[2]

The Doha Work Programme mandated a systematic survey and analysis of the provisions in order to assess the meaning and legal value of each one. Such a comprehensive study was never undertaken. The closest document is the listing of the provisions and implementation data compiled by the Committee on Trade and Development (CTD).[3] The CTD established a typology of SDT provisions depending on the primary objective of the provisions:

- provisions aimed at increasing the trade opportunities of developing countries,
- provisions under which WTO Members should safeguard the interests of developing countries,
- flexibility of commitments, of action, and use of policy instruments,
- transitional time periods,
- technical assistance, and
- provisions relating to LDCs.

This classification is now a standard reference at the WTO and will be used here with some modifications: SDT provisions for LDCs will not be considered as a separate category but will be addressed alongside other provisions that have the same substantive objective. A critical overview of the CTD's findings is presented below as a backdrop to the legal analysis in the remainder of this chapter.

1.1 Increasing the trade opportunities of developing countries

The synthesis document elaborated by the CTD denotes fourteen provisions aimed at increasing the trade opportunities of developing countries[4] and six additional LDC-specific provisions to that effect. It finds that only three of these embody a legal obligation, namely GATS Articles IV:1 and IV:2, and Article 2.18 of the now defunct Agreement on Textiles and Clothing.

Overall, there are very few provisions meant to increase the trade opportunities of developing countries and LDCs that have any legal effect at all. Regarding

---

[2] See B. Hoekman, "Operationalizing the Concept of Policy Space in the WTO: Beyond Special and Differential Treatment" 2005 *Journal of International Economic Law* 8(2) 405, at 407–10.

[3] WTO Committee on Trade and Development, *Implementation of Special and Differential Treatment Provisions in WTO Agreements and Decisions*, WT/COMTD/W/77 (25 October 2000) (and subsequent correcting documents).

[4] GATT Arts XXXVI:2–5, XXXVII:1, XXXVII:4, XXXVIII(c), and XXXVIII(e); Enabling Clause; Preamble, Agreement on Agriculture; Art 2.18 ATC; GATS Arts IV:1 and IV:2.

the substance of these provisions, one notable common feature is that the obligation is on developed members to implement measures that would foster the trade of their developing counterparts.[5] Developing members and LDCs, as ultimate beneficiaries, are never in the position to trigger the measures or to make any claim regarding increased trading opportunities for themselves. However, at least with respect to the GATT provisions, a more substantive legal meaning may be read into the provisions than has traditionally been the case, and such an interpretation could inform the future of similarly worded SDT proposals tabled during the Doha Round. That said, the relative lack of practice by GATT parties over the years makes it politically unlikely to reverse the trend now. The opportunity cost for developing countries to push for a strengthened interpretation and implementation of these provisions may also be too high compared to what the provisions can deliver.

1.2 Safeguarding the interests of developing countries

With fifty-four provisions and ten more specifically for LDCs, this is by far the largest category of SDT clauses, and also the one with the highest number of binding provisions (twenty-one according to the CTD, many of which are in the TBT Agreement).

Provisions to safeguard the interests of developing members in the face of possibly adverse trade patterns include GATT Articles XXXVI:6–7 (expressing the need for international cooperation to further economic development of developing members), XXXVII:3(a) (on maintaining developing countries' trade margins), XXXVII:3(b) (on increasing imports from developing countries), and XXXVII:3(c) (on exploring "constructive remedies" with developing countries prior to imposing trade-restrictive measures allowed under the GATT).

1.3 Flexibility of commitments, of action, and use of policy instruments

While developed members strive to adhere to the liberal ethos at the core of the WTO, macroeconomists have long theorized that some measure of government support and investment is necessary to jump-start developing economies. Whether this theory has been proven true by history is a matter of debate that is not the subject of the present study. Indeed, the current revival of theories similar to infant industry protection have been vigorously contested in some quarters.[6] Suffice it to say that flexibility provisions in the WTO agreements are premised on the notion that government intervention and support measures normally prohibited by WTO disciplines should still be allowed for developing countries.

---

[5] In addition to the provisions mentioned above, see also Art 66.2 TRIPS.

[6] In favor of industry support, see, eg, H.-J. Chang, *Kicking Away the Ladder—Development Strategy in Historical Perspective* (London: Anthem Press, 2002); Lee, above Ch 3 fn 38, and see contra J.N. Bhagwati, *Development and Interdependence* (Cambridge: MIT Press, 1985), at 350.

In the area of trade in goods, Article XVIII of the GATT, allowing government support to emerging industries (XVIII:A) and restrictions to protect the balance of payments (XVIII:B), is the main "flexibility" instrument. They have been a prominent instrument (and for some time the only one) to adjust GATT and later WTO obligations to the challenges of economic development. The use of Article XVIII has now receded in favor of other legal instruments allowing protection of domestic industries, in particular in anti-dumping actions.

Two factors may have combined to spell the demise of Article XVIII. First, the provisions of the article itself may have been inadequate to provide the safeguards that developing members needed. The relatively poor track record of Article XVIII in dispute settlement supports that claim. Second, it may be that as a tool of economic policy, Article XVIII:B (balance of payments restrictions) has outlived its utility. With the diversification of economies towards trade in services, an imbalance in trade in goods may be better remedied with currency adjustments or increase of activities in services than by restricting imports of goods.

The Agreement on Agriculture[7] and the Subsidies and Countervailing Measures (SCM) Agreement[8] include the vast majority of the flexibility provisions available to developing countries. This is not surprising since many developing members' economies rely on exports of agricultural commodities and since both the Agreement on Agriculture and the SCM Agreement deal with the thorny issue of government support.

1.4 Transitional periods

Transitional periods were included in the agreements that were most problematic to developing and least developed countries at the close of the Uruguay Round,[9] giving these members more time for implementation. The TRIPS and TRIMS agreements also offered longer implementation periods for LDCs. Overall, the length of transitional time periods was set rather arbitrarily, with no serious attempt, during the Uruguay Round, to quantify the cost and time necessary for developing members to adjust to the new disciplines. Almost all of them have now expired.

Transitional periods did not mean that developing members were excluded from the disciplines of the agreements until the set period expired. Rather, beneficiaries could choose whether to undertake the full commitments before the end of the period and it was presumably up to them to decide which parts they wished to start implementing. In some cases, developing countries were even required to notify the Director General of their intent to delay implementation within the limits of

[7] Arts 6.2, 6.4, 9.2(b)(iv), 9.4, 12.2, 15.1; Annex 2, para 3, and fn 5; Annex 2, para 4, fn 5 and 6; Annex 5, Section B.

[8] Art 27.2(a) and Annex VII; Arts 27.4, 27.7, 27.8, 27.9, 27.10, 27.11, 27.12, 27.13.

[9] For developing countries generally: Agreement on Agriculture (Art 15.2), SPS Agreement (Arts 10.2 and 10.3), TBT Agreement (Arts 5.9 and 12.8), TRIMS Agreement (Art 5.2), Implementation of Article VII of GATT 1994 (Customs Valuation) (Arts 20.1, 20.2, Annex III.1 and Annex III.2), Import Licensing Procedures (Art 2.2, fn 5), SCM Agreement (Arts 27.2 (b), 27.4, 27.14, 27.5, 27.6, 27.11), TRIPS (Arts 65.2 and 65.4). For LDCs: TRIMS (Art 5.2), TRIPS (Art 66.1), Enabling Clause, at para 1.

the transitional period (Customs Valuation, Articles 20.1 and 20.2). However, in practice, the gradual implementation that was envisioned often gave way to an all-or-nothing approach as the deadlines loomed.

Some transitional periods or the extension of transitional periods were conditional. Such was the case for the SPS Agreement (Article 10.3), the TBT Agreement (Article 12.8), and the Customs Valuation Agreement (Annex III.1).

Finally, some transitional periods were "soft" recommendations rather than rights, inviting members to give more time to developing countries for implementation but leaving it to their discretion whether to do so. The SPS Agreement provides an illustration:

Where the appropriate level of sanitary or phytosanitary protection allows scope for the phased introduction of new sanitary or phytosanitary measures, longer time frames for compliance should be accorded on products of interest to developing country Members (Article 10.2).

The term "should" clearly indicates a different level of obligation than the binding language used in other transitional provisions. Since a number of provisions gave a clear term of years during which developing countries or LDCs were not expected to be in full compliance with their commitments, such a "soft" provision must be distinguished.

A noteworthy feature of transitional period provisions is that they often do not treat all developing countries equally. A number of provisions differentiate between developing countries depending on their GDP per capita (SCM Agreement), the time when they became party to a particular agreement (Customs Valuation, Import Licensing Procedures), or whether they are LDCs. Moreover, when the decision to extend or to grant a transitional period is up to the committee administering the agreement, the committee's mandate often is to take into consideration the specific, individual conditions of the requesting developing country. This is a clear indication that differentiation was actually built into a number of the Uruguay Round agreements long before the Appellate Body explicitly used the term in the dispute between India and the EC regarding the latter's preference program.[10]

At present, virtually all transition periods have expired and only a few have been prolonged on a case-by-case basis due to the protracted negotiations; they constituted nearly a quarter of all SDT provisions. Most expired as the Doha Round was starting, which is no coincidence. Indeed, as developing countries realized the full burden of their commitments and their difficulties or incapacity to implement them, the need for a reconsideration of the agreements was an important force in the early years of the Doha Round. Many developing countries are still experiencing difficulties with implementation of the agreements, and it is generally recognized that the transitional periods were insufficient to allow them to come into full compliance within the allotted time given the technical hurdles and limited financial and human capacity available. This is particularly true as the

---

[10] Appellate Body Report, *EC—Tariff Preferences.* See a full discussion of the case in Ch 7.

technical assistance that was expected to boost the transitions was lagging or not forthcoming.

1.5 Technical assistance

Technical assistance comes in three main varieties: assistance to be given (1) under the auspices of the WTO; (2) under the auspices of other international organizations; and (3) by developed country members in the course of their dealings with developing members. Most clauses involve the third scenario and leave it to developed members to decide how, when, and to which members they will provide technical assistance.

Some provisions, essentially devoid of any legal obligation, only call on members to "facilitate the provision of technical assistance" (SPS Agreement, Article 9) or to give consideration to requests for assistance by developing members. By contrast, the TBT Agreement, the Customs Valuation Agreement, and the TRIPS create specific and detailed obligations and clearly delineate the subjects and goals of the assistance to be provided by developed members. The Customs Valuation Agreement further reinforces its technical assistance clause by requiring that developed countries draft technical assistance programs. This drafting not only makes it more likely that some result will be achieved and increases transparency, but it also generates knowledge and knowhow that can be more readily shared and improved. Such a clause demonstrates that it is possible to draft a technical assistance provision in a way that creates clear and implementable legal obligations and standards.

The only agreement that puts the onus on the WTO itself to provide assistance is Article 27.2 Dispute Settlement Understanding (DSU) Agreement:

> While the Secretariat assists Members in respect of dispute settlement at their request, there may also be a need to provide additional legal advice and assistance in respect of dispute settlement to developing country Members. To this end, the Secretariat shall make available a qualified legal expert from the WTO technical cooperation services to any developing country Member which so requests. This expert shall assist the developing country Member in a manner ensuring the continued impartiality of the Secretariat.

While the WTO Secretariat is still struggling to fulfill its obligations, the Advisory Centre for WTO Law, a non-profit organization voluntarily funded by WTO members and independent from the WTO, provides both legal expertise for adjudication of cases at the Dispute Settlement Body (DSB) and training for legal personnel from developing countries. The Advisory Centre for WTO Law does not operate pursuant to DSU Article 27.2 or any other WTO provision, but it has emerged to help fill a substantive gap. It was officially launched in 1999 and became operational in 2001. Its services were immediately in high demand and it has expanded ever since, struggling to meet the demand.

As with the transitional time periods, little more is provided for LDCs with respect to technical assistance, despite the fact that the need is both greater and more urgent for these members. The Decision on Measures in Favour of Least-Developed Countries (para 2(v)) provides that:

least-developed countries shall be accorded substantially increased technical assistance in the development, strengthening and diversification of their production and export bases including those of services, as well as in trade promotion, to enable them to maximize the benefits from liberalized access to markets.

The vagueness of the requirement and lack of guidance regarding implementation substantially weaken this clause. Moreover, it is not clear what the legal link might be between the Decision on Measures in Favour of LDCs and other WTO agreements. In order to have any effect, paragraph 2(v) of the Decision would need to complement agreements such as the GATT and the General Agreement on Trade in Services (GATS). This may be done either by considering the Decision as an interpretative tool of relevant GATT and GATS provisions, or by considering the Decision to amend the GATT and GATS. However, the GATT and GATS have specific processes regarding amendments and interpretative decisions, which are different from the Decision. It is therefore questionable whether the latter could really be considered as a binding interpretation or an amendment of the agreements. The legal value of paragraph 2(v) of the Decision, inasmuch as it seeks to modify or enhance the obligations of other WTO agreements, is therefore probably nil.

The objective of technical assistance is to bring developing members to the level of regulatory sophistication that prevails in developed countries. The issue is how to best deliver technical assistance. The WTO has done remarkable efforts in this area, and every announcement that a country is contributing to the general fund for these programs is a welcome one. The diversification of sources for technical assistance, such as the Advisory Centre for WTO Law regarding litigation, is an equally laudable measure. However, much work, qualitatively and quantitatively, remains to be done.

Overall, then, SDT promised much and delivered unevenly, in part because the legal instruments chosen were not necessarily adapted to the policy objective. If SDT is asked to deliver on all aspects of the development dimension it is unlikely to fulfill its objectives. Because it takes the place of a more profound reconsideration of what a multilateral trade liberalization system viable for developing countries could be, it can only deliver marginal benefits. In this sense, current SDT is closer to the *ad hoc* paradigm discussed at the outset of this book than to the normative co-constituent paradigm. Yet, marginal adjustments are not what developing countries are demanding in the current negotiations or in previous rounds since the 1950s. The continued focus on legal instruments that are only meant to deliver at the margins, then, is largely misguided.[11]

While SDT cannot be an all-encompassing solution for addressing developing members' problems at the WTO, it may nonetheless deliver some benefits.

---

[11] See, eg, F.J. Garcia, "Beyond Special and Differential Treatment" 2004 *Boston College International and Comparative Law Review* 27(2) 291.

Developing countries are a varied group, in terms of the socioeconomic make-up as well as the political economy policies. It is therefore likely that, no matter how well tailored the rules are to the main concerns of developing countries, additional exceptions and allowances will be necessary and SDT could be a viable conduit for such exceptions. The objective of the following section is to propose a legal inter-pretation of SDT provisions to point to those that could be effective for a particular purpose, and to assess the limits of current drafting techniques. While the analysis acknowledges the traditional interpretation of these provisions, it offers a dynamic reinterpretation in light of public international law developments.

2. Trends in Legal Drafting of SDT Provisions: Towards a Reinterpretation

Some 145 provisions provide SDT for developing countries in the WTO legal corpus, yet their legal value and content is far from certain. While there would certainly be value in undertaking a systematic article-by-article review of SDT pro-visions in the Uruguay Round agreements, the objective of this section is somewhat different. Most SDT provisions fall into four types of drafting patterns discussed below: escape clauses, best efforts provisions, provisions defining an objective but devoid of specific implementation prescriptions, and accountability provisions. Each could fulfill an important role, but are often hindered by their drafting.

Focusing on recurrent drafting patterns in the provisions, the analysis presents a progressive reading of the provisions that would enhance the legal toolbox of treaty negotiators and those involved in litigating the agreements. This is particularly important in light of the dozens of proposals submitted by WTO members in the Doha Round for more special and differential treatment or for a redrafting or reinterpretation of existing provisions.

2.1 Escape clauses and derogations

A number of escape clauses, exceptions, or derogations are available to developing countries in recognition of the economic, social, and administrative challenges they face. Mostly corresponding to provisions creating "flexibilities" for develop-ing members, escape clauses are found in GATT Articles XII (balance of pay-ment) and XVIII (infant industry and balance of payment), in the Agriculture Agreement (different threshold of support allowed), and in the SCM Agreement (different threshold for government support, different allocation of the burden of proof on some issues, exemption from the prohibition on export subsidies, etc). Additional derogations are provided by the Enabling Clause, effectively creating exceptions to the MFN clause of the GATT for preferential trade agreements and South–South trade agreements, and a number of other *ad hoc* waivers. The many transitional time periods for developing and least-developed members can also be construed as escape clauses and derogations, if only temporary ones.

From a legal standpoint, these provisions are perhaps the most straightforward. For instance, clearly defined terms of years for implementing the agreements leave little room for interpretation (with the exception of accession issues discussed in Chapter 4). They use traditional treaty-drafting techniques, combining the language of legal obligations (words such as "shall") with a specific content and a predictable scope of implementation, also characteristic of a legal obligation. Unfortunately, such provisions can also be the hardest to negotiate precisely because they are the most unambiguous and they represent fairly tangible concessions. It is perhaps for that reason that most of the escape clauses built into the Uruguay Round agreements were valid only for a specific term of years.

Another category of escape clauses raises slightly more complex issues because they are permissive, but the members which would be allowed to take action are not the developing members which would be the beneficiaries. Such is the case for the preference schemes allowed by the Enabling Clause (Article 2(a) and 2(d) with respect to LDCs): The burden is on developed countries to implement the measures, but they have no obligation to do so. Similarly, the 1999 Decision on Waiver for preferential tariff treatment of LDCs allows developed and developing countries to make non-MFN concessions to LDCs but does not require them to do so.[12] A number of technical assistance provisions also reflect this asymmetry between beneficiaries and grantors, with grantors permitted but not obligated to give technical assistance, and no opportunity for the beneficiary member to require it. The question then becomes how much of a duty do members have to give effect to these permissive provisions for the benefit of other members.

In current and future negotiations, developing members may be wary of drafting provisions in which the beneficiary has no control over the implementation. At the same time, preferential regimes, for example, involve special market access concessions on the part of the granting country, and it would be equally awkward and impractical for the granting member to relinquish control over whether, when, and how it grants preferential access to its market. If a derogation or escape clause has economic consequences for the economies of both the member benefiting from the clause and the member which would have to implement the derogation, it would be preferable to use a bilateral trigger for implementation where both members have a role to play.

---

[12] *Preferential Tariff Treatment for Least-Developed Countries, Decision on Waiver,* WT/L/304 (17 June 1999) ("Subject to the terms and conditions set out hereunder, the provisions of paragraph 1 of Article I of the GATT 1994 shall be waived until 30 June 2009, to the extent necessary to allow developing country Members to provide preferential tariff treatment to products of least developed countries, designated as such by the United Nations, without being required to extend the same tariff rates to like products of any other Member."). To date, only one notification has been submitted by Korea, which unilaterally decided to grant preferential access to a number of products from LDCs. WT/COMTD/N/12/Rev.1 (28 April 2000).

2.2 Best efforts provisions

Many SDT provisions (and in the Doha Round, a number of SDT proposals) mix the language of legal obligation with a "best efforts" substance. For instance, GATT Article XXXVII:3 is prefaced by "[t]he developed contracting parties shall," which cannot be mistaken for anything other than an unconditional legal obligation. Yet the substance of the purported obligation is more problematic: "make every effort," "give active consideration," and "have special regard" are the operative words of each subparagraph. A number of other SDT provisions use similar drafting patterns.[13] The issue is whether such language essentially eviscerates the purported obligation despite the use of the word "shall."

Historically, clauses indicating hortatory language, or clauses intimating countries to exercise best efforts or to endeavor to accomplish a stated goal have not been understood to embody any legal obligation.[14] More generally, commentators have cautioned that not all treaty provisions contain legally binding obligations and that political and policy statements of aspiration should be distinguished from legal obligations.[15]

However, the interpretation of "best efforts" has evolved and is increasingly considered to express a legally binding obligation, particularly in the human rights and environmental law fields. Because of the long-standing connection between development and human rights, and because most SDT clauses were drafted in the 1990s when "best efforts" provisions became commonplace in other areas, we argue that they now express a legal commitment and that the historical view no

---

[13] Art XXXVI:9 GATT (mandating some "conscious and purposeful efforts" towards the adoption of measures to enhance the trade of developing countries); Art XV:1 GATS ("take into account the needs of Members, particularly developing country Members, for flexibility in [the area of subsidies]"); Arts 10.1 and 10.4 SPS Agreement ("encourage and facilitate the active participation of developing country Members"); Art 12.2 TBT Agreement ("shall give particular attention to the provisions of this Agreement concerning developing country Members' rights and obligations and shall take into account the special development, financial, and trade needs of developing country Members"); Arts 10.3, 12.5 TBT Agreement ("Members shall take such reasonable measures as may be available to them"); Art 12.9 TBT Agreement (developed country Members shall "bear in mind the special difficulties experienced by developing country members"); Art 15 Antidumping Agreement; Art 4.10 DSU ("Members should give special attention to the particular problems and interests of developing country Members"); Arts 21.2 and 21.7 DSU ("in considering what appropriate action might be taken, the DSB shall take into account, not only the trade coverage of measures complained of, but also their impact on the economy of developing country Members concerned").

[14] J.E.S. Fawcett, "The Legal Character of International Agreements" 1953 *British Yearbook of International Law* 30(1) 381, at 390.

[15] See eg, E. Lauterpacht (ed), *International Law: Being The Collected Papers of Hersch Lauterpacht, Vol. 4: The Law of Peace* (Cambridge: Cambridge University Press, 2004), at 110–13. A vision of international law as essentially contractual, equating treaty interpretation with the expounding of common law commercial obligations, has also been used to bolster the position that the use of hortatory language deprives a clause of any legal meaning. However, it is now well established that the law of treaty interpretation diverges from contractual and statutory interpretation for a number of reasons having to do with the practice of international law making and that Arts 31–33 of the Vienna Convention on the Law of Treaties are a uniformly recognized embodiment of relevant customary law regarding treaty interpretation.

longer holds as firmly in the trade law context. That said, there are different ways to operationalize a best efforts provision.

A substantive obligation

In some cases, a textual interpretation of the WTO agreements supports the view that a "best efforts" clause is in fact meant to have some legal effect. The chapeau of GATT Article XXXVII:1 provides an illustration. It states "[t]he developed contracting parties shall to the fullest extent possible—that is, except when compelling reasons, which may include legal reasons, make it impossible—give effect to the following provisions." Historically, the whole of the provision might have been dismissed due to the phrase "to the fullest extent possible." However, the provision actually limits situations in which non-compliance would be excused to the cases where "compelling reasons" make it impossible to comply. While not defining specifically what reasons might count as "compelling," the clause indicates that they might be "legal reasons," a defense also available in some instances in the law of state responsibility. Moreover, GATT Article XXXVII:2 sets forth a mechanism for remedying non-compliance through reporting and consultations not only between the interested parties but possibly also under the aegis of the contracting parties acting jointly under Article XXV. Arguably, then, the drafters fully intended that the provisions of paragraphs 1(a)–(c) have legal effect and be subject to the procedures and remedies available in the agreement (see also paragraph 5 of the Article, referring to consultation procedures for dispute settlement).

The GATT and WTO panels and AB have typically avoided references to other fields of international law. Nonetheless, analyzing WTO provisions in the context of evolving international regulation holds valuable lessons.[16] While no direct import into the WTO system is legally possible or politically likely in the near future, such analogies provide valuable conceptual and theoretical insights. Moreover, with the growing spectrum of conflicts between the WTO and other agreements or regimes,[17] it is possible that the WTO will have to be increasingly cognizant of external evolution.

Flexible and conditional treaty obligations have been examined by domestic courts in the context of international environmental law. The Tasmanian Dam case and its progeny, in Australia, are perhaps the foremost example. It involved a

[16] For an examination (and advocacy) of the possible "cross-fertilization" between WTO law and other norms of public international law, see J. Pauwelyn, "The Role of Public International Law in the WTO: How Far Can we Go" 2001 *American Journal of International Law* 95(3) 535. This view remains controversial among WTO members.

[17] The quickly expanding body of literature on the possibility of such conflicts cannot be reviewed exhaustively here. See eg, G. Marceau, "Conflicts of Norms and Conflicts of Jurisdiction—The Relationship Between the WTO Agreement and MEAs and Other Treaties" 2001 *Journal of World Trade* 35(6) 1081; J. Pauwelyn, *Conflicts of Norms in Public International Law—How WTO Law Relates to Other Rules of International Law* (New York: Cambridge University Press, 2003), at 522; I. Van Damme, "Jurisdiction, Applicable Law, and Interpretation," in D. Bethlehem, D. McRae, R. Neufeld, I. Van Damme (eds), *The Oxford Handbook of International Trade Law* (Oxford: Oxford University Press, 2003), at 299–343. See also Panel Report and Appellate Body Report, *Mexico—Taxes on Soft Drinks*, and the recent truckers controversy pitting the United States against Mexico in a NAFTA/WTO conflict.

dispute between the government of Australia and the State of Tasmania regarding Australia's power to enact certain laws and prevent the building of certain projects by protecting the underlying natural space, ostensibly in application of the World Heritage Convention.[18] The issue was whether any obligation arose out of the relevant provisions of the Convention. Much like some SDT clauses in the WTO agreements, most of the Convention's provisions are couched in conditional terms rather than in the bright-line and strict language of contractual obligations or legislative commands.

The relevant articles of the World Heritage Convention read in part:

Article 4:

Each State Party to this Convention recognizes that the duty of ensuring the identification, protection, conservation, presentation and transmission to future generations of the cultural and natural heritage referred to in Articles 1 and 2 and situated on its territory, belongs primarily to that State. *It will do all it can to this end, to the utmost of its own resources* and, where appropriate, with any international assistance and co-operation, in particular, financial, artistic, scientific and technical, which it may be able to obtain.

Article 5:

To ensure that effective and active measures are taken for the protection, conservation and presentation of the cultural and natural heritage situated on its territory, *each State Party to this Convention shall endeavor, in so far as possible, and as appropriate for each country*: [list of actions]. (emphasis added)

The majority of the judges found that these terms created some legal obligations for Australia that supported the exercise of the government's external affairs powers in enacting the disputed legislation and regulations.

Mason, J. focused on the wording of the Convention to conclude that despite the absence of "undertake" as the command verb used in other provisions, Articles 4 and 5 are not simply statements of intention but rather, legal obligations. He found that the qualifications "in so far as possible" and "as appropriate for each country," far from eviscerating the provisions, helped delineate the exact duty of each state. Quite strikingly, he concluded that "there is a distinction between a discretion as to the manner of performance and a discretion as to performance or non-performance. The latter, and not the former, is inconsistent with a binding obligation to perform."[19] The discretion afforded to the states confirmed, in his view, that states did, in fact, have an obligation under Article 5, otherwise the qualifier would be superfluous. Mason, J. found further support for his interpretation in the procedural aspects of treaty-making, noting that states chose to enact a treaty rather than a resolution or a recommendation with respect to the content of Articles 4 and 5.[20] Finally, Mason, J. noted that the objectives of the Convention could only be achieved by means of legal commitments, so that interpreting the Convention as not creating legal commitments would be incompatible with its declared object and purpose.[21]

---

[18] *Commonwealth of Australia v State of Tasmania ("Tasmanian Dam Case")* (1983) 158 CLR 1.
[19] Ibid at para 132.   [20] Ibid at para 134.   [21] Ibid at para 135.

Following a different approach, Murphy, J. took stock of the scholarly debate regarding the nature and form of international legal obligations and applied the Vienna Convention on the Law of Treaties. Looking at the terms in the context of their object and purpose, he concluded that Articles 4 and 5 imposed a legal obligation on states.[22] Brennan, J. followed the same methodology. Those opinions are most germane to the WTO context since panels and the AB are bound to interpret the treaty language in light of customary rules of international law on treaty interpretation.[23]

Deane, J. also gave particular weight to the process of treaty-making (as opposed to the passing of a resolution by the United Nations Educational, Scientific and Cultural Organization) as proof of the states' intent to be bound by some legal obligations:

[U]nless one is to take the view that over seventy nations have engaged in the solemn and cynical farce of using words such as "obligation" and "duty" where neither was intended or undertaken, the provisions of the Convention impose real and identifiable obligations and provide for the availability of real benefits at least in respect of those properties which have, in accordance with the procedure established by the Convention, been indisputably made the subject of those obligations and identified as qualified for those benefits by being entered...on the World Heritage List.[24]

In two subsequent cases, the Australian courts reaffirmed the ruling of the landmark *Tasmanian Dam* case.[25]

In the environmental law area, "best efforts" and "endeavor" clauses are now commonly understood to translate into an obligation of due diligence by the states, a concept more readily acceptable because it is familiar to common lawyers and falls broadly within the category of obligations of conduct ("*obligation de moyens*" in French) in civil law systems. Enforcement of due diligence obligations is also well recognized, particularly regarding trans-boundary pollution. SDT clauses requiring developed members or WTO institutions to "take into consideration" the needs of developing members in a particular area, or to consider alternate remedies, could similarly be construed as obligations of due diligence on their part. This is particularly true where there is an accompanying reporting obligation, as is the case for the panels under DSU Article 12.11.[26]

---

[22] Ibid at para 177–8.
[23] Art 3.2 DSU specifies that the dispute settlement system serves, inter alia, "to clarify the existing provisions of [WTO] agreements in accordance with customary rules of interpretation of public international law." It is generally accepted and recognized that most of the Vienna Convention is a codification of the customary law on treaties and that is certainly the case with the Vienna Convention provisions to which references are made in the present analysis.
[24] Ibid at para 263.
[25] *Richardson v Forestry Commission* (1988) 77 ALR 237, 289; *Queensland v Australia* (1989) 167 CLR 232 (The *Tasmanian Dam* dissenters joined the majority position).
[26] Reading in part: "the panel's report shall explicitly indicate the form in which account has been taken of relevant provisions on differential and more-favourable treatment for developing country Members." See also the possibility of review under Art 27.15 of the SCM Agreement.

A progressive obligation

The practice in the field of human rights is also helpful to substantiate the argument that SDT clauses enjoining members to "take into account" certain circumstances, to "endeavor" to enhance the trade of developing countries, and other similar formulations do not necessarily render the provisions devoid of any legal substance. Indeed, many human rights treaties are drafted with "best efforts," "reasonable efforts," "endeavor," and similar language. In some cases, the provisions trigger a progressive obligation to achieve the required objective over time. The obligation is therefore inherently dynamic. The Covenant on Economic, Social and Cultural Rights provides an example at Article 2.1, one of the core provisions of the treaty:

Each State Party to the present Covenant undertakes *to take steps*, individually and through international assistance and co-operation, especially economic and technical, *to the maximum of its available resources, with a view to achieving progressively* the full realization of the rights recognized in the present Covenant by *all appropriate means*, including particularly the adoption of legislative measures. (emphasis added)

The italicized language has been the subject of intense debate, with the traditional view being that the paragraph was devoid of any legal obligation because of its cautious and almost exploratory wording. The opposite view is that the clause is a "progressive legal obligation," and that the lack of a "bright-line" rule in the article did not mean that it lacks legal meaning altogether. The Committee administering the treaty has made that clear in its General Comment 3.[27] Regarding the phrase "to take steps," the Committee notes:

The full meaning of the phrase can also be gauged by noting some of the different language versions. In English the undertaking is "to take steps," in French it is "to act" ("s'engage à agir") and in Spanish it is "to adopt measures" ("a adoptar medidas"). Thus while the full realization of the relevant rights may be achieved progressively, steps towards that goal must be taken within a reasonably short time after the Covenant's entry into force for the States concerned. Such steps should be deliberate, concrete and targeted as clearly as possible towards meeting the obligations recognized in the Covenant. (Paragraph 1)

Regarding the phrase "with a view to achieving progressively the full realization of the rights recognized," it specifies:

The concept of progressive realization constitutes a recognition of the fact that full realization of all economic, social and cultural rights will generally not be able to be achieved in a short period of time. In this sense the obligation differs significantly from that contained in article 2 of the International Covenant on Civil and Political Rights which embodies an immediate obligation to respect and ensure all of the relevant rights. Nevertheless, the fact that realization over time, or in other words progressively, is foreseen under the Covenant should not be misinterpreted as depriving the obligation of all meaningful content. It is on the one hand a necessary flexibility device, reflecting the realities of the real world and the difficulties involved for any country in ensuring full realization of economic, social and cultural rights. On the other hand, the phrase must be read in the light

---

[27] Committee on Economic, Social and Cultural Rights, General Comment 3, *The Nature of States Parties' Obligations*, UN Doc E/1991/23 (5th Sess 1991).

of the overall objective, indeed the raison d'être, of the Covenant which is to establish clear obligations for States parties in respect of the full realization of the rights in question. It thus imposes an obligation to move as expeditiously and effectively as possible towards that goal. (Paragraph 9).

The Committee also characterizes Article 2.1 as an obligation of result, albeit one that is implementable over a relatively long time frame.

Alston and Quinn, in their landmark 1987 article, give a persuasive analysis of Article 2.1 and other provisions of the Covenant as carrying legal duties.[28] They identify the obligation as one of conduct, which is a more flexible interpretation than the one adopted by the Committee in its General Comment 3. The authors acknowledge that the commitment, while it is "clearly to be distinguished from, and is less demanding than a guarantee, nonetheless represents a clear legal undertaking. The key point is that the undertaking to take steps is of *immediate* application."[29] The fact that the full implementation of the designated rights may only be achieved progressively over time does not diminish the states' clear and immediate duty to take steps towards that goal.

Next, the words "achieve progressively" in Article 2.1 of the Covenant have also been used to deny the existence of a legal obligation. Alston and Quinn explore whether they make the obligation so contingent that it is devoid of normative value.[30] Drafting history shows that the proponents of the concept saw it as a practical necessity, rather than an escape clause as feared by the opponents of the terms. The authors note that, somewhat ironically, the countries of the delegates that insisted the most on the meaningfulness of the phrase at the time of drafting eventually became those arguing that Article 2.1 was meaningless.

Arguably, SDT provisions such as those meant to promote or safeguard the trade interests of developing countries necessitate a mix of short-term and longer-term measures and can only be implemented progressively. It is therefore not surprising that guarded and conditional language is used in these SDT provisions, as in the Covenant, which is also concerned with economic rights. The analysis put forward of the Covenant should apply, *mutatis mutandis*, to similarly drafted WTO provisions.

An obligation contingent on the obligor's capacity

Last, best efforts provisions can also be seen as variable depending on the implementing state's capability. While all state parties are obligated to work towards the same objective, the scope, nature, and extent of individual duties depend on each state's capacity. Article 2.1 of the Covenant provides a further illustration. According to Alston and Quinn, language such as "to the maximum of its available resources" denotes a large measure of discretion for the state but nevertheless helps to "determin[e] the thresholds it must meet in discharging its obligations."

---

[28] P. Alston and G. Quinn, "The Nature and Scope of States Parties' Obligations Under the International Covenant on Economic, Social and Cultural Rights" 1987 *Human Rights Quarterly* 9(2) 156.   [29] Ibid at 166.
[30] Ibid at 172.

This language does not mean that the states are free to do as little or as much as they please while being accountable only to themselves. Rather, it emphasizes "the non-absolute nature of states' discretion in the allocation of sufficient resources to meet their obligations under the Covenant."[31] In international environmental law, the notion of "common but differentiated responsibility"[32] may also translate into obligations that vary depending on states' capacity.

Here again, the reasoning can be transcribed to the WTO context, with the committee administering each agreement at times playing a role in determining what can reasonably be expected of a member. In many cases, states' obligation to extend SDT is contingent on the state's "ability" to do so. The phrase could be viewed as a standard in the same way that "reasonableness" is a legal standard in common law systems.[33] In the context of economic rights, what may be reasonable for one state might constitute an insurmountable hurdle for another. A reference to available resources would, however, be preferable. In the words of Alston and Quinn:

a plea of resource scarcity *simpliciter*, if substantiated, is entitled to deference especially where a state shows adherence to a regular and principled decision-making process...and remains open to some sort of objective scrutiny by the body entrusted with responsibility for supervising states' compliance with their obligations.[34]

In fact, the WTO agreements themselves and the dispute settlement system have adopted flexible standards that set different thresholds depending on the circumstances. For example, when the least-restrictive alternative measure is required, compliance is assessed in reference to what the country enacting the measure could have done, rather than by reference to what any WTO member could have done. There is no clear bright-line rule as to what constitutes a more or less trade-restrictive measure, but the requirement is no less enforceable, as shown in the case of the ban on genetically modified organisms by the EC[35] and in numerous other cases. State discretion in choosing from a range of available measures is restricted by the obligation to adopt the least-restrictive one that can achieve the objective.

Developments in the human rights and environmental law fields have led to a reconsideration of the legal nature of treaty clauses that use language of conditional obligation. As states recognize that complex obligations cannot be immediately implemented, the language of progressive obligations has become commonplace. With the diversification of WTO regulation, its expansion to the field of administrative regulation, and its focus on non-quantifiable commitments, implementation requirements inevitably must vary from country to country. Not all members need to undertake the same actions in order to achieve the objective, nor can they all achieve it within the same time frame. The many transitional periods for

---

[31] Ibid at 179.

[32] Rio Declaration on Environment and Development, Principle 7; Kyoto Protocol to the United Nations Framework Convention on Climate Change.

[33] For a review of the literature on standards in international law, see S. Boutillon, "The Precautionary Principle: Development of an International Standard" 2002 *Michigan Journal of International Law* 23(2) 429, at 447.   [34] Alston and Quinn, above fn 28, at 181.

[35] Panel Report, *EC—Approval and Marketing of Biotech Products.*

developing countries and even longer implementation periods for LDCs also testify to the progressivity of WTO commitments. The interpretation of SDT provisions formulated in terms of best efforts and other conditional language therefore can and should follow the trend set in other areas of international law. These clauses can be read as meaningful and substantive legal obligations. In many cases, such an evolution need only be framed under customary rules of treaty interpretation, an uncontroversial proposition.[36] As such, the present analysis does not propose to import extraneous rules into the WTO legal regime, but rather it suggests that trends emerging in other areas of public international law could be mirrored at the WTO.

Additionally, WTO members that have an interest in fostering such an evolution can also learn from contemporary practice in human rights and environmental law when drafting, tabling, and negotiating proposals at the WTO.

2.3 Provisions defining an objective but lacking specific prescriptions

A number of WTO provisions identify the need to increase the trade opportunities of developing countries without requiring any implementation action. Traditionally, such provisions have been read as purely hortatory and essentially devoid of any legal obligation. However, alternative interpretations could give legal substance to these provisions. In the context of the treaty the provisions may be read as giving members a mandate for future specific action. Much like a framework convention, the provisions serve to open a field of regulatory activities by the members even if they do not initially specify particular implementation obligations. Similarly, reading the provisions jointly with more specific treaty clauses could create a guide for the interpretation of the latter. In other words, the more specific obligations may be interpreted in light of the purpose defined by the more general provision.

GATT Article XXXVI:2–5[37] and Article XXXVI:6–7 expressing the need for international cooperation to further economic development of developing members illustrates such interpretative methods. These clauses identify certain trade concerns of developing countries and the need for action in these domains; they read like treaty preamble clauses.[38] As such, they do not appear to trigger any legal obligation. Article XXXVI can be interpreted as giving a mandate to the GATT

---

[36] Panel Report, *Korea—Procurement*, at para 7.96 ("[C]ustomary international law applies generally to the economic relations between WTO Members. Such international law applies to the extent that the WTO treaty agreements do not 'contract out' from it.").

[37] Stating in part "There is need for a rapid and sustained expansion of the export earnings of the less-developed contracting parties...There is need for positive efforts designed to ensure that less-developed contracting parties secure a share in the growth in international trade commensurate with the needs of their economic development...There is need to provide in the largest possible measure more favourable and acceptable conditions of access to world markets for these products...There is, therefore, need for increased access in the largest possible measure to markets under favourable conditions for processed and manufactured products currently or potentially of particular export interest to less-developed contracting parties."

[38] See, eg, GATT Art XXXVI:1; Preamble, Agreement on Agriculture.

parties, individually and collectively, to act towards the objectives of increasing trade from developing countries. Considering that the GATT had no development mandate before the addition of Part IV and that the 1964 amendment was specifically aimed at making the GATT more cognizant of the needs of developing countries, such a reading is fully in keeping with the object, context, and purpose of Part IV. Unlike the traditional reading that views Article XXXVI as devoid of legal meaning, this reading would give substance to the provisions of the article, a result also preferred by the law of treaties. Indeed, it would likely be "unreasonable" or "manifestly absurd"[39] to suppose that the parties intended no legal obligation to flow from the addition of an entire part to a treaty. In light of the increased use of framework conventions (in international environmental law, for example) it is also an interpretation that is in line with contemporary legal practice, and a technique with which states are very familiar.

Such an interpretation is potentially far-reaching. If the parties to the GATT could rely on such a mandate to take unilateral, bilateral, or multilateral measures, the issue would then become whether these measures could derogate from other GATT disciplines. Article XXXVI indicates no hierarchy between measures taken pursuant to Article XXXVI:9 and those taken under other GATT provisions.

Article XXXVI:9, referring to the general objectives of Article XXXVI, states: "The adoption of measures to give effect to these principles and objectives shall be a matter of conscious and purposeful effort on the part of the contracting parties both individually and jointly." While Paragraph 9 is more specific than Paragraphs 2–5 and 6–7, it still does not explicitly state what members must do to implement the general obligation. Borrowing from EU law techniques, Article XXXVI:9 can be read as mandating "secondary legislation." In other words, Article XXXVI:9 creates an obligation to take regulatory measures downstream, rather than to set a substantive obligation directly in the treaty. Article XXXVII:1(a) and (c)(ii) directing developed countries to reduce or eliminate restrictions on the import of products of interest to developing countries, as a matter of priority, can also be read as more specific mandates for future action, also undertaken in pursuance of the overarching objectives of Article XXXVI.

Given how little relevance Part IV of the GATT has had to date, any claim to give more legal force to its provisions may seem spurious. Yet, it is precisely because it is the hardest case to make that it should be seen as a powerful one. Even if states' practice regarding Part IV is unlikely to evolve for political reasons, the analysis presented here can serve to recast other similarly drafted provisions, and to inform the drafting of future proposals. Indeed, in the Doha Round, a number of SDT proposals set a general objective without specifying what members are obligated to do, or are allowed to do, in furtherance of this objective. Such proposals raise the same interpretative and operationalizing issues as Part IV of the GATT. Moreover,

---

[39] See Vienna Convention on the Law of Treaties (Vienna, 23 May 1969; 1155 UNTS 331). Panels and the AB have referred to the Vienna Convention in over 200 reports (Panels and AB combined since the inception of the GATT).

with many SDT provisions having expired, Part IV remains one of the few available flexibility mechanisms. As such, it may be premature to shelve it entirely. In fact, China, in recent disputes, has raised development arguments under Part IV, perhaps signaling a renewed interest in the provisions.

That said, not every provision that sets a general objective can be read as a mandate for future action. For example, the provisions of the GATS concerning increase of trade opportunities for developing countries do not lend themselves to such an interpretation. GATS Article IV:1 essentially declares that trade liberalization in the service sector will benefit developing countries and that technology should be made available to them by developed countries on a commercial basis (meaning at normal market prices). This provision does not have any legal substance as it neither creates any duty or obligation for any party, nor seeks to modify the behavior of any party. The only obligation stemming from Article IV is the requirement that developed countries, and others if possible, establish a "point of contact" where developing members can seek information regarding technical and logistical aspects of trade in services. Although the GATS is generally considered to be more development-friendly than other WTO agreements, it is difficult to see how it provides any special treatment to developing countries regarding an increase of their access to trade in services.

2.4 Accountability provisions: The role of reporting and notification obligations in operationalizing SDT

Several SDT provisions include a reporting requirement. The primary right, obligation, or prohibition might be vague, or there may even be some doubt whether they create a legal obligation, but the reporting requirement is typically much more straightforward. For instance, Article 12.11 of the DSU indicates: "Where one or more of the parties is a developing country Member, the panel's report shall explicitly indicate the form in which account has been taken of relevant provisions on differential and more-favourable treatment for developing country Members." The clause contains two obligations: first, that some account be taken of relevant provisions on SDT for developing members involved in the case, and second, that the panel report explicitly indicate how that was done. While the first obligation (to take into account) poses all the problems discussed above with respect to "best efforts" provisions, the second obligation (reporting) is quite unambiguous. It clearly defines who has the obligation (the panel) and what is to be done (indicate the form in which SDT has been taken into account).

Contemporary international law teaches us that reporting requirements might fulfill a number of goals: They assist in gathering information to be used for particular prescriptions or mandates later, they are useful to monitor implementation and improve states' accountability for compliance, and they assist in the development of the law, to help build state practice with respect to a particular norm that was previously considered as soft law.

Returning to the DSU, the reporting obligation of Article 12.11 can play several of these roles. The accumulated panel reports on disputes involving developing countries would yield some information on the usefulness and interpretation of SDT clauses. This might help members to reshape the clauses in the future. The reporting requirement may also yield information as to the willingness of members in dispute to take into account the relevant SDT provisions, which is an avenue for monitoring implementation. By generating information on what members have done, or could have done, it may also identify areas where members are not compliant or not as compliant as they could be. At first, members may merely pay lip service to reporting requirements, but over time, if it is stringently controlled by the AB, reporting could help to build at least an awareness by members that one or more SDT provisions apply.

Reporting provisions take a variety of forms at the WTO. Some create obligations for the institution (the Secretariat or other bodies). Article 12.11 of the DSU, creating a reporting obligation on the panelists, is an example.[40] Alternatively, the reporting requirement might be on WTO members individually or collectively. GATT Article XXXVII:2(a) requires "the contracting party not…giving effect [to Article XXXVII:1(a), (b) or (c)]" or "any other interested contracting party" to report to the Contracting Parties acting jointly.[41] GATT Article XXXVIII:2(d) requires the WTO membership acting jointly to:

keep under continuous review the development of world trade with special reference to the rate of growth of the trade of less developed contracting parties and make such recommendations to contracting parties as may, in the circumstances, be deemed appropriate.

However, reporting requirements can be weakened by the omission of critical elements such as who has an obligation to report, or to whom. Annex III:5 of the Agreement on Implementation of Article VII of the GATT 1994 illustrates the difficulty with identifying *who has an obligation to report*, when it merely states "If such problems [relating to the implementation of Article 1] arise in practice in developing country Members applying the Agreement, a study of this question shall be made, at the request of such Members, with a view to finding appropriate solutions." The clause does not specify which body shall make the study.[42] Article 12.10 of the TBT Agreement, on the other hand, illustrates ambiguities in identifying *to whom the reporting is to be made*: "The Committee shall examine periodically the special and differential treatment, as laid down in this Agreement, granted to developing country Members on national and international levels."[43] While it is plausible to construe this obligation as including a reporting requirement (how else is the committee going to "examine periodically" SDT granted to developing members?), it is unclear to whom the Committee will account. In these instances, the clauses are substantially weakened as a result of the omissions.

---

[40] See also Art 2.18 Agreement on Textiles and Clothing; Art 10.6 TBT Agreement; Arts 27.6 and 27.15 SCM Agreement.
[41] See other notification and reporting requirements for individual members in relation to SDT provisions in Art 9 and fn 2, Agreement on Safeguards.
[42] See also Enabling Clause, paras 2(i) and 3.
[43] A similarly drafted provision is included at Article 27.14 of the SCM Agreement.

This section demonstrated that clauses mixing the language of legal obligation ("shall") with "soft" obligations, while historically seen as merely hortatory provisions, may now be read as binding and operational when considered along with other more targeted provisions, or in light of an overall objective of the agreement. They can be read as a mandate for "secondary legislation" by the WTO or implementation for individual members to fulfill the provisions' objective. They can be read as progressive obligations that are to be implemented in the long term. They can be read as contingent obligations.

Comparisons with the evolution of treaty interpretation in the field of human rights and international environmental law offers some avenues for a more progressive analysis than would give legal meaning and operational force to these SDT provisions. Human rights treaties and interpretation, climate change regulation, and the case law of Australian courts with respect to the World Heritage Convention provide particularly helpful guidance.

Finally, reporting obligations are critical in cementing the consideration of development issues when mandated by the WTO agreements. They provide accountability, they enhance transparency, they support capacity building. They are also a widely used instrument in other fields of international regulation, where they are not treated as merely advisory or hortatory. Clearly, states know how to operationalize reporting requirements and could do so at the WTO as well.

3. SDT: What Use by Developing Members?

The analysis of SDT would be incomplete without an examination of the use of SDT provisions by developing members.

While not all SDT provisions lend themselves to this analysis, particularly when there is no notification requirement for the invocation of particular provisions, the available record does provide helpful clues, particularly regarding the use of derogations. Where notifications are required, the accuracy in reporting may also be an issue. The following analysis may therefore not be of perfect scientific and statistical accuracy, but it is based on the best available data. The volume of records, where available, is such that there is reasonable confidence in the correctness of the trends.

Overall, the recourse to SDT exceptions and derogations by developing members has decreased in recent years. The use of SDT provisions has focused on a few clauses which have been invoked by developing members for vastly different economic development purposes. GATT Article XVIII and the SDT provisions in the SCM Agreement are salient examples. The concentrated usage of only a few provisions strongly suggests that SDT is not tailored to the range of circumstances of developing members.

The following exceptions and derogations are considered in this section:

- import restrictions for balance-of-payments purposes,
- subsidies,
- public health compulsory licensing scheme of the TRIPS.

While the balance-of-payment restrictions and the subsidies allowance are not restricted to use by developing members, both clauses have been of particular importance for these members.[44] Such provisions, as well as the compulsory licensing scheme, all carry notification requirements that make their usage traceable.

3.1 Balance of payments

Beginning in 1962 and continuing during the GATT years, Article XVIII:B allowing restrictions on imports in response to balance of payments difficulties was used in numerous instances by developing countries. Although recourse to Article XVIII is not expressly limited to developing countries, it is that group that has used it most frequently.

Based on the data from reports by the Committee on the Balance-of-Payments Restrictions during the GATT years, Asian countries emerged as the main users, accounting for the same number of consultations as all Latin American, African, and Middle Eastern countries combined until 1994. Annex 2 provides a breakdown by country and by decade.

Four countries were the biggest users of the balance of payment restrictions. India and Ceylon (later Sri Lanka) constantly had import restrictions under Article XVIII from the middle of the 1960s to 1994, and Pakistan had restrictions for most of that period; Korea also had measures in place constantly from its accession to the GATT in the late 1960s until 1989. Interestingly, they pursued very different models of development but used the same legal instrument to ease the tension between their development strategies and the multilateral trade disciplines: Indeed, it was virtually the only instrument available under the GATT.

In Latin America, Brazil had recourse to Article XVIII throughout the 1970s and 1980s, corresponding to the country's period of heavy debt after the rapid export-oriented economic growth between 1968 and 1973. The IMF had imposed policies of austerity between 1979 and 1984 in response to Brazil's growing debt. Peru also frequently used Article XVIII:B in the 1970s and 1980s and Argentina imposed some trade restrictions, albeit for more limited periods of time.

Among African countries, Egypt, Tunisia, and Ghana made recourses to Article XVIII:B for extended periods of time in the 1970s and 1980s.

Under the WTO, the Committee aggressively phased out the restrictions. Some countries, such as India, Sri Lanka (until 1998), and Pakistan, continued to impose restrictions to protect their balance of payments. A number of others "disinvoked" (the Committee's term) Article XVIII (by setting a timetable for eliminating the restrictions) either independently or as a result of consultations with the Committee. In some cases, the Committee requested or recommended that countries cease their restrictions within a certain date or not impose the restriction at

---

[44] See Annexes 2 and 3 at <http://ukcatalogue.oup.com/product/9780199600885.do>.

all.[45] In the late 1990s and until 2000, a number of Eastern European and Central European countries also imposed trade restrictions under Article XVIII. By 2001, however, Bangladesh was the only country mentioned in the annual report as being regularly reviewed, and the restrictions were being phased out as of 2007.

Overall, trade restrictions for balance of payments purposes were used by very diverse countries: large and small, whether they were using inward or outward-oriented economic development policies. The oil shocks of the 1970s and the deterioration of the terms of trade in the 1980s, when the price of a number of agricultural primary commodities plummeted, also fueled Article XVIII usage. The provision has emerged as the instrument of choice for developing countries to control their liberalization commitments in periods of domestic economic and social transformation. The restrictions were often implemented in consultations with the IMF, which made its views known to the Committee. However, the nature of such transformations and the accompanying trade policies varied greatly. For example, Korea's use of the restrictions in the 1960s and 1970s was clearly part of its policy of reinvesting the surplus from its exports into the economy, rather than paying for imports. By contrast, Latin American countries or sub-Saharan countries were responding to external pressure that put their economies on the verge of collapse.

Another perhaps surprising feature is that only a relatively small number of countries had recourse to this safeguard clause, but they generally invoked it for prolonged periods of time. The users also seem to be the same that invoked development-oriented provisions regularly in dispute settlement (see Chapter 7) and that have generally been most active in GATT negotiations on behalf of groups of developing countries (see Chapters 5 and 9).

This evidence begs the question whether Article XVIII was used because it was a good response to the difficulties faced by developing countries or because it was virtually the only safeguard mechanism available. Given the socioeconomic diversity of the countries that used it, the varying success that they had in their economic growth at the time of the restrictions, and the variety of purposes for which they used it, it is likely the latter.

The WTO now has all but eliminated the use of Article XVIII restrictions, thereby strengthening the application of the prohibition on quotas of GATT Article XI. While the safeguard clause of Article XII is still available, its standards are slightly more stringent than Article XVIII:B. Unlike Article XVIII, Article XII was not designed with developing countries in mind. While it is for economists to determine whether the escape mechanism of Article XVIII:B was beneficial to developing economies and should be revived, the conclusion from a legal perspective is that this instrument has fallen into disuse, if not *de jure*, then certainly *de facto*.

---

[45] See, eg, Report (1995) of the Committee on Balance-of-Payments Restrictions, WT/BOP/R/10 (4 December 1995), requesting that Slovakia and Poland stop invoking Article XVIII within a year or two, and recommending that Sri Lanka not impose certain restrictions.

3.2 Subsidies

The SCM Agreement provides to developing countries listed in its Annex VII (and others for a now-expired period of eight years) an exemption from the prohibition on certain subsidies. This is a rare instance where the beneficiaries of a development-oriented provision are specifically listed. A separate article also allows specific transitional periods for members switching from centrally planned economies to market economies. All WTO members are required to make regular notifications of their subsidies, which are included in the annual reports of the SCM Committee. Annex 3 offers a compilation of the notifications required under Article 25(1) for the period 1995–2011. It provides an interesting picture of developing countries' activities regarding subsidies and, indirectly, regarding compliance with the notification requirements.

The first striking feature of this data is that developing countries have a poor record of compliance with the notification requirement. The worst offenders include all LDCs, as well as a number of other sub-Saharan African countries and a few Asian and central Asian countries. Members with a somewhat patchy record include small Caribbean island-states, which began to consistently notify their subsidies in 2001, and a number of Central American countries. This may indicate a stronger engagement with WTO obligations, and it is interesting to note that notifications began in earnest just before the expiration of the exemption from certain prohibitions was to take effect. Regarding the Caribbean island-states, an increase in technical assistance in recent years may also have contributed to their improved performance.

Another group provides less cause for optimism. It includes countries that started off by making notifications in the first few years of the WTO but have since then given up on consistent reporting. Countries as diverse as Bahrain, Bolivia, India, Mexico, Namibia, Zambia, and Zimbabwe are examples. Whereas compliance with the notification requirement seems correlated to a large extent with the economic wealth of the members, the positions of India and Mexico in that group are an anomaly that is difficult to understand. Brazil straddles the two groups, with a good notifications record in the first few years of the WTO, then an interruption in notifications, and finally a recent resumption of the practice. India, Mexico, and Brazil are highly engaged in the activities of the WTO, certainly more so than many other developing countries. Their inconsistent records may still be due to insufficient capacity, but may also result from a reluctance to disclose politically sensitive information and expose themselves to litigation.

Most developing countries that comply with the notification requirement state that they have subsidies in place. Only a few members regularly claim that they have no subsidies: Benin, Bolivia, Botswana, Burundi, Cuba, Ghana, Macao, Suriname, Zambia, and Zimbabwe. Other countries claiming that they have no reportable subsidies are Hong Kong, Liechtenstein, New Zealand, and, until recently, Oman and Singapore. Here again, the economic profile of the countries that claim no reportable subsidies are at odds, including both very poor and very rich countries.

If the notifications are accurate (which may be doubtful in some cases), the types of countries that have subsidies suggests that the exemption on the prohibition of certain subsidies benefited only the middle-income countries (that had subsidies in place), but not the poorer countries (that had no subsidies to protect).[46] Although this conclusion seems logical and corresponds to the data, an important caveat is that the poorest countries, the LDCs, generally have not made any notification whatsoever. Nonetheless, additional circumstantial evidence to support the theory that the subsidies exemption benefited mostly middle-income developing members may be found in the recent initiative to extend the transitional period for the phasing out of export subsidies by developing country members (Article 25.4 of the SCM Agreement). With the Doha Round carrying on for longer than initially anticipated, in July 2007 the General Council adopted a recommendation to extend the transitional period to the end of 2007[47] and, on request, on a case-by-case basis pending the conclusion of the Round. Because such initiatives are generally driven by the middle-income developing countries, it is likely that they were indeed the ones with a significant interest in the matter, rather than the poorest members.

3.3 TRIPS and public health emergency

Among the many controversial issues surrounding the TRIPS, developing countries have been concerned that they would not be able to address national public health emergencies such as the HIV/AIDS pandemic because they could not afford the high-priced drugs patented by American, Japanese, and European pharmaceutical firms (for example) now benefiting from reinforced intellectual property protection under the TRIPS. Article 31, now dubbed the "compulsory licensing" mechanism, addresses the issue in part, but the modalities for implementation and the exact scope of the provision remain uncertain. During the 2001 Doha Ministerial Meeting, developing countries, backed by non-governmental organizations and media campaigns, pushed for a clarification of the provision that would allow them to produce generic drugs in certain cases and to import drugs produced abroad under the compulsory licensing mechanism. Eventually, the controversy led to the adoption of paragraph 6 of the Doha Declaration on the TRIPS Agreement and Public Health, mandating the WTO to take measures to ensure implementation of Article 31.[48] The General Council Decision of 2003 fulfilled this mandate on a temporary basis.[49] On 6 December 2005 the WTO made

---

[46] Some subsidies remain allowed under the SCM Agreement if the subsidies are non-specific, not export contingent, and not conditioned on the use of domestic over imported products (Arts 2 and 3 SCM Agreement).

[47] General Council, *Article 27.4 of the Agreement on Subsidies and Countervailing Measures—Decision of 27 July 2007*, WT/L/691 (31 July 2007); see SCM Committee 2007 Report, G/L/840 (12 November 2007), at para 17.

[48] WTO Ministerial Conference, *Declaration on the TRIPS Agreement and Public Health*, WT/MIN(01)/DEC/2 (20 November 2001).

[49] WTO General Council, *Decision on Implementation of Paragraph 6 of the Doha Declaration on the TRIPS Agreement and Public Health*, WT/L/540 and Corr.1 (1 September 2003).

permanent the changes in the Decision, thereby proposing for the first time an amendment to a core WTO agreement.[50] It will take effect when two-thirds of the members (102 members) ratify the change. As of October 2011, thirty-three countries (including most industrialized countries) and the EU (twenty-seven members) have accepted the TRIPS amendment. In the meantime, the waiver continues to apply, so that the mechanism devised by the 2001 Declaration and 2003 Decision is already usable by members.

The requirement for notifications by the importing and the exporting countries wishing to use Article 31 and the 2003 Decision makes it easy to track the use of this mechanism. So far, only one country has notified its intent to produce some generic drugs (Canada)[51] and one country has notified its intent to import these drugs (Rwanda).[52] The three drugs covered by this 2007 authorization were for HIV and AIDS treatment. It is not surprising that Canada has moved quickly to use the system because it already has extensive facilities and procedures for producing generic drugs. As an early mover, it could have become an important producer of generic drugs under the TRIPS public health mechanism. However, Canadian generics producers have instead hinted that they were unlikely to make use of the facility, due to the burdens of the authorization and reporting procedures combined with additional domestic Canadian regulatory requirements.

Both with respect to the TRIPS amendment and regarding the actual use of the 2003 Decision, WTO members are moving very slowly. Numerous complaints have emerged regarding the cumbersome procedures and limitations imposed by the 2003 Decision; prognostics are that it is unlikely that other developing countries will follow in Rwanda's tracks. Instead, it appears that the early Doha moves on public health leading to the 2003 Decision combined with domestic litigation in South Africa in particular have spurred direct negotiations with manufacturers for patented drugs to be available on developing country markets at cheaper prices than in developed country markets.[53]

At the same time that highly visible negotiations were taking place at the WTO where developing countries appeared to take the upper hand, the United States and Europe introduced more stringent provisions regarding intellectual property protection and sought to limit the effect of the 2001 Declaration and 2003 Decision in bilateral and regional trade agreements. Such limitative clauses

---

[50] WTO General Council, *Decision on Amendment of the TRIPS Agreement*, WT/L/641 (8 December 2005).

[51] Council for TRIPS, *Notification Under Paragraph 2(c) of the Decision of 30 August 2003 on the Implementation of Paragraph 6 of the Doha Declaration on the TRIPS Agreement and Public Health*, IP/N/10/CAN/1 (8 October 2007).

[52] Council for TRIPS, *Notification Under Paragraph 2(a) of the Decision of 30 August 2003 on the Implementation of Paragraph 6 of the Doha Declaration on the TRIPS Agreement and Public Health*, IP/N/9/RWA/1 (19 July 2007).

[53] A coalition of Caribbean countries first concluded a deal to obtain AIDS drugs at a discount price and a group of middle-income Latin American countries led by Brazil later secured a deal with Abbott Laboratories, Inc., a US pharmaceutical firm, in October 2005. See also E. Benvenisti and G.W. Downs, "Distributive Politics and International Institutions: The Case of Drugs" 2004 *Case Western Reserve Journal of International Law* 36(1) 21.

typically provide that the developing country partner will refrain from having recourse to compulsory licensing. The clauses have been dubbed "TRIPS-plus" because they preclude the use of derogations allowed under TRIPS. The potential conflict of these provisions with TRIPS obligations came under scrutiny both within the US government and beyond, ultimately prompting the US Trade Representative to issue a unilateral letter stating that "TRIPS-plus" clauses were not intended to and could not limit the application of TRIPS. The legal value and effects of the letter are uncertain and the issue remains problematic to date.

Finally, in a recent development, shipments of unpatented generic drugs produced in India that were destined for other developing countries were seized while they were transshipped through EU ports.[54] Although these drugs did not trigger the TRIPS' compulsory licensing system (because they were not patented in the place of production), these developments bear on the broader issue of the impact of WTO disciplines on access to medicine by developing members. A settlement was reportedly negotiated in December 2010 after India had filed a request for consultations with the EU and the Netherlands in May 2010.

This saga reflects the complexity of the multilateral trading system, both politically and legally. The interplay between multilateralism and regional or bilateral deals is pervasive and the potential for conflicts is increasing.

4. Conclusion

Three main issues are recurrent with respect to SDT provisions. First, the use of ambiguous language casts uncertainties as to the meaning and legal value of some provisions. However, modern developments in international environmental law and human rights law, as well as a more nuanced application of traditional canons of treaty interpretation, could give a much more operational interpretation to many of these provisions, even without any redrafting.

The second issue is the allocation of obligations. In a number of cases, it is unclear who has an obligation to do something in favor of developing countries. In other cases, SDT in favor of developing members is left to the discretion of developed members with no opportunity for developing members to jointly trigger the application of the provisions.

Third, most provisions leave to members a large margin of discretion with regard to the manner, extent, and timing of implementation. In itself, this is not necessarily fatal to the provision. Such leeway becomes much more problematic when it is coupled with a lack of accountability and reporting by the members who have a duty to implement.

---

[54] Third World Network, "Concerns Voiced at TRIPS Council Over Seizure of Drugs," (published online 11 June 2009) <http://www.twnside.org.sg/title2/wto.info/2009/twninfo20090611. htm>; "EU Offers Out of WTO Settlement on Drug Seizure Row," (published online 1 December 2010) <http://www.business-standard.com/india/news/eu-offers-outwto-settlementdrug-seizure-row/117841/on>.

The reluctance of panels and the AB to engage in a teleological interpretation of general (non-SDT) WTO provisions that would be mindful of development objectives reinforces the culture of treating development as a side-issue rather than an essential consideration affecting the trade policy of the vast majority of WTO members. It must be remembered that the Marrakesh Agreement's preamble makes supporting development a purpose of the WTO. The core tension in the WTO regime regarding whether the law is a reflection of the balance of power of economic interests or whether it plays a moderating role is, to some extent, reproduced in the context of disputes involving development considerations.[55] While the historical reluctance of the panels and AB to incorporate extraneous norms of international law in their reasoning is well documented, a shift in the interpretation of many SDT provisions to give them more legal strength would not necessarily require such a recourse to extraneous norms. In most cases, a re-examination of SDT provisions in light of customary rules on treaty interpretation would allow a dynamic interpretation. The option of reconsidering existing provisions to satisfy developing members' current demands may ultimately be a more practical alternative than amending the WTO agreements to redraft existing provisions or to add new ones. Considering the ongoing TRIPS amendment process regarding compulsory licensing and the deadlocks of the Doha negotiations, a dynamic interpretation of existing provisions may well be the only functional option.

Some commentators have argued that the AB in particular should fully acknowledge and embrace its role as a watchdog for the systemic interests of the WTO.[56] Where those systemic interests lie is in part a legal question, but it is also a political question that members must resolve more explicitly. While there is ample evidence regarding the shortcomings of the dispute settlement system, developing countries also acknowledge that the adjudicatory system is a benefit of the WTO[57] and there has been no allegation of systematic anti-developing country bias in panels or the AB. Hence, the dispute settlement system has credibility in principle and could deliver if developing countries were able to utilize it to its full potential.

More broadly, the limited utilization of SDT provisions by developing countries and the implementation problems of many existing provisions raise questions as to the validity of the SDT approach to addressing development issues. In practice, the use of SDT best illustrates the idiosyncratic approach to the trade and development relationship, where exceptions or derogations are used on an *ad hoc* basis, with no underlying principle. Yet, the gap between what SDT has

---

[55] D. Ierley, "Defining the Factors that Influence Developing Country Compliance with and Participation in the WTO Dispute Settlement System: Another Look at the Dispute Over Bananas" 2002 *Law and Policy in International Business* 33(2) 615, at 617–18 (empirical study based on interviews with diplomats from WTO developing members).

[56] P.M. Gerhart and A.S. Kella, "Power and Preferences: Developing Countries and the Role of the WTO Appellate Body" (2005) *North Carolina Journal of International Law & Commercial Regulation* 30(3) 515.

[57] Ierley, above fn 55, at 621–3; C.L.N. Amorim, "The WTO from the Perspective of a Developing Country" 2000 *Fordham International Law Journal* 24(1–2) 95, at 96.

enabled and what developing countries have asked the trading system to deliver, as discussed in the first part of this book, suggests that this approach, on its own, is bound to fail with respect to the integration of development concerns in trade regulation. The dynamic reinterpretation of many SDT provisions that has been proposed here may assist in bridging that gap, without precluding other avenues for reform.

7

Invoking Development in Dispute Settlement

The shortcomings of developing country participation in dispute settlement and the limited usefulness of the dispute settlement process for developing countries to protect their rights is well documented.[1] This chapter takes a different approach. It compiles and analyzes cases to identify trends in the interpretation and enforcement of development-oriented provisions and norms in dispute settlement. The systematic review of all cases involving development arguments show that cases cluster around a few SDT provisions: the Antidumping Agreement Article 15, the SCM Agreement Article 27, the Enabling Clause, and preference waivers. Recurring legal questions focus on the scope of the obligations, the relationship between SDT, development, and other WTO disciplines, and the allocation of the burden of proof.

Overall, panels and the AB have been more receptive to development argument when they were tied to a specific SDT provision, particularly when the latter embodied well-defined obligations. Where the wording of SDT clauses was ambiguous, adjudicators have often shied away from rigorous treaty interpretation exercises and have not attempted to develop tests, standards or methodologies that would be useful for future cases. The *EC–Tariff Preferences* case is an exception to this trend.

These issues are critical on a forward-going basis when considering how to interpret SDT provisions in future disputes, and how to amend them and draft new ones as many proposals have done in the Doha Round.

Section 1 presents a brief overview of developing members' participation in dispute settlement at the GATT and WTO. Without engaging in an extensive empirical study, it presents basic data regarding the number of cases where developing members have been involved in disputes and the geographical allocation of cases. Section 2 analyzes arguments related to development made in disputes during the GATT years and under the WTO's dispute settlement system. Section 3 considers the role of development in implementation proceedings, specifically DSU Article 21.3 and 22.6 arbitrations. Lastly, Section 4 assesses the role that development plays or can play in interpreting WTO provisions other than SDT clauses.

One caveat must be mentioned at this time. Despite the extensive references to earlier cases, both in GATT and WTO panel and AB reports, the WTO system

---

[1] See eg, C.P. Bown and B.M. Hoekman, "Developing Countries and Enforcement of Trade Agreements: Why Dispute Settlement is Not Enough" 2008 *Journal of World Trade* 42(1) 177.

does not apply *stare decisis*, the principle under which "a judge *must* decide a case at bar in accordance with any applicable precedent that cannot be distinguished on valid grounds."[2] International jurisdictions typically consider that the findings in a decision are binding only for the parties involved in that case, and only with respect to the elements of the dispute; the WTO operates on the same principle.[3] That said, Jackson has argued persuasively that precedent should not be understood as a binary concept[4] and that it plays a variety of roles at the WTO. This chapter is inscribed in this broader approach.

1. A Brief Overview of Developing Country Practice in Dispute Settlement at the GATT and WTO

Prior to the adoption of Part IV of the GATT in 1965, only eight disputes involved developing countries and one case presented a development argument, argued by Italy.[5] Between 1965 and 1995, developing countries made development-related arguments (either general or based on a particular SDT provision) in about twenty cases. Since 1995, development arguments have been made in nearly forty cases.

1.1 Developing country activity in disputes during the GATT years

While a relatively large number of cases involved developing countries during the GATT years, only a few countries were actual litigants and repeat users of the dispute settlement process: Brazil topped the list as a main party in eight cases and a third country in four cases; Argentina and India also had a noteworthy third country practice (about eight cases each). However, these members did not always present development arguments. In particular, Brazil often made claims without recourse to any development provision. A handful of other developing countries, mostly Central and South American and a few Asian nations, participated in a few disputes and often made development arguments.[6] In a number of cases, they

---

[2] R. Bhala, "The Myth About Stare Decisis and International Trade Law" 1999 *American University International Law Review* 14(4) 846, 849 fn 9.

[3] See the series of cases on zeroing and the ensuing controversy regarding panels' persistence in disregarding repeated findings by the AB that the US' zeroing methodology was inconsistent with its WTO obligations.

[4] J.H. Jackson, *Sovereignty, The WTO, and Changing Fundamentals of International Law* (Cambridge: Cambridge University Press, 2006), at 173–5; J.H. Jackson, "Process and Procedure in WTO Dispute Settlement" 2009 *Cornell International Law Journal* 42(2) 233, at 237–8, discussing a range of precedent from *stare decisis* at the top, to "something less weighty with burdens of proof ... to the case where we do not pay attention to it except for its titillating effect."

[5] GATT Panel Report, *Italy–Agricultural Machinery* (Italy claimed that the measure was necessary for its economic development and labor conditions. The panel "recognized ... that it was not the intention of the General Agreement to limit the right of a contracting party to adopt measures which appeared to it necessary to foster its economic development or to protect a domestic industry, provided that such measures were permitted by the terms of the General Agreement. The GATT offered a number of possibilities to achieve these purposes through tariff measures or otherwise" but the measure in question was not appropriate.).

[6] The United Kingdom acted on behalf of Hong Kong in a number of disputes. The United States and Italy also made some development arguments in one case each, defending policies in support of local and rural development.

only reserved the right to intervene as a third party, but failed to make oral or written submissions to the panel. No LDC participated in disputes, and virtually no African members participated. While the most economically developed of developing countries seem to account for most of the participation in dispute settlement, South Africa stands out by its absence (only one instance of third country participation).

By comparison, the United States was a complainant in twenty-seven cases and a respondent in twenty-eight cases during the GATT years. This accounts for over 50 percent of all disputes where a panel report was adopted (a number of these recorded a negotiated settlement rather than a full adjudication). The other main litigants were Western European countries (eventually participating as the EC), Canada, and, to some extent, Japan and Korea.

These patterns signal a tendency by developing countries (and then only a small group of these) to act as observers of the process, rather than as active, regular participants. Regarding the geographic distribution of developing country participation, the absence of Africa may be explained by an extreme scarcity of resources and lack of diversification in exports, such that the trade interests of African members were narrow in scope. More generally, the level of participation in dispute settlement seems correlated to the openness of a country's economy: Countries where foreign trade accounted for a comparatively smaller part of the domestic economy had limited incentives to devote resources to GATT litigation.

Qualitatively, development arguments tended to be very general, calling for the panel to take into consideration the economic and social circumstances of a party as a developing country,[7] or the broader actual or potential impact of the dispute on developing members, in the case of interested third parties.[8] The only legal

---

[7] India, as a third party, noted that "the maintenance of illegal quantitative restrictions was all the more serious as these adversely affected the trade interests of less-developed contracting parties which had serious balance of payments problems, whose leather industry was also manned by backward communities, and whose social uplift was a concern of the government." GATT Panel Report, *Japan–Leather II (US)*, at para 39. See also GATT Panel Report, *US–Superfund*, at paras 4.2.2 and 4.5.2, where Indonesia argued that the levies of funds for the Superfund "made developing countries pay for the protection of the environment in an industrialised country" and where Nigeria stated that "developing countries, faced with serious debt and commodity price problems, should not be denied their rights under the General Agreement."

[8] Eg, GATT Panel Report, *UK–Dollar Quotas*. In a dispute between the United Kingdom and the United States, the countries included in the "Dollar Area" expressed concern that the settlement between the main litigants would affect them adversely due to their circumstances as developing countries. These countries were Bolivia, Canada, Colombia, Costa Rica, Cuba, Dominican Republic, Ecuador, El Salvador, Guatemala, Haiti, Republic of Honduras, Liberia, Mexico, Nicaragua, Panama, Philippines, and Venezuela. In another case, Argentina acting as a third party pointed out that although the main parties to the dispute were two developed countries "the provisions and arguments invoked against Canada were not necessarily those which could legitimately be invoked against developing countries, considering the protection which those countries had the right to grant under the General Agreement to their developing industries" (GATT Panel Report, *Canada–FIRA*). The panel acquiesced that there may be some particular issues in that respect but declined to make a determination in this case because the dispute involved developed parties, ibid at para 5.2. This case illustrates the advantages and limitations of raising issues as third parties, even in cases such as this one, where Argentina had no alternative.

provisions that could form the basis of a development argument were Part IV of the GATT, Article XVIII and the Enabling Clause.

Despite the transformation of the dispute-settlement process, the trends in developing country participation and the type of arguments they made under the GATT endure under the WTO.

1.2 Developing member participation in the WTO's dispute settlement process

The advent of the WTO marked a notable increase in the level of developing country participation in disputes. In the eighteen years since the WTO was formed there were 194 instances of a developing country being a complainant, 179 instances of a developing country being a respondent, and 913 instances of interested third party participation. These figures suggest that the creation of the WTO's dispute settlement process has given much greater access to developing countries.

Nonetheless, these aggregate figures are misleading in several respects. First, the developing countries that used dispute settlement provisions under the GATT are still the main users under the WTO. Brazil alone totals 114 instances of participation in a dispute as complainant, respondent, or third party, and India totals 129 instances. Mexico participated in 104 cases. Argentina and Thailand come next, as they did under the GATT, with over 60 instances each. China is the major newcomer, with 139 instances of participation, nearly half of which as a main party. A few other Latin American and South Asian countries also account for moderate participation. However, as in the GATT, the bulk of developing countries, particularly African ones, have virtually no record of participating in disputes; participation as third parties remains the most popular means of access to the process. Of the thirty-four LDCs that are WTO members, Bangladesh is the only one that participated in a dispute as a main party (complainant or respondent),[9] but in the past five years, a few have participated as third parties.

Second, the likelihood that a developing country will face a complaint has grown exponentially,[10] despite their proportionally lower participation in disputes overall. From an economic perspective, Michalopoulos found that developing countries under-participated in dispute settlement compared to their share of

---

[9] Request for Consultations by Bangladesh, *India–Antidumping Measure on Batteries from Bangladesh*, WT/DS306/1 (28 January 2004) (The parties notified the DSB of a mutually satisfactory settlement in January 2006 and the case was closed).

[10] G. Shaffer, "How to Make the WTO Dispute Settlement System Work for Developing Countries; Some Proactive Developing Country Strategies," in G. Shaffer, V. Mosoti and A. Qureshi (eds), *Toward a Development-Supportive Dispute Settlement System in the WTO* (ICTSD Resource Paper No 5, 2003), at 14; M. Busch and E. Reinhardt, "Testing International Trade Law: Empirical Studies of GATT/WTO Dispute Settlement," in D.L.M. Kennedy and J.D. Southwick (eds), *The Political Economy of International Trade Law: Essays in Honor of Robert E. Hudec* (Cambridge: Cambridge University Press, 2002), at 466–7; B. Hoekman and M. Kostecki, *The Political Economy of the World Trading System: The WTO and Beyond*, 2nd edn (Oxford: Oxford University Press, 2001), at 394–5.

world trade.[11] Between 2005 and August 2011, disputes between developed and developing countries amounted to more than half of the total number of disputes, with China (as a complainant or respondent) overwhelmingly accounting for the fastest growing volume of litigation. These figures do not take into account the continued prevalence of developing country participation as third parties.

Third, the number of disputes between developing countries has also grown. During the first three years of the WTO, those represented 7 of 114 filed disputes. Between January 2005 and October 2011, 25 of 102 new disputes were between developing countries. The latter figure is comparable to the number of disputes between developed countries during the same period.

Fourth, and perhaps even more importantly, the number of instances where developing countries made development arguments has not grown proportionally with their overall participation, compared to the record of the GATT years. This is all the more surprising given that the proliferation of SDT clauses in the WTO agreements now provides many more opportunities for making development-oriented arguments than under the GATT.

Several reasons have been advanced for the number, type, and distribution of disputes involving developing countries: scarcity of resources, domestic dynamics of WTO litigation, and the problem of remedies.[12]

The overall availability of resources to pursue a case varies greatly from country to country, not just in absolute terms, but also in terms of the nature of the resources. Rich countries with a permanent staff have a low variable cost for bringing disputes. By contrast, poor countries with no permanent staff have to bear the cost of each dispute as variable cost. The resources therefore must be found anew for each dispute; there is no permanent, predetermined pool of resources to draw from. Developing countries that participate more regularly (and successfully) in disputes at the WTO have fully taken stock of the need for some, if only minimal, institutional expertise at the governmental lawyer level, from which to organize, coordinate, and manage WTO litigation. Brazil and Argentina, for instance, have built some level of institutional structure domestically and in their Geneva mission, as well as coordinating with the private sector to harness the resources to defend and challenge trade measures.[13]

The resource issue in turns bears on the domestic dynamics for WTO litigation. The concern here is not so much how many disputes will be brought or defended, but which ones. If the costs are variable, rather than built into the regular budget as fixed costs, the incentive is to bring or defend only disputes that can be self-funded. Governments become conduits for domestic industries willing to pay to bring or defend a particular case. If the industry cannot pay, cases are unlikely to go forward. That is particularly true in Caribbean countries. Others, such as

---

[11] Michalopoulos, above Ch 3 fn 26, at 167.

[12] See eg, G.N. Horlick and N. Mizulin, "Developing Countries and WTO Dispute Settlement" 2005 *Integration and Trade Journal* 23(1) 125.

[13] For these case studies and others, see G. Shaffer and R. Meléndez-Ortiz (eds), *Dispute Settlement at the WTO—The Developing Country Experience* (Cambridge: Cambridge University Press, 2010).

Argentina and Brazil, with a strong practice of industry-sponsored disputes, use a mix of government and private sector resources.

Finally, the incentive to bring a dispute depends on the likelihood that the disputed measure will be brought into conformity with the losing member's obligations. The issue of trade asymmetries between members and their effect on the implementation of remedies has been extensively discussed in the literature.[14] The main issue is that countries with a small portion of the world trade will not have the market power to coerce the losing member into compliance by suspending concessions on imports from that member. In other words, the exports of the losing member to the winning member will not be significant enough that higher tariffs on these products will create an incentive for the losing member to comply. Moreover, the member suspending the concessions may be doing more harm to its domestic market by imposing the higher tariffs if it is dependent on cheap imports to fuel its economy.

The advent of the WTO has transformed the legal grounds for development arguments. With the proliferation of SDT provisions, the opportunities for an offensive or defensive use of development or developing country status in dispute settlement has grown exponentially. Although the litigants tend to be the same countries as during the GATT years, and the number of development arguments has not grown proportionally with the participation of developing countries in dispute settlement, the legal basis for development claims has diversified compared to the GATT years.

2. Development Arguments in Disputes

This section discusses disputes where a right, obligation, defense, or other legal element of the WTO agreements was in dispute because of its relationship to a development policy or claim. In most cases, a developing country either advanced a claim, or presented a defense that its actions or omissions were motivated or excused by its development situation. This section will therefore not consider all the disputes where a developing country was involved. The objective is to show how the WTO agreements have been interpreted in relationship to an explicit development claim or implication.

Annex 4 summarizes instances of development arguments made in GATT and WTO disputes and the responses by the panels and Appellate Body.[15] The remainder of this section examines the evolution of the case law in three specific areas that constitute the bulk of development arguments in disputes:

- Part IV of the GATT (section 2.1),

---

[14] See eg, Bown and Hoekman, above fn 1; G.N. Horlick, "Problems with the Compliance Structure of the WTO Dispute Resolution Process," in *The Political Economy of International Trade Law*, above fn10, at 641–2; G. Shaffer, "How to Make the WTO Dispute Settlement System Work for Developing Countries: Some Proactive Developing Country Strategies," ICTSD Resource Paper No. 5 (March 2003), at 1 <http://ictsd.org/downloads/2008/06/dsu_2003.pdf>.

[15] Annex 4 at <http://ukcatalogue.oup.com/product/9780199600885.do>.

- the Enabling Clause and preferential schemes (section 2.2),
- specific development-oriented provisions in the WTO Annex 1 agreements (section 2.3).

While some panel reports addressing Part IV gave hope that these provisions might gain traction over time, arguments based on Part IV have been abandoned since 1995, until China raised it in the recent *China–Raw Materials* dispute. Instead, development arguments focus on the more technical SDT provisions scattered throughout the WTO agreements. That is not to say that all SDT provisions enjoy the same amount of attention. Articles 13 and 15 of the Antidumping Agreement, Article 27 of the SCM Agreement, Article 6 of the now-defunct Agreement on Textiles and Clothing, Article 9 of the Agreement on Safeguards, and Article 12 of the TBT Agreement all concerning SDT,[16] cover virtually all the development arguments made since 1995. Conspicuously absent are disputes involving SDT clauses in the TRIPS. One explanation is that the last transitional implementation periods accorded to developing countries only recently expired (particularly in the case of LDCs). Consequently, it may be that disputes involving the TRIPS and development issues will emerge in coming years. As the dispute between India, Brazil, and the EU over the seizure of generic drugs destined to a third country market and transshipped through EU ports showed, TRIPS disputes involving development issues may be so sensitive that countries have a higher incentive to settle their differences without a full-blown adjudication.

2.1 Adjudicating Part IV of the GATT

Part IV of the GATT constituted for many decades the only avenue for developing countries to balance GATT disciplines against development considerations. Was it used and could it be used in dispute settlement? While accepted wisdom typically portrays Part IV as devoid of any real legal implication, the evidence shows that developing countries actually attempted to give it operational effect in a number of disputes during the GATT years. Those efforts have mostly been hindered by the panels' reluctance to even consider the argument, with some notable exceptions. Technically, panels could often shy away from responding to a Part IV claim because third country interveners made the argument; panels were then not required to issue a formal decision on the issue.

This section argues that the limited usefulness of Part IV to support development arguments and its ultimate fall into disuse were not inevitable; opportunities existed for a more robust implementation and interpretation of Part IV. In fact, the recent disputes brought by the EU, the United States, and Mexico against China relating to its restrictions on exports of raw materials put Part IV in the

---

[16] Except Art 13 Antidumping Agreement.

limelight again, with China relying explicitly on Article XXXVI of the GATT.[17] These recent cases bolster the argument in Chapter 6 showing that Part IV could be interpreted in a more operational fashion. This analysis is particularly relevant for other SDT provisions and the slew of Doha Round proposals that use hortatory language.

Overall, Part IV has been used in offensive litigation strategies, where the developing country invoking it was the complainant, rather than as a defense against a claim that a developing country had violated its obligations. Hence, Part IV seems to have been understood to create additional rights and protections for developing countries, rather than to alleviate the burden of their general obligations.

A cluster of three cases is particularly illuminating, and probably the closest the GATT system ever came to giving legal substance to Part IV. In 1980, two panels issued decisions within days of each other. The third case was a sequel to one of these cases nearly a decade later.

The first case, *EC–Sugar Exports (Brazil)*, was a complaint by Brazil when the EC increased its sugar exports as a result of increased subsidies. The EC argued that it had to re-export additional quantities of sugar to make up for the sugar that was imported into the EC from ACP countries under the Lomé preferential agreement. Brazil and other signatories to the International Sugar Agreement had taken action to try to maintain the world price of sugar, which was dramatically plummeting at the time. Brazil argued that the EC, through its exports subsidies, was exporting more than its fair share of sugar to the prejudice of Brazil and other sugar exporters in breach of GATT Article XVI (on subsidies). Brazil further claimed that the EC's actions, by essentially counteracting the International Sugar Agreement's measures, were also in breach of its obligations under Part IV.[18]

The Panel found that Article XXXVI ("Principles and Objectives" of Part IV) and Article XXXVIII ("Joint Action") imposed an obligation of cooperation on the EC that had not been met. The Panel ultimately found against the EC both on the Article XVI claim and on the Part IV claim:

The Panel recognized the efforts made by the European Communities in complying with the provisions of Articles XXXVI and XXVII. It nevertheless felt that increased Community exports of sugar through the use of subsidies in the particular market situation in 1978 and 1979, and where developing contracting parties had taken steps within the framework of the ISA to improve the conditions of the world sugar market, inevitably reduced the effects of the efforts made by these countries. For this time-period and for this particular field, the European Communities had therefore not collaborated jointly

---

[17] Panel Reports, *China–Raw Materials*. China argued that Art XXXVI of the GATT was "relevant context for interpreting Article XI:2(a))" at para 6.21; see also paras 7.264, 7.265, 7.271, 7.389, and see the Panel response at para 7.280. China also argued that Art XXXVI should be used as context for Art XX(g): see paras 7.399, 7.403, and see the Panel response at para 7.400.

[18] GATT Panel Report, *EC–Sugar Exports (Brazil)*, at para 2.2. An earlier case was brought against the EC by Australia on the same issue. GATT Panel Report, *EC–Sugar Exports (Australia)*. Brazil and a number of other developing countries parties to the GATT reserved interested third party rights, and Brazil shortly thereafter brought its own case against the EC.

with other contracting parties to further the principles and objectives set forth in Article XXXVI, in conformity with the guidelines given in Article XXXVIII.[19]

Although the Panel recognized that the EC was not a party to the International Sugar Agreement, and therefore was not bound by its obligations, it effectively construed Articles XXXVI and XXXVIII as a superseding obligation to cooperate with members of the Sugar Agreement. The Panel took this approach presumably because sugar was also covered by GATT obligations and commitments.

Hence, Articles XXXVI and XXXVIII apparently required the EC to refrain from actively countering developing countries' efforts in support of exports crucial to their economies (sugar in this case), and to cooperate with these countries and other international groupings in furtherance of the development objective embodied in Part IV of the GATT. The Panel read Articles XXXVI and XXXVIII to include both a negative and a positive obligation based solely on the evidence regarding trends in sugar exports and on the fact that Brazil was a developing country. This reading of Part IV is quite progressive; it is in line with interpretative developments in other areas of international law that use "best efforts" style drafting, as discussed in Chapter 6.

More generally, this was a rare case where conflicting trade policies came to a head. Effectively, the Panel allowed a multilateral commodity agreement open to a wide variety of countries to prevail over a unilateral, discriminatory, trade preference scheme. As such, this case also foreshadows the debate about development, preferences, and non-discrimination.

Unfortunately, the Panel's reasoning is cursory at best, giving little guidance on the exact scope of the legal obligations under Part IV. The Panel's finding regarding the EC's duty to collaborate begs the question: How far does such a duty extend? Some answers are provided in the case of *EEC–Apples I (Chile)*, adopted by the Contracting Parties on the same day as the sugar case.

In the first iteration of the *EEC–Apples I (Chile)* case, Chile's claim was two-fold: Implicitly there was a question whether the measure taken by the EC was consistent with Part IV, and second, Chile suggested that Part IV imposed some level of procedural obligation on the EC to cooperate with Chile to resolve the situation that adversely affected Chile.[20]

The Panel recognized both aspects of the claim but focused its reasoning almost entirely on Article XXXVII:1(b) stating that "the developed contracting parties shall to the fullest extent possible…refrain from introducing, or increasing the incidence of, customs duties or non-tariff import barriers on products currently or potentially of particular export interest to less-developed contracting parties." The Panel found that the EC's measure "did affect the ability of a developing country to export into the EEC market." However, it went on to say "the EEC had taken certain actions, including bilateral consultations in order to avoid suspending imports of apples from Chile. After a careful examination, the Panel could not determine that the EEC had not made serious efforts to avoid taking protective measures

---

[19] Ibid at 30 (Conclusions).
[20] GATT Panel Report, *EEC–Apples I (Chile)*, at para 3.30.

against Chile."[21] The Panel concluded by finding no breach of the EC's obligations under Part IV. Several elements emerge from this ruling, despite the fact that the Panel failed to detail its reasoning.

First, inasmuch as Article XXXVII:1(b) includes a substantive obligation for developed members not to adopt measures that adversely affect products from developing countries, it may be overridden by compliance with what appears to be a procedural obligation to consult with, and inform, the affected countries. Here, the Panel did not dispute Chile's assertion that it was a developing country; it also found that the EC's measure operated to the detriment of Chile. Yet these conclusions were insufficient to find a breach of Part IV. According to the Panel, the fact that the EC engaged in consultations with Chile and had undertaken other actions to mitigate the effect of the measure needed to be read jointly with the substantive restrictive measure, and the two taken together did not amount to a violation.

Because Article XXXVII:1(b) only says the developed members "shall to the fullest extent possible . . . refrain from" introducing the restrictive measures, the Panel would have been hard-pressed to find in Chile's favor solely on the basis that the EC has introduced a restrictive measure that affected a developing country. However, Article XXXVII:1 gives more guidance on how to interpret this seemingly vague language. The clause "to the fullest extent possible" is the only limitation to what would otherwise be a straightforward prohibition on the imposition of the measures contemplated by paragraph (b). The Panel seized this to balance out the measure against the EC's procedural efforts to consult with Chile.

Article XXXVII:1 specifies that "to the fullest extent possible" means that only "when compelling reasons, which may include legal reasons, make it impossible" can the developed country derogate from the obligation to refrain from imposing the measure. Taken on its face, the language of the Article suggests a simple method for applying its provisions:

- By imposing the measure at stake, has a developed country "introduc[ed], or increase[ed]the incidence of, customs duties or non-tariff barriers on products currently or potentially of export interest to less-developed contracting parties"? (paragraph (b))
- Is there a "compelling reason, including a legal reason," for the developed country to take the measure? (paragraph (1))

Article XXXVII:1(c) lends itself to the same reasoning, *mutantis mutandis*. The Panel undertook no such analysis.

Second, while Article XXXVII:3 arguably includes some obligation of cooperation and consideration of alternate measures that would have a lesser negative impact on developing countries, Article XXXVI:1 focuses on the substance of the measures and says nothing regarding procedural obligations, cooperation, or consultation.

The Panel therefore read into it a defense for developed country members that is nowhere to be found in the terms of the provision. Undoubtedly, other provisions

---

[21] Ibid at para 4.23.

of Part IV (Articles XXXVII:3(b) and (c)) are closer to imposing a flexible procedural obligation, or "*obligation de moyen*" in civil law terms, rather than a substantive obligation, or "*obligation de résultat*." The Panel could also have relied on the
vaguer paragraph (a) stating that developed countries shall "accord high priority
to the reduction or elimination of barriers to products currently or potentially of
particular export interest to less-developed contracting parties."

The last specific discussion of Part IV is the 1989 case of the *EEC–Dessert
Apples*,[22] where Chile presented arguments similar to its 1980 case discussed
above. Chile argued that in restricting imports of apples from Chile, the EEC had
breached its obligations under Part IV because it failed to take into account the
"special needs" of Chile as a developing country, particularly one facing a foreign
external debt. More specifically, Chile claimed that the EEC had:

made no conscious and purposeful effort to ensure that Chile secure a share of growth in
international trade in apples commensurate with the needs of its economic development. It
did not provide in the largest possible measure more favourable and acceptable conditions
of access to world markets for these products, as required under Article XXXVI. Nor did
the Community refrain to the fullest extent possible from introducing non-tariff import
barriers on apples, which were of particular export interest to Chile, a less-developed contracting party, as required under Article XXXVII:1(c).[23]

Chile further argued that the EEC had in fact taken a series of measures to discriminate against Chilean imports of apples vis-à-vis imports of apples from other
developing country suppliers. Chile also relied on the standstill commitment
of the Punta Del Este Declaration launching the Uruguay Round negotiations,
whereby contracting parties undertook not to take any new restrictive trade measures until the completion of the negotiations. This is the most technical argument
yet regarding a specific provision of Part IV. Still, it does not engage in the sort of
logical, methodical, and systematic reasoning outlined above as an alternative to
the panels' 1980 cases. The Panel's report in *EEC–Dessert Apples* suffers from the
same shortcomings. As in the two 1980 cases, the Panel focused on what it saw as
procedural obligations under Part IV without taking into account the different
provisions.

However, the case provides an interesting insight on the balance and intercon-
nection between contracting parties' obligations under Part IV and under Parts I,
II, and III of the GATT. The Panel stated that "the commitments entered into
by contracting parties under Article XXXVII were additional to their obligations
under Parts I–III of the General Agreement, and that these commitments thus
applied to measures which were permitted under Parts I–III."[24] Hence, a measure
must first be authorized under Parts I–III before it can be examined under Part IV
and, presumably, must then satisfy the additional requirements of Part IV with
respect to developing contracting parties. Indeed, the Panel in this case concluded
that, while the EEC had fallen short of its Part IV obligations, the determining

---

[22] GATT Panel Report, *EEC–Dessert Apples*.   [23] Ibid at para 8.4.
[24] Ibid at para 12.31.

factor was that the measures in question primarily failed to pass muster under Part III of the GATT. Hence, no further inquiry was required with respect to Part IV.

The Panel's reasoning forecloses the possibility that measures taken under Part IV could be recognized as valid exceptions to obligations under Parts I–III of the GATT. This interpretation is consistent with the EEC's argument that "Part IV did not, and could not, mean that the ECC should forego its rights and be obligated to discriminate against other contracting parties."[25] The first part of that statement implies that Part IV does not constitute a basis for a developed country to claim an exception to a discipline of Parts I–III. The second part of the statement reflects what seems to have been the EEC's usual response to Part IV arguments: It can decide which trading partner to give more favorable market access conditions to, particularly when it comes to developing countries. The Panel's reasoning and the EEC's position fail to distinguish between the cases where the implementation of Part IV would require a member state to violate a commitment under Parts I–III, and the cases where Part IV would allow a member to make an exception to its obligations under Parts I–III.

The Panel's approach is similar to the decision in *US–Sugar Quota* where Nicaragua complained that US quotas on sugar imports violated Part IV, specifically Article XXXVI:1(a), (b), (d), (e), Article XXXVI:2-4, Article XXXVI:9, Article XXXVII:1(b), and Article XXXVII:2(a).[26] The Panel decided that the quota reduction was inconsistent with US obligations under Part II of the GATT and therefore "saw no need to pursue the question whether the actions was also contrary to the United States' more general commitments under Part IV."[27] A violation of a Part II obligation effectively overrode a possible cumulative violation under Part IV.

American legal commentators might call the Panel's approach "judicial economy." International law analysts may stress the Panel's qualification of commitments under Part IV as being more general in nature than those under Part III, in reference to the *lex specialis* rule of treaty interpretation. If in fact the Panel is referring to the *lex specialis* rule, it recognizes that obligations from the different Parts regulate the same object and may conflict so as to warrant the application of the rule. Yet, the Panel in the 1989 *EEC–Dessert Apples* case saw the obligations of Part IV as supplementary to those of Parts I–III, which would not call for the *lex specialis* rule.

More recently, China made several arguments based on Article XXXVI:5 in *China–Raw Materials*. First, with respect to the interpretation of GATT Article XI:2(a), China stated:

Article XXXVI:5 and its Ad Note support the view that Article XI:2(a) may be applied to address a product that is important to domestic processing industries. China submits that Article XXXVI:5 shows that the essential nature of a "primary product" for a developing country may derive from the product's role in securing economic diversification through the development of domestic processing industries. According to China, the customary

---

[25] Ibid at para 8.5.   [26] GATT Panel Report, *US–Sugar Quota*, at para 3.7.
[27] Ibid at para 4.6.

norm in international law of sovereignty over natural resources was developed in recognition of the "essential" role that natural resources play in the progress and development of states that possess those resources. China considers that Article XXXVI:5 applies to China in the same manner as it applies to other Members, and that China did not forgo—either through its Accession Protocol or Working Party Report—any particular treatment that may accrue to it under this provision as a developing country. (para 7.265, footnotes omitted)

Second, China used Article XXXVI:5 as a modifier to Article XX(g), arguing that the development provision of Part IV allowed China to impose different restrictions on domestic and foreign suppliers for measures relating to the conservation of exhaustible natural resources.[28] The EU, United States, and Mexico (complainants in this case) vigorously opposed these interpretations.

The Panel responded to these arguments in what perhaps constitutes the most extensive discussion of Part IV and general development arguments in a report. On the one hand, it rejected China's use of Article XXXVI to assist in the reading of Article XI, concluding that "GATT Article XXXVI:5 and its Ad Note does not assist the Panel in its interpretation of the meaning of 'essential products' in Article XI:2(a). Regardless of the particular status of China's development, as the complainants note, neither Article XI nor Article XXXVI:5 provide that Article XI should hold a different meaning or be applied differently for developing countries." On the other hand, it did agree that the determination whether a product is "essential" to a Member under Article XI:2(a) "must take into consideration the particular circumstances faced by that Member at the time that a Member applied the restriction."[29] With respect to the Article XX(g) argument, the Panel also rejected the use of Article XXXVI as "context" to be used for interpretation pursuant to the Vienna Convention rules on the interpretation of treaties by simply stating:

The Panel has a certain difficulty in seeing how a reference to the right to diversification set out in Article XXXVI:5 can assist it in its interpretation of Article XX(g). Even assuming that China has properly identified an interpretative ambiguity in Article XX(g), and that Article XXXVI:5 includes a right to economic diversification—which we are not suggesting it does—we cannot agree with China that such a right could undermine or even contradict the terms of paragraph (g) that require even-handed domestic restrictions on production or consumption.[30]

However, the Panel also engaged in an extensive discussion of the right to permanent sovereignty over natural resources and the Preamble to the Marrakesh Agreement to guide its interpretation of Article XX(g). In other words, in both instances, the Panel declined to rely on Part IV but used general rules of public international law regarding development to reach a similar result. The move is somewhat surprising in light of the preference for textual analysis that typically pervades panel findings. It is perhaps explained by a reluctance to open the door to development arguments grounded in the WTO agreements specifically, which

---

[28] Panel Reports, *China–Raw Materials*, at para 7.403.
[29] Ibid, para 7.282; see also para 7.306.   [30] Ibid, para 7.400.

would be harder to limit in the future, whereas looking to extraneous international obligations allows the panel to retain more flexibility and discretion.

What lessons may be drawn from the adjudication of Part IV for other provisions drafted in the language of endeavor or best effort?

Developing countries seemingly showed little faith in the enforceability of Part IV in disputes. When intervening as third parties, they made fairly general references to Part IV, without even claiming a particular remedy to the alleged breach of Part IV. Probably because the arguments were often marginal in the case, the panels often failed to address the issue. Had developing country litigants been more assertive in their Part IV claims, or had they better honed their arguments, it is possible that a more robust jurisprudence could have emerged. The ambiguities in the drafting of Part IV may account for that tentativeness in the arguments. Chapter 6 offers some avenues for a sharper interpretation, but it relies on more modern evolutions of international law and treaty interpretation that would not necessarily have been available to GATT members in the 1980s. The professionalization of dispute adjudication is also a recent evolution. In the past, lawyers or scholars with a comprehensive knowledge of public international law interpretation were rarely on GATT panels. Similarly, developing country representatives arguing their cases before panels potentially lacked the necessary background to make technical international law arguments. It must also be remembered that the GATT legal system was then seen as relatively insular from the rest of public international law. While it is now commonplace to make references to methods of interpretation exogenous to the WTO, such was not the case in the GATT years.

While the political importance of Part IV has receded as other sectors took the strategic lead over trade in goods, valid points remain regarding treaty interpretation and the development of a robust case law in the face of drafting ambiguities. GATT panels have passed on the opportunity to confront the language of Part IV and members have not sought to give substance to the provisions where it was possible to do so. The 2011 case of *China–Raw Materials* provides an interesting counterpoint. Generally, China has been increasingly forceful in making development arguments in recent disputes and it will be interesting to see whether this strategy will spur a reconsideration of Part IV. In the meantime, framework or conditional language such as that used in certain provisions of Part IV is still used in SDT proposals submitted in the Doha Round (see Chapter 10). In a number of cases, these proposals also pose problems of conflict and coordination with other WTO obligations similar to the issues in Part IV cases.

2.2 Disputing trade preferences and the application of the Enabling Clause

Implicit in the cases involving Part IV of the GATT are issues of differentiation between developing members. The Enabling Clause, with its reference to GSP, requires that preferences be granted to developing countries on a general and non-discriminatory basis.[31] However, most post-colonial European preference programs flew in the face of those requirements. In fact, the compatibility of preference programs with the GATT and the Enabling Clause has been identified as an issue in several cases since the late 1980s,[32] but only reached full adjudication with the *EC–Tariff Preferences* dispute in 2002–2004.[33] Some developing countries, particularly India, have been keenly aware over the years of the risks and questions posed by preferential schemes beneficial to some but not all developing countries, both in economic and legal terms.

The focus of this section is to assess how preferences, as a legal tool, have been implemented and what legal issues they have raised regarding the coherence of the international trade regime. It does not concern itself with the debate on the economic value of preferences, which is best explored in the economics literature.

A case with many precedents

Preferences were first discussed in dispute settlement by Australia in the *Australia Waiver* case adjudicated shortly after Part IV came into effect.[34] In that case, Australia sought a waiver from its MFN obligation in order to grant preferential tariffs to certain manufactured and semi-manufactured goods of export interest to developing countries, without reciprocity, up to a defined quota. Australia presented a list of products and an indicative list of potential beneficiaries, along with queries regarding how to determine which countries should be beneficiaries. The consultations with the Working Party focused on:

- the risk of arbitrary discrimination between beneficiaries and non-beneficiaries;
- the risk of trade diversion of products from non-beneficiaries to products of beneficiaries;
- whether the varying level of development amongst developing countries should be taken into account in determining the beneficiaries and whether this evaluation should focus on the state of the industries producing the covered goods or the state of the economy generally. Developing countries argued that an approach focused on "infant economies" rather than "infant industries" should be preferred. The issues raised in the *Australia Waiver* case largely foreshadow the current concerns regarding preferences.

---

[31] Enabling Clause, at para 2(a), fn 3.

[32] The EC tried to counter Brazil's claims in the GATT Panel Report, *EC–Sugar Exports (Brazil)*, by stating that its measure was a result of the support it was giving to sugar-producing countries under the Lomé agreement. The GATT Panel Report, *UK–Dollar Quotas* case required a systematic enquiry into the trade advantages enjoyed by Commonwealth Caribbean countries and territories included in the "dollar area quotas" compared to the trade conditions for third countries applicable to the same products. Both cases are posterior to the 1971 temporary waiver or the subsequent Enabling Clause of 1979, yet neither examined the legality of the measures at stake under the temporary waiver or the Enabling Clause.

[33] Panel Report, *EC–Tariff Preferences*, Appellate Body Report, *EC–Tariff Preferences*.

[34] *Australia Waiver*, at Annex B.

Many delegations from developing countries participated in the Working Party in that case. While the waiver was eventually granted with their support, most of them stated that a non-discriminatory generalized system of preferences should still be preferred over alternative schemes. India, in particular, noted that Australia's scheme differed from the generalized, non-discriminatory system of preferences unanimously proposed by developing countries at UNCTAD.[35] Argentina and the Ivory Coast underlined that Australia's scheme should not be used as a precedent. Some noted that the preferences in this case largely could have been implemented by MFN tariffs since two-thirds of the products that would benefit from the scheme were items that were not produced by industrialized countries (carpets and coir matting). One delegation noted that Article XIII of the GATT required non-discrimination in the administration of the quotas to be defined in the waiver. Here again, the question of how to resolve potential conflicts between various obligations loomed large. The final list of beneficiaries included over 130 countries (many of which were not parties to the GATT) considered to be developing countries. Although the waiver was not officially dubbed a general system of preferences, no developing country could be identified that had been excluded from the scheme. In practice, the waiver negotiations had mitigated the concerns regarding possible discrimination between developing countries, but many legal issues remained unanswered.

The first substantial analysis of the Enabling Clause transpired from the case *US–Customs User Fee*.[36] The contested measure was a new customs fee applied to all products except those from LDCs and from certain beneficiary countries pursuant to the Caribbean Basin Economic Recovery Act, a US program granting trade preferences to certain Caribbean countries. While the principal litigants (the United States, Canada, and the EC) did not consider the Enabling Clause, India, Singapore, and, to a lesser extent, Australia took it up as third party interveners. All three argued that the fee was discriminatory. India further reasoned that the discrimination was prohibited by GATT Article I:1 and was not covered by an exception such as the Enabling Clause.[37]

The Panel offered a crisp analysis in response to these arguments. It established first, that the customs fee was a measure covered by Article I:1 and that the exemption of some countries from payment was discrimination in violation of Article I:1. The Panel then found that the derogation from the discipline of Article I:1 had not been authorized by a waiver. The *Australia Waiver* case suggests that such a waiver could have been sought but that the selection of beneficiary countries may have been problematic. Nor did the Enabling Clause authorize the derogation, according to the Panel, because the exemption of the Caribbean Basin countries violated the requirement of conformity "to the Generalized System of Preferences or to instruments multilaterally negotiated under GATT auspices." Finally, the exemption in favor of LDCs was not covered by the Enabling Clause because it was not

---

[35] Ibid at 35.   [36] GATT Panel Report, *US–Customs User Fee*.   [37] Ibid at para 63.

taken "in the context of any general or specific measures in favour of developing countries" as required by the Clause.[38]

The method laid out by the Panel gives a clear template for dealing with preferential measures. First, it must be established whether a violation of the MFN obligation has occurred, and second, the resulting discrimination must be excused by the application of another rule such as a waiver, the Enabling Clause, or some other applicable multilateral agreement.

Yet, the Panel declined to give the weight of a formal finding to its conclusions regarding the violation of Article I:1 and discrimination, deciding the case instead on separate grounds. The Panel explained that "GATT practice has been for panels to make findings only on those issues raised by the parties to the dispute,"[39] and third parties are not considered as parties to the dispute.

The Panel's reasoning regarding the interaction between Article I:1 and the Enabling Clause was soon confirmed, this time in a formal finding, in the case of *US–MFN Footwear*.[40] The issue there was the scope of the Enabling Clause and whether it applied to non-tariff measures. The case had involved a non-tariff measure that gave an advantage to beneficiary countries designated in the United States' GSP scheme, but did not extend to other signatories of the Subsidies Agreement in violation of GATT Article I:1. The Panel agreed with Brazil to find that the Enabling Clause exclusively allowed derogations from Article I of the GATT:

[T]he "Enabling Clause", permits, in paragraph 2(a) thereof, "preferential tariff treatment accorded by developed contracting parties to products originating in developing countries in accordance with the Generalized System of Preferences" ... notwithstanding the provisions of Article I. It was clear that the Enabling Clause expressly limits the preferential treatment accorded by developed contracting parties in favour of developing contracting parties under the Generalized System of Preferences to tariff preferences only.[41]

India, which made the discrimination argument as a third party in the *US–Customs User Fee* case, was again a third party in this case, siding with Brazil.

After these two cases targeting American measures, it was the EC's preferential schemes that came under attack in the early years of the WTO, with two cases brought by Brazil in 1998 and 2000.[42] Neither case was adjudicated, nor was any settlement notified to the DSB. In these cases, Brazil alleged that two measures of the EC's GSP scheme violated the Enabling Clause and the MFN clause: the graduation clause, whereby preferences were reduced or eliminated with respect to certain products or certain originations; and the special additional preferential treatment for products covered by the so-called "drugs regime" designed to provide

---

[38] Ibid at para 122.
[39] Ibid at para 124.   [40] GATT Panel Report, *US–MFN Footwear*.
[41] Ibid at para 6.15. The panel refers to the GATT Panel Report, *US–Customs User Fee* at paras 6.16–17, noting that since no formal finding was issued on that question in that case, there is no decision by the CONTRACTING PARTIES that could be deemed inconsistent with the panel's finding in the *US–MFN Footwear* case.
[42] Request for Consultations by Brazil, *EC–Measures Affecting Differential and Favourable Treatment of Coffee*, WT/DS154/1 (11 December 1998); Request for Consultations by Brazil, *EC–Measures Affecting Soluble Coffee*, WT/DS209/1 (12 October 2000).

incentives to certain Central and South American countries to combat drug trafficking. As in the earlier cases involving the Enabling Clause, the preferential program was allegedly in violation of the Clause because it discriminated amongst developing countries.

While the EC did not have to face a Panel finding in these two cases,[43] the claims eventually came to full-fledged adjudication in the *EC–Tariff Preferences* case brought by India. In that case, two theories surfaced regarding the legal status of the Enabling Clause. In line with its arguments in earlier cases, India claimed that the Enabling Clause allowed certain derogations from GATT Article I:1. In other words, the Enabling Clause was to be construed as a limited exception to Article I:1. Therefore, while the complainant's claim (India) was grounded in an alleged violation of Article I:1, for which it carried the burden of proof, the respondent might raise the affirmative defense that the measure was allowed under the Enabling Clause (as did the EC), bearing the burden of proof in that respect.[44] By contrast, the EC argued that the Enabling Clause was an "autonomous right" and not a defense, so that the burden of proof was on the complainant to prove that the measure was not in conformity with the Enabling Clause. The EC argued that the Enabling Clause language "notwithstanding the provisions of Article I of the General Agreement" entirely excluded the application of Article I:1. According to the EC, the fact that the Enabling Clause was not fundamentally a positive right for developing countries did not mean that it must be an exception. Instead, it should be read as a mix of a "negative right" for developed countries to grant developing countries tariff preferences, and a "positive right" for developing countries to compel the preferences to be granted in a certain manner.[45] The EC gave significant weight to the shift from the "waiver" status of the 1971 temporary clause to the "enabling" permanent regime of the 1979 Decision.

An unprecedented number of substantive third party submissions were made in this case, particularly by developing countries. Several Andean countries (beneficiaries of the EC's preference scheme) agreed with the EC that the Enabling Clause should not be seen as an exception but rather as a "self-standing regime which affirmatively establishes how developed countries are to assist developing countries."[46] Panama appealed to the theory of *lex specialis*, arguing that "the Enabling Clause is special legislation governing the general legislation of the GATT 1994 with respect to differential and more favorable treatment of developing countries in accordance with the arrangements outlined in paragraph 2."[47] Some Central American countries, also siding with the EC, seemed to make a similar argument, though less explicitly: They "claim[ed] that the Enabling Clause does not annul the principle contained in Article I:1 of GATT 1994; simply it does

---

[43] The EC's preference schemes date to the first Lomé agreement signed in 1975 between the EC and forty-six ACP countries, and renewed in 1979, 1984, and 1990. It was replaced by the Cotonou agreement in 2000, valid between the EC's twenty-seven members and seventy-nine ACP countries. Because these agreements covered only certain developing countries for political and historical reasons, there is little doubt that they would not have passed muster under the GATT or the Enabling Clause. Eventually, the EC sought a waiver in October 1994.

[44] Panel Report, *EC–Tariff Preferences*, at paras 4.163–4.171.

[45] Ibid at paras 4.212–4.220.   [46] Ibid at para 5.1.   [47] Ibid at para 5.92.

not apply in this particular case because the Drug Arrangements are covered by the Enabling Clause."[48] Pakistan, also a beneficiary, similarly argued that:

Article I:1 of GATT 1994 is inapplicable to the Enabling Clause in light of the wording of paragraph 1 of the Enabling Clause…Accordingly, the Enabling Clause enables special and differential treatment of developing countries. Therefore, if preferential treatment is covered by any subparagraph of paragraph 2, then Article I:1 of GATT 1994 does not apply.[49]

The United States, aware of the implications of this case for its own preference schemes and having already had a taste of litigation, agreed with the EC that the Enabling Clause was not an affirmative defense to a violation of GATT Article I:1, but rather that the "Enabling Clause forms part of the GATT 1994 as an 'other decision' pursuant to paragraph (1)(b)(iv) of GATT 1994. Therefore, the Enabling Clause has co-equal status with the GATT 1947 (part of the GATT 1994 pursuant to paragraph 1(a) thereof)"[50] and "is a positive rule providing authorization and establishing obligations in itself."[51] The basis for its reasoning is much the same as the arguments made by the EC.

EC–Tariff Preferences: *The legal findings*

The Panel relied on the Appellate Body's report in the *US–Wool Shirts and Blouses* for a test on determining whether a provision is an exception: "first, it must not be a rule establishing legal obligations in itself; and second, it must have the function of authorizing a limited derogation from one or more positive rules laying down obligations."[52] It found that the two criteria were met, because:

the legal function of the Enabling Clause is to authorize derogation from Article I:1, a positive rule establishing obligations, so as to enable the developed countries, *inter alia*, to provide GSP to developing countries. There is no legal obligation in the Enabling Clause itself requiring the developed country Members to provide GSP to developing countries. The word "may" in paragraph 1 of the Enabling Clause makes the granting of GSP clearly an *option* rather than an obligation. The panel considers that this is also a *limited* authorization of derogation in that the GSP has to be "generalized, non-discriminatory and non-reciprocal."[53]

Accordingly, it decided that the EC must bear the burden of invoking and proving that the Enabling Clause applied to the disputed measure.

The Appellate Body upheld the Panel's finding, based both on an examination of the terms of the Enabling Clause and of GATT Article I:1, and on the object and purpose of the WTO Agreement and the Enabling Clause. The AB therefore also concluded that the EC bore the burden of proof that the Drug Arrangements fell within the ambit of the Enabling Clause. The AB, however, recognized the particular nature of the Enabling Clause as something more than a traditional exception in the sense of GATT Article XX, for example. The AB noted that if a dispute

[48] Ibid at para 5.64. See also arguments by Mauritius, para 5.74.
[49] Ibid at para 5.80.   [50] Ibid at para 5.144.   [51] Ibid at para 5.146.
[52] Ibid at para 7.35.   [53] Ibid at para 7.38.

raised an issue of compatibility under the Enabling Clause, the complainant had the duty to allege the violation in the complaint, before the burden shifted to the respondent to prove the compatibility of its measure with the Enabling Clause.

Overall, these conclusions are not surprising in light of the earlier cases where panels had broached the subject of the Enabling Clause. It is also perhaps not surprising that the case was brought by India, which had already drawn attention to the issue in earlier cases but had been impeded from obtaining a full litigation of the issue by its limited status as a third party. Perhaps more disconcerting was that the Panel, far from recalling earlier reasoning on the Enabling Clause in the *US–Customs User Fee* and *US–MFN Footwear* cases and finding that only the legal technicality of the third parties' status prevented the panels from making some formal findings in those cases, relied instead on tangential cases and reasoned by analogy in reference to GATT Article XX.

The other important aspect of the adjudication of the Enabling Clause is defining the scope of the non-discrimination requirement of footnote 3 of the Enabling Clause. In short, the issue is whether the requirement for non-discrimination in GSP schemes (Paragraph 2(a)) is modified by Paragraph 3(c) reading: "Any differential and more favourable treatment provided under this clause:...shall in the case of such treatment accorded by developed contracting parties to developing countries be designed and, if necessary, modified, to respond positively to the development, financial and trade needs of developing countries."

If Paragraph 3(c) means that the preference must be designed to respond to the need of individual developing countries, then the Enabling Clause only prohibits discrimination between developing countries with similar needs. Along those lines, the EC argues that if countries are not similarly situated, treating them differently is not actually discriminatory because non-discrimination does not necessarily mean formal equality. By contrast, if the term "developing countries" is to be taken as a single, undifferentiated group, then India's argument that Drug Arrangements are discriminatory because they include some but not all the countries designated under the GSP scheme should prevail.

Since a strictly textual interpretation was not determinative, the Panel resorted to a contextual reading of the Clause relying on the drafting history of the GSP system at the UNCTAD in the early 1960s. It concluded that the only allowed differentiation was between developing countries and LDCs.[54] Hence, while the reality is that individual developing countries may indeed have different needs "the only appropriate way [under paragraph 3(c) of the Enabling Clause] of responding to the differing development needs of developing countries is for preference-giving countries to ensure that their [GSP] schemes have sufficient breadth of product coverage and depth of tariff cuts to respond positively to those differing needs."[55]

The AB focused its inquiry on the meaning of "similarly situated" and reframed the parties' arguments in that context, finding that both parties agreed that discrimination was prohibited only between similarly situated countries. It read India's argument to mean that all GSP beneficiaries were similarly situated, whereas the

---

[54] Panel Report, *EC–Tariff Preferences*, at paras 7.80–7.116, 7.151.   [55] Ibid at para 7.149.

EC argued that only countries with similar development needs were similarly situated as a group distinct from countries with other development needs.[56] Because it found the Panel's position that Paragraph 3 could not have meant "the needs of *individual* developing members" unwarranted, the AB opened the door to some measure of differentiation. In a finding that was hotly contested by many developing countries, the AB announced that Paragraph 3(c) of the Enabling Clause "authoriz[es] preference-granting countries to 'respond positively' to 'needs' that are *not* necessarily common or shared by all developing countries. Responding to the 'needs of developing countries' may thus entail treating different developing-country beneficiaries differently."[57] The AB also found support for its finding in the preamble to the WTO Agreement. Yet, not just any kind of differentiation will pass muster: Only differentiations that are objectively linked to the development, financial, and trade needs of developing countries will be acceptable.[58] The AB then extended its conclusions regarding the interpretation of "developing countries" in Paragraph 3 to the terms as used in Paragraph 2(a). Hence, there too, "developing countries" need not be considered strictly collectively so that "paragraph 2(a) does not prohibit preference-granting countries from according different tariff preferences to different sub-categories of GSP beneficiaries."[59]

While the *EC–Tariff Preferences* case certainly is a major landmark in the WTO's case law, many aspects of the decision were foreshadowed by a string of cases dating back to the early years of the Enabling Clause that had never reached full fruition for legal, technical, or political reasons. The main departure from earlier cases is the AB's announcement of a principle of differentiation between developing countries. While the ruling is limited to the Enabling Clause, lengthy discussions by the parties and in the reports regarding the role of the Enabling Clause as the paramount SDT provision give differentiation a potentially much broader impact. Indeed, if the Enabling Clause is the conceptual forefather of all SDT and it is now interpreted as allowing differentiation between developing countries, it seems likely that differentiation will permeate all other SDT clauses as well.

Undoubtedly, developing countries have taken full stock of that possibility. Some resented the AB's finding as creating a legal basis for fragmenting a group of members that found legitimacy for its demands and weight in negotiations in its common belonging to a single category of "developing countries." As a counterpoint, others applauded the AB's decision as a move to bring the law closer to the political and economic reality of the diversity of developing countries. Inasmuch as their possible recourse to SDT waivers and exceptions has hurt the credibility of some developing countries in gaining valuable MFN concessions, the acceptance of a general differentiation may help them overcome that hurdle. This is usually understood to be true for middle-income developing countries. However, the empirical validation of this argument is ambiguous: India and Brazil have spearheaded the non-discrimination fight regarding the Enabling Clause; at the same time, Mexico, also a middle-income developing country, has made it clear that it

---

[56] Appellate Body Report, *EC–Tariff Preferences*, at para 153.
[57] Ibid at para 162.   [58] Ibid at para 163.   [59] Ibid at para 175.

was staying away from SDT because it felt it put it in a better economic and political position vis-à-vis trading partners.

What impact for addressing development through preferences?

On a forward-going basis, what is the likely impact of the AB's decision in the *EC–Tariff Preferences* case on the implementation of the Enabling Clause? One obvious effect is that developed countries will have a legitimate basis for excluding certain WTO members from preferential schemes. Beyond that narrow—yet critical—aspect, the consequences fall into two broad categories.

First, individual beneficiaries will see their "development, financial and trade needs" and their position vis-à-vis other developing countries assessed by the benefit-granting members. Whether they are better situated than the beneficiary countries to do so is questionable. For example, a preference scheme that offers broad product coverage would allow beneficiaries to shift from one product to another as their economies diversify and evolve. By contrast, a multiplicity of preferential schemes narrowly tailored to subsets of countries that are deemed by the preference grantor to be similarly situated does not allow such a dynamic evolution over time. In a broad scheme, beneficiaries "graduate" naturally as their economies and export interests evolve. In the narrow schemes the evolution and "graduation" from one scheme to another will be entirely controlled by the preference grantor. This may be problematic if the grantor's economy relies on cheap imports from particular countries, thus creating an incentive to maintain those countries in their current economic situation.

The second category of consequences concerns the relationship between developing members that are excluded from a preference scheme and those that are beneficiaries. Two cases must be distinguished: the impact on North–South trade and the impact on South–South trade.

With respect to trade between developed and developing countries (North–South trade), some economists have raised the question of trade diversion, though others contest the empirical validity of the concept. Trade diversion[60] describes situations where trade of a product is displaced from a more efficient exporter towards a less efficient one by the formation of a trade agreement between the importing country and the less efficient exporting country. If two developing countries produce the same good but only one country has a preferential tariff to access the preference-granting country's market, the theory of trade diversion predicts that the imports of the product from the non-beneficiary country will dwindle, to the benefit of the product from the beneficiary country.

Whether empirically verified, trade diversion concerns have been echoed by a number of submissions from developing countries in the Enabling Clause litigation. In the *EC–Tariff Preferences* case, much was made of India and Pakistan's positions on opposite sides of the issue. While the two countries often have adopted coordinated positions on trade issues, this was a rare occasion where

---

[60] The term was coined by J. Viner, *The Customs Union Issue* (New York: The Carnegie Endowment for International Peace, 1950).

they came head-to-head because textiles from Pakistan benefited from the Drug Arrangements preferences but competing like products from India were excluded. Similarly, a number of Latin American countries benefited from the scheme, but Paraguay was excluded (and sided with India in the dispute).

The other aspect is the impact on South–South trade. In economic terms, the concern is that a beneficiary could "subsidize" its exports of a product covered by the preferential duty by selling the product at a lower price to other markets as well and thus become more competitive in the South–South trade of that product, compared to non-beneficiary producers. Another destabilizing effect on South–South trade is that a beneficiary country may have an incentive to develop its economy in a particular direction to match the preferences and hinder an alternative economic development track that would have promoted South–South trade in the longer term. In an age where economists fairly uniformly claim that the biggest gains from trade to be had for developing members will originate from South–South trade, rather than from North–South trade, the impact of segmented trade preferences needs to be considered carefully. In the meantime, a uniform preference system may be less distortive on South–South trade.

An important issue is to determine how the "development, financial, and trade needs" of developing members will be defined, and particularly whether this is to be done on an economy-wide basis or on a sector-by-sector basis within each country. A similar question was raised in the *Australia Waiver* case. There, developing countries argued that the concept of "infant economies" should be preferred to that of "infant industries," so that countries with some economically advanced sectors would still qualify as beneficiaries. The final list suggested that the more inclusive approach had been adopted. The AB in the *EC–Tariff Preferences* case merely stated that the positions of individual developing countries should be evaluated against objective criteria. Whether these criteria should be applied to the country's economy at large, to some global development index, such as the UN's Human Development Index, or to the economic development of particular sectors or industries remains an open question. Looming large is the tension between different theories of development discussed in the first part of this book.

"Upping the antes": Procedural hurdles to future preferences disputes?

Beyond the many substantive issues raised by the *EC–Tariff Preferences* case, procedural aspects also have a bearing on future disputes. Overall, the *EC–Tariff Preferences* case suggests that the presumption has shifted from self-determination by members as "developing countries" to *ad hoc* determinations on development made by preference-granting countries. The burden would then shift onto non-beneficiaries to prove that they are covered by the set criteria in order to become beneficiaries, possibly by having recourse to the dispute settlement system. As a result, from a litigation perspective, future disputes involving claims of discrimination incompatible with the Enabling Clause likely will be more resource-intensive for developing countries claiming they should be beneficiaries. Developing country litigants will have to prove either that the criteria for granting the preferences violates the non-discrimination requirement of the Enabling Clause or that their situation warrants inclusion in the group of beneficiaries, assuming that the criteria are lawful. Table 7.1 illustrates the successive burdens that fall upon each party before the AB ruling in the *EC–Tariff Preferences* case (Case 1), and two hypothetical future scenarios taking into account the AB ruling (Cases 2 and 3).

Non-beneficiary developing members can potentially now bring two distinct types of cases (Cases 2 and 3 in Table 7.1). First, they may allege that the criteria used to differentiate between groups of beneficiaries or non-beneficiaries are not objective such that they are discriminatory within the meaning of the Enabling Clause footnote 3, or are not tailored to the "development, financial, and trade needs" of developing countries also in violation of the Enabling Clause (as was the case in *EC–Tariff Preferences*). In this case, it is likely that an extensive factual burden will ensue for the complainant to make their case. It is not clear from the AB's report who bears the burden of proving that the measure is objective, and at any rate, objective is not defined in any way in the report. Is it enough for the

Table 7.1 Before and after *EC–Tariff Preferences*: A shift in the allocation of the burden of proof in preference disputes?

		Pre *EC–Tariff Preferences*	Post *EC–Tariff Preferences*	
STEP 1	Complainant	Allege & prove violation of GATT I:1 by showing that other members benefit from the measure and complainant is denied benefit.	Allege & prove violation of GATT I:1, AND "raise the Enabling Clause" (AB report).	
STEP 2	Respondent	Deny violation of GATT I:1. OR Prove that the Enabling Clause provides a defense by proving that all requirements of the Clause are met.	Deny violation of GATT I:1. OR Prove that the Enabling Clause provides a defense by showing that the differentiation is based on objective criteria and that the complainant does not meet the criteria.	
STEP 3	Complainant	Rebut defense by showing that the non-discrimination requirement of the Enabling Clause is violated because complainant is a developing country (or an LDC) and is excluded from the benefit.	Rebut defense: prove that the criteria are not objective or not tailored to the "development, financial or trade needs" of developing members?	Rebut defense: prove that the complainant meets the criteria?
		CASE 1	CASE 2	CASE 3

beneficiary grantor to show that it had prescribed some sort of criteria? Presumably, the criteria must be tailored to the "development, financial, and trade" needs of developing countries, in keeping with the spirit of the Enabling Clause, but again, it is unclear how much, if anything, the respondent must prove in that respect. At any rate, the complainant will likely bear a heavy burden proving or disproving that the criteria are incompatible with the requirements of the Enabling Clause as interpreted by the AB. By contrast, in Case 1 the developing country complainant needed only show that it was a developing country and thus was entitled to benefits accruing under preference schemes allowed by the Enabling Clause (Step 3).

Second, non-beneficiaries may allege that although the criteria are objective, the complainant meets the criteria and should therefore benefit from the preferences. The AB report did not indicate whether the burden would be on the respondent to show that the complainant did not meet the criteria, or on the complainant to show that it did meet the criteria. Potentially, the complainant could be faced with having to bring forward a heavy factual record on that issue.

Another ambiguity stemming from the AB report concerns the initial burden of proof regarding the violation of GATT Article I:1, common to Cases 2 and 3 in Table 7.1. Although the AB formally upheld the Panel's finding that the burden is on the complainant to prove an Article I:1 violation and that the Enabling Clause is an exception to that provision, the new requirement that the complainant "raise" the issue of the Enabling Clause in fact has a deeper impact on how a complainant might structure its case. It effectively shifts some of the onus of proving the case on the complainant compared to Case 1. Indeed, if the purpose of the new requirement of "raising the Enabling Clause" is to notify members of all the core elements of the case, as stated by the AB, the complainant probably needs to identify at that stage why it thinks that the Enabling Clause would not provide a defense. Hence, the complainant will have to make a *prima facie* case in the complaint either that the criteria were inappropriate (Case 2) or that the criteria were applied incorrectly so as to wrongfully exclude the complainant (Case 3), and potentially both in the case of pleadings in the alternative. If it failed to do so, it could be barred from making those arguments at a later point. The AB's requirement of "raising the Enabling Clause" at the stage of the initial complaint, therefore, is not as trivial and innocuous as it seems at first sight.

When it comes to rebutting the respondent's Enabling Clause defense (Step 3), developing country complainants will also find themselves bearing a heavier burden than in Case 1. Whereas in Case 1, a simple proof by contradiction was required (showing that at least one developing country benefited from a tariff preference and the complainant did not), Cases 2 and 3 would require an extensive factual and perhaps policy inquiry regarding the objectivity of the criteria for differentiation, the adequacy of the criteria in regards to the object and purpose of the Enabling Clause, and the specific situation of the complainant vis-à-vis the criteria and probably vis-à-vis the beneficiaries. Moreover, the respondent will succeed in their defense if they can prove that one element of these new multiple requirements of the Enabling Clause was not met by the complainant, whereas the respondent will have to rebut each aspect of the defense in order to win the case. Therefore, the relative ease of making a simple proof by contradiction has shifted from the complainant in Case 1 to the respondent in Cases 2 and 3. Developing countries, typically the parties with the least resources, will now be forced to make the hardest arguments. The combination of the changed standard in the Enabling Clause allowing differentiation between developing countries and the shift in the procedural allocation of arguments creates an exponentially greater burden for developing country complainants.

Aside from the economic questions raised by preferences (diminishing value of preferences as MFN tariffs decrease, trade diversion, and cross-subsidization), the Enabling Clause litigation shows that preferences are a problematic instrument for developing members from a legal standpoint. While the *EC–Tariff Preferences* case eventually established some baseline regarding discrimination, it left many unanswered questions regarding the allocation of the burden of proof and the possibility of legal differentiation between developing members.

Ultimately, it is possible that litigation of the Enabling Clause has reached its apogee with the *EC–Tariff Preferences* case. This may be true not so much because the case puts to rest the questions that had emerged over the years (in fact it opened more questions) but rather because it sought to exclude the developing members with the higher resources while simultaneously making it more onerous for members with limited resources to successfully bring a case. As the developing countries with the most resources historically were the ones who brought cases and probably would have continued to do so in the future, the *EC–Tariff Preferences* case will likely create a chilling effect on Enabling Clause litigation. From a practical perspective, the EU policy of converting its preference programs into "economic partnership agreements" in the form of bilateral or regional treaties may also move the preferences debate to another legal arena altogether. Preference programs remain used by members in Asia and the Pacific region.

2.3 Enforcing technical SDT provisions

Over a hundred technical SDT provisions are to be found across the Uruguay Round agreements.[61] These include exemptions and derogations to particular trade disciplines, transitional time periods, and technical assistance. However, disputes are limited to a handful of SDT provisions. This section will analyze the trends for each cluster of disputes.

In the early days of the WTO, Egypt stated it was "witnessing a trend towards stricter interpretation" of SDT provisions.[62] Several years later, a study by Footer confirmed such a trend in the areas of import restrictions for balance of payments

---

[61] This research is limited to the Annex I agreements. Such a restriction is justifiable inasmuch as developing countries have generally not signed on to plurilateral agreements not included in Annex I.

[62] WTO Committee on Trade and Development, *Communications from Egypt*, WT/GC/W/109 (5 November 1998), at para 93.

purposes and of the use of export subsidies by developing countries.[63] With the benefit of more than a decade of WTO dispute settlement, there is now a more substantial body of evidence available regarding the interpretation of SDT provisions. As the remainder of this section shows, interpretation issues often turn on whether the drafting of a provision is specific enough. In general, panels are inclined to give no effect to provisions that do not set forth a clear right or obligation, but they do seek to substantiate provisions that include more readily applicable tests and standards. Inasmuch as provisions with less determinate language are still intended to have legal meaning, panels are unduly restrictive in their interpretation. However, because panels often fail to engage in rigorous treaty interpretation, it remains unclear where the limits of the law really stand.

GATT Article XVIII

Far from being a source of many disputes, GATT Article XVIII has prompted only a few cases focusing mostly on the provision's procedural aspects. There has been no dispute on the meaning and scope of Article XVIII:C (support for infant industries) or on the type of trade restrictions that fall within the scope of the balance-of-payment safeguard clause of Article XVIII:B. One explanation is that utilization of these mechanisms requires consultations with other GATT members acting jointly or with specifically affected GATT members so that potential disputes may be resolved without formal recourse to the dispute settlement system. In fact, it has even been argued that such consultation procedures should preempt the general dispute settlement procedures of Article XXIII. In *India–Import Restrictions on Almonds*, India had initially opposed the establishment of a panel on that basis, arguing that "the procedures in Article XVIII:B12(d), when available, should be followed, rather than that provided in Article XXIII."[64] Yugoslavia seconded that argument, which was also a concern for Egypt. The Panel's terms of reference ultimately did not include any reference to Article XVIII and the dispute was settled prior to the issuance of a panel report. The question arose again in three 1989 cases involving restrictions on beef imports by Korea. Korea contended that the compatibility of its trade restrictions imposed under Article XVIII:B "could not be challenged under Article XXIII because of the existence of special review procedures in paragraphs 12(b) and 12(d) of Article XVIII:B."[65] The Panel replied that procedures under both Article XVIII:B 12(d) and Article XXIII were available and that the parties could resort to either.

With respect to Article XVIII, the lack of disputes may reflect the fact that balance-of-payment measures or infant industry protection would have been examined and approved upstream in the relevant committees. It perhaps also

---

[63] M.E. Footer, *An Institutional and Normative Analysis of the World Trade Organization* (Leiden: Martinus Nijhoff, 2006), at 84–7.

[64] Unadopted GATT Panel Report, *India–Import Restrictions on Almonds*.

[65] GATT Panel Report, *Korea–Beef (US)*, at 37. See also parallel disputes brought by Australia and New Zealand and adjudicated on the same day: GATT Panel Report, *Korea–Beef (Australia)* and GATT Panel Report, *Korea–Beef (New Zealand)*.

testifies to a certain restraint by developed countries not wishing to challenge too heavily the use of a rare development provision of the GATT.

In the case of *Korea–Beef (US)* the complainants argued that the restrictions originally imposed for balance of payments purposes were no longer necessary because Korea's balance of payments difficulties had ended. The Panel agreed, concluding that economic circumstances no longer justified the measure under Article XVIII:B. The only other case adjudicating the propriety of an Article XVIII measure pitted India against the United States, the EC, Australia, New Zealand, Switzerland, and Canada (and Japan as a third party) regarding restrictions on imports of a number of agricultural, textile, and industrial products. India claimed that the measures were for balance of payments purposes pursuant to periodic consultations with the Committee since 1957. The Panel found that the measures violated Articles XI:1 and XVII:11 and were not justified under Article XVIII:B.[66] As with the Enabling Clause, Article XVIII has been interpreted as an exception to GATT disciplines.

Antidumping Agreement Article 15

As early as 1992, cases emerged concerning the SDT provisions (Article 15) of the Antidumping Agreement, which pre-dated the WTO Agreements as a Tokyo Code.[67] Article 15 states:

It is recognized that special regard must be given by developed country Members to the special situation of developing country Members when considering the application of anti-dumping measures under this Agreement. Possibilities of constructive remedies provided for by this Agreement shall be explored before applying anti-dumping duties where they would affect the essential interests of developing country Members.

In the first case, involving a dispute between the United States and Mexico, the former argued that, under the Agreement, domestic administrative remedies had to be exhausted. In reply, Mexico queried under what domestic US rules it could receive the special and differential treatment guaranteed by the Antidumping Agreement, in particular under Article 13 on SDT (now Article 15).[68] The Panel, established after consultations within the framework of the Committee on Anti-Dumping Practices, did not address the issue.

A more extensive examination of former Article 13 of the Antidumping Agreement emerged in *EEC–Cotton Yarn*. Brazil alleged that the EC had breached Article 13 for two reasons. First, it should have taken into consideration the special situation of developing countries when comparing normal value and export price, specifically by factoring in the combination of inflation with a frozen exchange rate affecting Brazil during the relevant period.[69] Second, the EC should have considered Brazil's position as a developing country more generally and considered the "constructive remedies put forward by the Brazilian Exporters."[70]

---

[66] Panel Report, *India–Quantitative Restrictions*.
[67] The Antidumping Agreement is formally known as the Agreement on the implementation of Art VI of the GATT.
[68] GATT Panel Report, *US–Cement*, at 4, 7.
[69] GATT Panel Report, *EEC–Cotton Yarn*, at 38–39, 58–59.   [70] Ibid at 91–92.

The EC had several arguments in reply. As a general matter, it argued that it had given consideration to the status of Brazil as a developing country in the decision whether to apply antidumping duties. This position is reminiscent of the EC's position in GATT Part IV and Enabling Clause cases where it simply stated that it had already given all due special consideration prior to the application of the disputed measure. In the antidumping cases, it deemed that special consideration was due only at the stage of deciding whether to impose an antidumping measure, and not in the crafting of the measure itself. The EC therefore argued that the provision did not cover the calculation of the dumping margin. Additionally, the EC emphasized that Article 13 required giving due consideration to "the special situation *of* developing countries" (emphasis added) rather than the special situation *in* developing countries. According to the EC, the word "of" in context refers to "the situation of developing countries in general, not a particular event or characteristic of the economy of the country under investigation. The 'special situation' was therefore the global one of being 'developing', as opposed to 'developed.'"[71] Interestingly, whereas the EC argued that development considerations should be tailored to individual countries when it came to the Enabling Clause, it made the opposite argument with respect to antidumping. Finally, the EC analogized Article 13 with Part IV of the GATT arguing that both should be construed as allowing only for general economic issues affecting developing countries, such as dependency on exports of primary commodities and lack of economic diversification.

The Panel failed to find a meaningful substantive obligation in the requirement that "special regard must be given by Developed country Members to the special situation of developing country Members" and that at any rate, "no operative language delineated the extent of the [assumed, *arguendo*] obligation." Rather, the only operative language was to be found in the second sentence of the provision mandating that constructive remedies other than antidumping duties had to be "explored," but only if the duties would affect "the essential interests of developing country Members."[72] Hence, after essentially agreeing with the EC's interpretation, the Panel dismissed Brazil's claim under former Article 13.

Two other cases involving Article 15 on SDT shed little additional light on the meaning of the provision. A 2002 case between the US and a number of developing countries included some arguments regarding the exact nature of Article 15 obligations. India and Indonesia argued that the Article was mandatory and binding on all members while the United States countered that it was a best efforts provision.[73] The Panel found the provision to be inapplicable to the facts of the case and did not elaborate further on these arguments. However, interpreting Article 15 as a best efforts provision is not inconsistent with the claim that it imposes an obligation. In a case between the EC and India, it was specifically proved that the EC had not provided any kind of special and differential treatment to India contrary

---

[71] Ibid at 95. [72] Ibid at 127.

[73] Panel Report, *US–Offset Act (Byrd Amendment)*, at 5, 7, 231, 318–19 (India and Indonesia's arguments), 232 (US arguments).

to what it had claimed, a fact the Panel specifically noted.[74] Egypt, intervening as a third party, also insisted that "the developed country member must show good intention to apply this [Article 15] as a part of their obligations under the WTO Agreements."[75] Here again, the Panel found that Article 15 did not apply to the facts of the case and did not provide further clarifications on the scope of the obligation.

Lastly, Article 15 also raised issues regarding differentiation between developing countries. In a case opposing Mexico to Guatemala, Guatemala unsuccessfully argued that it deserved a special kind of SDT to account for its position as a small developing country.[76] Mexico denied that there was any "small country exception to the [Antidumping Agreement]" and the EC, as a third party, pointed out that Guatemala's interpretation would lead to discriminatory outcomes particularly in the interpretation of other Antidumping Agreement obligations. Here again, the position of the EC is consistent with its argument in *EEC–Cotton Yarn* where it pushed for a consideration of developing countries as a single uniform group, but is inconsistent with its position regarding the Enabling Clause. The Panel found that there was no applicable SDT provision to the particular elements of this case that would protect small and developing countries and that Guatemala was seeking "to hide behind its status as a developing country in order to relieve itself of its obligation."

Article 15 disputes leave a number of questions open. First, the issue of differentiation amongst developing countries under the Antidumping Agreement offers an interesting contrast to the arguments made with respect to the Enabling Clause. In a notable reversal from their respective positions in the later *EC–Tariff Preferences* case, developing countries have generally argued in Antidumping Agreement cases that their individual situation and development challenges should be taken into consideration, whereas the EC argued that the reference to the situation of developing countries in Article 15 was a general one encompassing only issues that affected developing members as a whole, not their individual circumstances. More fundamentally, the inconsistency begs the question whether development and developing countries are meant to be treated in a legally consistent fashion throughout the WTO agreements or whether they are defined differently for each provision. The first option calls for a uniform normative understanding of development, whereas the second one allows an *ad hoc*, idiosyncratic treatment.

Second, Article 15 has not been interpreted as a general SDT provision that infuses the interpretation of the entire Antidumping Agreement. Rather it has been read to apply narrowly to the specific situations mentioned in its clauses: the determination of whether to apply antidumping measures and, under some circumstances, the exploration of constructive remedies. As a result, the substance and scope of the obligations, if any, embodied in the Article have not been tested to date, despite being invoked in a number of occasions.

---

[74] Panel Report, *EC–Bed Linen*, at 353–4.
[75] Ibid at Annex 3–7, 606.   [76] Panel Report, *Guatemala–Cement II*, at 106–7, 113–14.

Looking to the future, it is likely that the nature of Antidumping Agreement litigation will evolve because the users of antidumping duties have changed considerably in recent years. During the period 1985–1994, the United States, the EC, Canada, and Australia accounted for 73.1 percent of all antidumping duty investigations. Over the next ten years, these members accounted only for 36.4 percent of all investigations and 33 percent of all antidumping measures imposed. The main developing country users (Argentina, Brazil, Columbia, India, Indonesia, Mexico, Peru, Turkey, and Venezuela) accounted for 16.2 percent of all investigations between 1985 and 1994 but accounted for nearly 40 percent of all investigations over the next decade and almost 45 percent of all antidumping measures imposed. The worldwide number of investigations has also grown overall.[77]

As a result, antidumping cases are more likely to be brought between developing countries and it is unclear how the SDT provision, if it is triggered by the facts of the case, will be invoked and applied, particularly between the middle-income developing countries which are the main antidumping duties users, and other developing countries that may be targeted by those duties. The issue of differentiation is likely to come yet again to the forefront of the discussion if the poorer countries follow in Guatemala's footsteps when it invoked SDT against Mexico. It must also be noted that Article 15 is one of the few SDT provisions in the WTO agreements that was not time-bound and that is still in effect.

TBT Agreement

Although Article 12 (SDT) of the TBT Agreement also includes several "best effort" provisions, rather than specific exceptions and special procedures, at least one panel found that it still imposed some kind of obligation on developed members. In the case of *EC–Asbestos*, Brazil argued that the restrictive French ban had an increased effect on Brazil as a developing country and Zimbabwe as an LDC, which France had not taken into account. The Panel agreed, stating that Article 12.2 required France to "take into account the special development, financial and trade needs" of developing and least-developed countries when devising its technical regulations and that it had failed to do so.[78] The Panel did not specify, however, what measures France should have adopted to comply with its obligations under Article 12.

In another case, Argentina argued that Article 12 embodied more than an obligation to cooperate and contended that "the obligation applies to both the preparation and the application of technical regulations, standards, and conformity assessment procedures."[79] The Panel made no findings on those claims.

TBT Article 12 is still in force, as it was not a transitional provision. Assuming that members have not been dissuaded by these earlier cases, there would be opportunities for developing countries to continue to press for substantiating the

---

[77] C.P. Bown, "The World Trade Organization and Antidumping in Developing Countries," World Bank Policy Research Working Paper 4014 (September 2006).

[78] Panel Report, *EC–Asbestos*, at para 4.23.

[79] Panel Report, *EC–Approval and Marketing of Biotech Products*, at paras 4.306–4.308 (see also paras 74–77).

provisions of Article 12. Chapter 6 discusses how best efforts and "endeavor" provisions might be given enhanced legal meaning in light of contemporary evolutions of international law and the reasoning is applicable here.

SPS Agreement

Another SDT provision calling developed members to "take into account the needs" of developing country members, Article 10 of the SPS Agreement presents similar ambiguities to Article 12 of the TBT Agreement. The only panel to expound the meaning of the provision, in the *EC–Approval and Marketing of Biotech Products* case, found:

[T]he obligation laid down in Article 10.1 is for the importing Member to 'take account' of developing country Members' needs. The dictionary defines the expression "take account of" as "consider along with other factors before reaching a decision". Consistent with this, Article 10.1 does not prescribe a specific result to be achieved. Notably, Article 10.1 does not provide that the importing Member must invariably accord special and differential treatment in a case where a measure has lead, or may lead, to a decrease, or a slower increase, in developing country exports.[80]

Furthermore, the Panel found that the complainant Argentina carried the burden to produce "evidence and argument sufficient to raise a presumption that the [EC] had failed to take into account Argentina's special needs as a developing country Member."[81]

This issue of the burden of proof regarding compliance with SDT provisions is a recurrent problem. Meanwhile, the Panel gave no guidance as to how "special needs" are to be understood, though it did seem to indicate that the special needs of Argentina specifically were relevant, rather than the special needs of developing countries in general. This is also an ongoing question, with developed and developing countries often at odds on the question whether to contemplate development considerations on a country-by-country basis or on a group basis.

SCM Agreement

The set of SDT provisions that has triggered the most litigation is Part VII (consisting of Article 27) of the SCM Agreement. Article 27 is perhaps one of the most technical and specific SDT provisions in the WTO agreements. As with Article 15 of the Antidumping Agreement, attempts to invoke a generally relaxed enforcement of the agreement's disciplines for developing countries have been unsuccessful[82] and panels generally require that SDT be granted only in circumstances

---

[80] Ibid at para 7.1620; see also paras 7.1618–7.1626.   [81] Ibid at para 7.1622.

[82] Eg, GATT Panel Report, *Brazil–EEC Milk*, (adopted by the SCM Committee). The EC claimed that Brazil had violated procedures when it imposed countervailing duties against certain products from the EC (an unusual situation generally). Brazil admitted that there had been some mistakes in the procedures, though not such as to vitiate major elements of the decisions to impose the duties, but claimed that its position as a developing country in the midst of a sweeping economic liberalization program should be counted as an excuse. The panel did not address this argument and found against Brazil.

specifically covered by Article 27. On the upside, the panels are more inclined to respond to SDT arguments involving the SCM Agreement than any other WTO agreements, perhaps because the technicality of Article 27 provides more guidance than most other SDT provisions. In a noteworthy departure from other WTO agreements, the SCM Agreement also provides some definition of which members are considered as developing countries.

As with the Enabling Clause, some issues have arisen regarding the relation between Article 27 and the main disciplines of the SCM Agreement. For instance, Brazil argued that the provisions of Article 27 were not exceptions to other obligations (particularly those of Article 3) but rather existed as co-equal obligations.[83] This is reminiscent of the EC's position in the *EC–Tariff Preferences* case. The issue is important as it may bear on the allocation of the burden of proof.[84] The panels and the AB have consistently replied that Article 27, when applicable, displaced the main disciplines of the SCM Agreement.

While the track record for implementation of Article 27 through dispute settlement seems encouraging, most of its provisions have lapsed, making it unlikely that more cases will be brought in the future.

More generally, disputes involving SDT and development arguments in the context of the SCM Agreement testify to a willingness by panels and the AB to give full force to SDT provisions so long as they are drafted essentially like the main disciplines and obligations of the WTO agreements. Adjudication of exceptions and derogations in SDT provisions are much less problematic if they are clearly delineated. By contrast, panels and the AB are not receptive to more systemic arguments regarding the broader impact of a rule and assessing it against the objectives of an SDT clause. These trends are particularly clear when considering the dozen cases dealing with development considerations and the SCM Agreement.

DSU

Article 12.11 of the DSU should perhaps have been the most transformative SDT provision in the WTO agreements. It provides that where developing countries are parties to a dispute "the panel's report shall explicitly indicate the form in which account has been taken of relevant provisions on differential and more-favourable treatment...that form part of the covered agreements which have been raised" by the developing countries in the dispute. Whereas cases pre-dating the WTO often failed to address arguments related to development-oriented provisions, panels progressively shifted their positions and began to address SDT arguments more systematically whether or not the parties had specifically raised them in the course of the dispute. Thanks to this evolution, a conclusion such as the one reached in the

---

[83] Panel Report, *Brazil–Aircraft*, at 44; Appellate Body Report, *Brazil–Aircraft*, at 18 (arguing that Article 27 is a transitional regime in its own right).

[84] Eg, Panel Report, *Indonesia–Autos*. The panel found that the presumption of serious prejudice for subsidies falling within the scope of Article 6.1 was not applicable when the subsidy was by a developing country, so that "a complainant must demonstrate the existence of serious prejudice by positive evidence" (372). See also Appellate Body Report, *Brazil–Aircraft*, at 39–40 (upholding the panel finding that the burden was on Canada to prove non-compliance by Brazil).

case of *India–Import Restrictions on Almonds* where the Panel sidestepped a development argument on the basis that it was not part of the Panel's terms of reference, would now be precluded.

The first WTO dispute involving a developing country was *US–Gasoline*, on a complaint by Venezuela. Venezuela made claims under the GATT and the TBT Agreement, specifically its Article 12 (SDT). Pursuant to Article 12.11 of the DSU, the Panel should have examined any applicable SDT provision in the GATT and the TBT Agreement. Instead, the Panel concluded that because it had ultimately decided the dispute under the GATT, it was not necessary to address the TBT arguments.[85] Similarly, in the case of *US–Steel Safeguards*, the AB declined to address the contested issue of China's status as a developing country and whether it was entitled to SDT under Article 9 because it upheld the Panel's findings against the United States on other grounds.[86] In the *EC–Approval and Marketing of Biotech Products* case, the Panel also made no substantive findings regarding Argentina's claim that the EC had violated Article 12 of the TBT Agreement.[87]

Despite these questionable omissions, panels have generally responded to arguments raised by developing countries regarding SDT provisions, as required by Article 12.11 of the DSU. The 1999 report in *India–Quantitative Restrictions*, was the first where the Panel explicitly referred to its obligation under Article 12.11, stating that the whole of its analysis on Article XVIII fulfilled the obligation.[88] Following the same trend, the Panel in a 2002 case noted that, although Article 15 of the Antidumping Agreement had not been specifically included in the terms of reference of the Panel, it still had to be considered because of Article 12.11 of the DSU requiring the Panel's report to address the relevant SDT provisions.[89]

By contrast, a 2005 case still cast doubts on whether panels should examine the applicability of SDT clauses when the developing country party to the case has not specifically raised any such clause. In *Mexico–Taxes on Soft Drinks*, Mexico made a number of general development arguments.[90] The Panel responded that it was "aware of the crucial importance of the provisions on special and differential treatment in the WTO agreements in general, and of Article 12.11 of the DSU in particular." It considered that it had fulfilled its obligation under that Article when establishing the timetable for submissions and adjudication. Such an interpretation essentially makes Article 12.11 redundant with Article 12.10 embodying a separate obligation to consider a flexible timetable when a developing country is involved in the dispute. Finally, the Panel concluded that "Mexico ha[d] raised no specific provision on differential and more favourable treatment for developing

---

[85] Panel Report, *US–Gasoline*, at 47.

[86] Appellate Body Report, *US–Steel Safeguards*, at 166–167, 170; see also Panel Report, *US–Steel Safeguards*, at 934–6 ("the panel recalls the provisions of Article 12.11 of the DSU…Nevertheless, the Panel believes that the principle of judicial economy also applies to a claim such as was made under Article 9.1 of the Agreement on Safeguards. The Panel, therefore, believes that it is not necessary to examine the additional specific claims raised under Article 9.1").

[87] Panel Report, *EC–Approval and Marketing of Biotech Products*, at 868.

[88] Panel Report, *India–Quantitative Restrictions*, at para 5.157.

[89] Panel Report, *US–Offset Act (Byrd Amendment)*, at 319.

[90] Panel Report, *Mexico–Taxes on Soft Drinks*, at 32.

country Members that require[d] additional consideration."[91] The Panel's reading of Article 12.11 shifts the burden on the developing country to raise any applicable SDT provisions, whereas the text of the Article requires the panel report to examine any SDT provision that is part of an agreement raised by the developing country in the dispute.

In very recent cases, the panels acknowledge their obligations under Articles 12.10 and 12.11 and pay more attention to SDT provisions. In many cases, however, the panel reports merely state that no SDT provision was raised, that none applied, and that at any rate, the panel had taken into account the litigant's particular status as a developing member without offering specifics.[92] One is left to wonder whether anything more than lip service will be paid to Articles 12.10 and 12.11 in the future.

One issue is whether the obligation to consider SDT provisions should overcome the principle of judicial economy that panels have sometimes referred to. A related issue is whether Article 12.11 extends only to considerations of SDT provisions that might affect the outcome of the case. The text of the Article includes no such limitation, which casts doubts as to the validity of the theory of judicial economy when applied to SDT. Moreover, if a disputed measure violates a general discipline of the WTO and an SDT provision, but the panel only addresses the violation of the general discipline, it is possible that the losing party bringing its measure in conformity with that discipline would still violate the SDT provision. In that case, the winning developing party would have to bring further proceedings to obtain compliance with the SDT obligation, and since the issue had been omitted in the original case, it is likely that the establishment of further panel proceedings would be required. Whether any judicial economy would actually be achieved in those circumstances is highly doubtful and the winning developing party would incur substantial costs in bringing its SDT claim a second time.

Another issue is whether Article 12.11's clause "where one or more of the parties is a developing country" includes third parties. The panels' practice offers little guidance. In one iteration of the *EC–Bananas III (Article 21.5–Ecuador II)* case, the Panel, in its discussion of Article 12.11, observed that a number of developing

---

[91] Ibid at 162.

[92] Panel Report, *Chile–Price Band System*, at 56 (Panel noting that "the parties in this dispute are both developing country Members. However, as was the case in the original proceedings, there were no provisions on special and differential treatment for developing country Members invoked by any of the parties. In any event we find that these provisions were not relevant for the resolution of the specific matter that was brought before this panel"), Appellate Body Report, *Chile–Price Band System*, at 62–3 (AB examining whether Art 5 on SDT of the Agreement on Agriculture is applicable even though neither party raised it), see also AB Report in the original case WT/DS207/AB/R, 63 (AB examined the applicability of Art 15 on SDT of the Agreement on Agriculture even though both parties had confirmed that the fact that they were both developing countries had no relevance in the dispute; Panel Report, *Turkey–Rice*, at 112 ("The panel notes that . . . Turkey did not raise any specific provisions on differential and more favourable treatment for developing country Members that require particular consideration, nor do we find these specialized provisions relevant for the resolution of the specific matter brought before this Panel."); Panel Report, *EC–Bananas III (Article 21.5–Ecuador II)*, at 32, 224 (Panel noting that no SDT argument was made by Ecuador, that no provision applies and that the requirements of the DSU in that respect are met).

countries and LDCs were third parties in the dispute and were affected by the EC's policies. It ultimately decided to open broader third party access than normal.[93] While the Panel apparently linked its decision to Article 12.11, it would be an over-statement to say that it acted out of a sense of obligation, rather than mere courtesy or a general sense of fairness. Moreover, opening broader third party access, inas-much as it had to do with extending deadlines for submissions, would be better related to Article 12.10 than to Article 12.11.

Finally, the DSU provides a second SDT provision at Article 24 specifically for LDCs.[94] The Article has never been addressed by panels or the AB. There is lit-tle doubt that this is due in large part to the fact that LDCs have very seldom been complainants or respondents. Their participation has generally been limited to third parties. Yet, Article 24 is phrased broadly and does not restrict itself to LDCs participating as main parties. In fact, Article 24.1 specifically includes "all stages...of dispute settlement procedures involving a least-developed country Member." Here again, the issue of the applicability of the DSU's special and differ-ential treatment provisions to third parties has a particular bearing on developing members of the WTO.

3. Development in Disputes Regarding Implementation of Panel and AB Reports

The treatment of development considerations in disputes does not cease once the final panel or AB report has been adopted by the DSB. The member maintain-ing measures not in conformity with WTO obligations must implement the rec-ommendations of the reports immediately if practicable or within a reasonable period of time, defined at DSU Article 21.3. Article 21.2 specifies that "[p]articular attention should be paid to matters affecting the interests of developing country Members with respect to measures which have been subject to dispute settlement." More generally, with respect to the DSB's role in monitoring and ensuring imple-mentation, additional obligations attach when developing countries are involved in the case. Under Article 21.7 "[i]f the matter is one which has been raised by a developing country Member, the DSB shall consider what further actions it might take which would be appropriate to the circumstances." Article 21.8 elaborates on such further actions: "the DSB shall take into account not only the trade coverage of measures complained of, but also their impact on the economy of developing

---

[93] Ibid at 224.
[94] Note in particular Article 24.1 stating: "At all stages of the determination of the causes of a dispute and of dispute settlement procedures involving a least-developed country Member, particu-lar consideration shall be given to the special situation of least-developed country Members. In this regard, Members shall exercise due restraint in raising matters under these procedures involving a least-developed country Member. If nullification or impairment is found to result from a measure taken by a least-developed country Member, complaining parties shall exercise due restraint in ask-ing for compensation or seeking authorization to suspend the application of concessions or other obligations pursuant to these procedures."

country Members concerned." If the reasonable period of time cannot be determined by mutual agreement amongst the parties or with the DSB, the matter may be submitted to arbitration.

Should implementation still not be forthcoming, members are entitled to negotiate for compensation and, failing that, to request the suspension of concessions against the non-complying member after the expiration of the reasonable implementation period.[95] Although Article 22 of the DSU does not provide any specific safeguard for developing countries, a number of noteworthy disputes have taken place regarding the level of suspension of concessions involving the interests of developing members.

Section 3.1 considers how development considerations have been taken into account in Article 21.3(c) arbitrations to determine the reasonable period of time for implementation. Section 3.2 then assesses when the circumstances of developing country litigants play a role in Article 22.6 arbitrations for determining the level of suspension of concessions and the agreements under which suspension can be implemented.

3.1 Determining the reasonable period for implementation when developing countries are involved

When involved in Article 21.3(c) arbitrations, developing members can avail themselves of the SDT provision of Article 21.2. WTO members (generally developing) have done so in twelve cases.[96] While it is quite unclear from this small sample whether the call for SDT had any impact on the length of time available for implementation, the arbitrators nonetheless did comment on the legal effect of Article 21.2.

As a matter of litigation strategy, two sets of issues emerge:

- Who can rely on Article 21.2? Can both the implementing party (the party found to be non-compliant, typically the respondent in the original dispute) and the complaining party (which typically brought the claim in the original dispute) equally invoke the provision? Can the interests of non-parties be raised in relation to an Article 21.2 argument? How have arbitrators ruled when both sides of the dispute invoked Article 21.2?

- How have Article 21.2 arguments been framed? What particular aspects of being a developing country have the litigants put forth as warranted special treatment under Article 21.2? How have arbitrators responded to the various types of arguments?

---

[95] Art 22 DSU.

[96] See Annex 5 at <http://ukcatalogue.oup.com/product/9780199600885.do>, also indicating how much time each party requested for implementation and how much the arbitrator granted. Research assistance by Nathaniel Paty is gratefully acknowledged.

Who can rely on Article 21.2?

Case law shows that Article 21.2 is least controversial when the implementing party is a developing country that explicitly invokes it against a complaining developed country.[97] In contrast, whether Article 21.2 applies to complaining or non-party developing countries was unsettled[98] until a recent arbitration answered in the affirmative.[99]

Generally, the applicability of Article 21.2 to complaining developing countries is hindered by a relatively high threshold issue. The reasonable period of time for implementation has traditionally been interpreted to mean the shortest possible period of time necessary to achieve implementation within the legal and administrative system of the implementing country.[100] For instance, if it typically takes six months to amend a public law in the implementing country and such a statutory change is required to comply with the panel or AB report, then that is the minimum time needed for implementation. Logically then, the fact that the opposing party is developing is irrelevant to this determination. In *US–Oil Country Tubular Goods Sunset Reviews (Article 21.3(c))*, Argentina argued that the Arbitrator should take "cognizance" of the fact that it was a developing country member who was being hurt by the US tariff regime, and that the Arbitrator should use Article 21.2 as "context" for determining the reasonable period of time granted to the US. The Arbitrator ruled that the reasonable period of time would be the "shortest period possible" within the US legal system, and that this fact was not affected by Argentina's status as a developing country. Similarly, in *EC–Chicken Cuts (Article 21.3(c))*, Brazil persuaded the Arbitrator that its interests as a developing country were affected by the EC measures at the core of the dispute, but failed to persuade the Arbitrator that those interests had any additional bearing on the reasonable period of time necessary for EC implementation, because the Arbitrator had already concluded that the reasonable period of time was the shortest period of time possible in which the EC could implement its obligations.[101]

In the *US–Gambling (Article 21.3(c))* arbitration, Antigua invoked Article 21.2 and gave the most specific explanation seen thus far as to how its interests as a developing country would be affected by the timing for implementation by the United States. The United States countered that the task of the Arbitrator is to "determine the shortest possible period for implementation within the legal system of the implementing member," and thus the status of a complaining party as a developing member had no impact on the determination.[102] The Arbitrator engaged in a contextual analysis to determine whether a complaining member could ever invoke Article 21.2, but failed to answer the question on the merits.

---

[97] Award of the Arbitrator, *Indonesia–Autos (Article 21.3(c))*, at para 24.

[98] See, eg, Award of the Arbitrator, *EC–Export Subsidies on Sugar (Article 21.3(c))*, at para 99; Award of the Arbitrator, *US–Oil Country Tubular Goods Sunset Reviews (Article 21.3(c))*, at para 52.

[99] See Award of the Arbitrator, *EC–Export Subsidies on Sugar (Article 21.3(c))*, at para 99.

[100] See eg, Award of the Arbitrator, *US–Oil Country Tubular Goods Sunset Reviews (Article 21.3(c))*, at para 52.

[101] Award of the Arbitrator, *EC–Chicken Cuts (Article 21.3(c))*, at para 82.

[102] Award of the Arbitrator, *US–Gambling (Article 21.3(c))*, at para 57.

Instead, the Arbitrator left open the possibility that a complaining member could invoke Article 21.2 by ruling that he was not persuaded that the criteria for Article 21.2 were satisfied by Antigua "in the absence of more specific evidence or elaboration" of Antigua's affected interests and "their relationship with the measures at issue."[103]

In practice, however, the delayed implementation might have disproportionately adverse effects on a developing country complainant, such that the standard interpretation might not be adequate. Indeed, it could be argued that Article 21.2 justifies deviating from the traditional standard for determining reasonable time periods in order to balance the hardship to the developed implementing party to further compress the time period for implementation against the hardship for the developing country complainant of a longer implementation period.

Additionally, no arbitrator has ever allowed an implementing developed country to invoke Article 21.2 to protect the interests of developing country beneficiaries of a challenged trade policy.[104] It may still be possible to make such arguments in the future, provided the developed country can present specific evidence as to how the interests of the developing country beneficiaries bear on the reasonable period for implementation.[105] Indeed, in *EC–Tariff Preferences (Article 21.3(c))*, the EC argued that it should receive more time to implement the DSB ruling against it under Article 21.2 because the beneficiaries of its Drug Arrangements (tariffs) were developing countries. India countered that the EC should have less time because Article 21.2 only applies to developing countries that are parties to the dispute. The Arbitrator avoided deciding whether Article 21.2 could extend to non-party developing countries, finding instead that Article 21.2 was inapplicable to his determination of a reasonable period of time for implementation because neither side had

provided a satisfactory explanation or evidence of the precise manner in which these countries are particularly affected, as developing country Members, by the European Communities' implementation of the recommendations and rulings in this dispute, nor how this should affect the reasonable period of time for implementation.[106]

Similarly, both the implementing party (the EC) and complaining developing parties invoked Article 21.2 in *EC–Export Subsidies on Sugar (Article 21.3(c))*. There again, the EC did so on the ground that Article 21.2 also applies to developing countries that are not parties to the dispute. The Arbitrator concluded that Article 21.2 required "to pay particular interests to matters affecting... *complaining* parties to the dispute" (emphasis added) and that Brazil and Thailand had sufficiently demonstrated that their interests as developing countries were relevant for a determination of the reasonable period of time for implementation. Regarding the non-party ACP countries whose interests were cited by the EC, and other developing countries generally, the Arbitrator concluded that the EC had not submitted

---

[103] Ibid at para 62.
[104] Award of the Arbitrator, *EC–Export Subsidies on Sugar (Article 21.3(c))*, at para 102; Award of the Arbitrator, *EC–Tariff Preferences (Article 21.3(c))*, at para 59.
[105] See, eg, Award of the Arbitrator, *EC–Export Subsidies on Sugar (Article 21.3(c))*, at para 102.
[106] Award of the Arbitrator, *EC–Tariff Preferences (Article 21.3(c))*, at para 59.

sufficient evidence to satisfy Article 21.2 criteria. The Arbitrator also declined to answer the question of whether Article 21.2 could ever be applicable to non-party developing countries.[107]

An equally contentious issue is the applicability of Article 21.2 when both complaining and implementing parties are developing countries, and both invoke the provision.[108] In every instance where that was the case, the arbitrator decided that the interests of both parties as developing countries offset each other and therefore Article 21.2 had no bearing on what constituted a reasonable period of time for implementation.[109]

Apparently, the only possibility for Article 21.2 to commend a particular result when both sides (developing countries) invoke it is when one party can show that it is more severely affected by its developing status than the other party. In *Colombia–Ports of Entry (Article 21.3(c))*, both implementing party Colombia and complaining party Panama invoked Article 21.2. Colombia gave specific evidence as to how its interests as a developing country would be affected by delayed implementation, and argued that unlike the complaining party in *Chile–Price Band System (Article 21.3(c))*, Panama was not experiencing "daunting financial woes" that would justify an offset.[110] In contrast, Panama argued that implementing party Colombia had failed to demonstrate that it was in a "dire economic or financial" situation sufficient to satisfy Article 21.2 criteria.[111] The Arbitrator held that the interests of the two parties as developing countries essentially offset each other because Article 21.2 "[was] of little relevance," unless "one party succeeds in demonstrating that it is more severely affected by problems related to its developing country status than the other party."[112]

Future arbitrations under Article 21.3(c) will undoubtedly reveal more regarding when, how, and for whom Article 21.2 should bear on an arbitrator's determination of what constitutes a reasonable period of time for implementation of DSB decisions. Two significant questions remain: whether a developing country can ever successfully invoke Article 21.2 against another developing country, and whether an arbitrator will ever consider the interests of non-party developing countries when determining what constitutes a reasonable period of time for DSB implementation.

How are development arguments framed under Article 21.2?

The question is to determine what "matters" can be taken into account, and what "interests of developing Members" warrant a special consideration under Article 21.2.

When the implementing country is the developing country claiming Article 21.2 benefits, arbitrators appear to have been persuaded more often when the

---

[107] Ibid at para 103.
[108] See, eg, Award of the Arbitrator, *Colombia–Ports of Entry (Article 21.3(c))*, at para 104.
[109] See Award of the Arbitrator, *Colombia–Ports of Entry (Article 21.3(c))*, at para 106; Award of the Arbitrator, *Chile–Price Band System (Article 21.3(c))*, at para 56.
[110] Award of the Arbitrator, *Colombia–Ports of Entry (Article 21.3(c))*, at para 32.
[111] Ibid at para 54.   [112] Ibid at para 106.

country asserted with specificity how its interests as a developing country bear on the reasonable period of time required for implementation. Claims that the implementing country is in the midst of a financial or economic crisis have also been persuasive.

Citing Indonesia's status as a developing country, and particularly one facing harsh economic conditions, the Arbitrator in *Indonesia–Autos (Article 21.3(c))* found that the "reasonable period of time" for Indonesia to implement the recommendations and rulings of the DSB was six months longer than the six months required for the completion of Indonesia's domestic rule-making process. The Arbitrator accepted Indonesia's assertion that its economy was "near collapse" and that its economic conditions were "very particular circumstances."[113]

In *Chile–Alcoholic Beverages (Article 21.3(c))*, the Arbitrator agreed that Chile's status as a developing country should factor into his "reasonable time" determination despite the fact that Chile had "not been very specific or concrete about its particular interests as a developing country Member nor about how those interests would actually bear upon the length of 'the reasonable period of time.'"[114] The Arbitrator observed that Article 21.2 "enjoins, *inter alia*, an arbitrator functioning under Article 21.3(c) to be generally mindful of the great difficulties that a developing country Member may, in a particular case, face as it proceeds to implement the recommendations and rulings of the DSB."[115]

The Arbitrator followed the reasoning in these two cases in the *Argentina–Hides and Leather (Article 21.3(c))* case: Argentina's interest as a developing country was a general factor to be considered in his determination of what would be a "reasonable period of time" for Argentina to implement the DSB ruling, despite the fact that Argentina had not identified how its interests would be specifically served by a longer time frame, and the Arbitrator's doubts that Argentina's economy was "near collapse." Indeed, the *Argentina–Hides and Leather (Article 21.3(c))* Arbitrator observed that Argentina was arguably "assimilating its 'interests' as a developing country Member with the severe economic and financial difficulties" that it was then facing.[116] Noting the general language of Article 21.2, the Arbitrator accorded Argentina special treatment, thereby implicitly accepting that an assertion of a general economic or financial crisis by a developing country is acceptable in lieu of "specific interests" to successfully invoke Article 21.2.

The *Chile–Price Band System (Article 21.3(c))* arbitration offers an interesting contrast. In the first Article 21.3(c) arbitration between two developing countries, both sides invoked Article 21.2 to support their positions. The Arbitrator refused to accord Chile any special treatment for two reasons: First, Chile had not identified additional "*specific* obstacles that it faces *as a developing country*;" and second, Argentina was also a developing country facing "daunting financial woes."[117] Whereas the failure to raise specific developing country circumstances had not

---

[113] Award of the Arbitrator, *Indonesia–Autos (Article 21.3(c))*, at para 24.
[114] Award of the Arbitrator, *Chile–Alcoholic Beverages (Article 21.3(c))*, at para 44.
[115] Ibid at para 45.
[116] See Award of the Arbitrator, *Argentina–Hides and Leather (Article 21.3(c))*, at para 51.
[117] Award of the Arbitrator, *Chile–Price Band System (Article 21.3(c))*, at para 56.

been an obstacle in *Argentina–Hides and Leather (Article 21.3(c))*, it apparently justified the negative treatment of Chile's argument in *Chile–Price Band System (Article 21.3(c))*.

A wide disparity in the reasoning and outcomes characterizes the treatment of DSU Article 21.2 in arbitrations awards rendered pursuant to Article 21.3(c). While the older cases seemed more flexible in their consideration of the impact of the circumstances of developing country litigants, more recent cases have been more restrictive, requiring a narrow tailoring between the development circumstances and the particular request for a longer or shorter time period for implementation. Some arbitration awards also seem to eviscerate Article 21.2 entirely when it is invoked by a complaining party, by defining the standard for a reasonable period as the shortest possible time in light of the legal system of the implementing party.

3.2 Development consideration for purposes of setting the level of retaliation: Article 22.6 arbitrations

Article 22 of the DSU controls the availability of "compensation and the suspension of concessions or other obligations" for a complaining party when an implementing party fails to comply within a reasonable period of time. If the complaining and implementing parties are unable to negotiate a mutually acceptable compensation agreement, the complaining party may appeal to the DSB for authorization to retaliate by suspending concessions or other obligations.[118] If the complaining party disagrees with the scope of the DSB's authorization, then the matter proceeds to arbitration under Article 22.6. Unlike Article 21, Article 22 does not include an SDT clause. Nonetheless, developing parties have made arguments based on their developing country status regarding both the levels of retaliation and the type of retaliation to be authorized. The latter is governed by Article 22.3 under which a complaining party would normally retaliate in the same sector in which the implementing party's measures were previously found to be in violation of WTO rules. However, if the complaining party can show that it is not "practical or effective" to retaliate in the same sector then it may retaliate in a different sector covered by the same agreement. Finally, if the complaining party can show that the "circumstances are serious enough" and that it is not "practical or effective" to retaliate under the same agreement, it may then retaliate under a different agreement. It is the interpretation of Article 22.3 that has raised development questions.

The number of instances where such disputes have involved developing countries is still small, but even in this minimal sample, no consistency in the parties' arguments and in the arbitrators' decisions emerge. Many questions remain regarding the standard of proof, the level and type of evidence that is required to make the case, and the types of factors that can be considered in weighing the type of retaliation, but arbitrators have shown little inclination to develop tests and standards.

---

[118] "Retaliation" will hereinafter be used as a short form for "suspension of concessions or other obligations." See S.D. Andersen and M.A. Taylor, "Brazil's WTO Challenge to US Cotton Subsidies" 2000 *Richmond Journal of Global Law and Business* 9(1) 135, at 138.

Guiding principles for the interpretation of Article 22.3

Article 22.3(d) lists some factors to take into account in determining which type of retaliation can be authorized under Article 22.3(c): They are economic in nature, both qualitative and quantitative. None of these factors specify the role or place of development considerations. Neither does Article 22.3(d) suggest that the listed factors are exclusive, which developing country litigants have taken as a license to introduce broader socioeconomic elements in their pleadings.

Arbitrators have diverged in their interpretations of Article 22.3(d)(i) requiring that the level and importance for the complaining party of trade in the sector or agreement where a violation was found in the underlying dispute be taken into account. The *EC–Bananas III (Ecuador) (Article 22.6–EC)* case interpreted the provision to relate primarily to the actual trade affected by the WTO-inconsistent measure at issue, particularly when the complaining party is a developing country and the measure affects a trade that is "much more important" for that country than the developed implementing party.[119] In contrast, the *US–Gambling (Article 22.6–US)* Arbitrator posited that the provision was meant to apply to all trade within the sector affected by the measure.[120] The *US–Upland Cotton (Article 22.6–US I)* and *US–Upland Cotton (Article 22.6–US II)* arbitrations followed the *US–Gambling (Article 22.6–US)* approach.[121]

In *EC–Bananas III (Ecuador) (Article 22.6–EC)*, Ecuador submitted trade statistics displaying the widespread inequality between itself and the EC and the importance of the banana trade as the "lifeblood" of its economy to demonstrate the importance of the specific trade affected.[122] The Arbitrators concluded that Ecuador had demonstrated that the banana trade was sufficiently important to it, relying on the difference in economic wealth between the two parties, and the fact that Ecuador's economy was "highly dependent" on bananas.[123] The Arbitrators then found that Ecuador had met the requirements of Article 22.3 in requesting authorization to suspend certain obligations under the TRIPS Agreement.

With respect to Article 22.3(d)(ii) requiring that the "broader economic elements related to the nullification or impairment and the broader economic consequences of the [retaliation]" be taken into account, the main ambiguity is whether the impact is that in the complaining or the implementing country. The Arbitrator in the first case to be decided, *EC–Bananas III (Ecuador) (Article 22.6–EC)*, declared that the "broader economic elements *related to the nullification or impairment*" primarily concerned the effect of the existing impairment on the complaining party, as opposed to the effect of retaliation on the implementing party.[124] The Arbitrator also concluded that the "broader economic consequences" of *retaliation* applied in part to the complaining party as well, particularly when the differences

---

[119] Decision by the Arbitrators, *EC–Bananas III (Ecuador) (Article 22.6–EC)*, at para 84.
[120] Decision by the Arbitrator, *US–Gambling (Article 22.6–US)*, at para 4.34.
[121] See Decision by the Arbitrator, *US–Upland Cotton (Article 22.6–US I)*, at para 5.86; Decision by the Arbitrator, *US–Upland Cotton (Article 22.6–US II)*, at para 5.86.
[122] Decision by the Arbitrators, *EC–Bananas III (Ecuador) (Article 22.6–EC)*, at para 129.
[123] Ibid at para 130.
[124] Art 22.3(d)(ii), at para 85 DSU (emphasis added).

in the "level of socio-economic development are substantial."[125] The Arbitrators in the three subsequent cases followed this approach, citing the *EC–Bananas III (Ecuador) (Article 22.6–EC)* arbitration.[126]

In *EC–Bananas III (Ecuador) (Article 22.6–EC)*, to demonstrate that it had considered the "broader economic elements related to nullification" and the "broader economic consequences" of retaliation, Ecuador argued that it was facing the worst economic crisis in its history.[127] Over the objection of the EC, which argued that Ecuador had failed to establish a causal connection between the trade measures at issue and the economic crisis,[128] the Arbitrator essentially accepted Ecuador's arguments *verbatim*.[129] In support of this decision, the Arbitrator cited Article 21.8[130] mandating the DSB to consider a party's developing country status. The Arbitrator failed to explain how Article 21.8 applied in the context of an Article 22.6 arbitration.

Development arguments that retaliation in the same sector is "not practicable or effective"

In *EC–Bananas III (Ecuador) (Article 22.6–EC)*, Ecuador's status as a developing country was one factor that the Arbitrator used in determining that retaliation under the GATT with respect to primary goods and investment goods would not be practicable or effective.[131] The Arbitrator noted that Ecuador accounted for a "negligible portion" of the EC's trade in those areas, hence retaliation in those areas would not have a significant impact on demand for EC exports.

Antigua raised its developing status in *US–Gambling (Article 22.6–US)* as a reason why retaliation in the same sector was not practicable or effective. Antigua noted that it was the smallest WTO member "by far" to have made a request for the suspension of concessions. Additionally, 48.9 percent of Antigua's imports came from the United States, and Antigua's economy was infinitely smaller than America's. Therefore, Antigua argued that if it were forced to retaliate in the goods or service sectors it would essentially be subjecting its own citizens to economic hardship, but the impact on the US economy would be negligible.[132] The United States responded that Antigua's assertion that it was a developing country was "conclusory," and that Antigua had not provided an adequate explanation of why it could not retaliate on specific services under the GATS.[133] The Arbitrator ultimately sided with Antigua, but he apparently relied more on statistical data than on Antigua's developing country status.[134]

In both *US–Upland Cotton (Article 22.6–US I)* and *US–Upland Cotton (Article 22.6–US II)*, Brazil argued that it was not practical or effective to suspend trade

---

[125] Ibid.
[126] See Decision by the Arbitrator, *US–Gambling (Article 22.6–US)*, at paras 4.45–4.37; Decision by the Arbitrator, *US–Upland Cotton (Article 22.6–US I)*, at para 5.88; Decision by the Arbitrator, *US–Upland Cotton (Article 22.6–US II)*, at para 5.88.
[127] Decision by the Arbitrators, *EC–Bananas III (Ecuador) (Article 22.6–EC)*, at para 132.
[128] Ibid.   [129] Ibid at para 135.   [130] Ibid at para 136.
[131] Decision by the Arbitrators, *EC–Bananas III (Ecuador) (Article 22.6–EC)*, at para 95.
[132] Decision by the Arbitrator, *US–Gambling (Article 22.6–US)*, at para 4.2.
[133] Ibid at para 4.50.   [134] Ibid at para 4.60.

in the goods sector with the United States because such retaliation would be contrary to its objectives as a developing country and thus "costly and impracticable by definition." Trade between the two countries was very imbalanced, and the economic differences between the two countries were considerable.[135] The United States stressed that regardless of whether a country is developing or not, if it has sufficient bilateral trade in the disputed sector to retaliate in that sector, then it must do so under the DSU.[136] The Arbitrator rejected Brazil's imbalance argument, partially on the grounds that Brazil did not sufficiently explain why it would not be practical or effective to target specific subsets of the goods sector, where total goods imports from the United States greatly exceeded the level of permissible countermeasures.[137] Similarly, the Arbitrator concluded that Brazil had not demonstrated that it would not be "practical or effective" to retaliate solely in the goods sector. Nonetheless, the Arbitrator examined "whether the circumstances were serious enough" if the level of countermeasures to which Brazil was entitled were to increase in the future to a level beyond Brazil's import level of US consumer goods. Neither party made any developing country arguments at that stage of the analysis.[138]

In sum, the standard of proof remains uncertain for a development-based argument that retaliation in the same sector is not practical. No specific test of type of evidence to be adduced has been developed by the arbitrators in the few available cases.

Development arguments that retaliation in a different sector under the same agreement is not "practicable or effective"

If retaliation in the same sector is not available, then the next preferred alternative is retaliation under a different sector, but under the same agreement. With only one case to consider, there are no trends to speak of, but, as with retaliation in the same sector, the Arbitrator has engaged in some measure of evaluation of the actual economic situation of the country making the development argument.

Addressing Ecuador's arguments that it would not be practicable or effective to suspend under a different sector covered by the same agreement, the Arbitrator in *EC–Bananas III (Ecuador) (Article 22.6–EC)* accepted that the only service sector in which Ecuador could retaliate was the "commercial service" sector, which

---

[135] Decision by the Arbitrator, *US–Upland Cotton (Article 22.6–US I)* sought to determine the appropriate retaliation for export subsidies and guarantees, whereas Decision by the Arbitrator, *US–Upland Cotton (Article 22.6–US II)* concerned itself with marketing loan and counter-cyclical payments. Decision by the Arbitrator, *US–Upland Cotton (Article 22.6–US I)*, at para 5.124; Decision by the Arbitrator, *US–Upland Cotton (Article 22.6–US II)*, at para 5.124. See also Decision by the Arbitrator, *US–Upland Cotton (Article 22.6–US I)*, at para 5.196; Decision by the Arbitrator, *US–Upland Cotton (Article 22.6–US II)*, at para 5.196.

[136] Decision by the Arbitrator, *US–Upland Cotton (Article 22.6–US I)*, at para 5.115; Decision by the Arbitrator, *US–Upland Cotton (Article 22.6–US II)*, at para 5.115. The US cited the Decision by the Arbitrators, *EC–Bananas III (Ecuador) (Article 22.6–EC)* in support of this assertion.

[137] Decision by the Arbitrator, *US–Upland Cotton (Article 22.6–US I)*, at para 5.139; Decision by the Arbitrator, *US–Upland Cotton (Article 22.6–US II)*, at para 5.139.

[138] Decision by the Arbitrator, *US–Upland Cotton (Article 22.6–US II)*, at paras 5.201–5.202.

includes foreign direct investment ("FDI").[139] The Arbitrator then concluded that the commercial service sector was not an appropriate one for retaliation given Ecuador's status as a developing country "highly dependent" on foreign direct investment, particularly in light of the inequality between the population and GDP per capita figures for both parties. Accordingly, it was determined that it was not practicable or effective for Ecuador to retaliate under a different sector covered by the same agreement.[140]

Development arguments regarding whether "circumstances are serious enough" to retaliate under another agreement

If neither retaliation in the same sector nor under the same agreement are practicable, then retaliation under another agreement may be considered. Here again, no clear standard has emerged to date regarding the relationship between development concerns and the "serious" circumstances required under Article 22.3(c). It is also unclear which party's circumstances are to be considered, and which types of circumstances are legitimate issues. The open-ended drafting of the provisions suggests that any development concern having any bearing on the proposed cross-sectoral retaliation would be admissible, beyond the principles set forth in Article 22.3(d).

In *EC–Bananas III (Ecuador) (Article 22.6–EC)*, the Arbitrator subsumed the Article 22.3(d) factors into his Article 22.3(c) analysis, and indeed relied almost entirely on an analysis of the Article 22.3(d) factors to conclude that Ecuador had demonstrated that circumstances were serious enough to justify retaliation under another agreement, in that instance the TRIPS.[141]

In *US–Gambling (Article 22.6–US)*, Antigua forcefully invoked its status as a developing country to justify that the circumstances were serious enough to retaliate under TRIPS.[142] It noted that its economy was totally dependent on the service sector in the form of tourism and financial services.[143] Antigua also explained that the provision of remote gambling services was meant to be a way to diversify its economy and accelerate its development, and it alleged that the United States had initially cooperated with it on that endeavor. Antigua further highlighted the disparity in size between the two economies and its limited natural resources.[144] The United States did not dispute any of Antigua's assertions in this regard. The Arbitrator agreed with Antigua that the circumstances were in fact serious enough, citing the unbalanced nature of trade between the parties, Antigua's heavy reliance on the United States in the sectors that would be immediate candidates for retaliation, and thus the adverse impact that retaliation under the GATS would have for Antigua, "including for low wage workers."[145] The factors considered here seem broader than those listed in Article 22.3(d).

---

[139] Decision by the Arbitrators, *EC–Bananas III (Ecuador) (Article 22.6–EC)*, at para 110.
[140] Ibid at paras 120, 125.   [141] Ibid at para 137.
[142] See Decision by the Arbitrator, *US–Gambling (Article 22.6–US)*, at para 4.3.   [143] Ibid.
[144] Ibid at para 4.110.   [145] Ibid at para 4.114.

Ultimately, and somewhat surprisingly, both the parties and the arbitrators have made developmental arguments, and factored a party's developing status into their analyses, despite the lack of any SDT language in Article 22. This willingness to take into account development considerations is all the more unexpected given the timidity that parties and adjudicators have shown in invoking SDT provisions where they do exist.

What is less clear is how a developing country party to a future Article 22.6 arbitration can successfully raise the issue, or indeed how an arbitrator is likely to factor the issue into his analysis. Two trends emerge based on *EC–Bananas III (Ecuador) (Article 22.6–EC)* and *US–Gambling (Article 22.6–US)*. First, arbitrators seem likely to be receptive to developmental arguments when the size of the complaining developing country's economy is dwarfed by the size of the developed implementing party, and thus retaliation in the goods or services sectors will impose more harm on the developing country that should be benefiting from the retaliation. Second, arbitrators may be receptive for similar reasons when exports in the sector or industry in question are particularly important to the developing country's economy.

4. Beyond SDT in Litigation:
"Interpreting WTO Agreements for the Development Objective?"[146]

In the very limited literature that considers the adjudication of development issues in the GATT and WTO, Qureshi's and Footer's respective studies stand out for their attempt at a comprehensive examination of the dispute settlement system's role in supporting the implementation of the WTO's development objectives. By contrast, most commentaries only address the development implications of particular cases.

Looking at the first five years of WTO practice, Footer offers a fairly pessimistic assessment of the dispute settlement system's success in protecting the rights of developing members.[147] She notes that dispute settlement has not been very effective at protecting developing countries' market access rights, particularly in the area of textile and primary agricultural commodities.[148] However, it is unclear whether the primary cause of these shortcomings are the inadequacies of the Agreement on Textiles and Clothing and the Agreement on Agriculture, or a flawed jurisprudence by panels and the AB in interpreting developing members' rights and obligations under these agreements.

Looking at litigation strategy, rather than the application of specific agreements or provisions, Qureshi points out that developing countries have invoked development either as a relevant factual consideration or as a justification for preferential

---

[146] The expression is borrowed from the eponymous article by A.H. Qureshi, "Interpreting World Trade Organization Agreements for the Development Objective" 2003 *Journal of World Trade* 37(5) 847.

[147] Footer, above fn 63, at 55–98.   [148] Ibid at 76–9.

implementation of an obligation, in particular when the argument was not related to an SDT provision. For example, Argentina suggested that inasmuch as "reasonableness" was relevant to the application of Article XX, what is "reasonable" for a developing country specifically should guide the interpretation of that country's obligation.[149] The Panel held that the fact that Argentina was "a developing country Member which had to contend with low levels of compliance with its tax laws [did not] provide a justification for discriminating against imported products under the facts of the present case."[150] In relation to a dispute regarding India's application of GATT Article XII:2, India argued that as "a developing country with a low standard of living, India simply did not have the financial and administrative resources to identify and administer the quotas for nearly 2,300 tariff lines."[151] The Panel still found that India was in breach of GATT Article XI. The notorious *US–Shrimp* case also involved development arguments premised on general provisions such as the preamble to the WTO Agreement to justify the application of different measures. The United States argued that "its measures were consistent with the objective of respecting the needs and concerns [of countries] at different levels of economic development," while Pakistan countered that it "was in the best position to determine the measures to be taken to protect sea turtles within Pakistani jurisdiction while taking into consideration ... Pakistan's needs and concerns based upon its level of economic development."[152] India, Pakistan, Thailand, and Malaysia also noted that pursuant to the preamble of the WTO Agreement, the goal of sustainable development was to be achieved "in a manner consistent with [developing Members'] respective needs and concerns at different levels of economic development."

Panels have generally not been receptive to development arguments lacking specific ties to the application or interpretation of an SDT provision. This position may be justified if one considers that the agreements reflect a carefully balanced set of obligations, which the dispute settlement system may not change in any way. Since parties may negotiate the inclusion of development considerations through SDT clauses, it is not the adjudicator's place to write additional SDT elements into the agreements without the benefit of the multilateral negotiation process. This approach also reflects a preference for the idiosyncratic, *ad hoc* treatment of the trade and development relationship. By contrast, if the two are considered as normative co-constituent, then taking into account development considerations in the interpretation of general trade disciplines would not be problematic.

In the primarily textual interpretation of the agreements embraced by panels and the AB, much emphasis is given to the "ordinary meaning" of the terms under Article 31 of the Vienna Convention on the Law of Treaties, with the further reference to the object and purpose of the treaty seen as secondary and not necessarily integral to the textual interpretation. A contractual perspective of the

---

149 Panel Report, *Argentina–Hides and Leather*, at para 8.301. 150 Ibid at fn 570.
151 Panel Report, *India–Quantitative Restrictions*, para 3.54.
152 Panel Report, *US–Shrimp*, at para 7.52.

WTO agreements, infused by the Anglo-Saxon "four corners of the document" interpretation, also supports this position.[153]

To this reasoning, Qureshi replies that the preamble to the Agreement Establishing the WTO provides ample evidence that the parties intended to take development into account and that the panels and the AB should take stock of this overall concern in their interpretation of the agreements. Qureshi therefore argues for a moderate (re)habilitation of a teleological approach to the WTO agreements for a development objective, and finds that such an interpretation is warranted by public international law regarding the law of treaties as well as WTO law itself.[154]

So how well has (and can) the dispute settlement system protect the rights of developing countries beyond SDT provisions? Increased awareness regarding the interests and hurdles encountered by developing countries seems to have initiated a shift in recent years, with panels and the AB more cognizant that the "special needs" of developing members warrant something more than lip service. However, some stumbling blocks are located upstream from the actual adjudication and in fact prevent potential disputes from reaching the adjudicators.

Bown and Hoekman have called attention to what they call the "missing developing country disputes:" the disputes that should have surfaced but that fail to materialize.[155] Their account sees a combination of several causes to explain the fact that developing countries are not seeking to protect their rights and interests through the dispute settlement system as much as their developed counterparts. They first point to the cost of litigation as a direct barrier to entry to the system. Indirectly, this cost issue also means that because countries do not expect to be able to bring disputes, they fail to develop the expertise and monitoring tools to assess whether their rights are violated and whether they could seek a legal remedy, a point also made by Shaffer.[156] The combination of these direct and indirect effects means that many developing members fail to bring disputes because they are not aware that they could bring them. Case studies of the experience of developing countries confirms that a country's successful use of the dispute settlement process hinges largely on the resources and institutional basis available to monitor potential claims, to liaise with the private sector, and, should litigation proceed, to successfully bring or defend the case.[157]

Busch and Reinhardt further identify a shift in litigation strategy towards the pre-trial and settlement negotiation stage. Here again, developing countries are often ill equipped to bargain and obtain a favorable outcome, and the DSU procedures have raised transaction costs. That initial weakness is further compounded, according to the authors, by the fact that the implementation mechanisms in the

---

[153] See eg, G. Marceau, "WTO Dispute Settlement and Human Rights" 2002 *European Journal of International Law* 13(4) 753, at 772.   [154] Qureshi, above fn 146, at 870–880.

[155] C.P. Bown and B.M. Hoekman, "WTO Dispute Settlement and the Missing Developing Country Cases: Engaging the Private Sector" 2005 *Journal of International Economic Law* 8(4) 861.

[156] Shaffer, above fn 10, at 17 (also noting the difficulty that developing countries encounter in retaining the persons that develop an expertise in the area).

[157] Shaffer and Meléndez-Ortiz, above fn 13.

aftermath of a dispute create incentives for powerful defendants to delay making concessions.[158]

The direct cost issue has been reported in many commentaries and some solutions have been offered, mostly in the form of financial aid. The more fundamental issue is the need to build human resources that will detect when a dispute should be initiated. Initiatives such as the Advisory Centre for WTO Law seek to address both the direct cost issue, by providing legal services at low and subsidized rates, as well as the indirect effect, by providing training services and seminars.

Another major impediment to the protection of developing countries' rights at the WTO is the remedies if they do win their case. Here again the hurdles and their deterrent effect on developing countries' ability to use the dispute settlement system are both direct and indirect. In the case of a dispute between a WTO member with a high value of trade and a member with a much smaller percentage of world trade, trade asymmetries might render available remedies essentially worthless because non-compliance by the member with the bigger trading power is of little consequence for that member while it may result in a high cost for the other member. This may be the case between developed and developing countries, as exemplified by the *US–Gambling (Article 21.3(c))* case, pitting the United States against a small Caribbean developing island state, but it could also increasingly be an issue between developing countries with a large market and trading power, such as India, Brazil, or China, and other developing members with much smaller economies. Indirectly, this prospect may also mean that developing countries find that the stakes, in terms of possible remedies, are too low to be worth the resources required to pursue a legal battle.[159]

The difficulty for developing countries to vindicate their rights at the enforcement stage is also exemplified by the fact that the bulk of DSU Articles 21 and 22 cases, on implementation and remedies, involve disputes in which developing countries were complainants. In particular, the high profile cases such as *EC–Bananas, EC–Tariff Preferences, EC–Sugar, US–Gambling, US–Upland Cotton, US–Offset Act (Byrd Amendment)*, and *Canada–Aircraft*, have all been subject to at least one proceeding under Articles 21 and 22 of the DSU. Busch and Reinhardt note that developing country complainants obtained compliance in 36 percent of the cases under the GATT and 50 percent under the WTO.[160] However, full concessions generally were gained only by the richest and most powerful developing countries, particularly Brazil, Argentina, Mexico, and Chile, under the GATT and even more so under the WTO.

Finally, in a number of cases, victories were gained against developing countries with smaller economies and shares of the world trade than these middle-income developing country complainants. As the politics of the WTO turn

---

[158] M.L. Busch and E. Reinhardt, "Developing Countries and General Agreement on Tariffs and Trade—World Trade Organization Dispute Settlement" 2003 *Journal of World Trade* 37(4) 719, at 720–1.

[159] Shaffer, above fn 10, at 15–16.

[160] Busch and Reinhardt, above fn 158, at 725.

towards the promotion of South–South trade, it is likely that more disputes will emerge regarding trade relations between developing countries. How development arguments will play out in that framework is an open question at this time. The limited empirical evidence available so far suggests that developing countries have generally not tried to invoke SDT provisions or made more general development arguments against each other. That would be consistent with their political attempt at maintaining a legally unified "developing country" status and rights. Whether the increased push towards differentiation will change the terms of the disputes amongst developing countries is an issue to keep in mind in the coming years.

5. Conclusion

At first sight, there seems to be little cause for optimism in the current record of adjudication of SDT provisions and development-based arguments more generally. Panels and the AB's reports are characterized by a narrow approach to exceptions and derogations, unwillingness to read WTO provisions in light of the object and purpose of the covered agreements and the Marrakesh agreement, and a tendency to ignore arguments based on anything less than bright lines clearly delineated by explicit language in the agreements. This is also largely true in arbitration proceedings, particularly DSU Article 21.3(c) arbitrations. These interpretative methods are obstacles to the implementation of SDT provisions and prevent reading WTO disciplines together with the Marrakesh Agreement's objective of sustainable development.

At the same time, it is encouraging to see developing countries pushing for a reading of the agreements that is embedded in a public international methodology, which would be more conducive to the consideration of development as a factual or legal element in the case. Such a strategy coincides with the analysis of SDT provisions that was presented in Chapter 6. While panels and the AB have endorsed the approach in a number of areas, it has not yet had the impact it could have with respect to development-related arguments.

Looking ahead to the future of litigation at the WTO and members' interpretation of development-related issues, the current state of affairs suggests two distinct strategies. On the one hand, developing members can stay the course, continue to build institutional, human, and financial resources, and consistently argue for an interpretation of the agreements in line with public international law canons. Repeated and systematic tying of the provisions to the object and purpose of the Marrakesh Agreement, as embodied by its preamble, and a dynamic reading of specific provisions in light of developments in international law can help to operationalize SDT and to modulate general disciplines of the WTO. On the other hand, members can move away from the current drafting of the provisions and push for more explicit drafting in the future. In the meantime, they could seek General Council decisions of interpretation setting out more clearly defined obligations deriving from existing provisions. The objective would be to impose a substantive shift in the panel's and AB's approach, based on a consensual, updated approach explicitly mandated by members. Considering the current lack of consensus regarding the Doha Round, it is unlikely that members could agree to interpretative decisions, or introduce new language in the agreements. The first strategy may therefore be the only politically viable one in the near term.

8

Reconsidering Special and Differential Treatment in the Global Context

The analysis of SDT provisions in the WTO agreements (Chapter 6) suggests that in many cases, a more legally operative interpretation can emerge if the provisions are construed in accordance with customary rules of treaty interpretation, and an even more dynamic interpretation is possible if contemporary evolutions in the practice of international law are taken into account. A particularly clear example is the treatment of best efforts provisions, which traditionally were given very little legal value at the GATT and WTO, but are now pervasive in international environmental law, where they are seen as a useful instrument. The interpretation of SDT provisions and other development considerations in dispute settlement at the WTO (Chapter 7) confirms these trends. Developing country litigants have already learned the value of using public international law when making arguments under the WTO agreements.[1] While those earlier chapters proposed a dynamic interpretation of commonly used SDT drafting techniques, this chapter explores the substantive treatment of development considerations in international law beyond the WTO. It brings to light creative mechanisms developed in other treaties to deal with development disparities.

Many of the themes that WTO members grapple with, such as the cost of implementing obligations, capacity constraints, and the need for technical assistance, are also pervasive in other treaties and institutions. However, some treaties and organizations take a much bolder stance on asymmetric commitments between members with different economic, social, and political conditions. The manner in which such asymmetric commitments are built into parties' legal obligations can also differ strikingly from the WTO's more limitative perspective. Section 1 presents a number of SDT instruments used in trade and non-trade treaties, many of which could be considered in the WTO legal system.

With respect to adjudication of development-related arguments, the main trends that have been observed at the WTO find echoes in other fora. Generally, as at the WTO, adjudicators are a step behind contemporary evolutions of international law. However, the wide disparity between international judgments and

---

[1] J.L. Pérez Gabilondo, "Argentina's Experience With WTO Dispute Settlement: Development of a National Capacity and the Use of In-House Lawyers," in *Dispute Settlement at the WTO—The Developing Country Experience*, above Ch 7 fn 13, at 118 (drawing from the Textile case experience).

arbitration awards dealing with development issues thwarts the emergence of any consistent practice on the interpretation of SDT provisions that might exist in similar forms in different treaties. Section 2 presents findings drawn from cases at the European Court of Justice, the International Tribunal for the Law of the Sea, the North American Free Trade Agreement, the International Court of Justice, and arbitrations at the International Commercial Court, the International Centre for Settlement of Investment Disputes, and some *ad hoc* international arbitration awards.

1. Special and Differential Treatment in Trade and Non-trade Treaties

For didactic purposes, this section distinguishes between trade and non-trade treaties. Trade treaties discussed in Section 1.1 are mostly regional trade agreements, which have been growing in number and importance over the past decade. Although they are distinct instruments from the WTO, and a number of them pre-date the WTO, the recent renewed interest in RTAs, free trade agreements, and customs unions does not exist in isolation from WTO developments. Indeed, WTO agreements and RTAs have been mutually influential. A comparative study of SDT provisions in non-WTO agreements, then, may hold lessons for the WTO.

Section 1.2 then expands the enquiry to a number of non-trade instruments, many of which have important bearings on trade regulation. For example, the Framework Convention on Climate Change and the Kyoto Protocol are increasingly recognized as creating new mechanisms with trade implications. With development tensions sometimes at the core of these treaty mechanisms, the issue is whether helpful SDT instruments have emerged that could be mimicked at the WTO.

1.1 SDT in regional trade agreements

Perhaps counterintuitively, many South–South trade agreements contain special and differential treatment obligations in favor of the weakest parties to the agreement. Some regional agreements involving both developed and developing countries also have SDT provisions. This section will examine how RTAs determine the beneficiaries of SDT and what type of special treatment is granted. A separate examination will focus on SDT in dispute settlement in RTAs.

Who benefits from SDT in regional trade agreements?

Some agreements specifically identify which countries will receive special treatment. Other agreements note that implementation will be more difficult for some members and provide compensatory mechanisms to offset particular hardships. Certain agreements recognize that the boundaries of development do not always fall along national borders and that some regions may be adversely affected within a particular country. Overall then, RTAs are much more purposeful than the WTO in determining who might be the beneficiaries of special treatment.

A number of regional trade agreements between developing countries specifically identify which countries will be recipients of special treatment or special regimes. The Common Market for Eastern and Southern Africa provides that members shall "recognize the unique situation of Lesotho, Namibia and Swaziland...and grant [them] temporary exemptions,"[2] and the Andean Community grants special treatment to Bolivia and Ecuador, in particular calling for efforts to "seek adequate solutions to the problems stemming from Bolivia's landlocked condition."[3] The Andean Community's Cartagena Agreement creates a special regime for Bolivia and Ecuador, "with a view toward gradually reducing the differences in development that currently exist in the region. This system shall enable them to attain more rapid economic growth through effective and immediate participation in the benefits of the area's industrialization and the liberalization of trade."[4] Such "differential treatments and sufficient incentives shall be established to compensate for Bolivia and Ecuador's structural weaknesses."[5] The special regime responds to "differences in development that currently exist" and aims at "effective and immediate participation."[6] The Caribbean Community (CARICOM) specifies which countries are "less developed countries."[7] The ASEAN–Australia–New Zealand Free Trade Agreement specifies which "newer ASEAN Member States" are eligible for special treatment.[8] The Asia-Pacific Trade Agreement provides special and differential treatment for countries with special needs, especially LDCs.[9] In some cases, special treatment is limited to a particular country and specific measures, as is the case in the Trans-Pacific Strategic Economic Partnership allowing special agricultural safeguard measures for Chile.[10]

Other agreements do not identify which countries will receive special treatment, but note that implementation will be more difficult for some members and set forth the principle of special treatment on a need basis. For example, the Economic Community of West African States (ECOWAS) provides that members, considering the

economic and social difficulties that may arise in certain Member States, particularly island and land-locked States, agree to grant them where appropriate, special treatment in respect of the application of certain provisions of this Treaty and to accord them any other assistance they may need.[11]

---

[2] Arts 4.1(f), 4.4(d) Treaty Establishing the Common Market for Eastern and Southern Africa (Kampala, 5 November 1993; 2314 UNTS 265).

[3] Arts 3(j), 4, and 109–112, Decision 563: Official Codified Text of the Andean Subregional Integration Agreement (Cartagena Agreement) (Quirama Recinto, 25 June 2003) <http://www. comunidadandina.org/ingles/normativa/D563e.htm> (creating special regime for Bolivia and Ecuador).   [4] Art 109 Cartagena Agreement.

[5] Art 110 Cartagena Agreement.   [6] Ibid.   [7] Art 4 CARICOM.

[8] Art 3 ASEAN–Australia–New Zealand Free Trade Agreement.

[9] The Asia–Pacific Trade Agreement (Beijing, 2 November 2005).

[10] Art 3.13 Trans-Pacific Strategic Economic Partnership.   [11] Art 68 ECOWAS.

Similarly, the CARICOM sets out special provisions for "disadvantaged countries," which, among other definitions, refers to those countries that will need special support measures due to "the adverse impact of the operation of the [single market] on their economies."[12]

In addition, certain agreements recognize that development constraints may affect certain regions, within a member state. Along those lines, the Common Market for Eastern and Southern Africa refers to the development of LDCs and "economically depressed areas"[13] with a special regime relating directly to the issues of development disparity and adverse impact at the regional level.

Overall, a notable trend is that, unlike the WTO agreements, RTAs often recognize that the different position of some developing members is structural, rather than circumstantial. The special treatment they receive is therefore often built as a permanent feature of the agreement, rather than a transitory regime. Along the same lines, it is not surprising that these RTAs also recognize different categories of countries beyond the simple "developing" and LDC categories of the WTO. Landlocked and island states, for instance, are additional classifications used in RTAs that could help tailor the WTO agreements.

SDT measures in regional trade agreements

RTAs employ a range of specific tools to compensate for development disparity or adverse impact on particular members or regions within the treaty's coverage. Some are similar to measures found in the WTO agreements. For instance, implementation delays or "transitional periods" are used to level the playing field in a number of South–South RTAs. Even those, unlike the blanket provisions in WTO agreements, tend to be more specific to particular aspects of the agreement that are likely to be more problematic to certain members. For example, the Southern Common Market (MERCOSUR) sets forth "differentials in the rate at which [Paraguay and Uruguay] will make the transition."[14] It also gives those countries more products on the schedule of exceptions to external tariff reductions, and a slower elimination of those exceptions.[15] Similarly, the South Asian Association for Regional Cooperation sets a timeframe and target tariff rates according to levels of development.[16] These transitional provisions are likely to have a more progressive phasing-in effect than the general deadlines for implementation used at the WTO, which tend to push the actual implementation to the eve of the deadline.

Also well known to the WTO regime are technical assistance provisions. The CARICOM, for instance, mentions "technical and financial assistance to address economic dislocation arising from the operation of the [single market]."[17] Like at the WTO, general technical assistance provisions, lacking in specificity regarding implementation, tend to yield little result. RTAs in Asia, by contrast, take technical

---

[12] Art 1 CARICOM.   [13] Art 6(c) Common Market for Eastern and Southern Africa.
[14] Art 6 MERCOSUR. Annex 1, Art 1 MERCOSUR gives Paraguay and Uruguay an extra year for elimination of internal tariffs.   [15] Annex 1, Arts 6–7 MERCOSUR.
[16] Art 7 Agreement on South Asian Free Trade Area (Islamabad, 6 January 2004).
[17] Art 143.2(a) CARICOM.

assistance and capacity building much more seriously. The ASEAN–Korea Free Trade Agreement provides assistance to Cambodia, Lao PDR, Myanmar, and Vietnam in developing their legal system by training professionals, sharing legal knowledge and experiences, and improving investment-related laws.[18] The agreement also covers cooperation in regional and sub-regional development, the process by which the parties intend to share experiences with development.[19] Likewise, parties to the ASEAN–China Free Trade Agreement recognize the importance of capacity building and technical assistance. In particular, human resource development stands out as one of the five priority sectors of cooperation.[20] The Asia–Pacific Trade Agreement provides technical assistance for LDCs in relation to trade expansion.[21] The China–Singapore Free Trade Agreement has an economic cooperation provision on human resource development that contemplates the two parties jointly extending technical assistance to third countries.[22] The Agreement between Japan and the Socialist Republic of Viet Nam for an Economic Partnership, meanwhile, has multiple provisions on technical assistance scattered throughout the agreement by topic.[23]

Other SDT provisions target specific sectors, or are aimed at very concrete issues affecting the weaker members. The sectoral focus on development measures is an original feature that distinguishes the approach to development in many RTAs. In particular, a number of RTAs promote a particular sector as a way to remedy development asymmetries within the region. The inclusion of such substantive areas in these agreements shows that countries feel that obligations in these particular areas are necessary to achieve their larger objectives. The CARICOM mentions special measures to attract investment. The Common Market for Eastern and Southern Africa generally obligates members to "take several measures designed to strengthen the capacities of [LDCs and economically depressed areas]" and specifically mentions encouraging new investments and new technologies, improving supply side, and strengthening institutional bodies.[24] It also identifies several "strategy and priority areas" as components of its industrial strategy, the objective of which is balanced growth, improved competitiveness, and overall socio-economic development.[25]

In Africa, ECOWAS notes that development of certain industries will be "essential for collective self-reliance"[26] and it pinpoints "the development of agriculture,

---

[18] Art 2(2)(c) ASEAN–Korea Annex on Economic Cooperation.

[19] Art 3.2 (4) ASEAN Korea.

[20] Art 7 (1) ASEAN–China. The other four priority sectors include agriculture, information and communications technology, investment, and Mekong River basin development.

[21] Art 15 Asia–Pacific Trade Agreement.

[22] Arts 2(g), 89(2)(c) China–Singapore Free Trade Agreement (Beijing, 23 October 2008). Art 1.1(g) Korea–India Comprehensive Economic Partnership Agreement (Seoul, 7 August 2009).

[23] See, eg, Arts 53, 55, 102 Agreement Between Japan and the Socialist Republic of Viet Nam for an Economic Partnership (Tokyo, 25 December 2008); Arts 9, 17, 20 Implementing Agreement Between the Government of Japan and the Government of the Socialist Republic of Viet Nam Pursuant to Article 10 of the Agreement Between Japan and the Socialist Republic of Viet Nam for an Economic Partnership (Tokyo, 25 December 2008).

[24] Art 144 Common Market for Eastern and Southern Africa.   [25] Ibid Arts 99–100.

[26] Art 3(a) ECOWAS.

transportation and communications, natural resources and energy" as priority areas for industrial development.[27] The ASEAN–Australia–New Zealand Free Trade Agreement sets forth special provisions on trade in services[28] and investment;[29] the trade-development-investment nexus is also a prominent feature of a number of Asian RTAs.[30] One interesting and very specific tool used by the Andean Community obligates members to give preferences to Bolivia and Ecuador when deciding on the location for new production capacity.[31] The creation of infrastructure is seen as crucial to development, and thus heavy emphasis is placed on provisions addressing transportation and communications systems.[32]

Another type of SDT involves facilities to increase production and export. Some are more akin to infant industry protection, such as the CARICOM provision allowing less developed countries, on application, to temporarily suspend Community origin treatment "to promote the development of an industry."[33] Others are more complex instruments, such as the SAARC's mechanism to enhance sustainable exports from LDCs through "long and medium-term contracts containing import and supply commitments in respect of specific products, buy-back arrangements, state trading operations, and government and public procurement."[34]

A radical solution to address the adverse impact of trade liberalization within a group of countries is illustrated by the Southern Africa Customs Union's (SACU) customs revenue sharing scheme. Unlike WTO-style SDT, customs revenue sharing amongst the members has redistributive and compensatory objectives. SACU Article 2(g) states that one objective of the customs union is "to facilitate the equitable sharing of revenue arising from customs, excise and additional duties levied by Member States." To that end, the revenue sharing scheme is weighted in favor of the weakest countries in the customs union.[35] Similarly, the South Asian Association for Regional Cooperation (not a customs union) recognizes that LDCs may experience loss of customs revenue due directly to the operation of the agreement. Therefore, members agreed "to establish an appropriate mechanism to compensate the Least Developed Contracting States for their loss of customs revenue."[36] This is a novel approach to the notion of equitable development and equitable sharing of

---

[27] Ibid, Art 26.2(b).

[28] Ch 8, Art 20 ASEAN–Australia–New Zealand Free Trade Agreement.

[29] Ibid Ch 11, Art 15.

[30] Art 1.1(b) ASEAN–Korea; Art 1(b), 2(c) ASEAN–China; Art 1(b), 2(c), 2(g) ASEAN–India.

[31] Art 111 Cartagena Agreement ("The industrial development programs shall give special consideration to the situations of Bolivia and Ecuador in assigning, on a priority basis, the production for their benefit and the consequent siting of the production facilities in their territories.").

[32] Arts 4.2, 145 Common Market for Eastern and Southern Africa ("one of the major pre-requisites for sustained economic growth of the least developed countries and economically depressed areas of the Common Market is the development of adequate and reliable infrastructure, especially transport and communications"); CARICOM Preamble ("Acknowledging the vital importance of land, air and maritime transportation for maintaining economic, social and cultural linkages; Recognizing further the importance of the establishment and structured development of transport links with third States for the accelerated sustained development of the [single market]").

[33] Art 164.1 CARICOM.

[34] Art 11(c) South Asian Association for Regional Cooperation Charter.

[35] Arts 32, 34.5(b) SACU.

[36] Art 11(e) South Asian Association for Regional Cooperation Charter.

trade benefits. It sets the precedent for the possibility of a partial pool of the gains from trade, to be redistributed to those regions that are adversely affected by trade liberalization within the WTO.

All these instruments approach development disparities squarely from a multilateral perspective. This is an interesting contrast to the WTO regime, which often leaves affirmative measures to members' discretion to act unilaterally, with the WTO providing at best an umbrella allowing the measure. The use of preferences as the main tool for building asymmetric commitments at the WTO is the most salient example. Developed (or indeed developing countries that wish to do so) are not obligated in any way to provide preferential treatment: It is left for each to decide unilaterally. RTAs, and particularly South–South RTAs, appear to build asymmetries much more structurally in designing their trade liberalization process. The Asia–Pacific Trade Agreement, for instance, points out that its role in establishing preferences among developing countries would prove complementary to other international trade promotion efforts.[37] The distinction between *ad hoc*, temporary preferences and a built-in asymmetric regime is also reflected in the procedural framework for commitments.

SDT in dispute settlement procedures in RTAs

While not all RTAs have formal dispute settlement mechanisms, those that do also have an SDT provision. For instance, the ASEAN–Australia–New Zealand Free Trade Agreement mandates that development be accounted for in dispute settlement, requiring panel reports to "explicitly indicate the form in which account has been taken of relevant provisions on special and differential treatment."[38] The formulation is reminiscent of DSU Article 12.11. Most other instances of SDT in dispute settlement procedures are provided by the EU's Economic Partnership Agreements with ACP countries.

The Interim Economic Partnership agreement between the EU and Central Africa sets out a dispute settlement system closely inspired by the WTO's DSU and includes limited SDT provisions. When dealing with the time period for implementation of the binding arbitration award issued as a result of a dispute, the Agreement specifies that:

[i]n determining the length of the reasonable period of time, the arbitration panel shall take into consideration the length of time that it should take the Party complained against or, as appropriate, the signatory Central African States, to adopt comparable legislative or administrative measures to those identified by the Party complained against or, as appropriate, the signatory Central African States, as being necessary to ensure compliance. The arbitration panel may also take into consideration demonstrable capacity constraints which may affect the adoption of the necessary measures by the Party complained against.[39]

[37] Preamble para 7 Asia–Pacific Trade Agreement.
[38] Ch 17, Art 18 Australia–New Zealand Free Trade Agreement.
[39] Art 75.3 Council Decision of 20 November 2008 on the signature and provisional application of the interim agreement with a view to an Economic Partnership Agreement between the European Community and its Member States, of the one part, and the Central Africa Party, of the other part [2009] OJ L57/1.

With respect to temporary compensation measures in case of non-compliance, members shall "take into consideration their impact on the economy of the Party complained against and on the various signatory Central African States" and the EU "shall show restraint when asking for compensation or adopting appropriate measures."[40] Identical language is used in the Economic Partnership Agreement with some Caribbean Forum states[41] and the interim agreement with the Southern African Development Community.[42] In the two "stepping stone" economic partnership agreements between the EU and singular states (Ghana and Cote d'Ivoire) articles concerning "Temporary remedies in the event of non-compliance" and "Language of submissions" are materially the same. The Cote d'Ivoire agreement provides that "[t]he EC Party shall show moderation in its requests for compensation or when adopting the appropriate measures in accordance with paragraphs 1 and 2 and shall take account of the fact that the Cote d'Ivoire Party is a developing country."[43] The only difference in the Ghana provision is the replacement of the words "show moderation" with "exercise due restraint."[44] Unlike DSU Articles 21 and 22 discussed in Chapter 7, the interests of other parties to the agreement that were not necessarily involved in the dispute are specifically mentioned. The temporary remedies article contains the strongest development language as it plainly identifies the non-EU party state as a developing country.

1.2 SDT and development in other treaties

A dozen environmental instruments, several commodities agreements, and one human rights pact contain SDT provisions for some members. As in the trade agreements discussed above, the beneficiaries, the form, and the extent of SDT varies greatly by treaty and also over time. Indeed, many instruments drafted in the late 1960s, 1970s, and early 1980s reflect the then-prevalent discourse for a New International Economic Order in their stated objectives, if not always in their provisions.

Overall, SDT provisions in these agreements are very much in line with the main features of SDT at the WTO. They call for treaty parties to provide technical assistance (including technology sharing, and research and development),[45]

---

[40] Ibid Arts 77.2 and 77.3.

[41] Art 211 Economic Partnership Agreement between the CARIFORUM states, of the one part, and the European Community and its Member States, of the other part [2008] OJ L289/I.

[42] Art 77 Interim Agreement with a view to an economic partnership agreement between the European Community and its Member States, of the one part, and the SADC EPA States, of the other part (2009) CE/SADC.

[43] Stepping Stone Economic Partnership Agreement between Cote d'Ivoire, of the one part, and the European Community and its Member States, of the other part (2009) Official Journal of the EU L 59 at 19 and Stepping Stone Economic Partnership Agreement between Ghana, of the one part, and the European Community and its Member States, of the other part CE/GH at 63.

[44] Ibid.

[45] See eg, Arts 27(1)(f), 27(2)(b), and 30(5) International Tropical Timber Agreement (ITTA) (Geneva, 26 January 1994; 33 ILM 1014); Arts 4, 6(e), 17, and 18 Convention to Combat Desertification in Those Countries Experiencing Serious Drought And/or Desertification, Particularly in Africa (UNCCD) (Paris, 17 June 1994; 33 ILM 1328); Arts 4(5) and 4(9) Framework

capacity building,[46] longer time-periods for implementation,[47] and some measures of exemptions,[48] typically combining language of legal obligation ("the parties *shall*") and endeavor or best efforts language ("fully take into account"). For the most part, these agreements also refrain from establishing criteria or a list of the beneficiary countries, using instead generic terms such as "developing countries" or "least-developed countries," the latter presumably in reference to the UN list.[49] In a number of cases, beneficiaries of SDT are defined in reference to an injury. For instance, several treaties provide special provisions for those developing countries that suffer adverse impacts or other injuries from the implementation of the treaty.[50]

However, a few original features are of greater interest to interpret and to move the WTO framework forward. Some may seem mundane, dealing with sponsored travel arrangements from LDC representatives; others are indicative of shifts in drafting style of SDT. A number of these novel SDT arrangements are examined below, from the most specific to the more general.

Convention on Climate Change (UNFCCC) (New York, 9 May 1992; 31 ILM 849); Arts 8 and 13.2(b) International Treaty on Plant Genetic Resources for Food and Agriculture (PGRFA) (Rome, 3 November 2001; 2400 UNTS 303); Arts 5.2 and 10.1 Montreal Protocol on Substances that Deplete the Ozone Layer (Montreal Protocol) (Montreal, 16 September 1987; 1522 UNTS 3).

[46] See, eg, Arts 22.1, 22.2, and 28.4 Cartagena Protocol on Biosafety to the Convention on Biological Diversity (Cartagena Protocol) (Montreal, 20 January 2000; 39 ILM 1027); Art 19 UNCCD; Arts 5(b), 5(c), 6(a)(ii), 9(2)(d) UNFCCC.

[47] See eg, Sch B, para 1 Agreement Establishing the Common Fund for Commodities (CFC) (Geneva, 27 June 1980; 19 ILM 896); Art 12(5) UNFCCC (tiered calendar for developed, developing, and LDCs to make report on their implementing measures); Art 5.1 Montreal Protocol (certain developing countries exempt for 10 years).

[48] See eg, Art 12(5) United Nations Framework Convention on Climate Change (LDCs to make communications on their implementation "at their discretion"); Sch B, para 2 CFC Agreement (no suspension of membership for LDCs for failure to meet their financial obligations).

[49] Some important exceptions are Annex, para 15(d) Agreement Relating to the Implementation of Part XI of the United Nations Convention on the Law of the Sea of 10 December 1982 (Part XI UNCLOS) (New York, 28 July 1994; 33 ILM 1309) (defining beneficiaries for purposes of the decision-making under para 3); Arts 7, 13 United Nations Convention to Combat Desertification (priority given to African state parties and LDCs); Art 5.1 Montreal Protocol (certain developing countries whose annual calculated level of consumption of the controlled substances is less than 0.3 kilograms per capita on the date of the entry into force of the Protocol benefit from certain delayed implementation provisions); Art 8 United Nations Framework Convention on Climate Change (listing nine categories of countries that are likely to suffer more critical adverse impact).

[50] See eg, Annex, para 7 Part XI UNCLOS (economic assistance may be provided to "developing countries which suffer serious adverse effects on their export earnings or economies resulting from a reduction in the price of an affected mineral or in the volume of exports of that mineral, to the extent that such reduction is caused by activities in the Area"); Art 4(10) UNFCCC (parties shall "take into consideration in the implementation of the commitments of the Convention the situation of Parties, particularly developing country Parties, with economies that are vulnerable to the adverse effects of the implementation of measures to respond to climate change. This applies notably to Parties with economies that are highly dependent on income generated from the production, processing and export, and/or consumption of fossil fuels and associated energy-intensive products and/or the use of fossil fuels for which such Parties have serious difficulties in switching to alternatives."); see eg, Art 32 International Tropical Timber Agreement (Geneva, 16–27 January 2006; TD/TIMBER.3/12); Art 48 International Cocoa Agreement (Geneva, 16 July 1993; 1766 UNTS 3).

Some agreements offer very practical technical assistance directly aimed at participation, which is also at issue in the WTO. This is the case in the climate change arena, where the Instrument for the Establishment of the Restructured Global Environment Facility provides that "the costs of Council meetings, including travel and subsistence of Council Members from developing countries, in particular the Least Developed Countries, shall be disbursed from the administrative budget of the Secretariat as necessary."[51] At the WTO, the cost of attending meetings, in particular for LDCs which do not maintain a permanent mission in Geneva, is a well-known obstacle to meaningful participation in negotiations and day-to-day committee work. In addition to sponsoring travel arrangements, the greater use of technology to limit the need for travel, while affording an opportunity to participate in meetings through video conference calls, are practical means of supporting members lacking in human and financial capacity.

Both technical assistance and capacity building largely hinge on the availability of financial resources. While specific budgetary allocations remain rare, several conventions, particularly those that are more in the nature of framework conventions, include numerous provisions mandating the parties to find financial resources to support the weakest parties in their implementation efforts and to compensate for asymmetric adverse impact resulting from the treaty implementation. These conventions typically call on coordination efforts with other multilateral and regional initiatives where more funds are available.[52] Leveraging resources from other international bodies and agreements is quite original and could hold some promise for the WTO. Indeed, the WTO budget and administrative capacities are extremely limited and do not afford the means to provide real support for developing members. Additional resources are garnered from members' voluntary contributions (see Chapter 11 discussing aid for trade), but enhanced coordination and cooperation with more cash-rich organizations could be helpful in achieving common or complementary goals. Additionally, interagency collaboration is also likely to reduce incompatible or mutually counterproductive policies and to improve agenda coordination on substantive issues.[53]

A number of WTO SDT provisions disconnect the beneficiary from the obligation so that the beneficiary member had no control over how, when, and for how long it would receive a benefit from another member. By contrast, several non-trade instruments, especially in recent years, seem more attuned to the drawbacks of such a system, and they place more power in the hands of the beneficiaries to decide what measures are needed to meet their development needs, even when the primary obligation falls on a non-beneficiary member. The United Nations Convention to Combat Desertification provides an example: Developed country parties undertake to "provide substantial financial resources and other forms of

---

[51] Section III, Art 19 Instrument for the Establishment of the Restructured Global Environment Facility (Geneva, 16 March 1994; 33 ILM 1273). See also Art 16 noting that of the thirty-two Council members, sixteen are from developing countries.

[52] See eg, Arts 20, 21 United Nations Convention to Combat Desertification; Art 11(5) UNFCCC Art 5.3 Montreal Protocol.

[53] Art 14 United Nations Convention to Combat Desertification.

support to assist affected developing country Parties, particularly those in Africa, effectively to develop and implement their own long-term plans and strategies to combat desertification and mitigate the effects of drought."[54] Other instruments place the onus on the treaty parties to craft the supporting measures, which allows the beneficiaries to participate in the planning.[55] The critical element then is the deliberative process and decision-making procedures in place. Finally, it is at times up to the developing countries to determine how they should balance their obligations and their development needs.[56]

Related but distinct are provisions where the obligations of developing countries are contingent on the implementation by developed countries of their own obligations. The United Nations Framework Convention on Climate Change takes an original position in that respect, linking commitments by developing countries to

the effective implementation by developed country Parties of their commitments under the Convention related to financial resources and transfer of technology and will take fully into account that economic and social development and poverty eradication are the first and overriding priorities of the developing country Parties.[57]

Non-trade treaties examined here provide some novel technical approaches to regulation that could mitigate some of the issues identified with respect to WTO-style SDT, such as the disconnect between the beneficiaries and the obligor, the lack of policy space for developing countries to define their development priorities, and, to some extent, the reduction of capacity and participation constraints.

2. Adjudicating Development in International Courts and Tribunals

A broad survey of international dispute settlement mechanisms yielded some thirty cases containing at least some reference to a development argument.[58] These cases originated from the European Court of Justice (ECJ), the International Tribunal for the Law of the Sea (ITLOS), the North American Free Trade Agreement (NAFTA), the International Court of Justice (ICJ), the International Chamber of Commerce's court of arbitration (ICC), the International Centre for Settlement of Investment Disputes (ICSID), a few *ad hoc* international arbitration awards, and some domestic courts.

As shown in Table 8.1, development arguments most often affected the outcome when raised by the adjudicator, rather than by a party. Development arguments

---

[54] Art 6(b) United Nations Convention to Combat Desertification.
[55] See eg, Art 10.3 Montreal Protocol; Arts 8, 12(7) UNFCCC.
[56] Part II, Art 2(3) International Covenant on Economic, Social and Cultural Rights (New York, 16 December 1966; 6 ILM 360) ("Developing countries, with due regard to human rights and their national economy, may determine to what extent they would guarantee the economic rights recognized in the present Covenant to non-nationals.").
[57] Art 4(7) UNFCCC.
[58] Research assistance by Taran Nadler is gratefully acknowledged.

Table 8.1 International adjudicators' treatment of development arguments

Type of development argument	Adjudicator ignored argument	Adjudicator acknowledged but dismissed argument	Adjudicator notes but does not incorporate argument into decision	Adjudicator affirmed argument	Argument referenced in dissent
Jurisdictional		3[1]		1	2
Merits	2	5	1	2	
Contextual		1	6	1	1
Restitution or award related		1	1	2	1

[1] Two of these cases include instances where developed countries attempt to use a development argument against a developing country for jurisdictional purposes.

were raised *sua sponte* by the court or arbitration tribunals in almost half of the cases. Defending developing countries brought up the argument in nine cases. Developed countries or corporations pitted against a developing country brought up development issues as claimants or defendants in five cases.

Although the invocation of developing country status or circumstances remains residual in international disputes (qualitatively and quantitatively), diverse arguments have been made, ranging from procedural and jurisdictional issues to substantive matters and compensation.

While a thorough discussion of each case is beyond the scope of this study, several key questions are explored to determine the role of development arguments within these cases:

- What role is the development argument playing within the case (is it a defense, part of the claim etc)?
- Who makes the development argument and against whom?
- How did the adjudicator treat the development argument?

This section first considers development raised as part of a procedural argument, and second, development aspects as part of a substantive claim.

2.1 Development to support procedural claims

Development has been raised in support of procedural arguments, particularly to interpret the court or arbitral tribunal's jurisdiction.

A number of ICSID arbitrations illustrate this strategy. In *Mihaly International Corporation v Democratic Socialist Republic of Sri Lanka*, Sri Lanka resisted a claim by a US corporation on jurisdictional grounds. At issue was whether the claimant could establish *ratione materiae* jurisdiction, which would exist only if the legal dispute arose out of an investment.[59] The claimant argued that, given the imprecise definition of "investment," the broadest interpretation should be applied so as "to encourage a freer flow of capital into developing countries. It submitted that otherwise the free flow of capital investment to developing countries would subside."[60] Effectively, the claimant (a developed country company) made a development argument against a developing country respondent. Sri Lanka responded that it would damage developing countries' ability to abide by the treaty if the court extended the interpretation of investment despite the lack of explicit consent from the developing country.[61] The tribunal decided that the claimant's argument lacked evidence to support it and found that the claimant's request for "initiation of a proceeding to settle an investment dispute [was] . . . premature."[62]

The case of *Vacuum Salt Products Ltd v Republic of Ghana* involved a company controlled by a foreign national bringing a claim for breach of rights to develop salt mining in Ghana.[63] The development argument was part of Ghana's affirmative defense against the tribunal's jurisdiction. However, the tribunal itself raised the argument, rather than the respondent. The tribunal, in interpreting the aspects of the treaty relevant to jurisdiction, noted a commentator's analysis that "the governments of particularly the developing States . . . wish[ed] to preclude a priori any possibility that they might later be pressured into settling disputes under the Centre with another government or with one of their own nationals . . ."[64] As often happens when the tribunal is the instigator of the development argument, it found for Ghana.[65]

Malaysian Historical Salvors, SDN, BHD v The Government of Malaysia is another example of a country using development as a part of its affirmative defense to jurisdiction. The case is unusual in that claimant was a company incorporated in Malaysia, bringing a claim against its home country.[66] The case then led to an annulment procedure brought by the respondent. In the original ICSID arbitration, Malaysia had resisted the tribunal's jurisdiction, arguing that the contract at issue did not qualify as an investment because it did not contribute to the economic development of the state. The sole arbitrator, a Singaporean national, agreed with Malaysia that the definition of an investment required that a significant contribution be made to the host state's economy, an interpretation bolstered by earlier ICSID arbitrations. The claimants then applied for an annulment on the grounds that the arbitrator had exceeded its powers in failing to exercise jurisdiction. The annulment committee, composed of three members, granted the annulment. The dissenting member, Judge Shahabuddeen, quoted *Amco v Indonesia*, discussed below, for the proposition that "the Convention is aimed to protect, to the same

[59] *Mihaly International Corporation v Democratic Socialist Republic of Sri Lanka*, ICSID Award ARB/00/2 (15 March 2002). [60] Ibid at para 36.
[61] Ibid. [62] Ibid at para 61.
[63] *Vacuum Salt Products Ltd v Republic of Ghana*, ICSID Award ARB/92/1 (16 February 1994).
[64] Ibid at para 36. [65] Ibid at para 55.
[66] *Malaysian Historical Salvors SDN, BHD v The Government of Malaysia*, ICSID Award on Jurisdiction ARB/05/10 (17 May 2007), at paras 2, 5.

extent and with the same vigour the investor and the host State, not forgetting that to protect investments is to protect the general interests of development and of developing countries."[67]

In *Southern Pacific Properties (Middle East) Limited v Arab Republic of Egypt* the issue before the tribunal was a claim for value of investment, cancellation costs, and interest. Development was only mentioned by the dissenting arbitrator who expounded the jurisdictional purpose of the convention in light of its development objective and noted that international development law was changing the investment climate in developing countries.[68]

In *Compañía de Aguas del Aconquija, S.A. & Compagnie Générale des Eaux v Argentine Republic*, development was only briefly mentioned in a footnote when the arbitrators referred to the ICSID Convention's drafting history. They noted that many developing countries had made statements regarding the role of political subdivisions in attracting foreign investments, which militated for a broad interpretation of ICSID's jurisdiction to hear disputes involving these subdivisions.[69]

A domestic US case, *Khulumani v Barclay Nat. Bank Ltd* involved South African nationals alleging that a plethora of US businesses supported apartheid by doing business in South Africa during that period. In contesting the court's jurisdiction, the respondents, the US-based businesses, "express[ed] concern over the chilling effect that actions of this kind may have on future foreign investment in developing countries." This was not the first example of developed country-based corporations using a development argument against developing countries. However, the argument was only noted in the dissent and did not have a bearing on the outcome of the case.

The High Court of Hong Kong also had an opportunity to address a development argument in an international trade dispute. In *FG Hemisphere Associates LLC v Democratic Republic of the Congo*, two ICC awards were issued against the Democratic Republic of the Congo. In seeking fulfillment of the awards, the plaintiff learned that the Democratic Republic of Congo had contracted with China whereby the Democratic Republic of the Congo received payment from China for the exploitation of its resources.[70] The plaintiff sought to enjoin China and Hong Kong from paying the Democratic Republic of the Congo and claiming title to those payments in the High Court of Hong Kong. In response, China and Hong Kong, joined by the Democratic Republic of the Congo, argued that the latter was immune from the court's jurisdiction. This is an interesting case because developing countries made a development argument on behalf of another developing country respondent, but were doing so clearly with their own best interests in mind

[67] *Malaysian Historical Salvors SDN, BHD v The Government of Malaysia*, ICSID Decision on the Application for Annulment ARB/05/10 (16 April 2009), at M. Shahabuddeen, dissent at para 19.
[68] *Southern Pacific Properties (Middle East) Ltd v Arab Republic of Egypt*, ICSID Award ARB/84/3 (20 May 1992), M.A. El Mahdi dissent, 4–9, 1993 ILM 32(4) 933, at 988–90.
[69] *Compañía de Aguas del Aconquija, S.A. & Compagnie Générale des Eaux v Argentine Republic*, ICSID Award ARB/97/3 (21 November 2000), at fn 15.
[70] *FG Hemisphere Associates LLC v Democratic Republic of the Congo*, Civil Appeal Nos 373 of 2008, 43 of 2009 (2010) 2 HKLRD 66 (Hong Kong Court of Appeal).

(to maintain the ability to contract with the Democratic Republic of the Congo for natural resources). The court, however, found against China and Hong Kong.

Development arguments also arise in annulment proceedings in relation to different procedural aspects: impartiality, procedures for compliance, and allocation of the burden of proof.

CDC Group plc v Republic of Seychelles involved an award and subsequent annulment proceeding. The claimant was a company based in England bringing a claim against the Seychelles for breach of guarantee agreements made between the parties.[71] The Seychelles' development argument was summarized in the annulment proceeding: The Seychelles invoked principles of "equity, contractual fairness, inequality of bargaining power, contributory negligence and the emerging jurisprudence in relation to international trade and investments between developed and developing countries."[72] The tribunal, in the original proceeding, rejected this analysis, noting that the Seychelles could cite to no legal authority in support of its arguments.[73] The Seychelles, after losing the original award decision, brought an annulment proceeding, alleging in part that the arbitrator lacked impartiality. Although the Seychelles did not relate the lack of impartiality directly to its development argument, the annulment tribunal, in rejecting the claim, noted that the award arbitrator "approached the issues with an open mind" and "was at pains to accommodate to the maximum extent humanly possible the desires of a very small developing state."[74] Specifically, the tribunal had allowed procedural flexibility when the Seychelles repeatedly failed to meet deadlines, and when it applied rules regarding submissions to the tribunal.

Amco Asia Corporation, Pan American Development Limited, PT Amco Indonesia v Republic of Indonesia involved an original arbitration award, a recourse for annulment, which was granted, and a second arbitration on the merits. The development argument came into play in the annulment proceedings brought by Indonesia, in relation to procedural issues. To make its case for annulment Indonesia claimed that the tribunal in the prior award failed to follow rules of procedure, exceeded its powers, and did not state sufficient reasons for its findings. The annulment committee noted that the tribunal seemed to have taken into account Indonesia's relatively low administrative capacity when "distributing the burden of proof between the parties"[75] and it ultimately dismissed the claim of inadequate treatment.

In the annulment phase in *Mr Patrick Mitchell v Democratic Republic of Congo*, the Democratic Republic of the Congo argued that it should not have to post a guarantee in order to request a stay of the award. The Democratic Republic of the Congo reasoned that such a requirement, because it is a significant burden to developing countries, deters them from seeking annulments.[76] The committee

---

[71] *CDC Group PLC v Republic of Seychelles*, ICSID Annulment Proceeding ARB/02/14 (29 June 2005).
[72] Ibid at para 22.　　[73] Ibid at para 26.　　[74] Ibid at para 55.
[75] *Amco Asia v Republic of Indonesia*, ICSID Decision on the Application for Annulment (16 May 1986), 1986 ILM 25(6) 1441, at para 236.
[76] *Mr Patrick Mitchell v Democratic Republic of Congo*, ICSID Decision on the Application for Annulment ARB/99/7 (1 November 2006).

agreed with the Democratic Republic of the Congo's analysis and granted the stay without a guarantee.

Development is brought up in two separate instances in the annulment proceedings in *Enron Corporation; Ponderosa Assets L.P. v Argentine Republic*: first by the developing country against the developed country corporation and, second, in the reverse. Argentina used a development argument as a defense against Enron's action to end a continuance of the award. Argentina described itself as "a developing country with high rates of poverty, extreme poverty and social exclusions."[77] Argentina further argued that failure to stay the award or a requirement to post security would cause the state harm because of these circumstances. The opposing party, Enron, responded that "Argentina [would] not suffer irreparable harm if the stay of enforcement is discontinued or if it is required to post security given its economic recovery, and that Argentina clearly [had] the resources to post security."[78] The *ad hoc* committee, in interpreting the ICSID Convention to determine when a stay could be granted and whether a security would be required, noted that:

[w]here a State is the applicant for annulment, a further relevant factor for the Committee is that, because security ordinarily would only be sought against a developing country, it would risk introducing into the ICSID system the unacceptable suggestion of discrimination between States, whether *de jure* or *de facto*, as to terms for security imposed on Article 52(5) applications.[79]

The second development argument addressed whether Argentina was obligated to voluntarily pay the award, should the annulment request be denied. Argentina interpreted Article 53 of the ICSID Convention to mean that the claimant would have to comply with formalities of arbitration award recognition and enforcement before Argentinean courts in order to recover. Promoting a voluntary award payment interpretation of the statute, the claimants countered that the *travaux préparatoires* of the ICSID Convention show that Article 53 is supposed to be used "for the benefit of the developing countries who were thus given a means to enforce awards in their favor against foreign investors."[80] The *ad hoc* committee ultimately agreed with the claimant's interpretation requiring voluntary payment without further domestic proceedings.

2.2 Development to support substantive claims

Three landmark arbitrations, a product of their time, testify to the deep-running conflicts between different perspectives on economic law and development in the late 1970s and 1980s.

Texaco/Calasiatic raised the issue of development in the context of a dispute over compensation for nationalized property.[81] The award came in the wake of the mul-

---

[77] *Enron Corporation; Ponderosa Assets L.P. v Argentine Republic*, ICSID Annulment Proceeding ARB/01/3 (7 October 2008), at paras 15(c) and 98.
[78] Ibid at para 14(e). [79] Ibid at para 44. [80] Ibid at para 73.
[81] *Award on the Merits in Dispute Between Texaco Overseas Petroleum Company/California Asiatic Oil Company and the Government of the Libyan Arab Republic*, Arbitral Award (19 January 1977), 1978 ILM 17(1) 1.

titude of UN resolutions and other soft law instruments attempting to frame a New International Economic Order (see Chapter 2). The sole arbitrator, René-Jean Dupuy, was presented with the difficult task of parsing out which instruments testified to evolutions in the law regarding sovereignty over natural resources and nationalizations, and which instruments were merely aspirational, not yet embodying obligations for states.[82] He ultimately decided that the principle of good faith, which was confirmed by several key UN resolutions on the New International Economic Order, meant that the contracting state that nationalized an asset was still bound by the terms of the agreement covering that investment. Regarding compensation, the tribunal reiterated the *Chorzów Factory* principles on reparations and the standards for *restitutio in integrum*, which it decided constituted the appropriate remedy in this case.

The *LIAMCO* arbitration, a few years later, offered a stark contrast. This dispute also concerned restitution from a concession agreement broken by nationalization. Here, the tribunal itself raised the question of development, describing the importance of nationalizations to "third world" states.[83] However, the sole arbitrator, Dr Sobhi Mahmassani, departed from the *Texaco/Calasiatic* tribunal to decide that in light of the development considerations and the "confused state of international law," the principle of equity emerging from other international decisions should be applied to the calculation of compensation:

This formulation is certainly in complete harmony with the general trend of international theory and practice on the concepts of sovereignty, destination of national wealth and natural resources, nationalistic motivations in the attitude and behavior of "Third World" nations, the lawfulness and frequency of nationalization, and the recent declarations affirmed in successive United Nations Resolutions by the majority members of the General Assembly.[84]

Finally, the *Arbitration Between Kuwait and the American Independent Oil Company (AMINOIL)* resolved a dispute over payments regarding an oil concession agreement. The tribunal viewed development considerations as background on the vital importance of extraction concession for the economic development of "third world" countries which emerged after the Second World War.[85] However, the tribunal appeared to set aside these concerns as merely political and therefore not having a bearing on the legal issues at stake.[86]

More recent arbitrations and decisions have been equally inconsistent regarding the bearing of development on substantive claims, absent specific obligations addressing development considerations.

---

[82] Ibid at paras 80–92.

[83] *Dispute Between Libyan American Oil Company (LIAMCO) and the Government of the Libyan Arab Republic Relating to Petroleum Concessions*, Arbitral Award (12 April 1977), 1981 ILM 20(1) 1, at 49

[84] Ibid at 76–7 (also quoting UN Resolution No 626 (VII) in support).

[85] *Matter of an Arbitration Between Kuwait and the American Independent Oil Company (AMINOIL)*, Arbitral Award (24 March 1982), 1982 ILM 21(5) 976, at 1031.

[86] Ibid at 1032.

Also, in the context of compensation for nationalization, the European Court of Human Rights addressed development in *Lithgow and Others v United Kingdom*. The dissent argued that developing countries involved in nationalizations should be given special leniency within a compensation analysis.[87] More generally, it claimed that international law had moved away from the strict rule applied in the Permanent Court of International Justice's *Chorzów Factory* case, and now supported a more equitable standard, which would be more just for "third world" countries.[88]

ICSID proves to be the most significant source of cases dealing with development arguments, with fifteen instances. However, little consistently emerges from the awards regarding claims that certain rights or obligations accrue from a state's developing status.

Société Ouest Africaine des Bétons Industriels v Senegal involved a claim for reparations from respondent's breach of contract. This was another instance where development arguments were brought up in dissent. The dissenting arbitrator, Kéba Mbaye, lamented that the tribunal's decision would likely be misinterpreted as "the manifestation of two totally different sensitivities on problems highlighting the conflictual relationship between developing countries and foreign investors"[89] since the majority and the dissent fell along the lines of the arbitrators' nationality—from developed and developing countries. Mbaye, who had pioneered the "right to development," then made an appeal to justice to justify a different analysis of the investor's obligations.

In the Matter of the Arbitration between Alex Genin, Eastern Credit Limited, INC and A.S. Baltoil and the Republic of Estonia involved a Texas-based company claiming against Estonia for the losses it suffered as a result of alleged violations of a bilateral investment treaty.[90] Estonia cited its status as a developing country as a defense to argue that its economic and political circumstances gave it a legitimate reason to terminate the contract. The arbitral tribunal agreed with Estonia, noting:

[t]he Tribunal further accepts Respondent's explanation that the circumstances of political and economic transition prevailing in Estonia at the time justified heightened scrutiny of the banking sector. Such regulation by a state reflects a clear and legitimate public purpose.[91]

The tribunal ultimately dismissed the company's claims. This is one of several cases in which proxy terms such as "economic situation" are used to refer to development considerations.

Sempra Energy International v Argentine Republic pitted a US-based company against a developing country in an investment dispute where the claimant alleged

---

[87] At 406.

[88] *Lithgow and Others v United Kingdom* Series A No 102, (1986) 8 EHRR 329, at 405.

[89] *Société Ouest Africaine des Bétons Industriels v Senegal*, ICSID Award ARB/82/1 (25 February 1988), in *ICSID Review—Foreign Investment Law Journal* 125, 6 (1991), at 235.

[90] *In the Matter of the Arbitration between Alex Genin, Eastern Credit Limited, INC and A.S. Baltoil and the Republic of Estonia*, ICSID Award ARB/99/2 (25 June 2001).   [91] Ibid at para 370.

that the respondent violated the bilateral investment treaty.[92] Argentina responded with a *force majeure* defense, pointing to its economic crisis as a circumstance which justified breaching the treaty. The arbitral tribunal, in addressing the development argument, attempted to take an even-handed approach, noting that "[i]f exceptions are made like these or other circumstances, the entire purpose of modern investment law, which is to accelerate the movement of private funds into developing countries for development purposes, will be frustrated."[93] However, the tribunal also underlined that the crisis situation in Argentina should not be ignored and must be taken into account when determining what compensation Argentina owed for the breach of the treaty.[94] With what seems to be mostly lip service to the situation in Argentina, the tribunal ultimately applied a standard compensation calculation to measure Argentina's liability.

The case of *Biwater Gauff (Tanzania) Limited v United Republic of Tanzania* is the sole instance of a development argument presented by a third party. The claimant was a company incorporated in England, claiming against Tanzania for a breach of the performance of the contract.[95] The development argument came up in an *amici* brief submitted by a coalition of five nongovernmental organizations. It argued that the claimant, having invested in multiple developing countries in the past, should have been aware of the inherent risks of such an investment.[96] Additionally, it submitted that when investments involve human rights and sustainable development, the investor owed the developing country the "highest level of responsibility to meet their duties and obligations as foreign investors, before seeking the protection of international law."[97] The brief is treated by the tribunal as contextual background to the case.[98]

In *Klockner Industrie-Anlagen GmbH v United Republic of Cameroon, Société Camerounaise des Engrais* claimants sought to recover the outstanding balance of the price of a fertilizer factory. This is another illustration of the tribunal actively bringing up a development argument without prompting by either party. The tribunal described the situation as one between unequal partners, where Klockner, a multinational European company, held all the knowledge, and Cameroon relied on Klockner's promises to further critical domestic agricultural development objectives.[99] The tribunal eventually found for the respondent, but the award was annulled two years later.

Two ECJ cases address development in relation to substantive claims: *Usha Martin v Council and Commission*;[100] and *HEG Ltd, Graphite India Ltd v Council*

---

[92] *Sempra Energy International v Argentine Republic*, ICSID Award ARB/02/16 (28 September 2007). [93] Ibid at para 396.
[94] Ibid at para 397.
[95] *Biwater Gauff (Tanzania) Ltd v United Republic of Tanzania*, ICSID Award ARB/05/22 (24 July 2008), at paras 1, 354. [96] Ibid at para 382.
[97] Ibid at para 380. [98] Ibid at para 392.
[99] *Klockner Industrie v United Republic of Cameroon*, ICSID Application for Annulment ARB/81/2 (21 October 1983), in R. Rayfuse, *ICSID Reports: Volume 2: Reports of cases decided under the Convention on the Settlement of Investment Disputes between States and Nationals of Other States* (Cambridge: Cambridge University Press, 1965), at 26.
[100] Case T-119/06, 9 September 2010 (OJ 2010/C 288/57).

of the European Union.[101] The cases are materially similar. In both, an Indian company contested antidumping duties imposed by the EU. The plaintiffs in both cases used their status as developing country industries to resist the antidumping duties. In *Usha Martin v Council and Commission*, the claimants argued that the response was not proportional to the conduct in light of India's developing status. Plaintiffs argued a narrower point in *HEG Ltd, Graphite India Ltd v Council of the European Union*, claiming that developing countries were exempt from antidumping duties under the Community Customs Code. In both cases the claimants' arguments were rejected and the court upheld the antidumping duties. The court in *Usha Martin* did not directly address the development argument, whereas the judge in *HEG Ltd* noted that the applicable rules made "no distinction in favour of developing countries."[102]

International Thunderbird Gaming Corporation (Claimant) v United Mexican States involved a US company bringing a claim against Mexico for breach of contract under NAFTA. Thunderbird alleged that Mexico "breached its obligations under NAFTA...under Article 1102 (National Treatment), Article 1103 (Most-Favoured-Nation Treatment), Article 1105 (Minimum Standard of Treatment), and Article 1110 (Expropriation and Compensation)."[103] The tribunal independently mentioned Mexico's status as a developing country in recognizing the difficulty of doing business in such countries. Specifically the tribunal noted that "[d]ealing with governments, including, but not only, developing countries is always a difficult matter, particularly for foreign investors."[104] The argument was otherwise incidental and did not appear to affect the outcome of the case.

In a case before the UK High Court of Justice, *Norsk Hydro ASA v The State Property Fund of Ukraine & Ors*, the respondents submitted a motion to set aside a prior judgment for breach of contract. The respondent relied on its status as a developing country as a *force majeure* argument to avoid paying interest on the award. Ukraine pleaded that "[f]or a developing State with limited resources facing enormous budgetary pressures this is a very real political and administrative problem which is deeply troubling to the Government of Ukraine."[105] The court did not address Ukraine's argument in its analysis.

In a very recent Advisory Opinion, the Seabed Dispute Chamber of the International Tribunal for the Law of the Sea determined the extent of states' legal responsibilities, obligations, and liabilities with regard to the "Area."[106] Multiple countries submitted statements on their interpretation of the relevant texts. In general, developing states promoted a standard which would take their economic status into consideration so that they could be included. Statements by the Philippines, China, Mexico, and Nauru all insisted on the need to take developing countries'

---

[101] Case T-462/04, 17 December 2008 (OJ 2008/C 32/46).   [102] Ibid.

[103] *International Thunderbird Gaming Corp v United Mexican States*, UNCITRAL Award (26 January 2006), at para 6.

[104] Ibid at A.J. Berg, separate opinion at para 116 (emphasis added).

[105] *Norsk HydroASA v The State Property Fund of Ukraine & Ors* 2002/441 (2002) EWHC 2120.

[106] *Responsibilities and Obligations of States Sponsoring Persons and Entities with Respect to Activities in the International Seabed* (Advisory Opinion by the Seabed Dispute Chamber), 1 February 2011, ITLOS Case No 17, at 5.

relatively limited capabilities into account when determining states' duties with respect to the "Area."[107] However, some developing countries, including Chile and Romania, submitted statements that did not mention development.[108] The Chamber devoted an entire section of the opinion to the "Interests and Needs of Developing States."[109] It focused on whether the preamble of the Law of the Sea Convention, read together with Articles 140 and 148 of the Convention, meant that developing parties should receive preferential treatment. Generally, the Tribunal declined to substantiate general obligations to grant special treatment to developing states except where these more general clauses were supported by specific differential obligations. It noted that specific provisions existed with respect to certain activities.

In some instances, the developing status of a country may give it specific rights in domestic courts in line with WTO special and differential treatment provisions. Such was the case at the United States Court of International Trade in *Royal Thai Government v US*. The court noted that "the two percent *de minimis* (and thus non-actionable) rate afforded developing countries like Thailand under U.S. countervailing duty law [was exceeded]."[110]

Beyond investment and economic disputes, development arguments have been marginal in other substantive claims.

Only one ICJ case explicitly addressed the development circumstances of a state party before the ICJ: the *Case Concerning the Continental Shelf (Libyan Arab Jamahiriya/Malta)*, a dispute over the boundaries to a continental shelf. Malta, in its memorial and counter-memorial frequently argued that its status as an "island developing country require[d] no decision be reached as to the delimitation of the continental shelf which would impinge upon Malta's delicate economic status."[111] However, the court briefly dismissed the argument, concluding "[n]or does the Court consider, contrary to the contentions advanced by Malta, that a delimitation should be influenced by *the relative economic position of the two States in question*."[112] The case is notable as a rare example of a developing country making a development argument against another developing country.

From the limited case law to date, international and regional courts have shown little sympathy to development arguments, particularly when couched in general terms. They have generally adopted a more limited textual interpretation

---

[107] NV 10/76 *Statement by the Republic of Nauru regarding the questions submitted to the Seabed Disputes Chamber for an advisory opinion on the responsibilities and obligations of States sponsoring entities with respect to activities in the international seabed area* (2010), NV NO DDA 106–10, *Proposed Philippine Statements on the Request for Advisory Opinion Submitted to the ITLOS Seabed Authority* (2010), *Written Statement of Mexico* (2010), and *Written Statement of the People's Republic of China* (2010).

[108] *Written Statement of Romania* (2010) and *Written Statement of Chile* (2010).

[109] *Responsibilities and Obligations of States Sponsoring Persons and Entities with Respect to Activities in the International Seabed Area* (Advisory Opinion) paras 151–63.

[110] *Royal Thai Government v US*, 30 CIT 1072, 441 F Supp 2d 1350, 1075 (2006).

[111] Memorial of Malta and Counter Memorial of Malta Re, *Case Concerning the Continental Shelf (Libyan Arab Jamahiriya/Malta)*, available at <http://www.icj-cij.org>.

[112] *Case Concerning the Continental Shelf (Libyan Arab Jamahiriya/Malta)* (Judgment of 3 June 1985) ICJ Reports (1985) 13, at 149 (emphasis added).

emphasizing specific development-related obligations, to the detriment of a more contextual reading of treaties where a general clause mandating special treatment would be read to infuse states' other obligations. In that, they are fairly aligned with the position of WTO adjudicators.

3. Conclusion

At first sight, the trends that have been observed in the drafting of SDT provisions at the WTO as well as in their adjudication seem largely in line with trends in other treaties and other adjudicatory bodies. Yet, several *caveat* belie this observation in important ways.

First, with respect to treaty provisions, RTAs provide many instances of more operational and more refined regulatory instruments to deal with development disparities. The understanding of development they respond to also appears more nuanced and diverse than the WTO's perspective. Even the EU's emerging Economic Partnership Agreements, which have often been criticized for not adequately responding to the development needs of ACP partners, have some relatively progressive provisions.

Second, agreements in non-trade areas appear closer to WTO-style SDT, both substantively and in the drafting; but at least in the environmental field, where much of the recent SDT activity takes place, the types of obligations and their formulation have evolved considerably so that the comparison is a misleading one.

Third, adjudication of development is so scattered that it is difficult to establish any trends. In general, adjudicators and parties alike display a certain timidity in making and analyzing development-related arguments. As at the WTO, one likely reason is the uncertainty regarding the scope and nature of the rights and duties of many SDT provisions. However, development considerations could often inform the interpretation of treaty obligations at large (not just SDT provisions) if the SDT provisions were considered as context, infusing states' obligations throughout the treaty. Indeed, developing countries at the WTO and elsewhere, and even developed countries or corporations, have realized the power of such a strategy.

The special case of RTAs' interaction with WTO commitments will be examined separately in Chapter 9 through the lens of WTO-plus commitments.

9

Institutional Processes:
What Impact on Developing Members?

Some fields of legal thinking have fully recognized the importance of process in determining regulatory outcomes, but much less attention has been given to this issue in the WTO context. Perhaps because pragmatism pervades the institution and informal processes are largely informed by politics and economics, the trade community has shunned a serious inquiry into the role of WTO institutions on the formulation of substantive rights and obligations. The much-touted transition from the power-based system of the GATT to the law-based framework of the WTO has largely focused on dispute settlement; yet there are a number of other critical processes in play that both foster and impede regulatory outcomes for developing countries. Indeed, the rights of developing countries at the WTO result from systemic features such as the institutional setting and culture of the organization (such as the committees and subcommittees, the dispute settlement system, and administrative bodies such as the Secretariat).

A number of theories from the social sciences emerged to account for the role of institutions in determining outcomes. Path dependency theory and New Institutional Economics are some examples.[1] Applying these frames to the position of developing countries at the WTO would be a social science exercise requiring a methodology and empirical analysis that differs from the legal analysis undertaken throughout this book. While such a study would clearly be very valuable, it is not the objective of the present chapter. Rather, taking a pragmatic approach, this chapter asks how the organizational and decision-making processes at the WTO affect developing countries' representation and participation. The premise for this enquiry is that effective participation is *sine qua non* to members' ability to influence outcomes. Indirectly, participation is also a test of the organization's legitimacy.

The themes of participation, representation, and legitimacy are ubiquitous in the discourse on trade and development at the WTO, but they have rarely been tested against the WTO's legal processes and institutional mechanisms. This chapter analyzes the impact of decision-making procedures on the representation of

---

[1] See, eg, D.C. North, "The New Institutional Economics and Third World Development," in J. Harriss, J. Hunter and C.M. Lewis, (eds), *The New Institutional Economics and Third World Development* (London: Routledge, 1995), at 17–26.

developing members (Section 1), the ability of the negotiation process to foster developing countries' substantive trade interests (Section 2), and the impact of emerging quasi-administrative bodies at the WTO on developing members' participation (Section 3).

1. Decision-Making Procedures:
What Representation for Developing Members?

At first sight the rules for decision-making at the WTO appear deceptively simple. Article IX:1 of the WTO Agreement provides that, by default, decisions are made by consensus in line with the practice developed during the GATT years: A decision will be adopted if no member present formally objects. Only if no consensus can be reached may a decision be submitted to the members' vote. A majority of the votes cast will generally suffice to adopt the decision and bind all members;[2] each member is entitled to one vote at the ministerial meetings and the General Council. While virtually no decision has been put to vote since the advent of the WTO, and voting was seldom used during the GATT,[3] significant decisions nonetheless have been made at the ministerial level.[4] The preeminent role of consensus[5] has even been further expanded in the early days of the WTO with a *Statement by the Chairman on Decision-Making Procedures under Articles IX and XII of the WTO Agreement*.[6] The decision agreed upon by the General Council states that:

On occasions when the General Council deals with matters related to requests for waivers or accessions to the WTO under Articles IX or XII of the WTO Agreement respectively, the General Council will seek a decision in accordance with Article IX:1. Except as otherwise provided, where a decision cannot be arrived at by consensus, the matter at issue shall be decided by voting under the relevant provisions of Articles IX or XII.

Accordingly, consensus decision-making is now the primary process in all instances except for amendments (Article X of the Marrakesh Agreement) and budget decisions (Article VII). In practice, the Statement on Decision-making Procedures is also a quasi-amendment to Article IX.3 (waivers) and Article XII (accessions). Because it was not adopted pursuant to the amendment procedures of Article X, it also overrode, to some extent, the procedures of Article X.

   Still, there are several reasons that make it worthwhile to examine more specifically the impact on developing country members of actual and "on the books" decision-making processes. First, the WTO, like many traditional international

---

   [2] For quorum rules, see Rules of Procedures for Meetings of the Ministerial Conference and the General Council, *Rules of Procedure for Sessions of the Ministerial Conference*, WT/L/161 (25 July 1996); WTO Secretariat, *Rules of Procedure for Meetings of WTO Bodies* (Geneva: WTO, 1997).
   [3] Steinberg, above Ch 5 fn 1, at 344 (noting that only decisions on waivers and accessions have been taken by vote since 1959 and discussing the United States' strategic role in reinforcing consensus practice after the accession of most developing countries in the 1960s).
   [4] Among decisions affecting developing countries, see the Enabling Clause, adopted as a Ministerial Decision.   [5] See, eg, Footer, above Ch 7 fn 63, at 135–49.
   [6] Decision-Making Procedures under Arts IX and XII WTO Agreement, WT/L/93.

organizations, is formally premised on the juridical equality of states. Unlike the World Bank, where votes are a function of the shareholdership in the Bank, WTO decision-making is not contingent on any economic benchmark. The tension between this formal equality and the obvious discrepancies in terms of economic power of the members and their respective shares of world trade is particularly germane to understanding developing members' institutional power at the WTO. Second, international relations theory has long established that even where the formal rules are not respected, the participants' actions and behavior are still influenced by the shadow of the law. In the case of the WTO, consensus can be defeated by a reversion to the voting rules. Yet, if, as is established below, the voting rules would not allow an effective empowerment of the dissenters, then the consensus is unlikely to be defeated even in the face of a genuine dissent. Such incentives can only be understood if the ubiquitous use of consensus decision-making is placed in the context of the default voting rules and their potential impact.

This section discusses both aspects.

1.1 The lure of formal equality

Although the WTO's decision-making procedures differ in many ways from traditional public international law practice,[7] the organization still relies on formal equality in line with the basic principle of the juridical equality of sovereign states in international law.[8] A closer examination of the WTO's decision-making procedures shows that the rules are, in fact, not neutral and ultimately raise concerns of bias against developing countries generally. Reliance on formal equality in decision-making procedures contrasts sharply with the power plays that have been historically prevalent. The underlying economic disparities between members also translate fairly directly into political inequality.[9]

The situation is not unique to the WTO. Some authors have argued that "invisible weighting" pervades international organizations where decision-making formally respects sovereign equality but allows powerful countries to dominate.[10]

---

[7] Silence generally is insufficient to constitute acquiescence in international law because respect for state sovereignty generally requires the explicit agreement of the state for it to be bound. Consensus decision-making as it is practiced at the WTO does not require express consent. Additionally decisions at the WTO by majority of votes cast mean that a numerical minority of members could adopt a decision binding on all members. Nonetheless, some other international organizations also provide for decision by majority of the votes cast. See Art 1/(2) International Labour Organization Constitution.

[8] Steinberg, above, Ch 5 fn 1, at 344–45 (stating that "U.S. policymakers thought it would be impossible to reach an agreement on a weighted voting formula and expand the GATT into a broad-based organization that could attract and retain developing countries. Moreover, decision-making rules that were consistent with the principle of sovereign equality carried a normative appeal, particularly for less powerful countries.").

[9] As noted by Kelsen, "equality does not mean equality of duties and rights, but rather equality of capacity for duties and rights." H. Kelsen, "The Principle of Sovereign Equality of States as a Basis for International Organization" 1944 *Yale Law Journal* 53(2) 207, at 209; see also Gerhart and Kella, above, Ch 6 fn 56, at 528.

[10] Steinberg, above, Ch 5 fn 1, at 346; see generally R.W. Cox and H.K. Jacobson, *The Anatomy of Influence: Decision Making in International Organizations* (New Haven: Yale University Press, 1973), at 497.

When combined with consensus decision-making, formal equality can become a double-edged sword. In theory it allows weaker states to voice concern and break the consensus (thus giving them a quasi-veto power), but it also has a chilling effect on these states because of the political cost of breaking the consensus.[11] The fact that no decision has been put to vote since the creation of the WTO (with the exception of one decision on accession),[12] suggests that developing countries feel unable to voice their concern.[13] As a result, the power given to each member through the equal vote/voice system, which could play in favor of developing countries (as it does at the UN General Assembly), remains purely theoretical and is overshadowed by political processes. As will be shown in the following subsection, the residual voting processes can also have a chilling effect.

Despite using complex voting structures meant to ensure a more practical representation of members, other large international organizations also tend to make decisions by consensus.[14] Zamora provides an interesting overview of decision-making mechanisms in a variety of international economic organizations, including commodity agreements and product cartels such as OPEC. The range of combinations is astonishing, as organizations or treaties strive to reflect the particular interests involved: producers and exporters, amount of financial contribution, relative population size, mitigated by political factors, economic development and political-economy system, geographic representation, etc.

With respect to "task-oriented" organizations, such as the GATT, Zamora finds a tension between ensuring that decisions have enough support to be put into practice, and maintaining an efficient decision-making process. The former requires support by members that are powerful with respect to the organization's subject matter, while the latter favors informal decision-making procedures, such as consensus, rather than strict voting rules.[15] Hence, consensus can satisfy the two aspects only if there is a high degree of convergence amongst its constituents regarding the organization's activity. Zamora considers it an anomaly that the most powerful industrialized nations did not reserve some kind of decision-making safeguard in the GATT through a weighted vote or a unanimity requirement, and he explains it by the fact that no directly enforceable measure could be taken by the governing body.[16] In fact, the GATT's Contracting Parties, acting as a governing

---

[11] Diplomatic practice also developed ways to stall a consensus decision procedure while avoiding the stigma of formally breaking the consensus. For example, a delegate might say he or she lacks the required orders from his or her capital to be able to make a decision on the issue.

[12] WTO, *Accession of Ecuador*, WT/ACC/ECU/5 (16 August 1995).

[13] Decisions up for adoption by consensus by the full membership normally have been negotiated in smaller groups. Practice shows that this stage generally is considered too late to engage in further negotiations.

[14] See, in particular, decision-making practices at the World Bank, the IMF, the International Labour Organization, and regional development banks. See generally A-M. M'Bow, "The Practice of Consensus in International Organizations" 1978 *International Social Science Journal* 30(4) 893; E. Osieke, "Majority Voting Systems in the International Labour Organisation and the International Monetary Fund" 1984 *International and Comparative Law Quarterly* 33(2) 381, at 392, 404–8.

[15] S. Zamora, "Voting in International Economic Organizations" 1980 *American Journal of International Law* 74(3) 566, at 589.   [16] Ibid at 591.

body, did make binding decisions. Later, some important safeguards were reinforced or reserved at the WTO with enhanced super-majority requirements.

Ultimately, consensus decision-making at the WTO has become tantamount to weighted voting where the largest industrialized members of the WTO have a dominant voice. Moreover, the "soft" nature of consensus and the lack of transparency it involves make it impossible to balance individual members' voices as would be the case in an official weighted system.

1.2 The residual importance of voting procedures

It may be argued that voting rules matter little since decisions are taken by consensus, a procedure seen as more conducive to political negotiation and the search for common positions, flexibility, and compromise, in contrast with the crystallization of positions often resulting from formal voting.

Political scientists argue in response that the mere existence of formal decision-making rules has an impact on the actual process because they affect the type of consensus that tends to be reached,[17] they influence the power balances with respect to decision-making, and they bear on the amount of political capital required to break the consensus and revert to voting. From a legal perspective, formal rules matter too: If the system is to maintain its legitimacy, it must provide a framework corresponding to its constituents' needs and capabilities.[18] The impact of, and incentives generated by, the legal rules as they currently stand therefore must be examined along with possible alternatives that might better account for the actual practice while correcting some of its deficiencies.

For these reasons, it is useful to assess how the formal rules would play out for developing countries if they were used. A number of features are noteworthy.

One aspect is that majority votes are counted by the number of *votes cast*, which would play disproportionately against developing countries. Indeed, an endemic problem is the inability of many developing countries to support a permanent (or sometimes even an occasional) diplomatic presence at the WTO or in Geneva. Hence developing countries, particularly the poorest among them, are much more likely to be unable to attend a vote than developed nations.[19] Depending on quorum rules, decisions on Article IX might even be adopted by a minority of members, with no assurance of adequate representation of least-developed and developing countries. Readily available solutions would mitigate that issue, such as

---

[17] Ibid at 568–9 ("[F]ormal [voting] procedures may profoundly affect the de facto decision-making process. Even where decisions are often taken informally, the resort to formal voting procedures remains a possibility and may have a profound effect on the willingness of members to arrive at a consensus, as well as on the type of consensus or compromise reached.").

[18] Kelsen, above fn 9, at 211–12 ("Members of the society of nations may be presumed to be equal as a general principle; but when it appears that in certain aspects of legal equality they are organically unequal, it would seem that the law must either take cognizance of the facts of else admit its unreality.").

[19] It is generally known that absence or abstention (formal or informal) due to lack of capacity is compounded by power plays whereby poor members are given incentives to refrain from intervening or from attending meetings on particular issues.

remote voting procedures. In fact, the one instance of voting at the WTO involved a ballot by mail.

Another aspect is the special procedure afforded to the EU skewing the one-member-one-vote process. Article IX.1 states, "Where the European Communities exercise their right to vote, they shall have a number of votes equal to the number of their member States which are members of the WTO." The EU is the only regional organization authorized to vote as a group (though the number of votes it is given may not exceed the number of its members). This block decision-making is a significant tool for the EU to gain collective political weight at the WTO. Effectively, it multiplies the number of votes of an entity that, in terms of external trade, functions as a single unit. Since the EU has one common external tariff, and foreign trade is within the jurisdiction of the EU, giving the EU twenty-seven votes (the sum of the votes of each EU member) is generally absurd.[20] It is the functional equivalent of giving one vote per US state.

Yet another important feature of voting rules is that binding interpretations of the WTO agreements are made by a three-fourths majority vote of members (not simply votes cast).[21] Additionally there is no default preference for consensus. The problems outlined above in terms of developing country participation therefore would be mitigated with respect to binding interpretations.

Article IX specifies decision-making procedures to grant a member a temporary waiver of some of its obligations. This is particularly relevant to developing countries, which are more likely to request such waivers. A three-fourths majority of the members generally is required for granting a waiver.[22] A similar waiver was available in the GATT under Article XXV:5, but the voting requirement was limited to a two-thirds majority. The increase in the majority requirement at the WTO corresponds to the shift in balance of the membership over time: By the time of the Uruguay Round, it became apparent that developed members could keep a blocking power in voting procedures only by increasing the super-majority requirement from two-thirds to three-quarters. Procedures for amendment to the WTO Agreement similarly reflect a shift from a two-thirds majority (for the equivalent procedure under the GATT) to a three-fourths majority requirement.[23] Regardless of the intent behind the shift, its effect is clearly to maintain a privileged position for the dwindling portion of the developed country membership.

Ultimately, developing countries find themselves caught between a practice of consensus that underrepresents them, and a disaffected majority voting system that

---

[20] Given that EU members remain sovereign states and that the EU is not a federation, it would be politically difficult to cease giving each EU member one vote. In some very residual instances, measures by member states that do not involve EU law have also come up at the WTO.

[21] Art IX:2 WTO Agreement. See also H. Nottage and T. Sebastian, "Giving Legal Effect to the Results of WTO Trade Negotiations: An Analysis of the Methods of Changing WTO Law" 2006 *Journal of International Economic Law* 9(4) 989, at 1002–3.

[22] Art IX:3 WTO Agreement (meaning that waivers to the major multilateral agreements, such as the GATT, the GATS, and the TRIPS must be first examined by the relevant Council, which then reports to the members assembled in the Ministerial Conference per Art IX.3(b)).

[23] Compare Art XXX GATT 1994 and Art X WTO Agreement. The procedures are tiered and do not necessarily require a vote.

would likely make the organization entirely unmanageable and where they would still lack proper representation because of insufficient resources and onerous super-majority requirements in the areas most pertinent to them.[24] The WTO has, since the Seattle Ministerial, focused on ways to improve procedural safeguards and transparency. These laudable efforts continue to date. While the current system is unlikely to be abandoned for practical[25] and political reasons, some adjustments could improve developing members' representation through group participation in decision-making. Leaving aside anomalies such as the EU bloc voting, systemic changes could provide for a more balanced decision-making process. Since reaching a consensus will most realistically remain the end-goal, efforts must focus on giving procedural guaranties to developing nations, improving their participation, and increasing transparency upstream.

2. The Negotiation Process: Creating or Hindering Opportunities for Developing Members?[26]

A crucial part of the institutional function of the WTO is agreeing on modalities for negotiations—the rules of the game that will frame substantive trade liberalization talks. The WTO agreements set the principles for multilateral trade negotiations but more detailed modalities are decided by members during each negotiation round. With the diversification of the GATT membership after decolonization and the proliferation of trade topics that came within the GATT's ambit during the Tokyo Round, the dynamics for negotiation changed considerably and, with it, the legal framework for negotiations. In particular, two major transformations are central to negotiation design for developing countries: the shift from non-reciprocity to reciprocity and trade linkage. This section analyzes how both became closely intertwined with the use of the single undertaking as the paramount modality for trade negotiations. It also demonstrates how the shift from non-reciprocity to reciprocity and linkage affected developing members' strategy at the WTO in the context of single undertaking negotiations.

2.1 Request-and-offer versus formula negotiations

Until the 1970s, the debate on the modalities for negotiations centered on the mechanism for cutting tariffs: request-and-offer by product and formula for cuts across the board. In the former, negotiations operate on a product-by-product basis (technically by tariff line), where members offer to cut their tariffs on designated

---

[24] See generally, Rolland, above Ch 5, fn 5.
[25] The difficulty in amending WTO law is a serious obstacle. See generally Nottage and Sebastian, above fn 21. The TRIPS Agreement mandated by the Doha Decision on Public Health is a case in point.
[26] This section largely draws from S.E. Rolland, "Redesigning the Negotiation Process at the WTO" 2010 *Journal of International Economic Law* 13(1) 65.

products in exchange for other members cutting tariffs on products of interest to the former. In the formula negotiations, members agree to cut tariffs across the board according to a formula. Request-and-offer was used in the first five rounds of the GATT (spanning 1947–1961), while the Kennedy and Tokyo Rounds (spanning 1964–1979) proceeded on a formula basis. The Uruguay Round reverted to a request-and-offer system at the United States' insistence.[27] Negotiations under the GATS proceed on a request-and-offer basis. While the Doha Round has proceeded mostly on a formulae-based approach (with respect to agricultural support and other quantifiable sectors), the United States and Canada proposed in 2008 to shift to a request-and-offer system in a poorly received attempt to overcome the current deadlocks.[28] This section examines what impact the two major modalities for negotiation (request-and-offer and formula-based) have on developing members.

Request-and-offer

In a request-and-offer system, countries list the concessions (on tariffs or market access) they would like to obtain and offer other concessions in exchange. However, because of the extension of concessions to all members through the MFN system, a protocol typically determines which country can participate in negotiations regarding a particular product. Although the GATT leaves it to members to decide on the modalities for negotiations, tariff negotiations were historically conducted between the principal supplier of a commodity and the importer.[29] Under Article XXVIII of the GATT, members can renegotiate their tariff commitments with the member with which the concession was initially negotiated and "with any other party determined by the Contracting Parties to have a principal supplying interest…and subject to consultation with any other contracting party determined by the Contracting Parties to have a substantial interest." The determination of initial rights holder (the party with which the tariff concession was first negotiated), principal supplying interest, and substantial interest remains vague but some

---

[27] S. Laird, "Market Access Issues" in B. Hoekman, A. Mattoo, and P. English (eds), *Development, Trade and the WTO: A Handbook* (Washington, DC: The World Bank, 2002), at 641. The Geneva Tariff Conference (1947), the Annecy Tariff Conference (1949), the Torquay Tariff Conference (1950–1951), the 1956 Geneva Tariff Conference, and the Dillon Round (1960–1961) used the bilateral item-by-item request-and-offer negotiation system. The Kennedy Round (1964–1967) used a linear tariff cut system (proposed across-the-board cut of 50 percent). The Tokyo Round (1973–1979) used a more complex "Swiss" formula applying a reduction coefficient to the initial tariff rates. In the Uruguay Round, various members (including the EC, Canada, Japan, and Switzerland) proposed various formulae, but the United States insisted on a bilateral per product request-and-offer system; A. Hoda and M. Verma, "Market Access Negotiations on Non-Agricultural Products: India and the Choice of Modalities," Working Paper 132, Indian Council for Research on International Economic Relations, 2004, at 10–14; Committee on Trade and Development, Note by the Secretariat, *Objectives of the Kennedy Round Negotiations for Less-Developed Countries*, COM.TD/W/69 (24 October 1967), BISD 14S/19; *GATT Ministerial Declaration*, MIN(73) (14 September 1973), BISD 20S/19, at paras 5–6.

[28] F. Williams, "US backs new approach to Doha negotiations," *Financial Times* (13 May 2009).

[29] On tariff negotiations, see generally A. Hoda, *Tariff Negotiation and Renegotiation Under the GATT and the WTO: Procedures and Practices* (Cambridge: Cambridge University Press, 2001), at 312.

guidelines have been elaborated over time.[30] The identification of these negotiation partners has important bearings on members' individual and collective bargaining positions. For example, a country might not individually reach the threshold for principal supplying interest, but the top two or three producers, if their interests are aligned, might be better off joining in and negotiating as a group. However, the absence of a mechanism for aggregating trading power between countries on a given product and making joint demands as a single "principal supplier" makes it easier for a powerful member to break potential coalitions by making side-payments or separate offers to weaker members. The EU is an exception, as it is able to aggregate the trade of its members.

This mechanism takes into account individual members' shares in exports or imports of a commodity. Nevertheless, the emphasis clearly is on the relative importance of share in the importing member's market, rather than the weight of a particular commodity in the exporting member's economy. This has a particular impact on small developing members relying on exports of one or two commodities, but with a volume of exports that is still too small to amount to a significant market share of any importing member's market. In these cases, a single product may be of huge importance to a member's economy, but its exports might still not meet the threshold when considered on a global basis, thereby excluding the member from the negotiations.

Hence, request-and-offer negotiations are biased toward bilateral or restricted plurilateral bargaining dominated by the individually powerful trading countries.

Formula-based negotiations

Another mode of negotiations developed under the GATT consists in formula-based tariff cuts and increased market access. In contrast to the request-and-offer system, formula-based concessions require the agreement of all members on the type of cut, its level, and its application.

Cotton negotiations in recent years provide an example of the different strategies involved in a formula-based negotiation and their impact on developing countries. With American and European domestic support programs for agriculture deadlocking multilateral negotiations in the Doha Round, the Cotton Four group proposed the "Cotton Initiative" in an attempt to move negotiations forward. The Cotton Four includes Benin, Burkina Faso, Chad, and Mali; all except Benin are LDCs, and, in 2001, cotton amounted to more than 50 percent of each country's

---

[30] Interpretative Note ad Art XXVIII (30 October 1947), at para 1.4; Understanding on the Interpretation of Article XXVIII GATT, LT/UR/A-1A/1/GATT/U/6 (14 April 1994), at para 1. The provision was to be reviewed five years later with particular attention to the effect on the negotiation rights of small and medium-sized exporting members. A review undertaken in 2000 did not result in any amendment to this Understanding and the Secretariat noted that the provision apparently had never been invoked. Committee on Market Access, *Minutes of the Meeting of 23 March 2000*, G/MA/M/23 (12 May 2000), at para 4.6. On substantial interest, see P.C. Mavroidis, *The General Agreement on Tariffs and Trade—A Commentary* (Oxford: Oxford University Press, 2005), at 92 (citing Committee on Tariff Concessions, *Minutes of Meeting held on 19 July 1985*, TAR/M/16 (4 October 1985), at para 55.10).

agricultural exports.[31] The FAO estimates that at the time, US cotton farmers (around 25,000 persons) benefited from USD3 billion to USD4 billion per year in direct support, which corresponds to more than the entire GDP of Burkina Faso, where two million people depend on cotton production. Between 1998 and 2001, cotton production in the United States increased by 40 percent and the volume of exports doubled, but the ensuing collapse in world prices cost West African producers (eight countries) approximately USD200 million in lost annual export revenues. In 2009, US cotton subsidies were still over USD2 billion.[32]

Because of their large share of cotton exports, the Cotton Four's total exports may have qualified the group as a principal supplier under the exception clause of the Interpretative Note ad Article XXVIII, but that would have been conditioned upon approval by the Contracting Parties acting jointly. The Cotton Four was unlikely to succeed in arguing that without US domestic support, they would make up a share of US imports sufficient to reach the threshold for substantial interest on an individual basis. On a collective basis, they were closer to reaching the threshold. Hence, negotiating on a request-and-offer basis would have put each of the Cotton Four members in a weak position vis-à-vis the United States. Instead, they proposed modalities for negotiation that would keep the bargaining at a multilateral level where their power as a cohesive coalition would continue to play in their favor. Indeed, the agreement in principle on the Cotton Four initiative was one of the principal achievements of the Hong Kong Ministerial Conference in December 2005 and a positive step for developing countries that export cotton.[33] The Cotton Four, acting within the framework of the Sub-Committee on Cotton, then proposed specific formula-based modalities for negotiation.[34]

Several lessons emerge from the Cotton Four experience.

First, developing countries (and in this case LDCs) that would be marginalized as individual members can gain significant leverage and visibility as a coalition.

Second, a coalition with an institutional home (committee or working group) is reinforced and its work product has a higher impact. As defining formula tends to push negotiations upstream to technical councils, committees, and subcommittees, access to the forum where the formula are elaborated therefore becomes the crucial issue. Coordinated group action is possible in these working groups only if a representative of the coalition has effective access to the negotiation forum (council or committee) and has the credibility or authority to speak for the coalition. The procedural framework (including notification rules, access to the working group, document dissemination) therefore must be considered very carefully to ensure equitable access and participation. In the case of the Cotton Four, the coalition members were part of the Sub-Committee on Cotton and were able to use that institutional platform to push their agenda forward.

---

[31] FAO, "State of Agricultural Commodity Markets," (2004), at 25 <ftp://ftp.fao.org/docrep/fao/007/y5419e/y5419e00.pdf>.

[32] <http://farm.ewg.org/progdetail.php?fips=00000&progcode=cotton>.

[33] Hong Kong Ministerial Declaration, at paras 11–12.

[34] Sub-Committee on Cotton, *Sectoral Initiative in Favour of Cotton–Proposed Modalities for Cotton*, TN/AG/SCC/GEN/4 (1 March 2006).

Third, multilateral formula-based modalities may give better access to the process to weaker countries than the bilateral-oriented request-and-offer system. However, they may be more complex from a technical point of view.

Modalities for negotiation have a significant impact on developing countries' ability to negotiate individually and collectively, and are an increasingly sensitive issue as developing countries' participation and level of commitments increase.[35] That is not to say that one type of system is always more development-friendly than another. Formula-based modalities have yielded positive results in some areas of the GATT, but in other areas, developing countries have preferred a request-and-offer system.[36] For example, the GATS is perceived as more development-friendly because it operates on a request-and-offer basis. In fact, the United States has been unsuccessful at extracting more offers from developing countries on services in the Doha Round.[37] Formula-based negotiation calls for more multilateralism and may result in less flexible results. Offer-and-request negotiation may put countries at the mercy of bilateral divide-and-rule tactics, but they are not forced to make an offer in the first place.

2.2 The role of the single undertaking

The single undertaking currently is a key element to the WTO negotiation structure. Under a single undertaking approach nothing is agreed upon until all members agree to all aspects of the negotiations resulting in a single package of multilateral commitments agreed upon simultaneously and inseparably. The single undertaking generally precludes side deals among some of the members or on some of the agenda items separately from the general negotiations.[38] Since the inception of the Uruguay Round in 1986, the single undertaking has been the overarching modality for trade liberalization negotiations.

Two main drivers underpin the recourse to the single undertaking. First, the single undertaking brings a large number of diverse member states into the fold of a common trade liberalization regime. While the single undertaking mostly benefited developed members during the Uruguay Round, developing members

---

[35] Hoda and Verma, above fn 27, at 20 (discussing negotiations on modalities in the Doha Round). Some developing countries have submitted proposals regarding formula-based tariff negotiations in the Doha Round. Ibid at 25–6, 31, 35–6.

[36] Developing countries also have chosen a request-and-offer mechanism in other fora. Such is the case, for example, in the Global System of Trade Preferences, a forum for South–South market access negotiations system operating on the basis of request-and-offer. UNCTAD, *Global System of Trade Preferences among Developing Countries* (1985) <http://www.unctadxi.org/templates/News_____1723.aspx>.

[37] M. Khor, "WTO Services talks caught in webs of "horizontal process" and blame game," (10 March 2008) Third World Network <http://www.twnside.org.sg/title2/wto.info/twninfo20080309.htm>.

[38] The single undertaking may also be viewed as a characteristic of the WTO legal system beyond negotiations. For example, it is a powerful mechanism to strive toward consistency in the interpretation, application, and enforcement of WTO rules across the various multilateral agreements. See G. Marceau, "Balance and coherence by the WTO Appellate Body: who could do better?" in G. Sacerdoti, A. Yanovich, and J. Bohanes (eds), *The WTO at Ten: The Contribution of the Dispute Settlement System* (Cambridge: Cambridge University Press, 2006), at 326.

are increasingly feeling that it now safeguards them against unwanted commitments because they have gained enough political and, in some cases, economic weight to hold out until they get a satisfactory deal. Second, the single undertaking allows the integration of multi-faceted, multi-topic regulation in a single regime. As a result, the single undertaking and trade linkage have been largely assumed to be inseparable, the former being the conduit for the achievement of the latter.

There has been some consideration among practitioners of the broader implications and the limits of the single undertaking.[39] The academic literature has mostly focused on informal negotiating and bargaining tactics[40] to unveil the utilitarian[41] or the constructivist[42] impact of the single undertaking. This section focuses on the systemic design of the negotiation process to highlight its implications for the various constituencies of the organization (developed, least-developed, and developing members) and its effects on the outcomes that they are likely to gain from the negotiations.

The ongoing Doha "Development" Round provides a stark illustration of the major hurdles that can result from disagreements amongst members regarding the process for trade liberalization. It may well be that the core underpinning of the negotiations, the single undertaking itself, has become an obstructing, rather than facilitating, factor. Beyond the specific impact of negotiation design on the most vulnerable WTO members, particularly LDCs, the issue is a systemic one that affects the balance of the organization and the future of multilateral trade liberalization for all members.

From the reciprocity debate . . .

With the Tokyo Round (1973–1979), the nature of trade liberalization expanded and diversified through a series of agreements that states could choose to subscribe to or not. This "à-la-carte" system resulted from developing countries' insistence on non-reciprocity as a guiding principle for the negotiations. The à-la-carte approach also makes it difficult, if not impossible, to bargain across agreements. In effect, non-reciprocity as implemented in the Tokyo Round prevented linkage of vari-

---

[39] See in particular the critique in P. Sutherland and others, "The Future of the WTO" <http://www.wto.org/english/res_e/publications_e/future_wto_e.htm> (hereinafter "Sutherland Report"); Warwick Commission, "The Multilateral Trade Regime: Which Way Forward?" <http://www2.warwick.ac.uk/research/warwickcommission/worldtrade/report/uw_warcomm_tradereport_07.pdf> (hereinafter "Warwick Commission Report").

[40] See, eg M. Elsig, "Agency Theory and the WTO: Complex Agency and the 'Missing Delegation'"? (submitted to The Political Economy of International Organization Conference held 2 February 2008 through 8 February 2008, on file with the Center for Comparative and International Studies at <http://www.cis.ethz.ch/events/past_events/PEIO2008/Elsig_PAWTO>); J.S. Odell, "Chairing a WTO Negotiation" 2005 *Journal of International Economic Law* 8(2) 425.

[41] See eg Steinberg, above, Ch 5 fn 1 (focusing on "invisible weighting" as it affects consensus decisions at the WTO, but not specifically discussing the single undertaking).

[42] See, eg, R. Wolfe, "Arguing and bargaining in the WTO: Does the Single Undertaking make a difference?" (Prepared for the Canadian Political Science Association held 4–6 June 2008 <http://www.cpsa-acsp.ca/papers-2008/Wolfe.pdf>). More generally, the analysis and critique of the single undertaking in the literature tends to come from the social sciences.

ous agreements in a single package of commitments to which all members had to subscribe.[43]

The Uruguay Round, by contrast, shifted to the single undertaking.[44] While there is still some debate as to the timing of the introduction of the single undertaking, all agree that by 1991, when the delineation of the scope of the negotiations was fairly crystallized, the single undertaking was seen as key to closing the Round with a series of interdependent agreements.[45] Ultimately, the once-separate negotiations on services (Punta del Este Declaration Part II) and the negotiations on intellectual property all became part of the single undertaking during the Uruguay Round. While the adoption of the single undertaking in the Uruguay Round was initially motivated by the return to a reciprocal system,[46] it quickly became a powerful device to manipulate the negotiation agenda and the outcome of the commitments. Some have even argued that the pharmaceutical industry was a main beneficiary of the single undertaking approach.[47] While the Tokyo Round allowed different levels of commitments and participation based on non-reciprocity, a single undertaking approach fosters convergence in the level of participation and commitments.

The shift from non-reciprocity in the Tokyo Round to a reinforced reciprocity approach with the single undertaking had effects on developing members both within the GATT and with respect to outside agreements such as trade preferences between the EC and certain ACP countries. The Yaoundé Convention of 1964 established non-reciprocal trade preferences between the signatory ACP countries and the EC.[48] The Second Yaoundé Convention (1971)[49] and the successive Lomé Conventions[50] also provided for non-reciprocal trade preferences. These agreements were covered by the 1971 GATT waiver and the 1979 Enabling Clause. By

---

[43] The single undertaking, which would likely have precluded the à-la-carte approach, was first mentioned in the Declaration Launching the Tokyo Round but had no bearing on the negotiations or outcome. G.R. Winham, *An Institutional Theory of WTO Decision-Making: Why Negotiation in the WTO Resembles Law-Making in the US Congress* (Toronto: Munk Centre for International Studies, 2006).

[44] See J. Croome, *Reshaping the World Trading System: A History of the Uruguay Round* (Geneva: Kluwer Law International, 1995), at 382–92; Part I of the Punta del Este Declaration (1986).

[45] Some date the introduction of the single undertaking to the Punta del Este Declaration in response to the G-10's resistance to negotiations on trade in services; others place it in 1990, in relation to the push by the United States to prepare the closing of the Round, and others yet see it as coming into play in 1991 to achieve the linkage of trade in goods, services, intellectual property, and the dispute settlement system; Wolfe, above fn 42, at 5.

[46] A. Lanoszka, "The Promises of Multilateralism and the Hazards of 'Single Undertaking': The Breakdown of Decision-Making within the WTO" 2007–2008 *Michigan State Journal of International Law* 16(3) 655, at 663–4.

[47] B. Savoie, "Thailand's Test: Compulsory Licensing in an Era of Epidemiologic Transition" 2007 *Virginia Journal of International Law* 48(1) 211, at 247.

[48] Convention of Association Between the European Economic Community and Associated African States (Yaoundé Convention I) (Yaoundé, 20 July 1963; OJ 1431, 2 ILM 971), (entered into force 1 June 1964).

[49] Convention of Association Between the European Economic Community and Associated African States (Yaoundé Convention II) (Yaoundé, 29 July 1969; OJ (L282) 1, 9 ILM 484) (entered into force 1 January 1971).

[50] ACP–EEC Convention of Lomé (28 February 1975; 14 ILM 327); Second ACP–EEC Convention of Lomé (31 October 1979; 19 ILM 327); Art 18 Third ACP–EEC Convention of Lomé

contrast, the return to reciprocity during the Uruguay Round resulted in a fundamental reshaping of EC–ACP relations and a shift away from non-reciprocal trade preferences.[51] The Cotonou Agreement[52] inaugurated the shift and the more recent Economic Partnership Agreements have firmly anchored reciprocity in the EU–ACP trade relations. These post-Uruguay Round cooperation agreements are covered by the regional trade agreement exception of GATT Article XXIV.[53] Unlike the Enabling Clause, Article XXIV is not premised on non-reciprocity and in fact assumes reciprocal trade relations.

Non-reciprocity survived the Uruguay Round only in a residual and temporary form through SDT provisions that allow, among other things, additional implementation periods for developing and LDCs. During the transitional periods, their relationship with other members is non-reciprocal inasmuch as they benefit from other members' full implementation while they have not fully implemented their own obligations. Virtually all transitional time periods have now expired.

. . . to the linkage debate

With non-reciprocity being largely pushed aside during the Uruguay Round, the purpose of the single undertaking became the expansion of bargaining across an ever-increasing set of topics of interest to various segments of the WTO membership. The interdependent regulation of trade and other fields that are deemed to have an impact on trade is now generally encapsulated in the literature by the term "linkage." Linkage brings together trade and trade-related topics, such as intellectual property, labor standards, and environmental protection into a single regulatory regime.

While the use of the single undertaking during the Uruguay Round undoubtedly had a coercive effect on developing countries that were not eager to agree to the GATS and TRIPS, the dynamics of negotiations have evolved since then. Specifically, developing members have recognized the importance of the negotiation agenda and have succeeded, in the years since the Uruguay Round, in using the single undertaking as a tool to block negotiations on topics they did not want to see regulated under the aegis of the WTO. The single undertaking has become a double-edged sword whereby any WTO member or a coalition of members can hold all negotiations hostage. It is therefore not surprising that an increasing number of delegates from developing countries now embrace the single undertaking as a prime line of defense against the erosion of their agenda by more powerful players.

(8 December 1984; 24 ILM 588); Art 174 Fourth ACP–EEC Convention of Lomé (15 December 1989; 29 ILM 783).

[51] J.C. Nwobike, "The WTO Compatible ACP-EU Trade Partnership: Interpreting Reciprocity to Further Development" 2008 *Asper Review of International Business and Trade Law* 8(1) 87 at 87, 121, 123.

[52] Partnership Agreement Between the Members of the African, Caribbean and Pacific Group of States of the one part, and the European Community and its Member States of the Other Part (ACP–EC Partnership Agreement) (Cotonou, 23 June 2000; OJ (L/317) 3), (entered into force 1 April 2003).   [53] Nwobike, above fn 51, at 101–4.

The battle led by India over the "new issues"[54] at the Singapore Ministerial Meeting was a remarkable example of the efforts by some developing members to exclude certain items from the negotiation mandate and hence from the future single undertaking package. While a reluctant compromise included investment and competition on the agenda, the trade–labor linkage was more resolutely excluded as a result of pressure from developing countries.[55] The single undertaking facilitated developing members' resistance because it gave these countries the assurance that no negotiation could proceed unless they had agreed to the issue's inclusion on the agenda.

Conversely, strategic or opportunistic linkage enabled developing members to insist on resolving matters of primary interest to them (in particular the issue of agricultural subsidies) as a precondition to any other negotiation. They arguably achieved a total linkage hinged on agriculture that now holds the negotiations at a standstill. In that respect, developing members have accomplished an unprecedented feat in asserting a coordinated, solid stance that is possible only in the context of strategic linkage combined with a single undertaking approach.

Negotiation strategies and positioning at the Singapore Ministerial Meeting inform the road to the Doha Round. The United States supported launching a narrow round at the Seattle Ministerial Meeting, while the EU wanted to include a large number of topics including the environment, labor, trade remedies, investment, and competition, all of which developing countries had already opposed at Singapore. Developing members emphasized agriculture, trade in manufacture and tropical products, implementation issues relating to the Uruguay Round agreements, issues related to debt, technical assistance and capacity building, and the reform of the decision-making procedures. Ultimately, newly admitted China and the G-77 led the movement in favor of developing countries' agenda at the 2001 Ministerial Meeting at Doha by threatening to block the consensus. The Ministerial resulted in a very broad 'Doha Work Programme' that included virtually every issue raised. The battle over the agenda mattered primarily because all members took as a given that the negotiations would proceed on a single undertaking basis.

Paragraph 47 of the Doha Ministerial Declaration on the Organization and Management of the Work Programme formalizes this assumption:

With the exception of the improvements and clarifications of the Dispute Settlement Understanding, the conduct, conclusion and entry into force of the outcome of the negotiations shall be treated as parts of a single undertaking. However, agreements reached at

---

[54] Competition, investment, labor, government procurement, and trade facilitation issues. Investment and competition were eventually included on the Doha Work Programme only under the titles "Relationship between Trade and Investment" and "Interaction between Trade and Competition."

[55] See generally J.M. Salazar-Xirinachs, "The Trade-Labor Nexus: Developing Countries' Perspectives" 2000 *Journal of International Economic Law* 3(2) 377.

an early stage may be implemented on a provisional or a definitive basis. Early agreements shall be taken into account in assessing the overall balance of the negotiations.[56]

The Doha Work Programme and mandate for the Trade Negotiations Committee further provided that the negotiations were to be concluded by 2005 "as a single undertaking" with the expectation that negotiations on the Dispute Settlement Understanding (DSU) and on a registration system for geographical indications would be concluded by 2003.

In practice, the allowance for provisional or definitive implementation on issues agreed upon at an earlier stage has been virtually ignored. No agreement on the DSU has been implemented separately either. While deadlocks interrupted negotiations many times in recent years, there had been several opportunities for side agreements and early implementation envisioned by the Doha Ministerial Declaration. For example, reports identified that the Cancún Ministerial Meeting, widely seen as a failure, actually saw some agreements emerge in several areas, including modalities for agricultural negotiations and a preliminary agreement to eliminate agricultural export subsidies and trade-distorting export subsidies.[57] Similarly, at the 2005 Hong Kong Ministerial Meeting, several proposals garnered members' approval and many developing members took those issues to be approved in principle and not subject to reexamination or renegotiation as part of the remaining outstanding agenda items. For example, the cotton subsidies accord promoted by the Cotton Four group and the duty-free/quota-free initiative in favor of LDCs resulting from the EU's Everything-But-Arms proposal could have been implemented at least provisionally, if not definitively, since 2005.[58] Instead, those issues are now back on the table and subordinated to inflammatory agriculture and Non-Agricultural Market Access (NAMA) negotiations. These constitute clear examples where a strict application of the single undertaking, even beyond the Doha mandate, had an adverse impact on substantive outcomes for developing members.

The only exception to members' refusal to implement early agreed-upon commitments is the Decision on Public Health and the ensuing TRIPS amendment that is open for ratification.[59] The Decision and the amendment aim to improve

---

[56] Doha Declaration, at 28; See, eg "In the Twilight of Doha" *The Economist* (29 July 2006), at 63–4 (documenting the suspension of negotiations in 2006); P. Lamy, "Time Out Needed to Review Options and Positions" (Speech delivered on 24 July 2007) <http://www.wto.org> (documenting the suspension of negotiations in 2007).

[57] B. Mercurio, "The WTO and its Institutional Impediments" 2007 *Melbourne Journal of International Law* 8(1) 198, at 201.

[58] Agreement in principle was also reached regarding the extension of the implementation period of the Agreement on Trade-Related Investment Measures (TRIMS) for LDCs. Last, members also agreed to eliminate agricultural export subsidies by 2013.

[59] The Decision provides procedures for imports and exports of drugs made for a developing country under the compulsory licensing scheme of Art 31 of the TRIPS agreement. The Decision became effective in 2003 and will remain effective until 2009 (and possibly later if needed) pending the entry into force of the TRIPS amendment. WTO General Council, *Decision on Implementation of Paragraph 6 of the Doha Declaration on the TRIPS Agreement and Public Health*, WT/L/540 and Corr.1 (1 September 2003); WTO General Council, *Decision on the Amendment of the TRIPS Agreement*, WT/L/641 (6 December 2005).

access to drugs by developing members facing public health emergencies.[60] The political and human urgency of dealing with pandemics that were particularly irremediable in poor developing countries accounts for the fact that members were willing to make an exception to the single undertaking, while they failed to avail themselves of the opportunity in other areas of the negotiations.

The normative risks of combining strategic linkage and the single undertaking have been well identified. In the words of Leebron, "[l]inking disparate issues into a single regime...poses the risk that the policy goals of one of the issue areas will predominate, so that the goals of one are effectively sacrificed to the other."[61]

Failing to confront the difficult substantive and normative questions of what to include in the single undertaking makes it all too easy for members to block negotiations because they fear that the addition of a particular topic will only be a Trojan horse for protectionism. Effectively, the powerful tool of the single undertaking as an excluder or aggregator of topics has become a proxy for voicing concerns over the legitimacy of members' intentions. While a topic might well fit under the aegis of the WTO, the all-or-nothing requirement of the single under-taking as it is currently implemented overrides any serious consideration of the true normative implications of the topic and hence also precludes any negotiation of the underlying substantive issues.

Yet, as will be argued in Chapter 12, it is not necessary for the single under-taking to result in an all-or-nothing linkage. A broader spectrum of relationships between linkage and negotiation design exists. If partial linkage were recognized as a more desirable and realistic avenue, members would be forced to consider the substantive and normative nature of the linkage of particular trade topics.[62]

3. The WTO as an Administration: What Impact on Developing Country Participation?

Despite the ostensible functioning of the WTO as a "member-driven organiza-tion" which formally devolves virtually no rule-making power to its organs, there is in fact a norm-producing activity, binding in some cases, in the day-to-day oper-ations of the organization. The issue then is the role of developing members in the norm and rule-making activity.

A budding body of literature has considered the rise of quasi-administrative bodies at the WTO and their production of what has been dubbed "secondary legislation" in reference to the EU's rule-making processes. At the WTO, the

---

[60] See also WTO General Council, *Decision on Least-Developed Country Members—Obligations Under Article 70.9 of the TRIPS Agreement with Respect to Pharmaceutical Products*, WT/L/478 (8 July 2002).

[61] D.W. Leebron, "Linkages" 2002 *American Journal of International Law* 96(1) 5 at 25.

[62] S. Cho, "Linkage of Free Trade and Social Regulation: Moving Beyond the Entropic Dilemma" 2005 *Chicago Journal of International Law* 5(2) 625, at 638 ("The uncompromising nature of the con-ventional linkage narratives thus tends to thwart the development of an eclectic matrix of solutions that would be more feasible in reality.").

"primary legislation" consists in the multilateral agreements concluded as a result of a negotiation round involving all WTO members. The "secondary legislation" would encompass any binding undertaking by the members that happens outside of these rounds. Examples since the conclusion of the Uruguay Round include the 1996 Agreement on Information Technology,[63] the three protocols, under the GATS, on commitments in financial services and basic telecommunications, the Kimberley Waiver to allow bans on trade of "conflict diamonds,"[64] and the 1999 Decision on Waiver for LDCs. "Secondary legislation" could also be understood to encompass the growing activity of WTO Councils, Committees, Subcommittees, and Working Parties that produce guidelines, practices, understandings, and gentlemen's agreements that influence members' behavior.[65] This still hotly contested evolution intersects with the literature on international economic law governance, constitutionalism, transnational networks, global administrative law, and the role of technocracies and experts. Rather than reviewing these studies, the focus in this section is to point out the importance of such secondary rule- and norm-making practice on developing members through the lens of participation.

It is a truism that many developing countries and most LDCs do not have the resources to participate consistently—or even at all—in the numerous bodies administering the WTO agreements. The issue, then, is the implication for them of the administrative and legislative function of these bodies. For the rest of the members, the problem is the legitimacy and adequacy of norms that emerge from subgroups of members where there has been no real representation of vast portions of the membership.

The typical answer to these questions is that members unable to meaningfully participate account for a small portion of world trade, so that their absence is not a hindrance to elaborating sensible rules or to managing trade flows that bypass them anyway. Of course, this position ignores the political legitimacy implications, and, from an economic standpoint, it obviates the fact that a small portion of world trade in the aggregate might still represent an important portion of a (small) country's trade. In other words, while a particular country's participation might have little bearing on the global economy, it might have a huge impact on that country's economy and development. Moreover, such a position takes an essentially retrospective approach to managing the world's economy, forgetting that the trade flows of yesterday may be different tomorrow and that the WTO agreements are making rules for the future, not the past.

---

[63] *Ministerial Declaration on Trade in Information Technology Products*, WT/MIN(96)/16 (13 December 1996).

[64] WTO Council for Trade in Goods, *Waiver Concerning Kimberley Process Certification Scheme for Rough Diamonds: Communication*, G/C/W/432/Rev.1 (24 February 2003); WTO General Council, *Proposed Agenda*, WT/GC/W/498 (13 May 2003), at Item VI. WTO Members that are parties to the Kimberley Process need not be covered by a waiver, so long as the trade restrictions they implement among themselves are clearly in line with the Kimberley Process.

[65] For some examples from the Services Council and the Committee on Sanitary and Phytosanitary Measures, see A. Lang and J. Scott, "The Hidden World of WTO Governance" 2009 *European Journal of International Law* 20(3) 575.

This section argues that WTO bodies increasingly create hard and soft law that constrains members' trade practices. In this perspective, the issue of representation of all segments of the membership is particularly acute. Section 3.1 introduces the WTO's secondary rule-making activity. Section 3.2 then provides some empirical analysis of participation by developing countries in WTO bodies. Chapter 12 offers some proposals to reduce the participation gap in WTO bodies, with a view to ultimately enhancing developing country access and influence.

3.1 Rule and norm creation by WTO bodies

The WTO has not escaped the attention of global administrative law scholars, who point to a number of norm-creation processes within the organization that are more akin to administrative law.[66] Over the past decade or so, the field of global administrative law has emerged as a new account of norm creation in international law that bypasses traditional treaties and customary law processes. Others use EU "secondary legislation" as an analogy to describe rule-making by the subsidiary bodies of an organization, outside of the formal treaty-making process.[67]

In fact, the practice is not new to the WTO: During the last years of the Uruguay Round, the Trade Negotiation Committee adopted a number of decisions, which eventually became part of the Uruguay Round agreements.[68] After the creation of the WTO, this was the case very early on with the General Council Decision on Decision-Making Procedures under Article IX and XII of the WTO Agreement, which essentially amends the WTO Agreement to make consensus the default approach for decisions on accessions and on waivers.[69] This Decision is particularly crucial as it allows members to make further "secondary" rules as subsidiary bodies. Indeed, this extended secondary legislative power was used in 1999 for the Decision on Waiver for LDCs. A few years later, the Kimberley Waiver allowing bans on trade of "conflict diamonds" adopted by the Council for Trade in Goods and the WTO General Council became another example of "secondary legislation" activity by WTO bodies.

While the Information Technology Agreement does not create binding obligations for all members, it inaugurates a different track for regulation within the WTO system, where a subgroup of members can enter into sectoral agreements. During the Singapore Ministerial Meeting in 1996, thirteen members and the EU

---

[66] B. Kingsbury, N. Krisch and R.B. Stewart, "The Emergence of Global Administrative Law" 2005 *Law and Contemporary Problems* 68(1) 15, at 27.

[67] P. Mavroidis, "No Outsourcing of Law? WTO Law as Practiced by WTO Courts" 2008 *American Journal of International Law* 102(3) 421, at 423–7, 429 (Mavroidis differentiates between three categories of secondary law at the WTO: joint action by the WTO membership, including waivers, interpretations, and amendments; decisions and recommendations adopted by WTO organs; and international agreements signed by the WTO).

[68] Eg, Decision on anti-circumvention, LT/UR/D-3/1 (15 April 1994), Decision on review of Article 17.6 of the Agreement on Implementation of Article VI of the General Agreement on Tariffs and Trade 1994, LT/UR/D-3/2 (15 April 1994), Decision on measures in favour of least-developed countries, LT/UR/D-1/3 (15 April. 1994).

[69] Statement by the Chairman, *Decision-Making Procedures under Articles IX and XII of the WTO Agreement—As Agreed by the General Council*, WT/L/93 (15 November 1995).

issued a Ministerial Declaration on Trade in Information Technology Products, now known as the Information Technology Agreement. The Declaration sets out modalities by which the signatory members agree to bind their tariffs and eliminate duties with respect to a number of products specified in the annex. The commitments are stringent: In order to participate, members must undertake to reduce to a zero tariff level all products listed in the Declaration and to eliminate all other duties and charges. A subsequent Document on Implementation establishes a committee to monitor the agreement. This Committee, in turn, creates its own rules of procedures and meets on a regular basis to evaluate new participation as well as to review the product coverage (the expansion of coverage was envisioned in the original Declaration). There are currently forty-six members and the EU that are parties to the Information Technology Agreement. Here again, the intersection between institutional frameworks and regulatory outcomes comes to light: The small group of members which originally created the Information Technology Agreement deemed it necessary to create a Committee to support their work and help frame future negotiations.

The four protocols, under the GATS, on commitments in financial services, movement of natural persons, and basic telecommunications,[70] have also been cited by some as examples of secondary legislation. These protocols were adopted by groups of members which had made particular commitments. Their designation as secondary legislation is therefore not as clear since they were not adopted by a body of the organization. Unlike the Information Technology Agreement, they did not create a permanent body to support their administration. However, inasmuch as the WTO agreements are seen as a single package of commitments, such posterior side agreements amongst some members could be seen as affecting the rights, obligations, and opportunities of other members as well, who had little opportunity to influence it.

The secondary legislative and the quasi-administrative regulation undertaken by WTO bodies also take the form of softer instruments that are nonetheless intended to affect the practice of members and the dispute settlement adjudicators. Lang and Scott's work on the Services Council and the SPS Committee brings these dynamics to light. They identify several functions of theses bodies: information sharing, raising "specific trade concerns," monitoring harmonization activities in other international organizations, and norm elaboration.[71]

With respect to information sharing in the Services Council Committees, they note that although a number of developing countries participate in the discussion and make presentations on aspects of their services economy, these members are resistant to the findings of the committees, or insights shared by representatives of other organizations being made into regulatory or soft law instruments. Even coordination on standard setting has been received with skepticism, for fear that they

---

[70] WTO, *Second Protocol on the General Agreement on Trade in Services*, S/L/11(24 July 1995); WTO, *Third Protocol on the General Agreement on Trade in Services*, S/L/12 (24 July 1995); WTO, *Fourth Protocol on the General Agreement on Trade in Services*, S/L/20 (30 April 1996); WTO, *Fifth Protocol on the General Agreement on Trade in Services*, S/L/45(3 December 1997).

[71] Lang and Scott, above fn 65.

might eventually become part of WTO disciplines or interpretative guidelines in adjudication.[72] Nonetheless, information-sharing seems to operate in the shadow of negotiations, with members using opportunities for presentations in committees to signal to others what their future negotiation positions might be, and what might not be acceptable undertakings. Participation by a broad range of members, or at least, by members representing (formally or informally) different constituencies, would therefore appear critical. Conversely, it is likely that members which lack access to the information, tone, and spirit of information-sharing sessions and other committee discussions will be at a disadvantage when engaging in formal negotiations.

The SPS Committee, where activities relating to standard-setting and monitoring are a critical part of administering the agreement, appears to be received with similar ambivalence by developing countries. While they have been very active in raising specific trade concerns, the issue of their participation in standard setting, is still open. Still, the Committee has adopted a number of guidelines, recommendations, and decisions to support the implementation of the SPS Agreement.[73] The growing role of the *Codex Alimentarius* (created in 1963 by the Food and Agricultural Organization) is also a testimonial to quasi-administrative law emerging in the WTO context. According to some, it can be an opportunity to increase transparency and limit restrictions to trade by developed countries against products from developing countries.[74] For others, the use of *Codex* standards is just another example of legal imperialism because developed country industries have historically been more involved in standard setting, the participation by developing countries is weak (mostly due to capacity constraints), and the *Codex* Commission decision-making does not afford sufficient safeguards to ensure that the adopted standards reflect a true consensus involving developing countries.[75]

In some cases, an interpretative consensus emerges from a subsidiary body at the WTO, sometimes even leading to an informal agreement not to initiate a dispute on the issue. For example, the GATS read literally could be interpreted to prohibit differentiated state taxes in federal states such as the United States. After a discussion in the Services Council, members informally agreed to continue to explore the issue and, in the meantime, to refrain from bringing the matter for adjudication, as it had most likely not been the intention of the GATS drafters to prohibit differentiated state taxes.[76] Formally, WTO members are not actually bound not to bring such a dispute. The consensus is more in the nature of a "gentlemen's agreement." Where does that leave members that were not able to participate in the discussion in the Services Council meetings? In theory, they could still challenge the measure if it was in their interest to do so. Yet, there is likely to be some peer pressure for

---

[72] Ibid at 580.   [73] Ibid at 597–8.

[74] J. Steinberg and M. Mazarr, *Developing Country Participation in Transnational Decision-making: Lessons for IT Governance* (2003) (unpublished manuscript).

[75] B.S. Chimni, "Co-option and Resistance: Two faces of Global Administrative Law" 2005 *New York University Journal of International Law and Politics* 37(4) 799, at 811–18.

[76] Lang and Scott, above fn 65, at 587.

them not to do so, even though they had no part in shaping the consensus not to sue.

Without engaging an exhaustive review of the type and volume of secondary legislation and quasi-administrative law that is currently produced by the WTO, it is already clear that active, informed participation by members in subsidiary bodies is increasingly critical if they are to retain a voice in shaping WTO disciplines. This is perhaps even more true at a time when the formal multilateral negotiations are stalled. Now that the WTO has an institutional existence, it does what any bureaucracy does: It produces norms, practices, and even rules. Yet little attention has been devoted to the impact of that phenomenon for capacity-constrained developing members and the practical measures that could be taken to remedy their participatory gap. The next section provides some empirical evidence to paint a clearer picture of who participates in WTO subsidiary bodies. This in turn could help focus efforts on improving access for those who need it most.

3.2 Trends in developing country participation in WTO bodies

No less than three dozen bodies manage the WTO, including the General Council and its various configurations such as the Dispute Settlement Body and Trade Policy Review Body, the Councils for each main agreement and their myriad committees, subcommittees and working parties, the plurilateral committees, and the Trade Negotiation Committee and its bodies. A few inactive committees have not been counted. In theory, any member can participate in any body. Realistically, the organization would be paralyzed if 153 representatives attended every committee activity in person. In practice, only the larger delegations have the incentives and resources to participate meaningfully across the board.

This section presents some quantitative parameters of developing country participation in committees. This analysis is necessarily limited because there is no publicly available data on the identity of members present in committee meetings. However, alternative data can be used to paint a preliminary picture of developing country participation in the WTO bodies. Three data sources are considered. First, the nationality of Chairs appointed since 1995 provides some interesting trends regarding opportunities for appointment for representatives of developing countries. Second, meeting minutes reflect interventions by representatives in committees. While an imperfect proxy for actual presence, this data reveals at least the baseline of representatives present (those who made remarks that were reported in the minutes). Sociological research shows that representatives, especially from small delegations and developing countries, have a strong incentive to supply their home state with tangible evidence of their activities in Geneva.[77] Making interventions in committee meetings, even if fairly mundane (such as thanking another member for their presentation or answers), is one way to achieve such visibility. Third, the data on country of origin of Secretariat members provides another data set. Indeed, many are former diplomats from developing countries, who now hold

---

[77] Elsig, above fn 40, at 19.

civil servant positions within the Secretariat. As such, they are well versed in and sensitive to development issues and, while they are formally independent from their home countries, they typically have personal and professional ties with member representatives dating to their time in the service of their home countries. In light of the increasing Secretariat activity in preparing background materials and post-meeting reports for the Chairs and for members, these individuals play an important institutional role.

Statistical tools, such as a Bayesian analysis, help to compare the prevalence of developing country participation with that of developed countries based on these three data sets. While developing country participation might in fact be higher, the available data establishes a baseline. A finer analysis allows for a break down of the "developing country" aggregate to make regional comparisons.

Nationality of WTO subsidiary bodies' Chairpersons as an indicator of developing country participation

Some have argued that three sets of informal rules govern the allocation of leadership position at the WTO: First, the United States has "special privileges" as the world's largest trading country; second, the Quad (the world's four major trading powers) also have "special privileges;" last, the balance of chairmanships are allocated on a rotating basis amongst the rest of the membership, with an eye to regional balance (the existence of such a geographic weighting being contested by some).[78] Other evidence suggests that Chairs tend to be allocated preferably to smaller delegations.[79] Either way, chairmanships carry prestige, a privileged access to information, and, typically, a seat in the Green Room,[80] all of which give important participation and representation opportunities.

Table 9.1 presents the geographical allocation of Chairs and the total percentage of Chairs held by each category of developing countries at five-year intervals since the creation of the WTO.

Both in terms of world population and percentage of WTO membership, developed countries are significantly overrepresented. Instead, the Chair allocation is more representative of the percentage of world trade. To wit, in 2000, developing countries accounted for 30.57 percent of global merchandise exports and 27.8 percent of merchandise imports.[81] That year, developing countries held 41 percent of the Chairs. In 2008, developing economies' share in merchandise exports was 38 percent and their share in merchandise imports was 34 percent, compared with 46 percent of the Chairs in 2005. The percentage of developing countries in the world trade in services is somewhat lower (12.3 percent of total commercial services exports in 2008 and 31 percent of imports).

---

[78] J.K. Cogan, "Representation and Power in International Organizations: The Operational Constitution and its Critics," 2009 *American Journal of International Law* 103(1) 209, at 232.
[79] Elsig, above fn 40, at 19.   [80] Ibid.
[81] Committee on Trade and Development, Note by the Secretariat, *Participation of Developing Economies in the Global Trading System*,WT/COMTD/W/172/Rev.1 (21 January 2010), at 51, 55.

Table 9.1 Allocation of Chairs between developed and developing countries in absolute numbers and percentage

Year	Total number of Chairs serving that year	Developed Countries[1]	Africa	Asia	Latin America	Caribbean	Oceania
1995	22	13 (59%)	2 (9%)	4 (18%)	3	0	0
2000	27	16 (59%)	3 (11%)	3 (11%)	3 (11%)	1 (4%)	1 (4%)
2005	44	24 (54%)	6 (14%)	6 (14%)	6 (14%)	0	2 (4%)
2011	42	18 (42%)	9 (21%)	2 (5%)	8 (19%)	2 (5%)	3(8%)

Source: <http://www.wto.org/english/thewto_e/secre_e/current_chairs_e.htm>.

[1] European countries, the United States, Canada, Australia, New Zealand, South Korea, Singapore, Turkey, Japan, Switzerland, and Hong Kong are all counted as developed countries.

Considering representation by region, Asia appears to be underrepresented if the focus is on demographics and share in world trade. Developing Asia's share of world merchandise exports was over 21 percent, its share of merchandise imports was 20 percent, its share in exports of commercial services was 17.4 percent, and share of imports of commercial services was 18.38 percent in 2008.[82] By contrast, in 2011, Asia held only 5 percent of the Chairs.

Despite the paucity of publicly available information on the politics of allocation, it can be reasonably inferred that the economic weight of different world regions plays a significant role in the allocation of chairmanships, combined, most likely, with political considerations. This is a far cry from an allocation of the Chairs that would be based on sovereign equality. Here again, as in the case of decision-making rules, we observe a disconnect between the formal premises of the WTO as based on sovereign equality and the actual practice, much more grounded in economic power. This discrepancy is quite unique when compared with the IMF and the World Bank, where decision-making power is clearly pegged on economic benchmarks, rather than sovereign equality.

Reported interventions by members' representatives in WTO bodies as an indicator of participation

Using the minutes of a number of General Council subsidiary bodies in 2010, it is possible to identify which members actively participated by making remarks, which constitute a baseline of which countries were represented in committees. It is likely that other representatives were present in the room but did not make comments that were reported in the minutes. For this reason, the level of participation described here is a floor rather than a ceiling. For the reasons presented at the outset

[82] Ibid at 59, 63.

of this section, it is nonetheless a reasonable measure of the overall distribution of WTO members' participation.

The meeting minutes of the Trade in Goods Council, the Trade in Services Council and their subsidiary bodies, and the General Council (totaling 22 bodies) were examined for 2010. Each body met one to four times that year. Overall, the data described here was gathered from fifty-six meeting minutes. When a member representative made a comment, it was counted as a participant, but only once per meeting, even if that representative made several reported remarks. Because the objective is to identify who, at minimum, was present in the room, the qualitative content of the remarks (whether the comments were purely formal or more substantive) is irrelevant here.

Not surprisingly, the data shows the presence of Japan, the United States, and the EU in virtually every meeting. Canada, Norway, Taiwan, and Turkey were also present in the vast majority of the meetings. There is additionally a strong presence of Argentina, Brazil, Chile, China, and India, which participated in about half of the meetings, respectively. A few additional developing countries participated in more than a quarter of the meetings.[83] All other developing countries had a lower presence. Overall, African and Oceania countries had the lowest participation.

Statistical tools can help refine the interpretation of this raw data.[84] Empirical Bayesian analysis can be used to estimate the probability of an event occurring given information about its occurrences. Using the frequency of developed[85] and developing[86] members' participation in past meetings and the proportion of membership from each category in the WTO, the likelihood of a developing country participating in a meeting is calculated. The equation below shows the formula used. The probability estimates were calculated for each of the fifty-six past meetings and the results were averaged to arrive at a final estimate.

$$P(+ \mid D) = \frac{P(D \mid +)P(+)}{P(D)}$$

where $P(+|D)$ is the probability that the participating member is a developing country, $P(D)$ is the probability of a WTO member being a developing country, and $P(+)$ is the probability of a WTO member participating in a meeting.

The results show that the probability of a developing country participating is about 9 percent compared with about 16 percent for developed countries. Thus, developing country participation is significantly lower than would be expected given that they account for over 70 percent of the WTO membership. In this

---

[83] Colombia, Ecuador, Egypt, Indonesia, Mexico, Pakistan, the Philippines, South Africa, and Thailand. Barbados and the Dominican Republic participated in almost a quarter of the meetings, respectively.

[84] The assistance of Abinand Rangesh, PhD, MEng, MA (Cantab) for the statistical computations is gratefully acknowledged.

[85] "Developed countries" include WTO members that are high-income OECD countries, and Singapore, Hong Kong, and Taiwan.

[86] Developing countries were considered to be all other members.

computation, the EU participating as such was counted as a single member, but EU countries were also counted individually because some representatives' participation was recorded in meeting minutes as being that of the individual country, rather than the EU's. A more accurate representation is to consider the EU as a single member and to ignore the residual participation by individual EU countries. The group of "developed members" is then reduced by twenty-seven members (as is the overall number of WTO members) for purposes of the calculations. The probability of a developed country participating is now 37 percent. In other words, there is a more than one in three chance that each developed country will participate in a meeting, compared with less than one in ten chance that a developing country will participate.

The same analysis shows that meeting participation is approximately 2.2 percent for LDCs. In other words, each LDC is expected to participate once in every fifty meetings. This is significantly lower than would be expected in comparison to their 20 percent proportion of the WTO membership. Zambia, with a recorded intervention in eleven meetings, and Bangladesh, with five instances of participation, were the LDC members with the most intensive participation.

This data and the statistical analysis supports the widely held view that the vast majority of developing countries, and LDCs in particular are not very frequent participants in the quite intensive day-to-day activities of WTO subsidiary bodies.

Nationality of Secretariat members

The Secretariat has made particular efforts to diversify its staff since the inception of the WTO.[87] As international civil servants, Secretariat staff members must act independently of their home country and discharge their duties with impartiality.[88] They, in fact, take an oath to that effect. Nonetheless, there is a cross-pollination between the Secretariat and representatives of WTO members. A fertile recruiting ground is representatives from developing countries, who bring expertise as well as diversity, and an understanding of the workings of the organization. The internship programs also yield recruits from developing countries. Some 58 percent of professional positions that were staffed by people having previously completed an internship have been filled by nationals from developing countries.[89] Junior professional staff, in particular, tend to be hired from interns. More seasoned diplomats or policy-makers from developing countries who take up senior staff positions at the WTO inform their work with the experience they have previously gained as trade negotiators for their government.[90] While they

---

[87] This analysis excludes linguistic staff.

[88] Committee on Budget, Finance and Administration, *Report on Diversity in the WTO Secretariat*, WT/BFA/W/195(1 March 2010), at 2, citing Staff Regulation 1.4.   [89] Ibid at 4.

[90] For example, Deputy Director General Alejandro Jara was previously a member of the Foreign Service of Chile and led the Chilean delegation to the GATT for a number of years, as well as holding a number of top international economic relations postings throughout his career with the Chilean civil service. Similarly, Deputy Director General Valentine Sendanyoye Rugwabiza held a number of senior diplomatic postings for Rwanda prior to joining the WTO. Deputy Director General Harsha Vardhana Singh has gone back and forth between the GATT/WTO Secretariat and government work in India. Shishir Priyadarshi, Director of the Development Division, formerly was with South

clearly must (and do) act independently as WTO staff members, their previous career makes them more attuned to perspectives and issues that staffers from other backgrounds might ignore. That said, the increasing role of the Secretariat in the substantive work product of the WTO is not always welcomed by developing countries, despite the more diverse composition of Secretariat staff members.[91] Extreme caution must be taken not to equate the WTO members' participation as sovereign states and the indirect benefits of developing country nationals holding staff positions at the Secretariat.

In 1995, developed country nationals accounted for over 79 percent of the WTO professional staff. A steady decrease took place over the next fifteen years, with nearly 65 percent of developed country professional staff in 2010. In the meantime, the percentage of professional staff from developing countries increased from 20.7 percent to nearly 31 percent. LDCs, which were not represented at all in 1995 (no WTO member was an LDC at that time), now account for 4.4 percent of the professional staff.[92]

While diversity has undoubtedly increased significantly, 61 percent of the professional staff hired since 1995 was from developed countries. Still, considering that there is a much greater pool of qualified applicants from developed countries due to the vast number of trade, law, and economic graduate program graduates, for example, the number of recruits from developing countries and LDCs is impressive. There are seventy-five nationalities of members currently represented, or nearly half the total number of WTO members. Of the twenty-four members with over 1 percent of staff representation, ten are developing countries.[93]

Looking at a regional breakdown, Europe and North America (comprising Canada and the United States in this statistic) account for about 61 percent of the professional staff in 2010; Africa for nearly 10 percent of the professional staff, Asia for slightly over 14 percent, Latin America 11 percent, and Oceania nearly 4 percent.

The rise in number of developing country nationals at the Secretariat is not a direct measure of increased opportunities for developing country participation in the WTO. It is, however, relevant to their participation in a number of ways: It helps to build capacity and to increase the pool of highly qualified developing country trade specialists, it promotes a cross-fertilization of ideas, and it diversifies the range of policy and technical perspectives that will in turn inform the voluminous work product of the Secretariat. In the short and long run, then, the representation of developing countries and LDCs in the WTO staff can contribute to the positioning and opportunities of developing country members.

Centre an intergovernmental developing country think-tank, and served as a representative of the Indian government at the WTO. Ricardo Barba, of the Trade Policy Review Division, was a former senior member of the Mexican trade mission. These are but a few instances of senior WTO officials with earlier experience in the diplomatic or other governmental services of their home developing countries prior to joining the Secretariat.

[91] See, eg, Elsig, above fn 40, at 20–1.   [92] Ibid at 17.
[93] Ibid at 3. India, China, Colombia, Brazil, Philippines, and Egypt each accounts for more than 1.5 percent of the staff.

4. Conclusion

SDT is typically thought of as the natural and only legal space for development issues at the WTO, but the reality is that many institutional features of the organization have a critical impact on the opportunities for developing members in the trade regime. The institutions and decision-making rules at the WTO, while facially neutral in most cases, can and do have disparate impacts on various segments of the membership. The negotiation process itself empowers or disenfranchises members depending how it is designed.

The discriminatory effect of institutions, decision-making, norm elaboration, and agenda-setting processes is well known in the legal, sociological, and political science realms domestically. Some work has been done with respect to international institutions as well, but almost no literature focuses on these dynamics at the WTO.

From a normative perspective, the current institutional *status quo* appears to embrace a formal equality approach that is aligned neither with the economic and power weighting that controls in reality, nor with a legal and ethical notion of equity or actual equality. In respect to institutional dynamics perhaps even more so than regarding SDT, the normative implications of the trade and development relationship have been ignored in the WTO discourse. Yet developing members' increasing political and economic power clearly calls for a reexamination of the choices made by the institution. This chapter, by revealing some of the trends and implicit features of the WTO as an institution, hopes to give tools for members to engage in a reconsideration of the *status quo*.

IV

RETHINKING THE TRADE AND DEVELOPMENT RELATIONSHIP AT THE WTO

The introduction to this book presented two paradigms to use as benchmarks for assessing the trade and development relationship at the WTO. First, the *idiosyncratic approach* to development at the WTO represents an *ad hoc* approach largely devoid of overarching normative principles to inform when and how development considerations would be taken into account in drafting, interpreting, or implementing trade disciplines. Instead, development issues would be addressed on a case-by-case basis, if and when the need arose. In practice, it resembles more closely the current framework for SDT, with no real normative embedding of development as a core component of the WTO's mandate. Second, in the *normative co-constituent* paradigm, development is considered as normatively on par with the objective of trade liberalization. As such, WTO rules and institutions would be infused by a trade liberalization objective as well as the promotion of development. In practice, the preamble to the Marrakesh Agreement mentioning the objective of sustainable development can be seen as an embryonic illustration of this second paradigm.

This part takes a forward-looking perspective and asks whether the current efforts in the Doha Round are likely to transform the trade and development relationship at the WTO (Chapter 10), whether the WTO can be envisioned with a more integrated consideration of trade and development (Chapter 11), and finally offers a menu of legal tools that could help reconcile the current tension between developing members' needs and the design of trade disciplines and institutions at the WTO (Chapter 12). Throughout, the two paradigms are guides to help situate what members tried (and failed) to achieve in the Doha Round, and what could be done with the appropriate level of political willpower.

10

The Doha Round:
Chronicle of a Death Foretold?

Hindsight will tell us for certain whether the Doha Round will ever live up to its promises, but throughout the Round, it has been clear that despite developing countries' unprecedented level of participation, there has been no new approach to addressing development at the WTO. For all the originality of a "Development Round," the debate on the most contentious issues, particularly agricultural support, market access for products from developing countries, and preferences, seems frozen in time. Most of the proposals submitted by developing countries are strikingly similar in form and content to existing SDT provisions, and hence, are likely to be equally fraught with failure. Perhaps even more importantly, there has been little questioning of institutional and systemic issues alongside the substantive trade commitments. The combination of limited institutional opportunities and inadequate trade commitments undermines developing members' positions at the WTO, but attempting to change the law without rebalancing the institutional process is bound to fail.

The proposals submitted by developing countries in the first four years of the Round are now essentially shelved. An examination of developing members' activity in the Doha Round provides a cautionary tale against somewhat misguided proposals that cost those members some of their bargaining goodwill but would, in many cases, not accomplish the desired objectives. Developing members (certainly India, Brazil, and China among them) now have a political blocking power in the negotiations and will likely be increasingly successful in gaining control of the agenda. However, they have yet to formulate an effective "positive" law-making strategy ensuring that their needs and concerns are addressed in the multilateral trading system. This chapter takes stock of the progress and limitations of their work during the Doha Round and may serve to help avoid similar pitfalls in future negotiations. Indeed, while the Round is unlikely to reach even a semblance of the objectives set forth in the Doha Agenda, the underlying issues will not disappear. Rather, they will continue to haunt the multilateral negotiations as they have since the GATT's inception.

Developing members submitted a number of largely SDT-focused proposals in 2001, first as General Council documents and later in the framework of the Committee on Trade and Development in 2002 and 2003. In the run-up to the Cancún Ministerial Meeting, General Council Chairman Carlos Pérez del Castillo (then Permanent Representative of Uruguay to the WTO) circulated a document categorizing the proposals into three "baskets," depending on the degree of consensus and support that each proposal had garnered.[1] Since WTO members could not reach an agreement at the 2003 Cancún meeting, in 2005 at Hong Kong, or at the July 2008 Geneva mini-ministerial, the proposals have remained at a standstill to date. Between 2004 and 2006, some proposals have been presented within agreement-specific committees, but since no general agreement on negotiations has been reached at the committees level, the proposals have not been further disseminated.

According to several delegates as well as Secretariat members, while agreement-specific proposals (presumably those studied in committees, particularly proposals regarding the Agreement on Agriculture) had some likelihood of succeeding, more general proposals or cross-cutting proposals would probably not form part of the final negotiation package. This is in part the result of disseminating proposals in agreement-specific committees, rather than keeping the discussion centralized at the Committee on Trade and Development: Agreement-specific committees do not offer an appropriate forum for negotiating and refining cross-cutting proposals and institutional reform proposals because both are outside of their "jurisdiction."

An analysis of the proposals shows several trends in what they seek to achieve. Five main goals emerge:

- expounding the meaning of existing SDT provisions by giving more details on their scope and substance: with some fifty proposals, this is the most prevalent type. Additionally, proposals aimed at increasing the accountability of members and the WTO regarding their development-related obligations (about twenty proposals) are another way to reinforce existing provisions;
- creating new SDT clauses (about thirty proposals);
- extending transitional periods for implementation of the agreements, waiver periods, etc (about twenty proposals);
- reinforcing the obligatory value of SDT provisions (about eighteen proposals);
- protecting the "*acquis*" of the preferential regime (four proposals).

For each category, this chapter analyzes the legal techniques used, their legal value, and whether they are likely to fulfill their purpose.

---

[1] WTO General Council, *General Council Chairman's Proposal for an Approach for Special and Differential Treatment*, JOB(03)/68 (7 April 2003), at 2. Category I includes "Agreement-specific proposals which were already agreed in principle by Members in February 2003" and proposals most likely to garner support; Category II lists proposals relating to areas under negotiation pursuant to the Doha Development Agenda and other technical proposals considered in the relevant bodies, which were likely to be included in agreement-by-agreement negotiations; Category III includes proposals "on which we currently have wide divergences of views among Members," and are not likely to be adopted as they stood. See also Committee on Trade and Development, *Special Session: Report to the General Council*, TN/CTD/7 (10 February 2003) (hereinafter CTD Report), at Annex III (listing the proposals that were agreed in principle).

1. Proposed Amendments Expounding the Meaning of Existing SDT Provisions

Such proposals are directly in line with the Doha mandate and the call for "operationalizing" SDT; they strive to give obligatory and legal substance to clauses all too often limited to "best efforts." Only a few were ever "agreed in principle."

A number of clauses call upon developed members to "take into account" the development needs of members when devising domestic policies (Section 1.1). Other proposals give substance to SDT provisions by setting standards and procedures for implementation (Section 1.2). This is perhaps the most legally effective way to turn SDT into substantive binding commitments. A number of proposals also reinforce existing provisions by creating accountability mechanisms regarding the implementation of the provisions (Section 1.3). Finally, some proposals merely seek to confirm existing provisions (Section 1.4).

1.1 Programmatic provisions

A number of proposals refine the substance of SDT provisions by listing measures and programs that developed members should implement in favor of developing countries. This is particularly the case for SDT provisions that are for the benefit of developing or least-developed members but actually impose obligations on non-beneficiary members. While giving a more specific substance to broad and ill-defined objectives may render a provision more effective and implementable, a serious limitation remains since the provisions are subject to unilateral and mostly discretionary domestic implementation by developed countries. The issue has already been discussed in relation to trade preferences in Chapter 6.

One instance is the African Group's proposal to interpret GATT Article XXXVI paragraphs 2 to 7 as:

a binding commitment on the part of developed country Members in favour of developing and least-developed country Members to, (a) ensure a rapid and sustained expansion of export earnings of the developing and least-developed country Members; (b) ensure that developing and least-developed country Members secure a share of the growth in international trade commensurate with the needs of their economic development; (c) provide the maximum market access to products of export interest to developing and least-developed country Members and take measures to stabilise and improve conditions in world markets for these products particularly measures to attain stable, equitable, remunerative prices; (d) assist in the diversification of the economies of developed and least-developed country Members.[2]

---

[2] *Special and Differential Treatment Provisions: Joint Communication from the African Group in the WTO, Revision*, TN/CTD/W/3/Rev.2 (24 June 2002) (hereinafter African Group Proposal). The last language considered on this proposal, however, eliminated this programmatic guidance and was limited to a call for review by the Committee on Trade and Development of the implementation of Article XXXVI. See below discussion on proposals seeking to increase accountability.

Similarly, the African Group proposed that in implementing Article 66.2 of the TRIPS,

(i) developed country Members shall give incentives to enterprises and institutions in their territories through their laws or other administrative instruments; (ii) the incentives shall be of a magnitude and nature that will effectively operate as a motivation to transfer technology to least-developed country Members taking into account the actual conditions in the least-developed country Members and the difficulties expressed by enterprises and institutions.[3]

This example combines two techniques often used in the proposals to "operationalize" SDT: specifying the terms of the provision, and using words indicative of a binding commitment, such as "shall," instead of non-binding language such as "will." As noted in Chapter 6, both the legal and the political value of this drafting technique are limited.

The language of these fairly vague programmatic proposals is reminiscent of UN resolutions in the 1960s, 1970s, and early 1980s calling for more equitable exchanges, better terms of trade, and support of world prices particularly for primary commodities of interest to developing countries.[4] They call for a fundamental change in the way developed countries conduct their trade relations with developing countries, but developing countries are still framed as recipients of programs and policies to be formulated by developed countries. If earlier efforts by the UN are any indication, the political impact of these proposals likely will be limited, as will their legal effect.

1.2 Setting legal standards

Another set of proposals gives substance to SDT provisions by setting legal standards, specific procedures, and guidelines for implementation, sometimes even specifying avenues for recourse to the DSB. This is perhaps the most legally effective way to turn SDT provisions into binding commitments.

For example, a proposal on technical cooperation under the TRIPS Agreement (Article 67) fleshes out what technical cooperation might entail by requiring

comprehensive programmes comprising such components as improving the relevant legal framework in line with the general obligations of the Agreement, enhancing enforcement mechanisms, increasing training of personnel at the various levels, assisting in the preparation of laws and procedures in an effort to encourage and monitor technology transfer, making use of the rights and policy flexibility in the Agreement, and strengthening or establishing coordination between intellectual property rights, investment and competition authorities.[5]

The proposal does not give more legal value to the existing provision, but rather gives guidance on implementation. As such, it may reinforce the effectiveness of the provision, but it does not create any legal obligation regarding the quantity or

---

[3] Ibid at 23–4.   [4] See generally Ch 2.
[5] CTD Report, above fn 1, Annex III, at 8.

nature of technical cooperation programmes. This type of language is also useful to substantiate "best efforts" provisions discussed in Chapter 6.

Another interesting example is provided by a proposal on the Antidumping Agreement's Article 15 (on SDT). The African Group sought to give more specific modalities for the implementation of the requirement for "special regard" and the interpretation of "constructive remedies," "special situation," and "essential interests."[6] The proposal recommends a balancing test between dumping and injury against the background of "the WTO goals of improving living standards in developing and least-developed country Members through growth in the trade of these countries." Such balancing tests are imperfect but they are used in other legal systems, particularly in Anglo-Saxon common law. The proposal includes other procedural guidelines, such as a requirement of coherence between the Antidumping Agreement and the SCM Agreement. By giving some elements to interpret the requirement to account for developing countries, the proposal does give more legal value to this provision.

Similarly a proposal by India on Article 4.10 of the DSU seeks to operationalize the requirement that members "give special attention to the particular problems and interests of developing country Members."[7] First, it proposes to make the provision mandatory by using "shall," which in itself would not have a significant impact due to the vagueness of the substantive requirement. Second, regarding "giv[ing] special attention," a complainant developed country would be required to explain in the panel request and in its submissions how it has given particular consideration to the problems and interests of respondent developing countries and the panel would be required to rule on the issue as well. As discussed in Chapter 7, both issues (developed members' duty and the panel's duty) have found resonance in practice with respect to other DSU provisions.

Thus far, Article 4.10 DSU has not been cited in a single dispute. The proposed amendments might not be sufficient for parties and adjudicators to do much more than pay lip service to the provision. To avoid this, further guidelines would be necessary to specify what evidence is needed to support a claim of compliance with Article 4.10,[8] or the panels and possibly the AB would need to make robust rulings on the issue (drawing negative inferences from the lack of evidence) to influence members' future practice.

Several proposals seek to give a more specific (and more enforceable) substance to Article 21.2 of the DSU, on implementation measures (see substantive discussion of the case law in Chapter 7). The African Group wants the DSB to take into account "any economic or trade loss suffered by the developing country Member, by requiring that the developed country Member pay monetary compensation or make some other form of compensation to the developed country Member" and

---

[6] African Group Proposal, above fn 2, at 17.

[7] Committee on Trade and Development, *Communication from India*, TN/CTD/W/6 (17 June 2002) (hereinafter Communication from India), at 3–4.

[8] A further proposal by the African Group on DSU Article 4.10 specifies that "developed country Members shall present evidence of…how special attention has been given to particular problems and interests of developing country Members." See African Group Proposal, above fn 2, at 24.

to address "any difficulty that a developing country Member may face in seeking [enforcement], through authorizing collective suspension by the rest of the WTO Membership of obligations to the Member against which recommendations were made."[9] Meanwhile, a more modest proposal by India would require that taking into account "matters affecting the interests of developing country Members" be made a mandatory overarching provision in all disputes and that in practice, it translate into stricter "reasonable implementation periods."[10]

The African Group proposed that a binding interpretation of the Agreement on Agriculture's SDT provisions state:

It is understood that where developed country Members are to take measures of a special and differential treatment nature, they shall embody in their schedules of commitments or concessions specific special and differential treatment commitments in favour of developing and least-developed country Members, which shall be binding commitments.[11]

This proposal attempts to multilateralize measures that are otherwise often taken unilaterally (and hence are also unilaterally revocable). Including SDT concessions in schedules of commitments would make it much more difficult for members granting a concession to withdraw it at a later date, as they would have to offer compensation. Nonetheless, while such an amendment could play a role in shifting from unilateral preferential-style concessions to bilateral or multilateral actionable concessions, not every SDT measure can be translated into a tariff schedule.

Finally, some proposals shy away from specifying implementation procedures themselves but call for a WTO body to create such procedures.

Such is the case of an "agreed in principle" proposal on GATS Article IV. The proposal requires that "in all services negotiations, whether broad-based rounds of negotiations or separate negotiations on specific sectors, modalities shall be developed in order to allow the priorities of least-developed country Members to be presented and duly taken into account."[12] A proposal on GATT Article XVIII similarly aims at reforming procedures for recourse to this article by developing members. The proposal seeks to introduce a presumption that "the views of the developing and least-developed country Members concerned shall be fully accommodated and shall not be prejudiced or rejected except with the consensus of all Members." The proposal calls for members to create a multilateral framework for implementation of Article XVIII and Part IV of the GATT at the Fifth Ministerial Conference.[13]

1.3 Increasing accountability

Implementation procedures focus on accountability, typically by imposing a reporting requirement. As discussed in Chapter 6, increased accountability has several advantages: It allows for the generation of information on implementation

---

[9] Ibid at 25.   [10] Communication from India, above fn 7, at 4–5.
[11] African Group Proposal, above fn 2, at 12.
[12] CTD Report, above fn 1, Annex III, at 9.   [13] African Group Proposal, above fn 2, at 9.

and use of SDT, it increases transparency regarding members' undertakings and commitments, and it creates political leverage for developing countries when developed countries fall short of their obligations (the shaming effect of the reporting). Hence, while reporting requirements alone provide no guarantee that SDT will be better implemented, indirect effects may lead to improved compliance and may give political leverage to beneficiaries in the case of SDT obligations imposed on developed members for the benefit of developing members.

Virtually all proposals tending to increase accountability through reviewing and reporting mechanisms emanated from the African Group. This is the only category of proposals that is so uniform in its origin. Increased accountability has been proposed for GATS Article IV (Increasing Participation of Developing Countries), its Annex on Telecommunications (paragraph 6), TRIPS Articles 7 (objectives of the Agreement), 8 (principles), and 66.2 (technology transfer for LDCs). For the Enabling Clause, a more flexible mechanism was recommended, one aiming at increasing consultations and communication between developed and developing members on expansion of market access for products of export interest to developing countries.[14]

Other reporting mechanisms are designed to monitor the impact of certain obligations on developing or least-developed members. Such is the case for a proposal on paragraph 2(v) of the Decision on Measures in Favour of Least-Developed Countries aiming to assess the effect of trade measures on supply-side constraints for LDCs.[15] The proposal envisions building on the WTO's participation in the inter-organization Integrated Framework and the Joint Integrated Technical Assistance Programme by collaborating with the World Bank's country-specific Diagnostic Trade Integration Studies. A second step would require the Sub-Committee of the LDCs to biennially review implementation of the diagnostic tool in the context of the WTO, with particular emphasis on the impact of technical assistance provided in the field of export diversification. Here, the objective primarily is to generate information to better understand trade dynamics for LDCs, but the proposal also pushes towards a better integration of trade policies between the WTO, World Bank, United Nations Development Programme, UNCTAD, International Trade Centre, and the IMF. Efforts in this domain are crucial as uncoordinated policies may result in counterproductive results and programs that defeat each other.

Some proposals would introduce reporting requirements for all members. Such is the case for a proposal requiring all members to report biennially to the Committee on Agriculture any SPS measure that affects products from developing and LDC members.[16] The stated purpose of the proposal is to avoid the use of SPS measures to restrict trade in products originating from developing members. While the reporting requirement in itself would not prevent an SPS measure from being used in a reprehensible fashion, it would make the detection of such use easier, and hence it would expose the member to dispute consultations. Other suggested

---

[14] Ibid at 21.
[15] CTD Report, above fn 1, Annex III, at 10.
[16] African Group Proposal, above fn 2, at 12.

mechanisms for assessing and monitoring the impact of provisions include requiring impact assessments to be conducted before a measure is implemented to evaluate its likely impact on developing members.[17]

However, reviewing and reporting requirements are not always sufficient to promote transparency, accountability, or improved implementation: Reporting is meaningless if the underlying obligation is so vague that it is unclear what to report. For instance, an annual reporting requirement proposed concerning implementation of GATT Article XXXVI[18] may sound very straightforward, but considering that this article only sets out the general principles and objectives for Part IV of the GATT, it is difficult to see how to report on implementation at all.

Reporting requirements take many forms and would have varying degrees of success in improving the implementation and operationalization of SDT. While some are very technical (for example, the impact assessment requirement on SPS and TBT measures), others are too general and aim at even more indefinite clauses. The former truly may improve developing countries' position in international trade; the latter may lead to more disappointment by developing members as concrete results are unlikely to ensue. In many intermediate cases, reporting and reviewing mechanisms are a helpful instrument to generate information about measures taken by members and to increase transparency and ultimately accountability of all members.

1.4 Confirming existing SDT

A number of proposals simply reformulate or reiterate existing clauses, or correlate provisions across the agreements. These proposals are helpful to ensure consistency of interpretation throughout a complex set of interlocking agreements. Developing countries' interest in this issue is a testimony to their increased engagement and understanding of the WTO's legal regime.

For instance, a proposal on the TRIMS Agreement correlates the flexibility mechanism of Article 4 (Developing Country Members)—which itself operates by reference to GATT Article XVIII (and related Understandings and Declarations on balance-of-payment measures)—with the Doha Ministerial Decision of 2001 regarding Implementation-Related Issues and Concerns.[19] The Ministerial Decision provides a standard of interpretation on GATT Article XVIII that the proposal seeks to apply to the interpretation of TRIMS Article 4. The purpose is to confirm that, in accordance with the Ministerial Decision, recourse to GATT Article XVIII should be less onerous than recourse to GATT Article XII, so that the flexibility of TRIMS Article 4 should also reflect the lower threshold for measures taken under GATT Article XVIII. Along the same lines, Article 3 of the TRIMS Agreement incorporates "[a]ll exceptions under GATT 1994," and a proposal seeks

---

[17] Eg, requiring an assessment of the impact of developed country SPS measures proposed to be applied to developing country exports); see also ibid at 15–16 (requiring impact assessment prior to the implementation of standards under the TBT Agreement Arts 11 and 12).

[18] Ibid at 10.   [19] Ibid at 16.

to specify that this covers "cooperation arrangements, laws, measures and policies" adopted under the GATT and that operate as exceptions, including preferential regimes, quantitative restrictions under Articles XII, XVIII, and XIX of the GATT, and measures taken under Article XVIII.

In sum, proposals seeking to clarify the substance of existing SDT provisions succeed diversely in this effort. Proposals that set guidelines and procedures, or even those that merely replace vague declarations with binding legal standards are the most effective, particularly when they take into account possible impact at the dispute settlement level. These proposals make use of a number of different legal instruments, such as providing standards, creating reporting obligations, mandating existing technical bodies to develop procedures, setting bright-line tests, and mandating balancing tests to weight competing interests in disputes. By contrast, proposals relying on general, unilateral programs by developed members are less likely to reach their goal of substantiating SDT.

2. Proposals to Create New SDT Clauses

Given the dubious track record of SDT, the numerous complaints over the years that many SDT provisions are not useful or usable, and the flurry of proposals seeking to amend them, it may seem paradoxical that some thirty proposals suggest creating new SDT provisions. Moreover, the proposals are often strikingly similar in form to existing SDT clauses.

These proposals typically call for additional technical assistance, additional technology transfer, mechanisms to take into account developing members and LDCs' issues, waivers and exemptions in the case of obligations perceived as prejudicial to development, financial, or trade needs, or that would be too burdensome for these members' administrative and institutional capacities, and additional transitional periods for implementation of the agreements.

2.1 More of the same?

While developing members rightly complain that SDT has fallen well short of its promises, they are prompt to propose further SDT of the same genre. So, why want more of something that doesn't seem to work? One answer could be that although existing provisions fall short of their goals, the concept of SDT is valuable, and better drafted provisions that are better tailored to real needs are still necessary. The question then is to evaluate whether the proposals are apt to better fulfill developing members' demands. The illustrations below suggest varying degrees of success in that enterprise.

Several proposals aim at modifying GATT Article XVIII, a somewhat surprising strategy given that the provision has fallen into disuse over the past decades after its effectiveness as a development tool has increasingly come under criticism. For example, St Lucia proposes to make Article XVIII:C an instrument available in particular to "small and vulnerable developing country Members with limited administrative capacity."[20] The proposal suggests creating "a new distinct special and differential trade policy instrument" but fails to provide specific indications as to its contents or modalities.

A set of proposals by the LDCs focuses on creating mechanisms for ensuring that duty-free and quota-free preferential market access for LDCs becomes binding under the Decision on Measures in Favour of Least-Developed Countries.[21] One issue is whether the duty-free and quota-free treatment offered to products from LDCs in the Hong Kong Ministerial would be implemented on a voluntary, unilateral basis like preferences, or whether it will be multilateralized by inclusion in the granting member's schedule of commitments. The LDC proposal would require that commitments on duty-free and quota-free access become contractual (ie, multilateral and subject to the rules of renegotiation of the GATT).

Another proposal for new SDT by the LDC group is more problematic in terms of both its economic underpinnings and its political prospects. Framed in the context of paragraph 3(b) of the Enabling Clause, it notes that the reduction of tariff barriers through the MFN mechanism erodes preferential margins. Indeed, this is a natural consequence of the general lowering of tariff rates over the past fifty years, but it disproportionately affects developing and least-developed members. More broadly, it raises the question of the continued relevance of preferential schemes when, on the one hand, preference margins are small and dwindling, and, on the other hand, the political and economic cost of obtaining preferences remains high. Given the current tariff landscape, are preferences still worthwhile, or are they a losing battle? An increasing number of developing countries are reorienting their negotiation strategy away from preferences. Nonetheless, the LDC group's proposal offers a different solution:

> The LDC affected [by the erosion of preferential margins and the consequent loss of competitiveness for the affected LDC exports] would require compensatory or adjustment support measures in the trade, financial and technological fields to mitigate adverse effects on their export earnings as well as enable them to cope with increased global competition.[22] (List of proposed measures or target areas for compensation or other forms of assistance omitted.)

While appealing from an equity point of view, the proposal seems legally baseless in terms of current rights and obligations, politically improbable, and practically unfeasible. The economic implications of the proposals are problematic. First, the

---

[20] *Saint Lucia—Special and Differential Treatment Provisions*, TN/CTD/W/8 (24 June 2002) (hereinafter Saint Lucia Proposal), at 3.

[21] *Special and Differential Treatment Provisions: Joint Declaration by the Least Developed Countries*, TN/CTD/W/4 (24 May 2002) (hereinafter LDC Proposal), at 6. In another proposal, LDCs asked that duty-free and quota-free treatment be granted to all products from LDCs pursuant to paragraphs 1 and 2(d) of the Enabling Clause. See *Special and Differential Treatment Provisions: Joint Declaration by the Least Developed Countries, Addendum*, TN/CTD/W/4/Add.1 (1 July 2002) (hereinafter LDC Proposal, Addendum), at 2. However, the last language considered on this proposal reiterates only that the Committee on Trade and Development "shall review the progress made by [the developed] countries in providing access to the least-developed countries" on a duty-free and quota-free basis. WTO General Council, *General Council Chairman's Proposal on an Approach for Special and Differential Treatment*, above fn 1, at 22.

[22] LDC Proposal, Addendum, above fn 21.

value of preferences has never been precisely assessed and remains the subject of intense debates among economists.[23] Second, even if such value was quantifiable, it remains to be determined what baseline to take into account given that the value has varied over time. Third, the beneficiaries have varied over time, making it even more complicated to assess who should receive compensation and for what.

From a legal perspective, the question is the origin and nature of such an entitlement to compensation. Indeed, if preferences are a privilege, rather than a right or entitlement, it is difficult to see how compensation would be due in the event of the withdrawal of the privilege. Because the Enabling Clause does not mandate the establishment of preferential regimes, it is difficult to make the case that developing members are entitled to preferences as a general matter, much less to specific levels of benefits. Grantors must certainly abide by the terms of their own programs, and the Enabling Clause sets limits on the form of these programs, as shown by the *EC–Tariff Preferences* case. But preference schemes do not provide any guarantee or commitment that the margins of preference will be maintained. As a result, it is difficult to find a contractual or property right to the maintenance of a set margin of preferences.

In support of the proposal, one could say that the granting of preferences created certain expectations at the time of their granting, on which beneficiaries relied in structuring their vulnerable economies, and that grantors therefore should be estopped from subsequently nullifying the benefits, or should provide compensation. The estoppel argument is nonetheless rather weak, as all parties involved at the time of negotiation of the preferences were fully aware of the drive to reduce tariffs through MFN negotiations and its obvious effect on margins of preferences. As such, it is doubtful that there could be any expectation as to the maintenance over time of the value of the preference. Additionally, adjudicators at the WTO have been reluctant to recognize estoppel as an applicable general principle of international law.[24]

2.2 Proposals to promote South–South trade

Several proposals set out new legal instruments meant to promote South–South trade. This is particularly relevant in the context of the renewed interest in the

---

[23] S. Inama, "Trade Preferences and the World Trade Organization Negotiations on Market Access: Battling for Compensation of Erosion of GSP, ACP and other Trade Preferences or Assessing and Improving Their Utilization and Value by Addressing Rules of Origin and Graduation?" 2003 *Journal of World Trade* 37(5) 959; UNCTAD, *Trade Preferences For LDCs: An Early Assessment of Benefits and Possible Improvements*, UNCTAD/ITCD/TSB/2003/8 (30 January 2004), at 129.

[24] J. Cazala, "L'invocation de l'estoppel dans le cadre de la procédure de règlement des différends de l'OMC" 2003 *Revue Générale de Droit International Public* 107(4) 885. On estoppel in international law generally, see C. Dominicé, "A propos du principe de l'estoppel en droit des gens," in Faculté de droit de l'Université de Genève (ed), *Recueil d'études de droit international en hommage à Paul Guggenheim* (Geneva: Institut universitaire des hautes études internationales, 1968) at 327–65.

Global System of Trade Preferences[25] (GSTP) under the auspices of UNCTAD and the now widespread perception by developed and developing countries that South–South trade is an essential element of development through trade.

Estimates regarding the benefits of multilateral trade liberalization at present and in the immediate future stress that developing countries are bound to benefit more from increased South–South trade than from the reduction of impediments to trade with the wealthiest countries. In practice, the average level of tariff barriers and other trade obstacles between developing countries are substantially higher than they are between developed members, or between developed and developing members.[26] This is a natural result of the exemption of developing countries from making commitments in pre-Uruguay Round negotiations, combined with trade strategies focused on preferential access to rich markets or on inward-looking development such as import substitution.

As a number of developing country economies have diversified over the past two decades and virtually all countries have adopted trade-oriented policies, the landscape for potential trade partners for developing countries is evolving. While regional trade agreements between developing countries have been relatively unsuccessful in the past because of the limited product differentiation or product complementarity, they might now take on a new life in the changed economic context.

The Latin American economic integration experience, the South Asian Association for Regional Cooperation, the CARICOM, and some African experiences, such as the Southern African Development Community, are examples of the varyingly successful South–South integration. The ASEAN, which was very active in the early 1990s, is regaining vitality in the face of the faltering Doha Round, with additional free trade agreements signed with India and the Guangdong province of China.[27] More flexible frameworks such as the GSTP are still limited in terms of their membership and the extent of their activity, but they are gathering

---

[25] The GSTP is a forum where developing countries can negotiate and offer trade preferences to each other. The idea dates to the 1976 ministerial meeting of the Group of 77 in Mexico City and was further developed at ministerial meetings in Arusha (1979) and Caracas (1981). The Agreement on the Global System of Trade Preferences Among Developing Countries is a framework for cooperation on tariffs, para-tariffs, non-tariff measures, direct trade measures, and sectoral agreements. Currently, their cooperation covers tariffs negotiated during the First Round of negotiations in the mid-1980s. The tariff concessions are embodied as schedules in Annex IV of the Agreement. The Agreement entered into force on 19 April 1989. Forty-three countries are members.

[26] The post-Uruguay Round average bound tariff rates for all products for industrial countries was 4 percent, compared to 25 percent for developing countries. The difference is smaller when considering applied tariffs, with an average for all products of 3 percent for industrial countries and 13 percent for developing countries. IMF and World Bank, *Market Access for Developing Countries' Exports* (27 April 2001) <http://www.imf.org/external/np/madc/eng/042701.pdf>, at 18. Applied tariffs are the actual tariff that is applied by the member and which can be lower than the bound tariff set forth in the member's schedule of concessions. The MFN obligation of GATT Art I extends to applied tariffs as well as bound tariffs.

[27] ASEAN Secretariat, "ASEAN Secretariat Enters into Cooperation Agreement with Guangdong Province, China" (5 September 2008) <http://www.asean.org/21942.htm>; Agreement on Trade in Goods Under the Framework Agreement on Comprehensive Economic Cooperation between the Association of Southeast Asian Nations and the Republic of India (Bangkok, 13 August 2009).

more momentum, particularly in the context of uncertain multilateral outcomes. As the Doha negotiations have slowed down or come to a standstill, some WTO developing members have been able to dedicate more time and human resources to GSTP negotiations.

It follows quite naturally from this conjunction of modified economic circumstances, reconsideration of negotiation strategies and priorities, and the fairly strong consensus among all WTO members regarding the importance of South–South trade, that the legal framework within the WTO may need to be reassessed. As such, the African group proposal and another one from the LDC Group discussed below are laudable efforts. Whether these particular groups of countries would really benefit from enhanced South–South trade is less clear.

The African Group's proposal would essentially rewrite paragraph 2(c) of the Enabling Clause on preferential arrangements between developing countries.[28] The proposal stipulates that:

the arrangements can be for reduction or elimination of tariffs *or non-tariff barriers*, and that with respect to reduction or elimination of tariffs *no WTO body or Members can prescribe any criteria* relating to the arrangements. Members shall respect any such arrangements as an exercise of rights that developing and least-developed country Members have under the WTO Agreement. (emphasis added)

By contrast, the Enabling Clause provides a tiered system where arrangements for the reduction or elimination of tariffs may be entered into freely among developing and LDCs but arrangements regarding non-tariff barriers are subject to criteria set by the Contracting Parties acting jointly. The proposal garnered enough support to be classified as "agreed in principle" in Chairman Pérez del Castillo's 2003 summary document.

South–South trade mechanisms may also be pursued under GATT Article XXIV on customs unions and free trade areas. Indeed, the LDC Group has proposed that:

special treatment shall be accorded to the least-developed among developing countries in arrangements involving developed and developing countries or among developing countries in accordance with [the Enabling Clause] notwithstanding Paragraphs 5, 6, 7 and 8 of Article XXIV of GATT 1994.[29]

The proposal also calls for an interpretation of the *Understanding of Article XXIV* that would not be prejudicial to "the right of developing and least-developed country members to enter into arrangements for the mutual reduction or elimination of tariffs and non-tariff barriers to their trade." It is entirely unclear what is meant by "special treatment" for LDCs in this context. RTAs are already a categorical derogation from MFN treatment. The GATT certainly imposes some restrictions as to what is validly considered an RTA, but the proposal fails to clarify whether special

---

[28] African Group Proposal, above fn 2, at 21.
[29] LDC Proposal, Addendum, above fn 21, at 7. The proposal is made in the context of the Understanding on the Interpretation of Article XXIV of the GATT 1994.

treatment would result in more flexibility of this framework for LDCs or whether it would relate to something else.

While RTAs may be of growing importance for South–South trade, likely beneficiaries are medium-income developing countries with relatively diversified economies, rather than LDCs which still tend to rely on a handful of primary commodities for the bulk of their foreign trade. RTA members, if they produce the same raw product, will not be good trading partners because the products are insufficiently differentiated. If LDCs involved in an RTA produce different goods, there may be more opportunities for trade. Yet, many LDC exports of unprocessed commodities are geared towards rich industrialized markets and would be of little interest to neighboring countries with the same economic profile. This would be the case regarding, for instance, diamond exports or other high-value ores such as coltan, used in electronic products such as mobile phones. Hence, RTAs might not be the most useful trade instrument for most LDCs. That is not to say that the legal framework for RTAs should not be cognizant of, and adapted to, the specific situation of LDCs, but the main obstacle to successful LDC regional trade agreements may be structural economic features rather than the legal framework.

Overall, proposals to create new development-oriented exceptions to the main disciplines of the covered agreements may be valuable in principle but often come short in terms of their design and implementability. Additionally, proposals to promote South–South trade may be well taken but not necessarily for the members that put them forward. Flaws regarding the discrepancy between intended beneficiaries and the likely actual beneficiaries and lack of modalities for implementation are recurrent issues in the proposals for new SDT. Unfortunately, little debate is likely to take place to improve those proposals in the current Round of negotiations. As such, it is to be feared that developing members will re-table similar proposals in future Rounds without having taken away lessons from the current exercise.

3. Proposals on Transitional Periods

Several proposals indicate more specific time periods in lieu of existing provisions providing for "a reasonable period of time," a "limited period," or other similar language.[30] By contrast, other proposals reject the imposition of a specific term of years for waivers and other derogations.[31] In fact, the two are not entirely contradictory inasmuch as proposals setting a term of years usually are framed as a

---

[30] African Group Proposal, above fn 2, at 9–10 (regarding Art XVIII:B GATT); ibid at 14 and 15–16 (regarding Art 10.3 SPS Agreement and Art 12 TBT Agreement); ibid at 20 (on Art 27.13 SCM Agreement); ibid at 16 (regarding Art 4 TRIMS Agreement); ibid at 24 (regarding Art 12.10 DSU). See also, Communication from India, above fn 7, at 4–5 (on Art 21 DSU). For a proposed overhaul of the timing and delays in DSB procedures, see *Special and Differential Treatment Provisions: Joint Communication from Cuba, Dominican Republic, Egypt, Honduras, India, Indonesia, Kenya, Mauritius, Pakistan, Sri Lanka, Tanzania and Zimbabwe*, TN/CTD/W/2 (14 May 2002) (hereinafter Joint Communication from Cuba and others), at 2–3.

[31] See eg, Saint Lucia Proposal, above fn 20 (regarding Art XVIII:C GATT).

minimal term of years designed to give developing countries a minimal guarantee and some flexibility. A number of proposals simply require an extension of transitional time periods for implementation originally embodied in the Uruguay Round agreements, most of which now have lapsed.[32]

Indeed, a major problem with implementation is that the time needed by developing countries—particularly the least-developed amongst them—to adjust their regulatory framework and the cost of doing so has been grossly underestimated. The proposals generally cast the extension as an unconditional right. While members facing continuing implementation difficulties insist that they should be given additional time to implement their obligations, such requests have been met with some resistance by other members who feel that political motivation for implementation is lacking, and motivates the drive for further transitional time periods.

4. Proposals to Reinforce SDT Provisions' Obligatory Value

A set of proposals attempts to give effect to SDT provisions by using binding language instead of hortatory language or stating that a clause shall be interpreted as binding, but the proposals do not otherwise seek to change the substance of the provisions. The legal impact of these proposals is often limited.

4.1 From legalese…

In some cases, the mere substitution of "shall" for "would" does little or nothing to give enforceable substance to the provision. For instance, proposals to replace "would" by "shall" in Article 3.5 (j) of the Agreement on Import Licensing Procedures would result in the clause reading:

[I]n allocating licences, the Member *shall* consider the import performance of the applicant. In this regard, consideration *shall* be given as to whether licences issued to applicants in the past have been fully utilized during a recent representative period. In cases where licences have not been fully utilized, the Member shall examine the reasons for this and take these reasons into consideration when allocating new licences…[S]pecial consideration *shall* be given to those importers importing products originating in developing country Members and, in particular, the least-developed country Members.[33]

---

[32] African Group Proposal, above fn 2, at 21 (regarding Decision on Measures in Favour of Least-Developed Countries para 2); ibid at 12 (on Art 15.2 Agreement on Agriculture); ibid at 19 (on Art 27.4 SCM Agreement); ibid at 17 (on Art 5.3 TRIMS Agreement); ibid at 20 (on Art 9 Agreement on Safeguards); ibid at 18 (on Art 20 Valuation Code); ibid at 23 (on Art 65.4 TRIPS Agreement); LDC Proposal, Addendum, above fn 21, at 9 (proposing that requests from LDCs for extensions under Art 66.1 of the TRIPS Agreement be granted automatically by the TRIPS Council and that the burden of proof be shifted to members opposing the extension to prove that the objective of the transition period has been met for the member requesting the extension).

[33] New "shall" appears in italics. African Group Proposal, above fn 2, at 19; see also Communication from India, above fn 7 (suggesting either an authoritative interpretation of Art 3.5(j) to make it mandatory to enable the products from developing countries to benefit from the provision, or to replace "would" by "shall" in the last sentence, similar to the African Group proposal).

The provision might be made obligatory by the use of "shall" but its content and modalities are still so vague that it is unclear what obligation actually ensues.

DSU Article 4.10 is another illustration. It states that "[d]uring consultations Members should give special attention to the particular problems and interests of developing country Members." Taken in isolation, a simple change from "should" to "shall," as advocated by India,[34] is insufficient to significantly affect the framework. The phrase "give special attention" must be further defined (as India's proposal further elaborates) if legal benefits are to accrue from the provision for developing members.

Likewise, the deletion of "may" in Article 27.1 of the SCM Agreement does little to "give full effect to this S&D provision" notwithstanding the statement by the proposal's sponsors.[35] The clause would then read: "Members recognize that subsidies play an important role in economic development programmes of developing country Members." No right or obligation derives from the clause, and it is difficult to see how it could be used, if only as a guiding principle in dispute settlement.

4.2 ... to legal obligations

Nonetheless, some proposals that introduce "shall" or some other language of obligation may indeed make the SDT provision a binding commitment.

Such is the case for the proposed amendment to the SPS Agreement, Article 10.3, to read "the Committee *shall* grant to [developing] countries, upon request, specified, time-limited exceptions in whole or in part from obligations under this agreement" (rather than the existing "is enabled to grant").[36] Here, the simple change in the wording would have a legal effect, making it mandatory for the Committee on SPS to grant time extensions to developing countries, in contrast to the current optional and discretionary procedure.

The same holds true for a proposal by India on Article 10.2 of the SPS Agreement, which would make the granting of extended periods for implementation automatic for products of interest to developing countries in certain circumstances.[37] Another proposal regarding the SPS Agreement would make it mandatory for

---

[34] Communication from India, above fn 7, at 3–4; see also similar proposal regarding Art 21.2 DSU.

[35] Proposal by Cuba, the Dominican Republic, Honduras, India, Indonesia, Kenya, Pakistan, Sri Lanka, Tanzania and Zimbabwe, TN/CTD/W/1 (14 May 2002) (hereinafter Proposal by Cuba and others), at 11. Art 27.1 SCM Agreement states: "Members recognize that subsidies *may* play an important role in economic development programmes of developing country Members" (emphasis added).

[36] Joint Communication from Cuba and others, above fn 30, at 5; African Group Proposal, above fn 2, at 14 (proposing identical language).

[37] Communication from India, above fn 7, at 2. Surprisingly, the proposal is relatively similar in form and substance to the proposals on Art 10.3, but the latter were considered less controversial and easier to adopt, whereas the former is considered unlikely to be adopted in its current formulation. The rationale is difficult to understand and probably reflects occasionally arbitrary choices by the drafters of the Cancun document. Indeed, both the principle of the classification and the actual categorization of the proposals have been opposed by certain developing countries.

importing members to provide technical assistance to developing country exporters when needed to meet the SPS requirements of the importing members. Article 9.2 currently states that the importing member "shall consider providing such technical assistance." The proposal deletes "consider," thereby creating a binding obligation for importing members to provide technical assistance under the conditions described by the article.[38]

Likewise, a proposal on non-automatic import licensing procedures (Article 3 of the Agreement on Import Licensing Procedures) would provide a safe haven from commitments for developing countries ("developing country Members *shall not* be required to take any measures additional to existing measures" (emphasis added)) instead of the current ambiguous language ("would not be expected").[39]

Attempts at giving legally binding force to ambiguous existing SDT provisions simply by inserting the language of legal obligation is often not sufficient in itself to achieve that objective. Rather, the language of obligation must reflect a well-defined substantive obligation. Form and substance must be considered together for legal effect to ensue.

In sum, the many SDT proposals submitted in the Doha Round, most of which are shelved due to the lack of momentum in the negotiations and the focus on agriculture and non-agricultural market access, played several roles.

A number of proposals reflect a rolling back of Uruguay Round trends and a reintroduction of exceptions, temporary or permanent, meant to ensure some flexibility for developing countries in the implementation of their commitments. Other proposals would reshape, to some extent, the balance of power at the WTO and increase the profile of development concerns in every sector. This approach is, in a way, a departure from the notion of SDT as it seeks to "normalize" development considerations, rather than marginalize them as exceptions to be eventually phased out.

In terms of economic theory, the two approaches reflect the age-old debate discussed in Chapter 1 between the theory of development as a process of "catching-up," which translates into the type of legal instruments embodied in SDT, or the recognition of developing countries as structurally different, therefore calling for a different set of legal instruments than those applying to developed countries. It should come as no surprise that the "catching-up" theories emanated mostly from first world economists, as has the traditional approach to SDT, whereas the structural theories have been promoted by Third World economists and it is also developing countries that have sought a more structural approach to incorporating a development dimension at the WTO.

The purpose of this study is not to demonstrate the superiority of one theory over the other. Indeed, it seems plausible that both have some merit and that they should be considered jointly. The increase of domestic human and economic

---

[38] Joint Communication from Cuba and others, above fn 30, at 3–4.

[39] African Group Proposal, above fn 2, at 19; *Special and Differential Treatment Provisions: Communication from Thailand*, TN/CTD/W/7 (20 June 2002) (hereinafter Proposal from Thailand), at 2 (proposing identical language).

resources, the industrialization efforts, and the building of infrastructure, which pertain more to the "catching-up" theories, are widely recognized as *sine qua non* conditions to human and economic development. At the same time, failing to acknowledge that the human, political, and economic make-up of many developing countries fundamentally differs from that of rich, industrialized countries, at least as a starting point, is a fallacy. For instance, building bridges and telecommunications networks looks the same the world over, but micro-credit lending was designed specifically to remedy structural problems in particular developing countries and has little place in industrialized countries with a sophisticated banking sector and different social mores. Ultimately, both development theories may well have the same objective—the increase of well-being and opportunities for the population of developing countries—but the policies required for implementation, and hence the legal instruments needed, are different.

The same holds true for SDT at the WTO: The historical evolution of the shape and content of SDT, and the current divergence as to what SDT should do are indicative of a tension regarding the objective and purpose of SDT. Can SDT ever be anything other than a set of carve-outs and exceptions that are costly for developing countries to negotiate and that implicitly, if not explicitly, tend to marginalize them within the trading system? As designed in the WTO agreements, SDT largely pertains to the "catching-up" categories of instruments and policies. That may be appropriate in some areas, but it should not overshadow the need for legal instruments to achieve other policies.

5. Doha's Achievements and Shortcomings

In July 2006, the WTO Director General officially suspended the negotiations, which had been at a standstill. After another failed "mini-ministerial" in July 2008 and pessimistic statements from negotiators in 2010–2011, the prospects of completing the Doha Round seem ever more elusive.

Could some aspects of the Doha Agenda have been concluded earlier? Two days after the 2006 collapse, the EU Trade Commissioner proposed to continue talks on trade facilitation rules as they could be addressed separately from the more contentious substantive issues of agriculture, market access, and SDT. The proposal was unambiguously and immediately rejected by Director General Pascal Lamy, the United States, and a number of developing country members, thereby giving a strong signal that the sanctity of the single undertaking approach is to remain intact even at the cost of a potentially irreversible collapse of the talks. In other words, there can be no progress on the technical issues, where developing countries encounter comparatively more difficulties, absent payoffs by developing members in other substantive areas of the negotiations, presumably agriculture and NAMA.

Since the Tokyo Round, the single undertaking approach may have been useful to gather momentum for the creation of the WTO and the expansion of international trade regulation.[40] It came at a high price for developing countries. At the moment, the single undertaking approach no longer generates momentum. Rather, it has become a significant obstacle to the advancement of the WTO system on the many technical issues that could be agreed separately. It may even impose significant costs on developing countries by making it possible for more powerful countries to extract concessions in exchange for amendments to a legal system that initially failed to take into account the situation and capabilities of many members.

After the collapse of talks, the United States stated that it did not consider itself bound by the agreement in principle reached at Hong Kong regarding duty-free, quota-free access for LDCs[41] and the reduction of cotton subsidies, a position consistent with the restrictions embodied in the Annexes of the Hong Kong ministerial declaration. Since then, a number of developing countries insist that what had been agreed in the 2004 "July Package"[42] and at Hong Kong is not subject to renegotiations and that renewed talks would have to continue to build a package beyond that unquestionable "*acquis*." In fact, there is a genuine fear that the interruption in the negotiations might mean a *tabula rasa* on the items agreed in principle over the past years.

Surprisingly, delegates from developing countries seem content to maintain the single undertaking approach in spite of its inherent risks for their interests. Arguably, the single undertaking also enables them to resist what Cold War international relations analysts have called the "salami tactic:" the slicing away of opponents' margin of negotiation. Developing countries should carefully weigh the pros and cons of pursuing the single undertaking strategy, recognizing that their balance of interests and negotiation tactics change over time. Rather than to be taken for granted, the propriety of the single undertaking should be considered at the start of each round alongside the agenda. At the very least, it should be discussed jointly with the rest of the modalities negotiations. Pursuing negotiations under a single undertaking approach is, after all, the paramount modality that conditions much of the scope for bargaining.

In this context, the discreet relaunching of the negotiations in the early months of 2007 was less than promising. None of the substantive disagreements had been bridged and the parties' positions had scarcely evolved. New Chair Papers on agriculture circulated in May 2007 pointed out the lack of a foreseeable agreement

---

[40] S. Charnovitz, "Triangulating the WTO" 2002 *American Journal of International Law* 96(1) 28, at 31.

[41] A. Beattie, "Lamy snubs Mandelson on call to rescue parts of agenda," *Financial Times* (27 July 2006).

[42] *Draft General Council Decision of…July 2004,* JOB(04)/96 (16 July 2004); *Decision Adopted by the General Council on 1 August 2004,* WT/L/579 (2 August 2004). This so-called "July 2004 Package" consisted of a draft platform to relaunch the negotiations after the failure of the Cancún ministerial meeting. It sought to establish a baseline for continuing the negotiations on the modalities for the Doha Round, particularly with respect to the agriculture negotiations, the negotiations on cotton, and the NAMA negotiations. It also took stock of the progress made on development-related issues (general principles, SDT, technical assistance, implementation issues, LDCs) and other cross-cutting and institutional issues.

absent considerable evolution on a number of issues, many of critical importance for developing countries large and small.[43] Some degree of convergence was reported on amendment of the Green Box by the Chairman, but has not yet been reflected in the draft modalities. Deadlocks, some of which date from the inception of the GATT and certainly from the Uruguay Round, remain on agricultural exports subsidies, tariff escalation, and the setting up of specific safeguard mechanisms to address food security, net food importing poor countries, and product diversification in emerging countries.

While the leaders of the new WTO "Quad"—India, Brazil, the United States, and the European Union—as well as other members publicly expressed a strong desire to reinitiate discussion in the sidelines of large economic fora such as the Davos meeting,[44] and Director General Lamy strove to revive the talks, a new collapse took place as India and Brazil walked out of quadrilateral talks in Potsdam in June 2007 due to the lack of convergence on agricultural concessions from developed countries and industrial tariff reductions by the large developing countries.[45]

More generally, the effectiveness of developing country participation has been limited in many ways both by the overall negotiation strategy focusing on SDT and by the shortcomings in the drafting of their proposals. It is not surprising that developing members' first major attempt to shape negotiations encountered so many obstacles and ultimately enjoyed limited success. Yet, the Round was a paramount step in identifying political, strategic, institutional, and legal problems associated with developing country participation in negotiations and it may be hoped that the years to come will allow these members to draw lessons from the present experience and to adjust their future positions accordingly. Already, their refusal to proceed in the negotiations prior to obtaining a deal on agricultural subsidies signals some evolution compared to their position in the Uruguay Round.

6. Conclusion

Was the Doha Ministerial Meeting a turning point? The launching of a "Development Round" certainly elicited huge expectations, particularly as the WTO had come to represent the forum where development had to be addressed. The Hong Kong Ministerial Meeting yielded some encouraging results, the first after several years of unsuccessful negotiations, but that hope now has largely dissolved in the face of the core deadlocks. More than ten years after the inception of the Round and in the aftermath of a global economic crisis, the situation on the ground has also largely transformed members' political priorities and opportunities. Even new members in 2001, such as China, which then had a reasonable

---

[43] *Communication from the Chairman of the Committee on Agriculture, Special Session* (25 May 2007) <http://www.wto.org/english/tratop_e/agric_e/agchairtxt_25may07_e.pdf>.
[44] "WTO Powers Fail to Revive Trade Talks," *Associated Press* (27 January 2007).
[45] "OMC: le Brésil et l'Inde rompent les négociations avec les Etats-Unis et l'UE," *Le Monde* (with AFP and Reuters) (21 June 2007).

argument for resisting further concessions in light of their accession package, can no longer insist on that position.

The Uruguay Round occupied more than a decade, from its preliminary framing to its conclusion. The Doha Round seeks to address many problems inherited from the Uruguay Round and earlier, as well as some fundamental restructuring of the trading system and the place of developing members in the WTO. It is somewhat unrealistic to expect such ambitious undertakings to be achieved over a short period of time, especially with 153 members and constantly evolving political interplays. Rather than raising the paper tiger of failure and the organization's discredit at each faltering ministerial (every two years, under the WTO Agreement), the key players and the WTO Director General would perhaps better serve both causes by accepting that the negotiations will take a long time to come to fruition and devise ways to ensure political momentum for that length of time.

11

Strategic Challenges to Integrating Development at the WTO

The faltering Doha "Development" Round begs the question whether the multilateral trading system needs to fundamentally reconsider the place and role of development in the WTO's architecture. With SDT showing its limits, many of the Doha Round proposals attempting to do more of the same, and the politics of negotiations testifying to a deep malaise about the relationship between trade and development, it is clear that past assumptions about the normative objective of the WTO are tested to the breaking point.

As shown in Chapters 2 and 3, the fundamental questions regarding the appropriate form and forum for dealing with development issues are hardly new, but the expansion of the WTO's membership and regulatory ambit makes it an ever more pressing concern. The development constraints of the vast majority of the membership directly affect the multilateral negotiations. For instance, the politics and economics of Indian farmers conditions India's position regarding agricultural negotiations; together with Brazilian cotton lobbies, the West African Cotton Four countries may bring about a realignment of US cotton subsidies and industrial development policies in Brazil, and China have reshaped antidumping and countervailing duties litigation. The notion that development is the province of specialized development agencies, such as UNCTAD, the UN Development Programme, the World Bank, and the IMF is a convenient fiction, but it is far from the reality of international economic regulation.

Although members have raised the issue in the Doha Round, no reasoned methodology has emerged for deciding how development concerns should be addressed at the WTO and in relation to other areas of international regulation. This chapter provides a coherent mapping of the challenges most often raised. Starting with an assessment of what development provisions currently achieve, it widens the inquiry to examine how bilateralism and regionalism affect the framework for development at the WTO and how the broadening agenda of WTO regulation shapes the content of development provisions.

Section 1 derives broader principles from the black-letter law analysis of Chapters 6 and 7. It provides some perspectives on the objectives of development provisions as they currently stand and questions their continued validity.

Section 2 focuses on the fundamental debate of SDT versus "mainstreaming" development. Should some developing countries, or at least the richest among them, be excluded from SDT and fully join the general regime? Or, should the general regime itself be reframed to incorporate development concerns at its core rather than at its margins?

Another major debate goes to the appropriate forum for addressing development concerns: multilateralism at the WTO or bilateralism and regionalism. Section 3 addresses this set of issues. Multilateralism and bilateralism/regionalism both affect development undertakings and policies, and they are inseparable due to the regional trade agreement provisions of the GATT. A subset of that debate involves trade preferences awarded by developed members to developing and least-developed countries. While preferences technically are regulated outside of the WTO, they must conform to basic guidelines established by the Enabling Clause and other WTO Agreements. Conversely, the politics of preferences also affects the politics of MFN negotiations.

Section 4 examines how ambiguities relating to the WTO's mandate bear on its ability to respond to members' development concerns. What are the impediments to addressing development issues, at least the trade-related development concerns, at the WTO? Would coordination with development agencies provide some solutions to the WTO's shortcomings?

1. What is Development at the WTO?

A largely unspoken and non-negotiated understanding of what development means within the WTO transpires from the GATT and WTO practice regarding special and differential treatment. Chapter 6, in its analysis of the legal meaning of SDT provisions, found three main objectives:

- the promotion of North–South trade,
- allowances for domestic development policies that may be trade-restrictive, and
- the increase of South–South trade, though only in a very limited fashion.

The Doha Round proposals, discussed in Chapter 10, also largely fall along those lines. Are these three categories still valid to substantiate a development dimension at the WTO?

1.1 Promoting North–South trade

Traditionally, the promotion of North–South trade has been the main instrument to increase developing country exports, and it was hoped, their economic development. Although the policy instruments used to promote exports from the South to the North have changed, North–South trade is still of paramount importance for middle-income countries that have benefited from outsourcing of manufacturing and, more recently, services.

However, old and new challenges hinder the growth of North–South trade. Middle-income developing countries, which have abandoned infant-industry policies, still want to promote their domestic industries through other forms of subsidies that would be WTO-incompatible. Moreover, the nature of the products exported by many developing countries has changed from unprocessed commodities to semi-processed or manufactured products. Yet, tariff peak and tariff escalation clauses continue to hinder such a trade strategy, particularly for lower-income countries. Preference programs focused on primary agricultural products have also become inadequate. Finally, LDCs and middle-income countries have diverse and sometimes conflicting interests regarding North–South preferential trade agreements.

1.2 Preserving domestic development policies; "policy space"

The preservation of domestic development policy instruments remains high on developing members' agenda. Now often termed "policy space," it is a concern for all developing members. The pressure on domestic policy instruments has increased as transition time periods have expired and full WTO obligations apply to all countries regardless of their policy orientations. To put it simply, can one size of trade liberalization fit all members?

A growing number of economists now recognize that the search for a uniform model for economic development may be illusory and that countries in different situations, with different factor endowments and challenges, may be best served by different economic policies and tools. Brazil and Malawi, both WTO members yet worlds away in terms of their economic, social, and political make-up, can hardly both be best served by a single set of economic policies. The theoretical shift is critical when considering the historic importance of a single model, the Washington Consensus in particular, at the WTO, as well as development-oriented agencies such as the World Bank.

Yet, as was shown in Chapter 6, only a handful of provisions have been used by developing members to modulate their GATT and WTO commitments in pursuance of vastly differing domestic development models. For example, the balance of payments flexibilities of GATT Article XVIII have been used equally by members adopting import-substitution policies and export-driven development models and by members transitioning from a communist to a capitalist economy. More generally, the call for policy space at the WTO translates into demands for flexibility in the regulation of trade policies looked down upon by economic liberalism orthodoxy.

The issue of "policy space" and the use of development instruments such as subsidies, strategic tariff protection, local content requirements, limits on repatriation of capital, differentiated tax incentives, etc is quite contentious, with some economists arguing that such policies are risky and more distorting than beneficial, while others find historical evidence for their success. The case of South Korea's phenomenal growth since the 1960s is invoked by both sides. Chang argues that the Washington Consensus has resulted in "kicking away the ladder" that industrialized countries used to support their economic development, thereby denying developing countries the use of these same trade policy instruments because they now run counter to liberal economics orthodoxy.[1] Lee, building on Chang's analysis, argues that developing countries should be able to use tariff bindings and subsidies to promote their industrialization. He argues for the creation of a "development facilitation tariff" and a "development facilitation subsidy," though he is mindful of the risks of abuse.[2] On the other side of the debate, the World Bank has produced reports attributing the East Asian "miracle" (including South Korea) to a free-trade orientation and openness to foreign trade and investment, thereby interpreting the emergence of some South East Asian economies in the 1960s to the 1980s as proof that orthodox trade liberalization policies are the way forward for a trade-led development.[3] Economists also have expressed doubt whether infant-industry protection, for instance, is ever successful as a trade policy to promote development.[4]

1.3 South–South trade: The new promised land?

More recently, a new objective for development-related trade policy has emerged: the promotion of South–South trade. Heralded as a bonanza for developing countries, it has yet to yield concrete results. The common wisdom from economists is that most developing countries have more to gain from increased trade with other developing countries than they have to gain from increased trade with industrialized nations. However, a few assumptions and *caveat* must be considered.

First, the prospective measure of gains from trade is fairly speculative, as the Uruguay Round has shown.[5] Similarly, projections regarding the economic impact of the Doha Round have already been subject to debate and to downward revisions.[6]

---

[1] Chang, above Ch 6 fn 8. [2] Lee, above Ch 3 fn 38, at 62–81.

[3] World Bank, *The East Asian Miracle: Economic Growth and Public Policy* (New York: Oxford University Press, 1993) (also acknowledging the positive role played by "tailored government intervention"); for a critique of this report, see P. Krugman, "The Myth of Asia's Miracle" 1994 *Foreign Affairs* 73(6) 62.

[4] See eg, R. Alavi, *Industrialization in Malaysia: Import Substitution and Infant Industry Performance* (London: Routledge, 1993), at 213; Baldwin, above Ch 1 fn 5; J. Bhagwati and T.N. Srinivasan, "The General Equilibrium Theory of Effective Protection and Resource Allocation" 1973 *Journal of International Economics* 3(3) 259; J. Bhagwati and T.N. Srinivasan, *Foreign Trade Regimes and Economic Development: India* (New York: Columbia University Press, 1975).

[5] See comparative table of gains from trade projections for the Uruguay Round in S.B. Epstein, "GATT: The Uruguay Round Agreement and Developing Countries," Congressional Research Service Report <http://www.natlaw.com/pubs/gatt.htm>. The estimated range of worldwide gain after implementation of the agreement extends from USD140 billion to USD274.1 billion. For developing countries, income potentially will grow between USD36 billion to USD89.1 billion; estimates for developing country growth due to the Uruguay Round agreement range from 0.6 percent and 3 percent. See also J.F. Francois, B. McDonald and H. Nordström, "The Uruguay Round: A Global General Equilibrium Assessment," CEPR Discussion Paper No 1067 (November 1994); W. Martin and L.A. Winters, "The Uruguay Round and Developing Countries," World Bank Discussion Paper No 307 (1995).

[6] F. Ackerman, "The Shrinking Gains from Trade: A Critical Assessment of Doha Round Projections," Global Development and Environment Institute Working Paper No 05-01 (2005).

Second, the claim regarding the value of South–South trade is one grounded in marginal utility. The argument is not so much that developing countries stand to gain nothing or to lose from North–South trade, but that they would gain more for their input from South–South trade. The assumption is that North–South trade has already reached (or is nearing) its maximum efficiency. Hence, only a shift towards South–South trade would increase the marginal benefits. That may be true if North–South trade does not change, but is that such a foregone conclusion? The answer depends on whether Northern countries change their trade policies, the access to their markets, and other factors that determine the value of trading with them for developing countries. Inasmuch as developed countries are unwilling to yield to developing countries' demands regarding agriculture liberalization, the reduction of tariff escalation clauses, and other impediments to market access, the assumption will likely be verified. But if negotiations succeed regarding agriculture and NAMA, then the comparison between gains from trade to be had from South–South trade and from North–South trade respectively may need to be reevaluated.

Third, even if we are to assume that there is indeed a substantial gain to be had from South–South trade in the near future, the allocation of this projected gain between developing countries remains in question. Further economic research is needed to determine which countries or group of countries would benefit. Not all developing economies stand to gain from South–South trade in the short to medium term.

Fourth, a limiting factor to South–South trade is the size of many developing country markets. With the exception of a few large developing countries (including China, India, and Brazil), domestic markets are generally small, and trading with similarly sized countries might still not allow them to reach a critical mass in terms of market size. South–South trade is therefore more likely to involve trade between small developing countries and the handful of very large developing economies.[7] The experiences of South–South RTAs in the 1990s are another warning sign. These failures have been imputed to institutional limitations and the lack of diversification of economies producing similar unprocessed commodities. As a counterpoint, the recent revival of RTAs among developing countries could be an encouraging sign that the participating countries' institutions have gained enough strength to support trade policy-making at the regional level. The EU's reliance on existing trade groups in Africa as stepping stones for its new Economic Partnership Agreements may also serve to bolster these previously fledgling regional schemes.

Fifth, the push in favor of South–South trade assumes a shift in the allocation of resources devoted to trade liberalization. Because of limited human and financial resources, many developing countries are not able to pursue a trade strategy aimed simultaneously at developed economies and at other developing economies.

---

[7] A leading study on the economic forecast of developing countries shows that Brazil, Russia (since then a WTO member), and India are the only likely prospects to reach the level of economic wealth of G-7 countries over the next fifty years. Goldman Sachs Global Economics Group, *BRICs and Beyond* (2007), <http://www.goldmansachs.com/ideas/brics/BRICs-and-Beyond.html>.

The shift from the known framework of North–South trade to uncharted South–South trade is unlikely to occur simply on the say-so of economists and will probably require tangible incentives to be built into the multilateral and regional trading system. Who will provide these incentives? In financial terms, this is still an unanswered question; in political terms, the ongoing failure of the Doha Round may well provide the biggest impetus for South–South trade. The enormous activity deployed by India and China to position themselves as regional leaders in Asia and the Pacific region is perhaps the most salient sign of such a realignment.

As a result, while it may well be that the future of developing countries' economic promotion lies in South–South trade, it is also easy to use that rhetoric as a smoke screen to hide the reluctance of developed countries to do away with the market barriers that affect developing country exporters. In the meantime, the legal framework for the development dimension at the WTO must continue to address all three aspects of the trade needs of developing countries: North–South trade, South–South trade, and the ability to implement a broad range of domestic development policies that may not be compatible with some WTO disciplines.

2. Special and Differential Treatment *versus* Mainstreaming Development

This debate is increasingly prominent as developing members find themselves in a new conundrum. On the one hand, they face great difficulty in implementing their Uruguay Round commitments. On the other hand, they find that the fallback on waivers and exceptions is no longer available as most SDT provisions have expired. Moreover, developing countries' positions now diverge as some are shunning SDT as a thing of the past.

The analysis in Chapters 6 and 7 has shown that most SDT clauses failed to perform their stated purpose, either for legal reasons (they were not binding, or were not interpreted to impose a binding and substantial legal obligation) or for practical reasons (they did not adequately address actual needs or were too cumbersome or impractical to use). Yet SDT remains a core aspect of some developing countries' strategies in the current round of negotiations as discussed in Chapter 10. Not only is the reinforcement of SDT part of the Doha Work Programme, but a number of delegates made strong statements on the need to fulfill that mandate. As stated by the African Group:

The case for special and differential treatment in the WTO has long been recognised and a series of provisions in the agreements attest to this ... But on the whole the operationalisation, implementation or compliance with these provisions has been less than fully satisfactory and this is the reason the Ministers mandated further work in the Committee on Trade and Development.[8]

---

[8] *Special and Differential Treatment Provisions: Joint Communication from the African Group in the WTO, Revision*, TN/CTD/W/3/Rev.2 (24 June 2002), at 2.

Several explanations have been offered for this paradox. First, the traditional rationale is that developing countries, particularly LDCs, want to preserve as many escape clauses as possible in negotiated agreements. They may be willing to undertake commitments only if they can fall back on opt-out mechanisms as an insurance against unforeseen developments. Second, the demand for SDT clauses is seen as a sign that WTO disciplines need to be adapted to the particular constraints experienced by developing countries and SDT can provide some form of customization. While that strategy has been moderately successful at best in the past, it is hoped that the accumulated experience will result in better SDT provisions in the future.

These proffered explanations, while certainly relevant, seem insufficient to account for the extraordinary revival of interest regarding SDT since the inception of the Doha Round.

The traditional explanation framing SDT as an escape mechanism is largely discredited by theory as well as practice. An extensive international relations literature exploring why and under what circumstances states undertake international commitments comments on that type of strategy. The finding generally is that in a repeat game with the same set of players, those who use escape clauses destroy their international goodwill and make future commitments less credible. Past practice confirms that the value of SDT as escape mechanism is dubious. The traditional explanation also fails to explain the relative paucity of SDT provisions compared to the escape mechanisms historically used by developed members: Whereas SDT provisions are marginal in scope, antidumping and safeguards, which were the traditional escape mechanisms used by developed countries, are the object of full-fledged agreements. If developing countries' needs for escape mechanisms had been taken seriously, shouldn't we have seen similar agreements tailored to their needs? Finally, traditional explanations also fail to account for the relatively limited use over the past decade of waiver mechanisms that were actually available to developing members.

We argue that the drive to review and enhance SDT can be seen as the result of a causal relationship between capacity constraints and a shift in negotiating priorities during the Uruguay Round and back again since then. It also testifies to a debate on development that is backward-looking and frozen in time. Developing countries' position since the 1970s generally has been entrenched in seeking waivers from the general regime of obligations and securing special trade preferences outside of the MFN mechanism. A shift was initiated by many of them during the Uruguay Round, with broad trade liberalization programs often undertaken under the impetus of the World Bank and the IMF. However—and this is the critical element—as these developing countries undertook high levels of commitments in the Uruguay Round, the focus on SDT receded to some extent, largely due to their insufficient negotiation resources. Indeed, if resources allow for pushing only one strategy and the priority is to join the main regime of trade liberalization, no resources will be left for negotiating the back-up strategy of SDT. This shift accounts for the relatively insubstantial SDT provisions smattered throughout the WTO Agreements. In effect, developing countries were probably unable to devote resources to negotiating both substantive commitments (including, for a number of them, accession protocols) and SDT. They chose to devote their limited resources to the former. Faced with transitional implementation periods lapsing in the first few years of the twenty-first century and the impossibility of meeting their commitments, developing members suddenly found their traditional lifeline of escape clauses was no longer available. Developing countries' interest in negotiating robust SDT then resurfaces in the Doha Round as a reflex reaction to alleviate the pressure they are suddenly facing to fully implement their commitments. The resurgence of the SDT strategy, then, can be understood as reactionary rather than as a forward-looking strategy.

In the first few years of the Doha Round and in the aftermath of the *EC–Tariff Preferences* case, the terms of the debate for the place of developing countries in the WTO could be summarized by the following: Most developing countries want to maintain a special status in the WTO; they would not give up the possibility of having recourse to SDT as a matter of principle and as a matter of political cohesion. Most of them strongly rejected any notion of a general sliding scale, which would differentiate between members, but would also mark the end of the categorical distinction between developed and developing members.

Since the 2005 Hong Kong Ministerial Meeting, some developing countries realize that the political cost and drain on resources of negotiating SDT provisions at the margins of the trading system may not be worthwhile and is likely doomed to fail. While they maintain active SDT discussions for political reasons, their agenda and priorities have moved away to focus instead on substantive issues such as agriculture, NAMA, TRIPS, etc. The shift from SDT to substantive issues is reminiscent of the Uruguay Round negotiations, ultimately raising the question whether developing countries will fare better now than they did then. Is history about to repeat itself and to result in another failed attempt to fashion a multilateral trade regime mindful of development needs?

A systemic approach to mainstreaming development, although it is gathering increased support among some developing members, so far has found little translation in concrete proposals by negotiators. One notable exception is a 2005 proposal for an Agreement on Trade and Economic Development by Kenya, circulated prior to the Hong Kong Ministerial Meeting,[9] aiming at creating a legal framework and institutional home for addressing systemic issues. The proposal notes that while the GATT and WTO "have been helpful institutions towards achieving economic development objectives of developing countries," progress has been hampered by "underlying systemic issues." It then proposes that the Hong Kong Ministerial conference mandate the creation of an "Agreement on Trade and Development."

The proposal identifies a few development-oriented provisions of existing WTO agreements[10] upon which it would build to foster ties between economic

---

[9] Kenya, Proposal for an Agreement on Trade and Economic Development (non-public WTO document, on file with the author).

[10] Agreement Establishing the WTO, Preamble; Preamble, Art XVIII, and Part IV GATT; Preamble, Art IV GATS; Preamble, Arts 7–8 TRIPS.

development and trade policy at the multilateral level. The proposed agreement's role would include:

- adopting principles to facilitate the role of trade in the promotion of social and economic development in developing countries,

- elaborating general rules on SDT to serve as a framework for the negotiation, interpretation, and implementation of WTO commitments (similar to a separate proposal by Pakistan and others),[11]

- setting objective criteria to grant waivers and other flexibility mechanisms available through the agreements to developing countries with emphasis on trade performance,

- identifying and interpreting all development provisions (building upon the mandate of the Doha Ministerial Declaration, paragraph 44), and

- elaborating measures to address implementation issues relating to current development provisions.

The proposal is framed in very preliminary terms, clearly a call for reflection and an attempt to gauge the level of interest and support for such a project. It appears to have made an impression on the WTO Secretariat, though no concrete discussion has been undertaken at the negotiators' level.

In 2005, former WTO Ambassador for South Africa F. Ismail led a working group, bringing together a small group of academics from various fields (law, international relations, economics) to explore a broader conception of development at the WTO. His own contribution to the group identifies specific areas of concern for developing members and advocates "mainstreaming development" as a solution preferable to the piecemeal SDT approach, which alone "will not be effective and will be seen as a palliative for an unfair and unjust system."[12] He argues that developing countries' fundamental interests in the WTO are promoting fair trade, capacity-building, balanced rules and good governance, and that the trading system should be built around these systemic values and interests. Ismail further argues that "the development dimension is also the convergence between the needs and interests of developing countries and the broader systemic interests of developed countries."

The debate on SDT and mainstreaming development does not necessarily call for a monolithic answer. Some SDT provisions are likely to remain a necessary element of trade negotiations. However, they cannot be a substitute for a more

---

[11] *Proposal for a Framework Agreement on Special and Differential Treatment: Communication from Cuba, Dominican Republic, Honduras, India, Indonesia, Kenya, Malaysia, Pakistan, Sri Lanka, Tanzania, Uganda and Zimbabwe*, WT/GC/W/442 (19 September 2001). The proposal advocates treating SDT provisions "not as exceptions to the general rules but more importantly as an integral and inherent objective of the multilateral trading system;" it sets out various principles for implementation that overlap in part with the Kenyan proposal.

[12] F. Ismail, "Mainstreaming Development in the World Trade Organization" 2005 *Journal of World Trade* 39(1) 11, at 14.

in-depth reconsideration of the multilateral trade regime that would be more mindful of development issues.

More generally, it appears that the state of thinking on how to integrate development at the core of WTO policies is more one of identifying the problems than of proposing solutions. As the Doha Round lingers, even that approach is disappearing, with negotiations focusing instead on sectoral issues.

3. Multilateralism *versus* Regionalism and Bilateralism

While the Secretariat and the current Director General regularly express concern over the multiplication of RTAs and the organization's inability to implement GATT Articles XXIII and XXIV (vetting RTAs), the trend in favor of RTAs shows no sign of receding, particularly as multilateral negotiations have made little progress over the past ten years. The concern largely stems from the fact that RTAs give WTO members an alternative negotiation forum that might erode the importance of the WTO, both as an institution and as a defining ethos for trade liberalization.

From a developing country perspective, shifting trade negotiations from the WTO's multilateral forum to bilateral and regional fora has a profound impact on developing members' position in negotiations. First, in the case of RTAs between developing countries, it allows the groups to define common interests and positions and to then leverage that group power in multilateral negotiations at the WTO. Second, in the case of RTAs between developing and developed countries, it may raise issues of erosion of the developing members' rights under the WTO (as illustrated by negotiations on the TRIPS and public health). Third, developed countries can also offer RTA deals to developing countries to lure them away from multilateral positions unfavorable to the formers' agenda. Each aspect is discussed in the remainder of this section, using illustrative case studies.

3.1 Developing country RTAs' impact on WTO negotiations

Developing country RTA activity really boomed in the first years of the WTO, a trend that is not surprising given the atomization of developing country positions into smaller interest-based groupings, rather than the traditional large G-77 style alignments. The MERCOSUR,[13] the Caribbean Community Regional Negotiating Machinery[14] (formed in 1997), the South Pacific Forum (coordinating action among its WTO members on development issues and trade in fisheries

---

[13] Treaty Establishing a Common Market between the Argentine Republic, the Federative Republic of Brazil, the Republic of Paraguay and the Eastern Republic of Uruguay (Treaty of Asuncion or MERCOSUR) (Asuncion, 26 March 1991; 30 ILM 1041).

[14] Leading to the CARICOM, a regional trade agreement signed in 1991.

and marine resources),[15] and the African Group[16] offer examples of groups of developing countries using the structure of their regional economic agreements to pursue joint actions at the WTO. Moreover, the legal recognition afforded by Article XXIV of the GATT (and its counterpart Article V of the GATS) can play a role to support coordinated action at the WTO. Indeed, regional trade agreements are virtually the only way for groups to be legally recognized as such in the WTO legal architecture.

As many developing countries shift their efforts and resources to regional nego-tiations, RTAs, at least those involving countries with relatively diverse economies (generally mid-level income countries), appear to regain momentum. Whether a deepening regional trade liberalization agenda can later be used to reinvigorate multilateral negotiations remains an open question. The East Asian economic inte-gration experience provides interesting vignettes in that respect.[17]

The ASEAN Geneva Committee,[18] formed in 1973 with Hong Kong, Indonesia, Malaysia, Thailand, Singapore, Philippines, and Brunei, proved remarkably effec-tive at coordinating issues within its membership. Narlikar credits this success to the group's relative internal cohesion, common economic interests, and simi-lar geo-strategic concerns arising from their proximity to China.[19] The influence of the ASEAN reached its heyday during the Uruguay Round. Despite diverg-ing individual economic priorities (particularly on services), ASEAN members were successful in promoting a coordinated platform emphasizing the opening of commodity markets and some specific demands in certain sub-sectors (such as increased liberalization in telecommunications and financial services).

More recently, East Asia is engaged in a remarkable realignment of its regional economic groupings, motivated by exogenous factors, such as the slow pace of multilateral negotiations, and endogenous factors, such as regional preferences and experiences regarding the trade and development relationship. Building on past waves of regionalism,[20] new initiatives either revamp existing regional

---

[15] See *Papua New Guinea—Statement by Minister for Foreign Affairs and Trade,* WT/MIN(96)/ST/112/Rev.1 (1996).

[16] The membership corresponds to the Organization of African Unity (continued as the African Union since 2002).   [17] Research assistance by Hyejin Park is gratefully acknowledged.

[18] Representations of ASEAN in third countries are maintained through ASEAN Committees. The mission of such committees is described in ASEAN, Terms of Reference and Guidelines for the Organization of ASEAN Committees in Third Countries (Adopted by the 2nd Meeting of the 13th ASEAN Standing Committee) (Kuala Lumpur, 17 October 1979) <http://www.asean.org/14814.htm>, as follows: "committees shall be established in countries having dialogue with ASEAN to safeguard and advance ASEAN interests through joint consultation with the host gov-ernments...ASEAN Committee shall be the outpost of ASEAN in the capital of the host country. It shall be directly responsible to and shall act only upon the instructions of the ASEAN Standing Committee." The ASEAN Geneva Committee not only is the ASEAN liaison vis-à-vis the Swiss government but also vis-à-vis international organizations established in Switzerland, including the WTO.

[19] A. Narlikar, *International Trade and Developing Countries: Coalitions in the GATT and WTO* (New York: Routledge, 2003), at 173.

[20] R.V. Fiorentino, L. Verdeja, and C. Toqueboeuf, "The Changing Landscape of Regional Trade Agreements: 2006 Update," WTO Discussion Paper No 12 (Geneva: WTO, 2006) <http://www.wto.org/english/res_e/booksp_e/discussion_papers12a_e.pdf>, at 8.

schemes or consolidate them into broader—and in some cases continent-wide—integration arrangements. Some agreements build on existing regional cooperation structures, such as the ASEAN; others extend and reinforce existing economic relationships, such as India with the three northeast Asian states.[21] ASEAN member states are also increasingly active in seeking out bilateral RTAs with non-ASEAN member economies in the region. Such cumulative RTAs may build on the commitments the parties have already made within the ASEAN[22] or be completely separate from any ASEAN commitments.[23] As shown in Table 11.1, they use a combination of GATT Article XXIV, GATS Article V, and the Enabling Clause as legal cover with respect to the WTO, testifying that these RTAs recognize the need to manage their interaction with the WTO agreements.

The perceived need for adequate policy space,[24] combined with the need to form alliances with neighboring economies, is part of the motivation driving the many Asian RTAs. The parties may perceive RTAs as a better forum to reflect their particular needs, with better prospects for tangible, direct, quicker benefits as compared to multilateral fora.[25]

Table 11.1 WTO legal cover of East Asian RTAs

Agreement	WTO Legal Cover	
	Goods	Services
ASEAN–China (Goods 2005; Services 2007)	Enabling Clause	GATS Art V
ASEAN–India (2010)	Enabling Clause	Enabling Clause
ASEAN–Korea (Goods 2010; Services 2009)	GATT Art XXIV	GATS Art V
Asia–Pacific Trade Agreement (1979, China 2002)	Enabling Clause	n/a
China–Singapore Free Trade Agreement (2009)	GATT Art XXIV	GATS Art V
Agreement between Japan and the Socialist Republic of Viet Nam for an Economic Partnership (2009)	GATT Art XXIV	GATS Art V
Korea–India Comprehensive Economic Partnership Agreement (2010)	GATT Art XXIV	GATS Art V

[21] N. Kumar, "Investment Provisions in Regional Trading Arrangements in Asia: Relevance, Emerging Trends and Policy Implications," in UNESCAP, *Towards Coherent Policy Frameworks: Understanding Trade and Investment Linkages—A Study by the Asia-Pacific Research and Training Network on Trade* (New York: United Nations, 2007), at 1–2.

[22] See, eg, China–Singapore Free Trade Agreement (CSFTA) (Beijing, 23 October 2008).

[23] See, eg, Implementing Agreement Between the Government of Japan and the Government of the Socialist Republic of Viet Nam Pursuant to Article 10 of the Agreement Between Japan and the Socialist Republic of Viet Nam for an Economic Partnership (Tokyo, 25 December 2008).

[24] D. Rodrik, "Rethinking Growth Policies in the Developing World," Luca d'Agliano Lecture in Development Economics, Torino, Italy (2004), at 4–5. See, eg, Preamble para 10 Indian Korean Comprehensive Economic Partnership Agreement (Seoul, 7 August 2009).

[25] See Korean Ministry of Foreign Affairs and Trade (MOFAT) website <http://www.mofat.go.kr/english/econtrade/fta/issues/index2.jsp>.

Finally, regionalism can assist with capacity building in developing countries, and, as such, could translate into an increased ability of developing countries to achieve better results in the multilateral negotiations. For instance, Mexico's involvement in NAFTA negotiations has been a valuable learning experience for the country's trade negotiators, with that expertise ultimately benefiting Mexico's positions in multilateral negotiations. This type of experience is often best acquired in the context of RTAs between developed and developing countries, rather than between developing countries only.

3.2 North–South regionalism: Divide and rule? The example of the US–Morocco Free Trade Agreement

The term "New Regionalism" has emerged to describe the recent wave of predominantly bilateral trade agreements.[26] This "new regionalism" has resulted in a decrease in regional trade agreements such as NAFTA, and prioritization of negotiating bilateral trade agreements, mostly under the impetus of the United States and the EU. Since the US's shift in priority to trade agreements in the early 2000s, they have concluded bilateral agreements with seventeen countries.[27] With the objective to enter into more bilateral agreements, the United States has created a model agreement that encompasses its goals in pursuing economic integration. The United States–Morocco Free Trade Agreement (FTA) can be used as a proxy for the model that the United States has used as a negotiating platform. Analyzing this treaty reveals the ways in which recent US bilateral trade agreements both converge and diverge from the legal regime of the WTO, particularly with respect to the treatment of developing countries.

Preamble and general provisions

The main stated purpose of the US–Morocco FTA is to "promote mutually advantageous economic relations" between the United States and Morocco as parties to the FTA. The Preamble affirms "Morocco's commitment to reform to improve the lives of its people." Other stated purposes include raising living standards, promoting economic growth and stability, creating new employment opportunities, liberalizing and expanding trade between the parties, increasing the competitiveness of the parties' enterprises in global markets, and building on the parties' rights and obligations under the WTO agreements.

The Agreement also states that the free trade zone between the two parties will not affect legal rights and obligations under other agreements the two countries are

---

[26] C. O'Neal Taylor, "The U.S. Approach to Regionalism: Recent Past and Future" 2009 *ILSA Journal of International and Comparative Law* 15(2) 411. Research assistance by Andrew Angely is gratefully acknowledged.

[27] Australia (entered into force 2005), Bahrain (2006), Chile (2004), Dominican Republic–CAFTA (Costa Rica, El Salvador, Guatemala, Honduras, and Nicaragua) (2004), Jordan (2010), Morocco (2004), Oman (2009), Peru (2006), and Singapore (2004). Congressional approval for entry into force of free trade agreements with Panama, South Korea, and Colombia was obtained on 12 October 2011.

parties to, including the WTO agreements. This specifically includes rights and obligations that are more favorable to the parties than those contained in the FTA.

Goods

Provisions relating to goods apply to all trade in goods between the two parties, which contributes to the agreement passing muster under GATT Article XXIV.[28] Trade in goods under the FTA proceeds on an MFN basis[29] and benefits from national treatment. The parties cannot create any new tariffs or increase any existing tariffs on the other's goods and they should move to eliminate existing tariffs on the other's goods based on an agreed-upon schedule.[30] The FTA bans restrictions on exports[31] and ensures that administrative fees do not become a *de facto* market protection.[32] These commitments resemble GATT disciplines. The FTA also contains extensive rights covering the temporary admission of certain goods, goods reentering after repair, as well as commercial samples and negligibly valuable advertising materials.

Services

The services section of the FTA covers "measures adopted or maintained by a Party affecting cross-border trade in services by service suppliers of the other Party."[33] The terms "cross-border trade in services" are defined to cover what are known as Modes 1 (cross-border supply), 2 (consumption abroad), and 4 (presence of a natural person) under the GATS. Mode 3 of the GATS (commercial presence) is omitted. The FTA also excludes financial services, air services, government procurement, and subsidies or grants provided by a Party.[34] Like the GATS, it includes both an MFN and a national treatment clause, but it does not differentiate between specific commitments and general commitments. Other measures ensure transparency,[35] mutual recognition of educational attainment,[36] and unimpeded cross-border flow of currency and payment for services.[37] In these respects, they go further than the GATS.

Intellectual property

The intellectual property provisions of the Agreement are easily the most expansive and complex. At the outset, they require that the parties ratify or accede to eight other international treaties already in existence, as well as that they make every "reasonable effort" to ratify or accede to two others.[38] The legal technique is similar to that employed in the TRIPS Agreement, but while the TRIPS incorporated by

---

[28] Art 2.1 United States–Morocco FTA (Washington, 15 June 2004; 44 ILM 544).
[29] Ibid at Art 2.2(2).   [30] Ibid at Art 2.3(1)–(2).   [31] Ibid at Art 2.8.
[32] Ibid at Art 2.9.
[33] Ibid at Art 11.1.   [34] Ibid at Art 11.1(4).   [35] Ibid at Art 11.8.
[36] Ibid at Art 11.9.
[37] Ibid at Art 11.10. Note that Morocco does have an upper limit on the amount its nationals can transfer out of the country for the payment of services. This was agreed upon in a side letter.
[38] Ibid at Art 15.1(2)–(3).

reference the provisions of other IP treaties, the FTA actually binds the parties to ratify these additional treaties. None of these treaties are listed in the TRIPS, and, indeed, three of the mandatory treaties and the two optional agreements post-date the TRIPS. In this respect, the FTA goes much beyond the TRIPS, a typical example of the much-debated TRIPS-plus provisions found in many recent RTAs and bilateral investment treaties. The US–Morocco FTA also includes detailed regulation of trademarks, geographical indicators, Internet domain names, copyrights, encrypted satellite signals, and patents. Last, the provisions enumerate detailed enforcement measures for intellectual property rights.

With no commitments from the US on agriculture and heightened commitments on intellectual property, the US–Morocco FTA epitomizes the divergent agendas of developed and developing country in trade negotiations. Another element missing from most North–South FTAs is disciplines on protectionist trade remedies (antidumping, safeguards, and countervailing duties). During the Doha Round, the opposition to trade remedies was largely led by Chile and Japan. While developing countries decry the use of trade remedies by developed countries, they have increasingly implemented such remedies themselves, often against other developing countries.

RTAs such as the US–Morocco FTA also illustrate the vulnerability of individual countries to make commitments in the bilateral context that they otherwise resist in the multilateral forum. Whether the United States and the EU would be able to extract similar concessions from developing countries with larger markets, such as Brazil and India, is uncertain and may prove the limits of the bilateral strategy for developed countries.

3.3 Forum-shifting and the impact on WTO rights and obligations for developing countries: The TRIPS and public health example

Offering separate deals, either in the form of individual concessions within the WTO framework or in the context of bilateral trade agreements, has been a recurrent strategy to pull apart coalitions, starting in the Uruguay Round.[39] Negotiations on TRIPS, public health, and the so-called "Singapore issues" offer repeated examples of this strategy being used to divide the unusually united front presented by coalitions of developing countries. Braithwaite roots the trade negotiating power of the United States in part in its ability to move back and forth between multilateral and bilateral negotiations:

The United States manages to concentrate its power in trade negotiations by moving backwards and forwards between its multilateral agenda and, when that is momentarily thwarted, its bilateral negotiations, which include the individual picking off of politically and economically significant States. These bilaterals progressively lock more States into the

---

[39] That is not to say that bilateral trade agreements may not have been motivated by other factors such as more general political or economic partnerships, or the pursuit of a progressive regional integration strategy. Certainly, no single cause can be seen behind the conclusion of a bilateral trade agreement between a developed and a developing country.

preferred U.S. multilateral outcome until the point is reached where the United States can attempt to nail that multilateral agenda again.[40]

Recent multilateral trade negotiations offer several instances of developed countries making strategic use of bilateral trade deals to induce defection from developing country coalitions. Braithwaite argues that a number of bilateral or RTAs (such as the Central American Free Trade Agreement) were proposed and negotiated between the United States and members of the Cairns Group and the G-20 Group in an attempt to divert key players from these coalitions. He finds that a developing country's membership in these coalitions significantly increases its chance that the United States will propose a bilateral deal.[41] He concludes that only a networked, coordinated strategy will allow developing countries to maintain their positions, and that the G-20 must offer a constructive prospective vision to its members (as opposed to simply a blocking strategy) to keep them united.[42] In practice, however, the United States has only been moderately successful at concluding RTAs with developing countries, and when an agreement has been forthcoming, it was not with a major economic partner. The United States was unable to obtain the same level of concessions from Brazil, South Africa, and Thailand, for instance, leading to the failure of RTA negotiations with those countries. To some extent, negotiations for bilateral investment treaties, which increasingly include a broad range of disciplines touching on trade policy, follow the same trends.

   The negotiation of the Doha Decision on Public Health shows both developing country coalitions and defection inducements at play in what some commentators see as the test-case the G-20 has built on for negotiations on agriculture. Historically, developing countries' reluctance on intellectual property have prompted negotiations to move from one multilateral forum to another, culminating with the negotiation of TRIPS during the Uruguay Round.[43] At that point the United States used the threat of unilateral sanctions (Section 301 of the US Trade Act of 1974[44] and subsequent amendments) to pressure individual developing

---

[40] J. Braithwaite, "Methods of Power for Development: Weapons of the Weak, Weapons of the Strong" 2004 *Michigan Journal of International Law* 26(1) 297, at 313.
   [41] Ibid. The correlation is not perfect and some agreements pre-dated the country's activism in the Cairns Group or the G-20 (Mexico's membership in NAFTA, for example).
   [42] See also P. Drahos, "Developing Countries and International Intellectual Property Standards-Setting" 2002 *Journal of World Intellectual Property* 5(5) 765, at 784–5 (noting that loose groups are "more susceptible to divide-and-conquer tactics of strong States").
   [43] Ibid at 780. On coalition strategies leading to the negotiation of the TRIPS Agreement during the Uruguay Round, see also G. Sjostedt, "Negotiating the Uruguay Round of the General Agreement on Tariffs and Trade," in I.W. Zartman (ed), *International Multilateral Negotiation: Approaches to the Management of Complexity* (San Francisco: Jossey-Bass, 1994), at 44–54.
   [44] 19 USC § 2411. The Section "is the principal statutory authority under which the United States may impose trade sanctions against foreign countries that maintain acts, policies and practices that violate, or deny U.S. rights or benefits under, trade agreements, or are unjustifiable, unreasonable or discriminatory and burden or restrict U.S. commerce." Where the US Trade Representative determines that a foreign government is violating or denying US rights or benefits under a trade agreement, Section 301 requires retaliation against that country. Discretionary sanctions are also available if "a particular act, policy or practice of a foreign country is unreasonable or discriminatory and burdens or restricts U.S. commerce."

countries into cooperating in TRIPS negotiations and to break the coalition led by Brazil and India.[45]

Despite continuing disagreements among developing countries on the protection of intellectual property, they identified a strong common interest regarding access to medicines to fight large pandemics. The 2003 Decision on Public Health was a developing country initiative aimed at counteracting actions by the United States and the pharmaceutical industry that hindered the manufacture and distribution of generic AIDS medicines. Arguably, the 2003 Decision does not affect pre-existing legal rights,[46] yet it was heralded as a negotiating success by developing countries. This was partly because it gave high visibility to the issue, thwarted US and European retaliatory threats, and gave legitimacy to developing countries' recourse to compulsory licensing under TRIPS[47] for access to cheap drugs in certain cases.[48]

The United States belatedly attempted to roll back these developments through bilateral deals.[49] Indeed, free trade agreements negotiated after the adoption of the 2003 Decision included provisions limiting the use of the tools provided by TRIPS and the Doha Declaration regarding pharmaceutical products.[50] Restrictions include limitations on production of generic drugs that would be possible under TRIPS and the 2003 Decision, restrictions on parallel imports, and restrictions on the use of information contained in patents so as to limit the development of generic drugs in the country where a patent is held as well as in third countries. Additionally, the threat of sanctions under Section 301[51] and the negotiation of bilateral agreements continued to be used

---

[45] J.T. Gathii, "Patents, Markets and the Global Aids Pandemic" 2002 *Florida Journal of International Law* 14(2) 261, at 316–17. See also R.L. Okediji, "Public Welfare and the Role of the WTO: Reconsidering the TRIPS Agreement" 2003 *Emory International Law Review* 17(2) 819, at 844–6 (noting the role of domestic US private entities in the threat and use of unilateral sanctions and the role of the pharmaceutical industry in mirroring the coalition between the United States, Europe, and Japan at the industry level).

[46] The TRIPS Agreement already provided for compulsory licensing, which allows a developing country to acquire patented drugs manufactured by other than the patent holder, effectively creating generic drugs under certain conditions in cases of public health emergencies.

[47] The Declaration reiterated and reinforced the availability of compulsory licensing, but it failed to provide a clear position on parallel importing, which would enable developing countries lacking production capacity to have access to cheap drugs produced in a third country.

[48] See Benvenisti and Downs, above Ch 6 fn 53, at 27.

[49] C. Thelen, "Carrots and Sticks: Evaluating the Tools for Securing Successful TRIPs Implementation" 2005 *Temple Journal of Science, Technology and Environmental Law* 24(2) 519, at 539.

[50] These include agreements signed or negotiated with Australia, Bahrain, Chile, Morocco, Singapore, Thailand, members of the Andean Community, the Southern Africa Customs Union (SACU), and the plurilateral CAFTA agreement. Regarding CAFTA, see C.M. Correa, "Bilateralism in Intellectual Property: Defeating the WTO System for Access to Medicines" 2004 *Case Western Reserve Journal of International Law* 36(1) 79, at 85–94 (reviewing how US negotiations with CAFTA have resulted in increasing the intellectual property standards of CAFTA members). On TRIPS-plus provisions, see G.B. Dinwoodie, "The International Intellectual Property System: New Actors, New Institutions, New Sources" 2004 *American Society of International Law Proceedings* 98(1) 213, at 215–16.

[51] Section 1303 (dubbed "Special 301") of the Omnibus Trade and Competitiveness Act of 1988 is "designed to enhance the United States' ability to negotiate improvements in foreign intellectual

to splinter coalitions. The EC similarly introduced "TRIPS-plus" provisions in bilateral trade agreements.[52] The use of bilateral and regional agreements to limit the effect of WTO instruments regarding public health has raised concern, eventually prompting the US Trade Representative to issue side letters of understanding.[53]

A recent new chapter in this saga is the negotiation of the Anti-Counterfeiting Trade Agreement (ACTA) between 2008 and 2011. ACTA sets forth minimum standards for the enforcement of intellectual property rights but does not address substantive rights, the main subject of the TRIPS treaty. Generally, the provisions in ACTA apply across the board to all rights protected by TRIPS, resolving a longstanding dispute about the scope of the agreement. However, certain parts of ACTA have a narrower scope. ACTA largely mirrors TRIPS on the issue of civil enforcement of intellectual property rights, but it significantly expands criminal liability for infringement, in particular, by providing for criminal liability with regard to infringing labels and packaging, for aiding and abetting, and for legal persons, as well as the possibility of such liability for pirated movies. Additionally, the entire digital enforcement section is new, but is relatively weak compared to previous versions of the treaty and compared to the original objectives of the United States, which was to "export" the Digital Millennium Copyright Act. ACTA was negotiated by a small group of industrialized countries outside of the WTO, and largely out of the public eye. It is another example of forum-shifting to manipulate standards in intellectual property rights and enforcement, by creating a baseline that will eventually inform the multilateral negotiations. In fact, Japan recently suggested that ACTA rules should serve as a model for further disciplines in the WTO framework, while acknowledging that the countries promoting ACTA, the US and Japan included, had chosen to negotiate the agreement outside of the WTO in order to develop more stringent rules than would have been acceptable in the multilateral setting.[54]

Developing countries' negotiation success on access to drugs and public health suggests that a coordinated and united approach enables them to balance out more powerful members. Developing country group strategy can place and maintain

---

property regimes." Each year, the US Trade Representative "must identify foreign countries that deny 'adequate and effective' protection of intellectual property rights (IPR) or 'fair and equitable market access' to U.S. persons relying upon [intellectual property rights] protection." Most notably, a country can be designated under Special 301 even if it is in compliance with its TRIPS obligations. Those countries are then investigated and are subject to sanctions under Section 301. Other countries "not designated as 'priority foreign countries' may be placed on 'priority watch' or 'watch' lists if their intellectual property laws or enforcement practices are of major concern to the United States." Placing a country on the "watch list" is tantamount to threatening it with further investigation and possibly retaliation under Section 301.

[52] This includes trade agreements with the Palestinian Authority, South Africa, and Tunisia. See Correa, above fn 50, at 80.

[53] See F.M. Abbott, "The WTO Medicines Decision: World Pharmaceutical Trade and the Protection of Public Health" 2005 *American Journal of International Law* 99(2) 317, at 352–3 and note 255 (noting the limitations of CAFTA provisions and the US–Morocco FTA).

[54] R. Mitchell, "Intellectual Property: Japan Trade Official Suggests ACTA Should Serve as Model for WTO Rules" 2011 *International Trade Reporter* 28 575.

issues of interest to them on the agenda and obtain concessions in the face of bilateral incentives offered by trade partners to induce developing countries to defect from the common position.

In sum, the relationship between regionalism and multilateralism is a complex one for developing countries. While there is a definite potential to further their interests at the multilateral level through leveraging regional power, that negotiating card has also been used against them by more powerful members. As the structure and politics of multilateral negotiations now fully reflect the diversity—and divergence—of developing country interests, regional bases for promoting joint interests certainly have more potential for success than broad umbrella groups that lack the cohesion necessary to resist divide-and-rule tactics, and lack the credibility of a uniform agenda. Also, the possibility of using regional fora to develop institutional and human capacity is an important positive aspect of regionalism for developing countries.

4. Looking Beyond the WTO?
"The WTO is not a Development Agency"

WTO Director General Pascal Lamy and Secretariat members are often quick to point out that the WTO is not a "development agency" and that members should look elsewhere for international support of development policies. By contrast, others, particularly some development-oriented nongovernmental organizations have come to hold the WTO responsible for the development failures of its members and expect an increasing number of development challenges to be addressed within the WTO.

This section will discuss first the legal and the normative bases for addressing development in the WTO (Section 4.1); it will then assess whether the organization has the practical means to do so (Section 4.2); and finally enquire whether coordination with actual development agencies might provide a solution (Section 4.3).

4.1 Is development part of the WTO's mission?

The legal framework is ambivalent: On the one hand, the WTO lacks an explicit mandate to respond to the development needs of its members; on the other hand, the organization has no legally defined mandate and inasmuch as its guiding principles are to be found in the preamble to the Marrakesh Agreement, then development is an integral element of the organization's mission.[55] Beyond this relatively formalist—and inconclusive—approach to defining the WTO's mandate, some commentators have focused their inquiry on the WTO's mission, recognizing that

---

[55] Agreement establishing the WTO, Preamble: "*Recognizing* further that there is need for positive efforts designed to ensure that developing countries, and especially the least developed among them, secure a share in the growth in international trade commensurate with the needs of their economic development."

the concept goes beyond a strictly legal analysis of what it actually is and into a policy and prescriptive analysis of what it should be.

Charnovitz's seminal article offers a fresh perspective on this debate, drawing from the practice of the WTO in its first decade.[56] He builds on the distinction between strategic linkage and normative linkage. Strategic linkage, which largely fuelled the expansion of domains regulated by the WTO, suggests that better trade-offs can be achieved if there are more items on the table. Hence, any area affecting trade liberalization, if only indirectly, can fall within the WTO's ambit so long as members are interested in bargaining in this area. Since development bears on global trade, it could be a "trade topic" given as much consideration as competition, intellectual property, or services if it opens to strategic trade-offs. From a theoretical perspective, strategic linkage sets no boundaries to WTO regulation because almost all domains are interdependent with trade at some level, and strategic linkage does not set a threshold of minimal substantive relevancy of the linked domain to trade.

What is the effect of strategic linkage on developing countries' position and interests? Both practice and theory show that it is very much a double-edged sword.

On the one hand, developing countries have resisted the expansion of the negotiating agenda to new areas since the Singapore Ministerial Meeting (indeed, even the expansion to intellectual property and services in the Uruguay Round was a hard-won compromise). Their limited resources are stretched beyond the limits by complex negotiations across the board, the increased trade-offs dilute their specific areas of interest, and an expanded agenda will require more costly concessions of developing countries in core areas. By contrast, members with more diverse economies can spread the cost of concessions across domains, thereby minimizing the impact on strategic sectors of their economy.

On the other hand, strategic linkage enables developing members to insist on resolving matters of primary interest to them (in particular the issue of agricultural subsidies) as a precondition to any further negotiation. In fact, they have currently achieved a total linkage hinged on agriculture that holds the negotiations at a standstill. In that respect, developing members have accomplished an unprecedented feat in asserting a coordinated stance that is possible only in the context of strategic linkage combined with a single undertaking approach.

Normative linkage is defined as a situation where "trade and the other issues are governed by the same norm, or...one of the issues has consequences for the other."[57] Even if practice informs the determination of the normative linkage, it is a more top-down approach (where theory informs practice) than strategic linkage, which is purely a bottom-up approach where prescriptive positions arise from the actual practice.

With respect to development and the WTO, a normative linkage between trade and development would ensure that development is on the agenda as a core factor without requiring developing members to devote resources to negotiating

---

[56] Charnovitz, above Ch 10 fn 40.   [57] Ibid at 31.

it and maintaining it on the agenda. As such, normative linkage could be a powerful tool for them. That said, if the WTO system evolved toward a normative linkage framework but excluded development, the consequence would be dire for developing countries because the "back-door" introduction of development through strategic linkage would be precluded. In practice, a number of proposals tabled by developing countries in the Doha Round find their conceptual source in a normative linkage between trade and development, and some proposals explicitly formalize it.

Hence, the theoretical debate whether the WTO needs to concern itself with development may be resolved in several ways with vastly different consequences for developing members. Each approach involves both benefits and drawbacks that need to be carefully weighed by all actors involved.

In the end, the issue is not so much whether the WTO needs to encompass development, but how its members will decide to incorporate it in negotiations: By refusing to formalize a framework, they *de facto* pursue the strategic linkage route, with developing members having to constantly expend bargaining chips to maintain development-related issues on the agenda and inject development-friendly features in every relevant legal instrument, concession, and discipline. Eventually it is possible that such a practice will mutate into normative acceptance, contingent on developing members' sustained capacity to push their development agenda. Such a strategic linkage approach might foreclose a very important debate on the nature and extent of development needs, with more powerful developing countries' views potentially marginalizing or overriding different or divergent concerns of other developing members. By contrast, formalizing a normative linkage between trade and development will provide a focal point and legal basis for addressing trade-related aspects of development at the WTO.

4.2 Does the WTO have the means to respond to development challenges?

A first issue is whether the WTO has actual legal tools to address development; a second issue centers on whether it has the practical means to do so; a third aspect is the political animus.

Lack of legal instruments?

The WTO already administers legal tools that directly and indirectly affect development and members' development policies. For example, WTO rules bear on members' fiscal and revenue balance (through lowering of tariffs and national treatment requirements), on administrative management (through the valuation code and import/export licensing procedures), on public health (through the TRIPS and the SPS Agreement), on public aid and public works (through the SCM Agreement and the Agreement on Government Procurement).

Whether these WTO rules are supportive or even mindful of development issues is a serious concern. The number and breadth of proposals submitted by developing countries in the Doha Round suggest that many trade rules and disciplines are inadequate. Yet, members appear to be balking at what would be a pervasive overhaul of the covered agreements. As discussed in Chapters 6, 7, and 9, SDT can be a useful tool, if framed in legally operational ways, but it is limited. A more fundamental reshaping of the rules may be necessary. In turn, such a reshaping is unlikely to happen unless the institutional features of the WTO that affect the creation of trade rules (decision-making and negotiation in particular) are also reconsidered with a view to rebalancing access and participation.

At this juncture, it is unclear whether the WTO has the tools to further any kind of development mission in the framework of the agreements as they stand. Attempts to revisit the existing provisions in the Doha Round will likely prove a failure, but the exercise was a valuable one to begin mapping the possibilities.

Lack of resources?

A discussion on the WTO's capacity to address development also needs to consider the human and financial resources at its disposal.

The WTO Secretariat comprises a fairly small development division (12 staff members, relative to the full Secretariat staff of 637) and a somewhat larger economic division (50 staff members). Additionally, the Institute for Training and Technical Cooperation comprises 29 persons. A number of staffers in the development division are former trade negotiators from developing members, which is conducive to a more targeted examination of the issues, as well as a way to facilitate exchanges with current trade representatives from developing members.

Technical assistance and training activities offered by the Secretariat seek to address an endemic problem significantly undermining developing members' ability to successfully pursue their negotiation objectives: capacity constraints. The Trade Policy Review mechanism is also a resource, both human and institutional, for helping to identify the interplay between trade disciplines, trade policies, and development for each member or group of members. For instance, the review exercise provides much-needed opportunities for the various branches of government and regulators in the country under review to exchange information and work together.

The Committee on Trade and Development and the Sub-Committee on Least-Developed Countries constitute additional resources where members are directly confronting development questions. While these bodies are important, compartmentalizing development in specific committees presents serious drawbacks. A horizontal integration of development concerns throughout each and every institutional segment of the organization may produce more effective results.[58]

While Aid for Trade has become a rallying cry to make the trade liberalization process more palatable to developing countries, the numbers remain comparatively modest, and the financial resources depend on the goodwill of individual WTO members. Aid for Trade is understood differently in various international

---

[58] Rolland, above Ch 5 fn 5.

institutions but overall, it includes enhancing supply-side capacity for exports and trade, helping to manage the costs of the trading system for stakeholders, and supporting trade policy development. As such, it goes much beyond technical assistance. Aid for Trade at the WTO was endorsed as part of the Doha Development Agenda, with the Hong Kong Ministerial Meeting mandating the creation of an Aid for Trade Task Force to "provide recommendations on how to operationalize Aid for Trade."[59] While many agencies (multilateral, regional, bilateral, or even domestic) have developed trade assistance programs, the WTO is mostly involved in two efforts: the Integrated Framework for Trade-Related Technical Assistance for Least-Developed Countries (now known as Enhanced Integrated Framework, EIF) and the Joint Integrated Technical Assistance Program. The EIF is a joint initiative with the International Trade Centre, the IMF, the UNCTAD, the UN Development Programme, and the World Bank. It is funded by individual country contributions (currently twenty-two donors). Current funds stand at USD100 million, and pledges at USD182 million, well short of the 2007 funding target of USD250 million. The JITAP also brings together the WTO, UNCTAD, and the International Trade Centre to build trade-related capacity for African countries. In its first phase, until 2002, it supported eight countries. It now supports sixteen African countries (developing and LDCs), in programs extending to 2007.

Overall, Aid for Trade has grown significantly for the more advanced developing countries but less so for sub-Saharan countries, and has actually decreased, between 2001 and 2004, for LDCs.[60] Funding bodies and program managers are scattered amongst dozens of agencies, with activities involving both public and private stakeholders. The breadth of the undertakings cannot be summarized here, nor can the extensive literature on the subject be meaningfully discussed.[61]

While the WTO as an institution and its members are clearly aware of the need to account and provide for the many and varied costs of trade liberalization for its weakest members, it is not clear whether the Doha Round will fare any better than the Uruguay Round in quantifying the costs and understanding the nature of the support that will be required. There have been some suggestions of compensation for the opening of certain sectors by developing countries, but no real negotiation or principle on supporting trade capacity building has been built into the Doha talks.

Coherence between international economic agencies also remains a work-in-progress, with continued calls to avoid policy conflicts between IMF and World Bank loan conditionality and WTO-mandated trade policies, for example. The 2005 WTO Ministerial Meeting Declaration acknowledged:

Within the context of coherence arrangements with other international institutions, we urge donors, multilateral agencies and international financial institutions to coordinate

---

[59] Hong Kong Ministerial Declaration, at para 57.

[60] J.M. Finger, "Aid for Trade; How we Got Here, Where We Might Go," in D. Njinkeu and H. Cameron (eds), *Aid for Trade and Development* (Cambridge: Cambridge University Press, 2008), at 84.

[61] For qualitative and quantitative overviews, as well as a number of country case studies, see generally Njinkeu and Cameron above fn 60.

their work to ensure that LDCs are not subjected to conditionalities on loans, grants and official development assistance that are inconsistent with their rights and obligations under the WTO Agreements.[62]

Overall, the WTO has a number of human and institutional resources that could be mobilized for a development objective. Arguably, though, they remain meager compared to the combined expertise, know-how, and resources of the relevant UN agencies (UNCTAD, UN Development Programme, UN Environment Programme, etc), the World Bank, and the IMF, to name a few.

Lack of political motivation?

Political impetus may be the hardest element to identify due to the lack of quantitative and qualitative benchmarks. Its evaluation is best left to political science analysts. Suffice it to note here that the WTO is a member-driven organization so that the political animus depends on the 153 countries participating in the organization. The characterization, if in name only, of the Doha Round as a "Development Round," and the ubiquitous discourse regarding development in association with the WTO are some indications that the issue is on both the political and the legal agendas.

Given the lack of specific development mandate and the relative paucity of means to carry out a development agenda within the organization, it could be argued that not only is the WTO not a development agency, but also that it should not even aspire to be one. That, however, does not resolve the issue for developing members. Whether or not the WTO is presently equipped to deal with development, the reality is that it is confronted by it and must address it.

4.3 A possible solution: Cooperation with development agencies?

If development cannot and should not be addressed within the WTO, it follows that it should be addressed in the realm of general public international law and within the bosom of specialized international organizations. The issue, however, remains open until a study surveys and analyzes the legal framework for development outside of the WTO. Such is not the object of this book. Rather, the present study can hypothesize the existence of a set of norms and institutions pertaining to development that are external to the WTO; the question then becomes how WTO law interconnects with these external norms.

The issue is not unique to the relationship between trade and development. Indeed, substantial research and writing has explored the interaction between WTO rules and other rules of international law, particularly in the environmental and the investment context. Attempts have even been made to elaborate a general framework for addressing conflicts of laws between the WTO and other international legal regimes. Pauwelyn's study on that topic is the most comprehensive to

---

[62] Doha Ministerial Declaration, at Annex F, para 38.

date.[63] It mobilizes an arsenal of tools drawn from traditional international legal practice (*lex posterior*, *lex specialis*, and other general rules of treaty interpretation), as well as approaches more familiar to constitutional interpretation. There is no reason why this framework could not apply to development norms as well.

In addition to questions of conflict/coordination of norms or rules, the other concern is that of conflicts/coordination of institutions and policies. The first part of this book presented a reasoned historical overview of the role of various intergovernmental organizations with respect to development. As the WTO has become a focal point for demands of all types and a scapegoat for failing to provide answers, particularly in the development sector, the need for a more effective coordination with other institutions is becoming increasingly obvious. In recent years, the WTO secretariat has recognized this and has promoted a number of mechanisms to create the missing links. The Integrated Framework and the Joint Integrated Technical Assistance Programme are the most prominent examples of such budding coordination. While their institutional coverage is wide, their impact is still perceived as limited by some developing country delegates at the WTO.

Meanwhile, the WTO also has made efforts to increase participation by nongovernmental organizations, most notably via accreditation to observe meetings and a change in policy regarding the filing of *amicus curiae* briefs in dispute settlement proceedings. Leaving aside the fact that such organizations are neither accountable nor democratic in the traditional political sense, making their inclusion in the WTO process problematic, some have pursued conflicting agendas at the domestic level and at the WTO level.[64] Such conflicts might be reconciled, or at least subject to more scrutiny if NGOs' input is channeled through official and transparent mechanisms.

Finally, it should not be forgotten that the primary stakeholders regarding development are developing countries themselves. While an integrated chain of policies must be facilitated at the international level, the first and last links are between international agreements, policies, and domestic governments (not to speak of intra-national constituencies and actors). As such, the debate regarding the WTO's role and capability with respect to development must, first and foremost, make room for developing members to formulate and implement their own development policies. A number of proposals in the Doha Round reflect precisely that concern. As governments elaborate rules and disciplines within the WTO, they are not detached from development policy-making domestically. A normative linkage also exists between the domestic and the international spheres. Can and will the WTO provide the forum for reconciling domestic development policy-making with

---

[63] Pauwelyn, above Ch 6 fn 17.
[64] A case on point is the position of environmental NGOs with respect to the *US–Shrimp* dispute: While they actively lobbied governments of developing countries where harvesting of shrimps posed a threat to protected species of sea turtles to impose the use of harvesting techniques that would be less detrimental to the protected species, these NGOs also submitted briefs in support of developing countries disputing the US's "turtle exclusion device" requirements as a disguised protectionist measure.

international trade policy-making? That may be the more fundamental question regarding the WTO's mandate on development.

5. Conclusion

While earlier parts of this book have asked how the WTO deals with development and have questioned how it should deal with it, this chapter focused on whether the WTO can address development challenges.

The hurdles are manifold: legal, political, financial, institutional. The answers are ambivalent, suggesting that there may be many different models for managing the trade and development relationship at the WTO. For instance, the debate between mainstreaming development and relying primarily on SDT calls for different regulatory and institutional mechanisms depending which avenue is chosen. Similarly, the tension between multilateral regulation and bilateral or regional trade liberalization affects how development is addressed in all fora. Moreover, there are very real logistical, personnel, and financial constraints to what the WTO as an institution can provide to its members in support of its development role.

No single avenue unequivocally protects the interests of all WTO members, which means that even on an abstract, theoretical plane, there is no ideal solution. Ultimately, it is for members to balance out their preferences, keeping in mind that focusing purely on trade disciplines without taking into account institutional processes and structures is unlikely to produce a radically different result than what has been done over the past sixty years.

12

Towards Development-Oriented Rules at the WTO: Some Proposals

As the Chair for agriculture negotiations pointed out in his August 2008 Report: "like all fundamental political differences, there are consequent technical differences, but the impasse was not technical. It was political."[1] In the Doha Development Round the focus on SDT, reflecting an attempt to find technical solutions, contrasts with proposals advocating a more comprehensive approach. The trade community increasingly recognizes that some of the core concerns and priorities of developing countries go well beyond SDT and cannot be solved by limited carve-outs. In this spirit, this chapter offers a menu of proposals for recasting the trade and development relationship at the WTO. They range from limited, more technical reconsiderations of SDT to more systemic features, including differentiation of trade liberalization commitments tailored to members' circumstances, and the realignment of WTO institutions to create a more productive framework for negotiations. While these proposals do not pretend to solve the political differences that currently keep members apart, they aim to provide the flexibility to accommodate inevitable political divergences while enabling a workable legal framework for the multilateral trading system.

Section 1 presents options for reconsidering SDT. The objective is to remedy some of the flaws of SDT (discussed in Chapter 6) and similar shortcomings transpiring from a number of SDT proposals submitted in the Doha Round (addressed in Chapter 10). The first option is a "multilateral SDT" principle to administer general development exceptions. The second option is a "unilateral SDT" approach where members customize their commitments through reservations and declarations. In both scenarios, the concern is to provide a rational system of exceptions and derogations giving flexibility while not excluding developing members from the trading system and not undermining their credibility as concessions grantors.

Moving beyond SDT, Section 2 considers how scaled liberalization could be built into the agreements so that a variable geometry of commitments tied to development needs would permeate the multilateral trading system. In this perspective, it proposes a shift from the traditional valuation of members' concessions in absolute terms to a valuation of concessions in relative terms. The objective is to better

---

[1] *Report to the Trade Negotiations Committee, by the Chairman of the Special Session of the Committee on Agriculture, Ambassador Crawford Falconer*, JOB(08)/95 (11 August 2008), at 3.

correlate the different trade capabilities of various segments of the WTO membership to their level of commitments.

Regardless of which system is used, the rules must be supported by the WTO's dispute settlement system. Section 3 examines how development can be adjudicated more transparently, more predictably, and more effectively, building on the lessons drawn from Chapters 7 and 8.

Leaving the realm of trade rules and disciplines, Sections 4 and 5 propose avenues for dealing with the systemic and institutional aspects of the development dimension at the WTO. Sometimes called "cross-cutting issues," they are often relegated to the lowest negotiation priority, even though they condition the making of commitments. Indeed, if the development constraints of the vast majority of the membership are not taken into account by the WTO institutions and by the WTO's legal architecture, it is perhaps not surprising that the substantive work-product of the organization also does not cater to the interests and priorities of developing members. Section 4 presents avenues for rethinking the overarching modalities for negotiating trade rules, and in particular offers alternatives to the single undertaking. Section 5 focuses on institutional reforms that could improve the quality of participation by members, and thus the organization's legitimacy.

1. Exceptions and Derogations Revisited

While Chapter 6 has outlined the limitations of current SDT provisions and Chapter 10 has cautioned against a number of SDT proposals submitted in the Doha Round, both conclude that SDT is an adequate legal instrument for certain purposes. Indeed it is hard to conceive of a system where the rules fully accommodate large developing countries like Brazil and India, land-locked countries such as Moldova, and small island states such as St Lucia. If the WTO's regulatory paradigm is to apply the same default rule to all members regardless of development needs, SDT then becomes a useful and even a necessary tool to bridge the operational gaps that members will encounter.

SDT, understood as a set of *ad hoc* rules, exceptions, and derogations, best embodies the idiosyncratic paradigm presented at the outset of this book. Exceptions and carve-outs give members flexibility while minimizing the need to agree on a coherent normative framework for development at the WTO. *Ad hoc* derogations also allow for evolving circumstances in developing members over time and in response to trade liberalization. Without an overarching legal and normative framework for addressing development, then, how can members deal with the reality of their different development constraints when committing to WTO disciplines, implementing them, and adjudicating them? Several modalities can be envisioned for managing SDT more effectively.

First, SDT may be incorporated in the agreements with qualifying criteria, so that any country meeting the criteria may automatically avail itself of the provision. Several Doha Round proposals adopt this approach. The current debate focuses on what the qualifying criteria might be and what monitoring system, if any, would be appropriate. This format is essentially a *multilateral form of SDT* because it is accessible on a multilateral basis.

Second, exceptions and derogations may also be left to each individual country to modulate their commitments through declarations and reservations to specific agreements. Although this has not been a legal tool used in the past, nothing in the WTO agreements excludes it and it is possible that some individual members' problems could be more effectively solved through individual reservations than through multilateral negotiations. The international law on treaty reservations would apply. This option is a *unilaterally* driven type of SDT.

1.1 "Multilateral SDT": Administering development exceptions

If SDT provisions are available to members generally, two broad questions arise: the triggers that would allow and limit access to the provisions, and the provisions' administration. In terms of the legal framework for triggering and administering SDT, a loose framework agreement on SDT may be useful to increase predictability, transparency, and fairness.

Triggering, limiting access, and administering "multilateral SDT"

SDT provisions now tend to be limited in their application. The more powerful developed WTO members are increasingly unwilling to accept broad, open-ended exceptions that allow unchecked escape from the constraints of trade liberalization. In fact, a number of proposals, including some from developing members, have called for benchmarks that would automatically allow recourse to certain SDT provisions. The issue, then, is how to set the benchmarks to trigger access to SDT and to limit its availability. Rather than recommending the adoption of specific benchmarks, this section maps the different regulatory and institutional issues that would need to be considered by members if they engage in this type of reform.

Several types of benchmarks may be used: a list of qualifying countries, a set of economic indicators, a time-line, a list of qualified products or sectors to which the exception can apply at any given time, etc. Such qualifying criteria could be defined by members during rounds of negotiations. However, the political hurdles to finding common grounds on those matters should not be ignored.

In fact, several of these issues have arisen in the past and have been resolved on a case-by-case basis, without any consideration of a more general framework or uniform rules. For instance, GSP preferences have increasingly been subject to various graduation clauses[2] and qualifying criteria devised by the preference-granting

---

[2] Such clauses provide that preference beneficiaries can be excluded from the preference program at some point when they satisfy certain criteria or economic benchmarks. Graduation clauses are generally in place to limit access to preferences by developing countries that are not considered to be priority countries for receiving this indirect aid. See generally, J.H. Jackson, *The World Trading System* (2nd edn, Cambridge: MIT Press, 1997), at 322–5.

countries, generally to the dismay of developing country beneficiaries and some-times in violation of WTO rules as illustrated by the *EC–Tariff Preferences* case and its precursors (discussed in Chapter 7). No rules were provided or enforced regarding qualifying criteria for preferences, but a practice emerged nonetheless. Qualification conditions have also appeared in accession negotiations regarding "developing country" status (see Chapter 5).

Alternatively, if no agreement can be reached regarding objective qualifying fac-tors, limitations may be decided on an *ad hoc* basis. The issue then is who decides when an SDT provision can be invoked, and on what basis: Both are institutional issues. Should it be left to the appreciation of the country wishing to make use of the SDT provision, or to a monitoring body or committee that would accept or refuse the applicant member's request? How would the composition of such a monitoring body be determined?

Balance of payments safeguards of the GATT (technically two different articles, but we consider mostly Article XVIII here) provide an illustration of how the insti-tution has effectively governed (and restricted) access to SDT in the absence of a mandate or implementation criteria. Although the GATT does not make the use of Article XVIII subject to the approval of any monitoring body, the Committee on Balance of Payment Restrictions has acted as a moderator and a clearing-house for requests by GATT members to impose temporary trade restrictions to protect their balance of payments. Under the WTO the Committee has gone one step fur-ther by essentially winding down all balance of payments restrictions, even though no such mandate was ever given to it (see Chapter 6). The Committee therefore became a very crucial monitoring body. It formally reports to the General Council, but meeting minutes fail to reveal much discussion of the Committee's overall policies and objectives.

The question of qualification for SDT is still at the core of the Doha negotia-tions. With developing members officially united to reject further differentiation, the notion of qualifying criteria enjoys little support. However, in some areas, qual-ifying criteria are accepted with little protest from members. For example, provi-sions for LDCs are effectively subject to qualifying criteria. The SCM Agreement also specifies which developing countries qualify for certain differential treatment. While a number of members have rejected using a simple GDP/capita threshold, the use of composite indexes might be a better indication of a country's develop-ment needs.

Conversely, some developing members want to clearly signal that they will not have recourse to SDT, in an effort to gain more valuable concessions from power-ful countries. Mexico is an example of a developing country that has mostly fore-gone recourse to SDT and other development provisions in an effort to negotiate more valuable concessions on par with developed members. If it is clear from the legal framework that Mexico does not have access to escape clauses, it could be in a better position to gain more valuable concessions. Other developing countries that are moving away from SDT may also find that an idiosyncratic framework with overarching principles for deciding who can access SDT benefits them too. At present, those countries tend to be middle-income developing countries.

A framework agreement on the administration of "multilateral SDT"?

In the early days of the Doha Round, a group of developing countries proposed a framework agreement to set principles for the interpretation, use, and adjudication of SDT.[3] One principle is the notion that SDT "shall be mandatory and legally binding through the dispute settlement system of the WTO (including notification requirements and inclusion of these commitments in country schedules)" to enhance the legal predictability and transparency of derogations and exceptions.

Ultimately, a completely *ad hoc* application of SDT exceptions and derogations may prove a hindrance to trade liberalization by injecting uncertainty in the application of the exceptions, unpredictability as to which exceptions might be triggered by particular members, and by fostering a general lack of transparency regarding which rules apply to which members or which sectors. Moreover, the current focus on simplification of rules and the recognition that simpler rules improve importers and exporters' opportunities run counter to a possibly unruly expansion of exceptions and derogations. It may be possible to mitigate that risk by devising some general rules on the application of SDT, which would guide members and the dispute settlement system in interpreting SDT provisions. The adoption of procedural standards for ensuring a fair and uniform application of SDT would maintain the essentially *ad hoc* character of SDT whilst upholding the rule-based nature of the WTO.

1.2 "Unilateral SDT": Using reservations and declarations to customize WTO agreements

Incorporating derogations in multilateral agreements is not the only way to account for development concerns and hurdles in the spirit of the idiosyncratic paradigm. In general international law, the ultimate legal instruments for exceptions are reservations and, to a lesser extent, declarations. Although parties to the GATT and members of the WTO agreements have not made use of this option, it is nonetheless available and could be used by developing countries to modulate their commitments under a number of WTO agreements.

The Marrakesh Agreement establishing the WTO prohibits members from making reservations to it (Article XVI.5). With respect to the other multilateral agreements listed in the Marrakesh Agreement annexes, reservations "may only be made to the extent provided in those Agreements." Neither the GATT (1947 and 1994) nor the GATS mention reservations. The TRIMS, SPS, and Rules of Origin Agreements, the Rules on Preshipment Inspection, the Agreement on Agriculture,

---

[3] *Proposal for a Framework Agreement on Special and Differential Treatment: Communication from Cuba, Dominican Republic, Honduras, India, Indonesia, Kenya, Malaysia, Pakistan, Sri Lanka, Tanzania, Uganda, and Zimbabwe,* WT/GC/W/442 (19 September 2001). The proposal also advocates a systemic incorporation of development considerations at the WTO: conducting mandatory development impact assessments for future trade agreements (including, but not limited to, implementation costs), linking transitional time periods to the attainment of trade and development objectives, presuming that all trade policies aiming at promoting growth and development are allowed, and moving away from the single undertaking.

the Understanding on Balance of Payment Provisions, the DSU, and the Trade Policy Review mechanism similarly are silent with respect to reservations and declarations. The issue therefore becomes whether silence means that reservations are allowed, presumably within the confines of customary international law on treaty interpretation and reservations.

The TRIPS Agreement presents a slightly different case as it addresses reservations to some extent. With respect to Protection of Performers, Producers of Phonograms (Sound Recordings) and Broadcasting Organizations (Article 14), the TRIPS Agreement allows reservations to the extent permitted by the Rome Convention and the Berne Convention. Additionally, a general reservations clause provides that "[r]eservations may not be entered in respect of any of the provisions of this Agreement without the consent of the other Members" (Article 72).

Finally, the TBT Agreement provides: "Reservations may not be entered in respect of any of the provisions of this Agreement without the consent of the other Members" (Article 15.1). The SCM Agreement provides an identical clause at Article 32.2, as does the Agreement on Import Licensing Procedures (Article 8.1), the Customs Valuation Code (Article 21), and the Anti-Dumping Agreement (Article 18.2).

It is difficult to find a rationale for the inclusion or exclusion of reservation clauses in the various WTO agreements. Where there is a reservation clause, its notable feature is the requirement that all members must consent to reservations made by another member. Hence, the classic international law dilemma regarding the legal effect of an objection to a reservation will not be raised with respect to the six WTO multilateral agreements that have a reservation clause. Clearly, the restriction makes the use of reservations fairly cumbersome, but still possible.

Regardless whether members need to agree to a reservation by another member, the general rules of international law will still apply. The Vienna Convention on the law of Treaties may be used as an expression of applicable customary law on this issue. The requirement of consent by other members in six of the multilateral WTO agreements may be interpreted as a derogation to the default rules stated at Article 20 of the Vienna Convention.

With respect to reservations generally, the Convention provides in its Article 19:

A State may, when signing, ratifying, accepting, approving or acceding to a treaty, formulate a reservation unless:
- (a) the reservation is prohibited by the treaty;
- (b) the treaty provides that only specified reservations, which do not include the reservation in question, may be made; or
- (c) in cases not failing under subparagraphs (a) and (b), the reservation is incompatible with the object and purpose of the treaty.

Paragraph (a) confirms the analysis on the basis of the *Lotus* presumption. The *Lotus* case has set the general principle that if a conduct or activity is not prohibited by international law, then it is presumed to be allowed.[4] Although this principle

---

[4] *The Case of the SS Lotus (France/Turkey)*, PCIJ, Series A No 10, 7 September 1927.

has been reconsidered in some contexts, it is arguable that if a treaty is silent regarding reservations and does not explicitly restrict or foreclose parties' ability to make reservations and declarations, then the general rules of international law should provide the outer limit on parties' capacity to make such reservations and declarations. Except in the case of the Marrakesh Agreement, which expressly prohibits reservations, all other multilateral WTO agreements allow reservations under certain conditions.

Paragraph (b) covers the restriction of Article 14 of the TRIPS Agreement restricting the kind of reservations that may be made by reference to the Rome and Berne conventions.

Paragraph (c) is the most pertinent limiting factor here and requires specific reservations to be examined against the object and purpose of the particular agreement. Assuming a reservation is made for a development objective, the issue is whether that could be said to be incompatible with the objective of trade liberalization that permeates the WTO agreements. A decision on whether a development-oriented reservation is compatible with the object and purpose of the multilateral agreements takes us back to the more fundamental issue of the normative relationship between development and trade liberalization. Absent a clearly enunciated principle regarding that relationship, with the sole guidance of the preamble to the Marrakesh Agreement mentioning sustainable development, it is difficult to anticipate how members, the panels, or the AB would interpret it. Additionally, while one individual reservation might not threaten the objective of multilateral trade liberalization, members and adjudicators may be concerned by a possible floodgate effect of allowing reservations for development purposes.

The principle of *lex specialis* also confirms the theory that the silence of the WTO agreements must be interpreted as leave to make reservations within the limits of general public international law. Here, the WTO provisions on reservations constitute *lex specialis*, and general international rules on treaty interpretation should apply in the absence of special rules in the former.

The use of reservations in WTO agreements therefore falls into three categories:

- absolute prohibition (Marrakesh Agreement);
- silence (eg, GATT)—the Vienna Convention on the Law of Treaties applies;
- *lex specialis* on reservations in specific WTO agreements (typically those requiring express consent from all state parties to a reservation).

Another limitation to reservations is timing. Reservations are normally made at the time of signature, ratification, or accession. Only a few countries are not yet WTO members and they would be the only candidates for reservations. Therefore, with respect to the current agreements, the reservation option offers only limited possibilities for WTO members. It may be, however, that future agreements or packages resulting from a trade round may open new opportunities. For example, the Uruguay Round resulted in a set of "new" agreements such that reservations to the GATT 1947 arguably could have been possible.

Finally, reservation clauses in the WTO agreements are silent about interpretative declarations. As discussed in Chapter 10, a number of SDT proposals tabled by developing countries during the Doha Round merely seek to interpret existing SDT provisions without changing their wording. Interpretative declarations might be helpful to achieve the same objective without going through the cumbersome process of all members agreeing on a declaration of interpretation or other form of formal decision by the General Council. The downside is that it is unclear what legal effect if any such a declaration would have in dispute settlement.

The use of reservations and declarations for implementing a development dimension, though technically available, would be a shift in WTO culture. It would risk weakening the integrity of the agreements and would likely be politically costly for the members using those instruments. However, while it would certainly not respond to all developing members' needs and concerns, it may prove useful in some cases. At any rate, it is one more tool in members' legal arsenal.

In sum, relying primarily on exceptions and derogations to manage the trade and development relationship presents several advantages in theory. The lack of limitative principles means that any development clause or exception that members are able to negotiate can become part of the WTO disciplines. It also allows for vastly different understandings of what the meaning of development might be and would not require members to agree on a definite content for development at the WTO. It reflects most closely the idiosyncratic paradigm presented in the introduction.

The question is whether this approach would also provide a process to achieve those results. If not, it is questionable whether the potential benefits of this approach are likely to truly respond to the development challenges of WTO members. Rather, SDT should be reconsidered for its true purpose: providing effective safeguards for developing country members of the WTO. As a legal tool to "mainstream" development, it can only reflect the current power play amongst WTO members.

2. One Size Does Not Fit All: General Differentiation at the WTO?

Differentiation amongst developing countries and their trade commitments is not a new concept. Prebisch recognized that not all developing countries needed the same level and type of preferences and he understood preferences as a transitory instrument subject to "gradation."[5] Despite these auspicious beginnings, the concept of differentiation has now become controversial in diplomatic circles at the same time that it is acclaimed by economists. The AB's use of the term differentiation in the *EC–Tariff Preferences* case recently became a focal point inflaming some developing members.

As it often seems to be the case with sensitive issues at the WTO, practice has taken the lead on the political or legal acknowledgement of new trends. The agriculture and NAMA negotiations that took place between February and July 2008

---

[5] R. Prebisch, *Towards a New Trade Policy for Development: Report by the Secretary General of the United Nations Conference on Trade and Development*, E/CONF.4613 (1964), at 65–7.

are a case on point. Both propose different threshold and "bands" of commitments depending on the situation of members. Members would fall within one of several bands depending on the amount of domestic support, the level of their bound duties, etc, and would then be bound by different reduction/increase formula. The categorization of states in those bands roughly corresponds to the countries' wealth and economic makeup so that similarly situated countries generally fall in the same band. The stated objective is to impose less onerous commitments on some developing countries whilst still moving all WTO members in the general direction of trade liberalization.[6]

Differentiation, then, is deeply embedded in the proposed commitments and, importantly, it does not fall along the lines of the simple developed/developing/ LDC categories. The focus is already shifting from formal legal categories to economic benchmarks. Developing members, at least a good number of them, may not want to relinquish the legal harbor of the "developing country" designation, but the concessions they will gain or give in the future, it seems, are already fully "differentiated" on a continuous scale from the EU's richest to the poorest of LDCs.

A number of proposals have emerged from academia to devise scaling mechanisms designed to adjust the levels of commitments to each member's economic situation. The purpose of this section is not to review all of them, but rather to use a few as test cases to bring into the limelight some of the assumptions and issues that are currently not considered in the differentiation debate at the WTO (Section 2.1). This section then proposes a new valuation mechanism for assessing members' concessions, which would support differentiated commitments without the political and legal stigma of banning the developed/developing country categories (Section 2.2).

2.1 Scaling WTO commitments and disciplines

One way to produce different levels of commitments that are adequate to each member's situation is to recognize that even an agreement adopting a middle-of-the-road position may be impossible to implement or have undesirable effects on the trade positions of countries at both ends of the development spectrum. Mechanisms must therefore be created to allow members to continue participating in the system while not undertaking commitments that are too burdensome or exacting to them and, for those desiring a higher level of commitments, to account for that as well.

Allowing for higher level of commitments is an easier question to resolve. The WTO already allows groups of countries to enter into more favorable trade agreements without extending those conditions to all other members through free trade agreements and custom unions. Similarly the Enabling Clause permits the

---

[6] Committee on Agriculture, Special Session, *Revised Draft Modalities for Agriculture*, TN/ AG/W/4/Rev.3 (10 July 2008); TN/AG/W/4/Rev.2 (19 May 2008); TN/AG/W/4/Rev.1 (8 February 2008); Negotiating Group on Market Access, *Draft Modalities for Non-Agricultural Market Access*, TN/MA/W/103/Rev.2 (10 July 2008); TN/MA/W/103/Rev.1 (19 May 2008); TN/MA/W/103 (8 February 2008).

granting of more favorable concessions between developing countries only. The system of bound duties that may differ from actual, lower duties is another flexibility mechanism allowing a country to further lower its tariffs while technically subscribing to a general agreement with a less stringent standard.[7]

Enabling lesser levels of commitments without destroying the overall balance of concessions is more difficult. First, each member could be allowed to opt in or out of each agreement. Such an approach may conjure ghosts of the Tokyo Round where the lack of a single undertaking resulted in a patchwork of agreements with varying (and generally low) membership. Additionally, non-reciprocity in the Tokyo Round caused developing members to be largely excluded from gaining valuable concessions. A revised opt-out approach could, however, provide a more successful outcome in terms of meaningful participation by a large number of members.

Alternatively, all members could be integrated in all agreements, but each member's obligations under the agreements could be differentiated. This second option, which will be referred to as "general differentiation," evokes the Appellate Body Report in *EC–Tariff Preferences*, with developing countries taking exception to what they perceive as an attempt by the AB to do away with the unifying legal category of "developing members." However, lessons from the (recent) past are only partially helpful. If differentiation is based on unilaterally defined criteria, with only a very loose overarching principle, as in the *EC–Tariff Preferences* case, developing members' concern and ensuing lack of control over their own development policy may be legitimate. That scenario still reflects the idiosyncratic paradigm. By contrast, differentiation can be supported by an overarching normative principle agreed upon by the membership as defining the trade and development relationship, where differentiation becomes a tool to tailor the level of commitments to development needs and capabilities. This approach to differentiation would be more in line with the "normative co-constituent" paradigm described in the introduction of this book.

With respect to the mechanics for differentiation, Charlton proposed a system where the level of commitments depends on the *relative position of members vis-à-vis each other*. He suggests that each member make commitments in favor of countries poorer than itself, but those commitments or concessions would not necessarily extend to countries richer than it.[8] Such "asymmetric opt out provisions" would ratchet up the commitments of members depending on their economic position, while ensuring that the benefits trickle down to the poorer members. This mechanism would also be helpful to tackle counterproductive South–South protectionism.

---

[7] IMF and World Bank, *Market Access for Developing Countries' Exports* (27 April 2001) <http://www.imf.org/external/np/madc/eng/042701.htm>, at 15 (showing the differential between bound rates and applied rates at the conclusion of the Uruguay Round).

[8] A. Charlton, "A Proposal for Special and Differential Treatment in the Doha Round," Working Paper for WTO SDT Working Group (2005) (on file with the author). We use the terms "rich" and "poor" instead of "developed" and "developing" in this section because it is the terminology used by Charlton and it reflects a shift from development concerns to a categorization of members based solely on macroeconomic benchmarks.

Charlton does not necessarily view his proposal as a way to provide differentiation between all members since he still assumes that there is a uniform level of commitments applicable in principle to all members, with some members then opting out "asymmetrically." However, given the present evolution towards differentiation, it is possible to recast his proposal as asymmetric scaling rather than asymmetric opt-outs. To illustrate, his proposal calls for developing countries to implement only part or none of the tariff-cutting commitments on goods imported from richer or larger countries (assuming that the tariff cut is determined by an across-the-board formula). Recast as built-in scaled differentiation, a rule would provide that a member is never obligated to provide the same or a higher level of concession vis-à-vis richer members in a request and offer system. If negotiations are formula-driven, members would agree on a formula for the highest level of commitments and the formula would then be automatically scaled down for members depending on their economics. The modalities for opting out and asymmetric commitments is further explored in Section 4 below addressing negotiations.

This asymmetric scaling would allow members to lower the barriers to trade amongst similarly situated members, while members with less capacity would liberalize less, commensurate with their economic capabilities. Richer members wanting more liberalization would have to open their markets to all poorer members for free or for concessions of lesser value. Is that a price that the richer members would be willing to pay? Would such a mechanism result in excluding the poorer members from gaining concessions valuable to them from richer members because they would necessarily offer a lesser concession in return? There is certainly such a risk as the driver for liberalization would be the richer members' own priorities, rather than common, agreed-upon priorities amongst all members.

Whereas Charlton's proposal emphasized members' economic position vis-à-vis each other, most proposals call for *differentiation of commitments based on objective predetermined criteria.*

In this perspective, Lee, for example, has proposed two instruments: a development facilitation subsidy, and a development facilitation tariff, both designed to provide a sliding scale of commitments and concessions.[9] Both find their economic rationale in theories similar to infant industry protection and the notion that government support is crucial to jump-start economic sectors domestically.[10]

Lee's development facilitation tariff would allow developing countries to impose additional tariffs beyond the scheduled commitments to support their economic development in designated sectors. Abusive use of the facility could be prevented or minimized by requiring that a genuine industrial development plan be in place, publishing a clear schedule of the increased tariff along with a time limitation on its use and a phasing-out of the excess tariff keyed to the progress of the

---

[9] Y.-S. Lee, "Facilitating Development in the World Trading System—A Proposal for Development Facilitation Tariff and Development Facilitating Subsidy" 2004 *Journal of World Trade* 38(2) 935.
[10] Lee finds economic support for the legal instruments he proposes particularly in Chang, above Ch 6 fn 6.

protected industry. Transparency and fairness would be ensured by holding public hearings on the implementation of the temporary protective tariff and requiring notifications regarding recourse to the facility.

This excess tariff would vary depending on the country's level of development. A base threshold for having access to the facility would be defined, typically by objective benchmarks such as gross national income per capita. The maximum excess tariff would also be predetermined. The maximum excess tariff that a country could apply would be scaled according to that country's gross national income per capita relative to the defined threshold. Lee suggests a threshold of USD15,000 per capita above which a country would be considered "developed" and not have access to the facility. Figure 12.1 illustrates how the tariff could apply if the maximum excess tariff is set at 100 percent *ad valorem*, and the decrease of the tariff is linear. Thus, a country with a per capita income of USD1,500 would be at 10 percent of the threshold. It could avail itself of 90 percent of the maximum excess tariff, setting the tariff at 90 percent *ad valorem* on imports that compete or are likely to compete with the protected industry, for instance.

Lee's development facilitation subsidy operates along similar lines and would be built into the SCM Agreement.

Both Charlton's and Lee's mechanisms assume a "normal" commitment that would then be scaled down for certain members. However, if the scaling mechanism is built into the agreements then the result is essentially a general differentiation of the members' commitments, and the "normal" commitment is increasingly a fictional benchmark simply used to calculate the scaling. They also both tend to assume a baseline of commitments that is essentially the highest level of commitment, presumably undertaken by industrialized members. Poorer members'

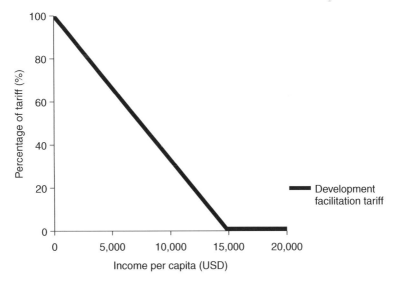

Figure 12.1 Y.-S. Lee's development facilitation tariff

commitments are then scaled down from that benchmark. This approach assumes that the richer members are always the ones driving trade liberalization and setting the highest level of commitments and disciplines. Historically, this has certainly been the case with respect to industrial tariff reductions and, more recently, with respect to liberalization of trade in services and the requirement of increased and harmonized intellectual property protection.

However, developing countries' complaints throughout the GATT and WTO history has been that the developed members have also consistently balked at lowering barriers to trade on products of interest to developing countries. Agriculture comes to mind with respect to subsidies, tariff escalation clauses on semi-processed goods are another example, as are tariffs on tropical products other than agricultural goods. This suggests that it may not always be appropriate to take the richest members' commitments as the benchmark to calculate other members' commitments, especially in sectors of interest to developing members. Instead, why not take the poorer members' commitments as the benchmark and scale commitments up for richer members? With scaling up, developing countries would have an incentive to lower the barriers to trade where they can because it would automatically trigger a correspondingly increased lowering of the barriers by all the richer countries. This would have beneficial effects on South–South trade liberalization and would prevent a Tokyo Round scenario, where lesser commitments by developing countries resulted in sidelining products of interest to them. In areas where developing countries do not wish to make commitments, or where they have no concessions to give, richer members would still be free to make enhanced commitments on a unilateral basis.

The issue of which benchmark to consider in order to differentiate between members ultimately relates to the control of the agenda and the pace of trade liberalization. In a scale-down scenario, the richer countries set the pace and determine which sectors are opened up. In a scale-up system, the poorer members have more control over these elements. Adopting one system or the other without being cognizant of these indirect effects on agenda-setting and prioritization of trade liberalization is likely to create more deadlocks in negotiations in the future.

If differentiation is built into the concessions system, what criteria are to be used to determine how to differentiate? The literature tends to refer to basic macroeconomic indicators such as GDP, GDP per capita, or gross national income per capita. This may be appropriate for some countries where the income inequalities are relatively low, but may be quite misleading in other cases, such as Brazil, which has some of the world's highest income inequalities, or oil producing countries. Similarly, if the differentiation targets a particular sector, it must be considered how far that sector's performance deviates from national economic indicators.

In many ways, general differentiation is already gaining ground in the WTO culture even though the topic remains politically taboo, particularly with some developing countries. However, unprincipled, *de facto* differentiation constitutes a hurdle to the consideration of more radical general differentiation models that would fundamentally transform the way in which members negotiate commitments and concessions. In a context where development is not a core value or a normative driver of the WTO system, developing members' reluctance to accept differentiation is understandable, perhaps even justified. However, incorporating development considerations at the core of negotiation design might make systemic differentiation a more attractive route than fighting for SDT provisions of dubious value. Shifting from an idiosyncratic paradigm to a normative co-constituent paradigm would support the viability and acceptability of differentiation.

2.2 Towards a relative valuation of members' concessions

Meaningful and successful scaling up may also hinge on a shift in the valuation of concessions. This section proposes a transformative approach to valuing concessions. The argument is that members may be more willing to recognize the legitimacy of differentiating commitments, through scaling or otherwise, if the value of concessions is expressed in terms relative to the offeror's economy, rather than in absolute terms. In the currency of concessions, relative terms may in fact be more important than absolute value. In practice, the issue is that it is not so much the value of the concession that counts but rather the fact that it may be the best a member has to offer. With the built-in asymmetry, concessions could become valued in terms of how much they are worth to the offering member, rather than what they are worth to the receiving member. This shift from absolute valuing of concessions to relative valuing would help mitigate poorer members' inability to gain concessions of value to them because they are offering less in return, in absolute terms.

For example, Japan may be offering concessions worth USD4 billion (absolute value), which represents 0.1 percent of Japan's GDP. If it were to require the same absolute amount of concessions from Mexico, the concession would account for 0.3 percent of Mexico's GDP.[11] Hence, the concession would be three times more costly for Mexico than it is for Japan, relative to their respective economies. Similar arguments can be made using members' GDP per capita. Essentially, the idea is to compare concessions based on their value relative to the offering member rather than to compare their absolute values.

Whether such a change in the culture and perception of WTO negotiators is likely to happen in the near future is another question. Only a combination of political and legal instruments can truly embed a development dimension at the WTO. The dispute settlement system offers a useful parallel to inform the discussion on relative or absolute valuation of concessions. Members and commentators now fully recognize that a major limitation to the effectiveness of the process is the different impact of an absolute level of retaliatory rights on large economies and on small ones. The case was particularly clear in the *US–Gambling* dispute

---

[11] Mexico's GDP in purchasing power parity (PPP) was estimated at USD1.56 trillion for 2010; Japan's GDP in PPP was estimated at USD4.31 trillion for 2010 (Source: *CIA World Factbook* <https://www.cia.gov/library/publications/the-world-factbook>).

where Antigua was allowed to retaliate against the United States but the dollar offset of the absolute value of the concession nullified or impaired by the losing party on its own was unlikely to coerce the United States into compliance. Instead, the qualitative nature of the retaliatory rights played a significant role. To some extent, the same is true for concessions, where even in the most traditional mercantilist system the bargaining is between more than simple dollar amounts of concessions.

To conclude, both differentiation and opting-out mechanisms appear to reduce trade liberalization (and in some cases increase protectionism) by the WTO's poorer members. While this seems to run counter to the main objective of the WTO, the reality is more subtle. Differentiation and opting-out devices go against the fundamental notion of reciprocity between equal concessions. As such, they displace the mercantilist ethos of the WTO where liberalization results from the exchange of equally valuable concessions. But perhaps the GATT and WTO's old mercantilist strategy is not the only way to bring about trade liberalization, and other mechanisms might better respond to current challenges. Are WTO members ready to abandon their mercantilist culture and embrace differentiated commitments, or will developing countries continue to "pay" for decreased commitments in one agreement by concessions in other sectors in the currency of the more powerful members, rather than their own valuation of the concessions?

3. Rationalizing the Role of Development in Dispute Settlement

An important part of giving life to the trade and development relationship is the dispute settlement system and the panels and the AB's power to interpret the covered agreements. Yet, the current approach that relies on limited SDT provisions to provide a level playing field for all litigants is fraught with failure.[12] Problems of participation identified in Chapter 7 and shortcomings regarding the current remedy system of Article 22 of the DSU would also require adjustments.

Dispute settlement may operate at several levels to support and enforce a development dimension at the WTO. First, if the relationship is limited to idiosyncratic derogations and exceptions, adjudication must play a critical role in fostering predictability and some measure of uniformity. Second, in the framework of a normative integration of development at the WTO, the dispute settlement system is best placed to expound the relationship between trade and development. Third, it would also be key to enforcing a new deal of differentiated rights and obligations. Last, regardless of the paradigm that frames the trade and development relationship, the dispute settlement system currently

---

[12] A. Alavi, "On the (Non-)Effectiveness of the World Trade Organization Special and Differential Treatments in the Dispute Settlement Process" 2007 *Journal of World Trade* 41(2) 319.

suffers from participation and procedural shortcomings that could be better addressed. Each aspect is examined in turn.

3.1 Litigating derogations and exceptions

From a dispute settlement perspective, multilateral or unilateral SDT explored in Section 1 have the spirit of common law at heart. Both would rely heavily on dispute settlement to preserve the coherence of the system. Absent overarching norms, adjudicators would be left with only general principles of treaty interpretation to address the implementation of exceptions, derogations, reservations, and interpretative declarations. With an overarching agreement on the modalities and processes of accessing SDT, adjudicators would have a stronger framework to rely on.

In domestic common law systems, balancing the emphasis on individual cases with the need to maintain a fairly uniform application of the law comes at the cost of a high volume of litigation. At the WTO, the string of zeroing cases suggests that cases can quickly multiply on similar issues. More generally, the dispute settlement system already deals with an extraordinary number of cases compared with other international jurisdictions. Endorsing the principle of *stare decisis* or a softer precedent principle could assist in limiting the relitigation of identical issues. Reliance on dispute settlement also requires a high level of compliance with decisions to ensure uniformity in the application of the law. Can the WTO dispute settlement system deliver on these three elements?

While the dispute settlement system has been successful both quantitatively and qualitatively, it is far from certain that it could absorb a surge in disputes if many members were to adopt their own interpretation of WTO provisions or make various declarations. The DSU calendar for a relatively quick resolution of disputes is already greatly strained: The average length of the panel proceedings is over thirteen months, compared to a statutory length of six to nine months.[13]

The distribution of cases is also to be considered. If provisions for developing countries are to be interpreted, harmonized, and enforced mainly by relying on dispute settlement, a greater number of disputes would likely involve developing and least developed countries. Yet, as discussed in Chapter 7, LDCs are virtually absent from the dispute settlement process, at least as main parties (they have a minor third party participation).

Alongside the availability of a forum for litigation, a case-by-case approach also requires reliance on precedent in order to ensure a uniform and coherent application of the law. International law generally limits the binding legal value of rulings by international courts and tribunals to the parties in respect to the specific dispute,[14] though in reality, the practice of referring to earlier cases still fosters coherence in international court's case law. In that sense, international adjudication

---

[13] H. Horn and P.C. Mavroidis, "The WTO Dispute Settlement System 1995–2006: Some Descriptive Statistics" (14 March 2008) <http://siteresources.worldbank.org/INTRES/Resources/469232-1107449512766/DescriptiveStatistics_031408.pdf>, at 28–9.

[14] See, eg, ICJ Statute, Art 59 ("The decision of the Court has no binding force except between the parties and in respect of that particular case.").

is more imbued by a civil law culture than a common law one. Precedent takes a variety of forms: In the words of Jackson, "it is a multilayered concept, or a ladder of concepts."[15] The WTO's DSU is no exception to the general public international law approach but the language of the DSU does not preclude, in theory, a shift towards a more common law inspired model: It merely specifies that the dispute resolution process is not to increase or diminish the advantages of the parties under the covered agreements.[16]

Recent developments in WTO case law highlighted members' fundamental ambivalence regarding the precedential value of panel and AB decisions. In disputes regarding zeroing methodology in antidumping cases, the AB consistently rejected all applications of zeroing.[17] A reliance on precedential culture was indeed taking hold of the WTO until a panel attempted to roll it back in the *US–Stainless Steel* case, arguing that panels "are not, strictly speaking, bound by previous Appellate Body or panel decisions that have addressed the same issue."[18] The AB ultimately responded with a ruling reversing the panel's decision and reaffirming the invalidity of zeroing both "as applied" and "as such."[19] With respect to precedent, the AB stopped short of enshrining a principle of *stare decisis* in WTO law, but effectively created a presumption of authoritative value. It stated that reports created "legitimate expectations" by members and should therefore not be departed from absent "cogent reasons."[20]

Developing members reacted vocally. Hong Kong and India, for instance, supported a strongly consistent jurisprudential approach, in line with the AB report.[21] Mexico used measured and ambiguous terms that seemed to support the AB's position. A few dissenting voices amongst developing members were not as supportive of the trend in favor of *stare decisis*. Chile expressed relief that the AB had not "cross[ed] the 'obligation' line" and concern that the need for

---

[15] J.H. Jackson, "Process and Procedure in WTO Dispute Settlement" 2009 *Cornell International Law Journal* 42(2) 233, at 237–8, discussing a range of precedent from *stare decisis* at the top, to "something less weighty with burdens of proof . . . to the case where we do not pay attention to it except for its titillating effect." See also, J.H. Jackson, *Sovereignty, The WTO, and Changing Fundamentals of International Law* (Cambridge: Cambridge University Press, 2006) at 177 ("In sum, it can be argued that there is quite a powerful precedent effect in the jurisprudence of the WTO, but that it is certainly not *stare decisis*, and it is not so powerful as to require panels or the Appellate Body considering new cases to follow prior cases, with the possible exception that once prior cases have been numerous regarding a particular issue and approach, and apparently accepted by all members of the WTO, then the language of the Vienna Convention about 'practice under agreement,' may suggest a stronger impact. But short of that situation, it appears that the 'flavor' of the precedent effect in the WTO is still somewhat fluid, and possibly will remain fluid for the time being.").

[16] Arts 3.2, 3.5, 19.2 DSU.

[17] Appellate Body Report, *US–Zeroing (EC)* (upholding the panel's findings against zeroing); Appellate Body Report, *EC–Bed Linen*; *US–Softwood Lumber V*; *US–Softwood Lumber V (Article 21.5–Canada)*; *US–Zeroing (Japan)*. See also Request for Consultations, *United States–Provisional Anti-Dumping Measures on Shrimp from Thailand*.

[18] Panel Report, *US–Stainless Steel (Mexico)*, at para 7.102. See also para 7.106 ("[W]e have decided that we have no option but to respectfully disagree with the line of reasoning developed by the Appellate Body regarding the WTO-consistency of simple zeroing in periodic reviews.").

[19] Appellate Body Report, *US–Stainless Steel*.   [20] Ibid at paras 159–60.

[21] DSB, *Minutes of the Meeting held on 20 May 2008*, WT/DSB/M/250 (1 July 2008), at para 62.

security and predictability required, according to the AB, not to depart from prior rulings absent "cogent reasons." Colombia felt equally ambivalent about the AB moving towards a *stare decisis* policy, reminding members instead that only the Ministerial Conference and the General Council were empowered to make interpretative decisions on this issue.

The ECJ, as the only other effective dispute settlement mechanism policing an international trading system, may provide valuable insights. The ECJ plays a crucial role in solidifying, enhancing, and even accelerating Europe's economic integration—and now increasingly its political and social integration. Yet, it is not governed by a strict application of *stare decisis*. What lessons could be drawn for the WTO? First, the complexity of WTO rules and the geographic scope of their application would result in a much more daunting task when it comes to consistency and harmonization in adjudication of *ad hoc* SDT provisions. Second, the ECJ benefits from a rigid and powerful enforcement mechanism as its decisions trickle down to the lowest levels of judicial, legislative, and executive enforcement with uncontested binding force. Not so for the WTO: Much more variance must be expected in the domestic implementation of panel and AB decisions. Third, the ECJ's integrating power has been exercised in large part through the preliminary ruling procedure of Article 267 of the Treaty of Lisbon.[22] When faced with a deluge of requests for ruling, particularly from the Italian courts, the ECJ decided that it would not issue a ruling in response to a question that it had already decided. Such a method is, for all practical purposes, essentially an application of *stare decisis*. The conformity to precedent has therefore been a powerful tool used in practice by the ECJ to further EU integration. It could play the same role at the WTO, but that may require an amendment to the DSU allowing panels or the AB to dispose of disputes presenting issues that have already been decided.

Reliance on the dispute settlement system to ensure consistency, fairness, and transparency in the administration of idiosyncratic SDT is certainly possible, but may require a reconsideration of some features. First, the value of precedents would be a key question: Less weight to precedent means a higher likelihood of serial litigation of the same issue or inconsistency in the interpretation of the provisions. Second, the complete lack of guidance regarding the relationship between liberalization and development leaves it to the discretion of the panels and AB to balance these possibly competing objectives. Third, if exceptions and derogations are multiplied, the volume of cases might also increase (though that did not materialize in the first decade of the WTO), further imposing on an already strained system. Fourth, the track record of cases so far suggests that the drafting of SDT provisions, waivers, and other derogations would need to be much more bright-lined (including tests, criteria, or standards that would provide clear benchmarks for adjudicators) if they are to have any effect. Some of these issues could be addressed in part by incorporating an overarching development norm in the covered agreements.

---

[22] Formerly Art 234 of the Treaty establishing the European Community, Official Journal C 325, 24/12/2002 p 0127–8.

3.2 Expounding development as a normative component of the covered agreements

Chapters 7 and 8 have shown that comparatively few development arguments are made at the WTO, that development-oriented provisions have not been exploited to the maximum of their availability in dispute settlement, but that giving more legal effect to SDT provisions may be possible in a number of cases by drawing analogies with other areas of international law. This section explores how an overarching normative principle for trade and development would affect dispute settlement.

Overarching interpretative principles are a familiar feature in WTO law. The notion of least trade-restrictive measure is an example of how a strong overarching principle guides judicial interpretation of WTO obligations. If development was mainstreamed as a normative pillar of the WTO, we could imagine panels and the AB developing similar notions for gauging the WTO compliance of particular measures. For instance, the interpretation of trade rules could be subjected to tests of development-fostering versus development-stifling measures. Compliance with WTO disciplines could require domestic measures to also be least development-restrictive.

Beyond the interpretation of substantive WTO obligations, incorporating development as a normative co-constituent also bears on procedural aspects, such as the allocation of the burden of proof. If the overall mandate specifies that the agreements shall not be interpreted or applied in a way that impairs the implementation of fundamental development objectives of members, the issue then is to determine which party bears the burden of proof to substantiate a claim that there is a "fundamental development objective" and that it is impaired by the application of a particular provision. If the process is tipped in favor of developing members, the developing country litigant would merely have to make a *prima facie* case that a fundamental development objective is impaired and the burden would fall on the non-developing litigant, to prove that there is no fundamental development objective or that it is not impaired by the application of the agreement (and the developing member could rebut the arguments). Alternatively, developing countries would carry the burden of proof regarding their fundamental development objective and possibly also regarding the impairment element of the claim. Such an allocation of the burden would be more onerous to developing country litigants. In the case of litigation between developing countries, the arguments could still be made, as competing development objectives and needs do not cancel each other out, contrary to what panels, the AB, and arbitrators suggested in some cases.

Traditionally, panels and secondarily the AB have determined how to allocate the burden on proof and the order of the proof. The general rule is that the claimant bears a burden of proof, whether the thing to be proved is a positive or a negative, and a party raising an affirmative defense similarly must prove it.[23] However,

---

[23] See eg, P. Lichtenbaum, "Procedural Issues in WTO Dispute Resolution" 1998 *Michigan Journal of International Law* 19(4) 1195, at 1248–52; A.W. Shoyer and E.M. Solovy, "Operation of

in some cases where a more subtle approach was required, panels considered the wording of the provision at stake, and relied on common sense and on the general objective of the provision or the agreement. How the burden of proof for development will be allocated is much more than a legal technicality, but is indicative of where the presumptions lie regarding development and liberalization.

3.3 Enforcing a "New Deal" of rights and obligations?

With the derogations and exceptions approach to development, a central issue is to determine which members could opt out and for how long. Criteria set through a framework agreement on SDT would help to guide adjudicators, or, absent that, the terms of the provisions themselves would be the sole reference. General differentiation relies perhaps even more heavily on the overarching codification of development as a normative co-constituent than the *ad hoc* approach. As discussed above, general differentiation may only be politically acceptable to developing members if it is part of a credible *quid pro quo* between giving up the "developing country" designation and offering a normative incorporation of development at the core part of the WTO system. The dispute settlement system would have a heavy burden in ensuring that the *quid pro quo* is upheld and that the differentiated obligations are truly cognizant of members' needs and vulnerabilities.

Perhaps most critically, general differentiation would entail a radical change in the understanding of what constitutes reciprocity and non-discrimination at the WTO. Inasmuch as both notions currently are based on the notion of equality pervasive in public international law, a different grounding would have to emerge.

So far, with the exception of SDT, WTO members are treated as formally equal and hence subject to the same obligations. Formal equality and formal reciprocity makes for a very Talion-like legal system (an eye for an eye). That legal culture is now becoming a source of inequity.

Another avenue, which might be helpful, is the reconsideration of the role of equity as compared to strict legalism. Decisions *ex æquo et bono* in arbitration proceedings and even at the ICJ pursuant to Article 38.2 of the Court's Statute pertain to a rich international law tradition. Some studies currently are being undertaken in the area of arbitration that could provide some useful perspectives for WTO adjudication.[24]

3.4 Procedural issues and participation

This body of research has repeatedly shown that if development considerations are to be included in the WTO legal framework, it must be done both through

---

the Appellate Process and Functions, Including the Appellate Body: The Process and Procedure of Litigating at the World Trade Organization: A Review of the Work of the Appellate Body" 2000 *Law and Policy International Business* 31(3) 677, at 689.

[24] M. Della Valle, *Das Decisões por Eqüidade na Arbitragem Comercial Internacional*, (São Paulo: Mimeo, 2008); *Task Force on Amiable Composition and ex æquo et bono, Interim Report*, ICC Doc 420/555, at 22 (2008); M. Sornarajah, "Power and Justice in Foreign Investment Arbitration" 1997 *Journal of International Arbitration* 14(3) 103.

substantive rights and obligations and through the empowerment of developing members at the institutional and procedural levels. That is also true with respect to the dispute settlement process.

Chapter 7 discussed the nature of developing members' participation in dispute settlement and its shortcomings. In particular, developing members' use of the process as third parties limits their ability to obtain remedies available only to principal parties. Either the process must be reconfigured to promote an increased participation as principal litigant, or remedies should be considered for third parties.

The cost of litigation combined with the lack of resources in most developing countries has resulted in a variety of coping mechanisms that raise issues of their own, particularly with respect to incentives to litigate. Chapter 7 analyzed the costing structure of dispute resolution for WTO members (predominantly fixed costs for rich countries, predominantly variable costs for poor members) and its effect on incentives to litigate. In Brazil, for example, the government typically will litigate disputes if the domestic industry interested in bringing the dispute (or, presumably, defending it) is willing to pay for litigation costs. Small developing countries without a strong local industrial base will be hard-pressed to replicate that model. Instead, they are more likely to join a dispute instigated by a large developing country or to become a third party in that dispute. The role of nongovernmental organizations in those cases is also important to identify the real drivers of disputes in some developing countries.

This lead-followers model is workable so long as the interests of the principle and third parties are congruent. That may be the case if the dispute is brought against a developed country regarding development provisions (although the *EC–Tariff Preferences* case shows that is not necessarily the case). However, such a model may be of little help as the interests of the middle-income countries increasingly diverge from those of other developing members and LDCs.

A number of suggestions have been made for bridging the participation gap between rich and poor members. They range from continuing to increase technical and financial assistance to amending third party procedures as well as procedures for joining as a co-complainant or co-respondent once another member has launched the case. These suggestions would play an important role in reinforcing the role of developing members in dispute settlement, which is crucial to substantiating a development dimension at the WTO.

Another major issue is remedies. Because the trade position of many developing countries vis-à-vis more powerful trading partners makes WTO remedies ineffective, members with small economies and a small share of world trade have a lower incentive to engage in a dispute and defend its interests, or, once a dispute has been won, to be able to effectively pressure the other member into compliance.[25]

---

[25] See eg, G.N. Horlick, "Problems with the Compliance Structure of the WTO Dispute Resolution Process," in D. Kennedy and J. Southwick (eds), *The Political Economy of International Trade Law: Essays in Honor of Robert E. Hudec* (Cambridge: Cambridge University Press, 2002); G. Shaffer, "How to Make the WTO Dispute Settlement System Work for Developing Countries: Some Proactive Developing Country Strategies," in "Towards a Development-Supportive Dispute

A number of proposals have been made to increase the impact of remedies as they currently exist and therefore make up for asymmetries between WTO members. One avenue is to auction the right to suspend concessions. Interestingly, this proposal has been developed both by academics and by the Mexican delegation at the WTO.[26] Another proposal that has also garnered support both amongst some WTO members and in academia is to monetize remedies such that a monetary compensation would be due to the winning member until the member in default brings its measures into compliance.[27] Such efforts show that there are solutions to the issue of remedies in an asymmetric trade environment.

Whether in the framework of the idiosyncratic paradigm or the normative co-constituent paradigm, the dispute settlement system has a critical role to play for the integration of trade and development. However, the types of reforms that would be required vary depending on the nature of the trade and development relationship that members wish to foster. Procedural issues as well as practical considerations (volume and cost of litigation, etc) must be considered jointly.

4. Moving Away from All-or-Nothing Negotiations

The negotiations shall aim to:... secure additional benefits for the international trade of developing countries so as to achieve a substantial increase in their foreign exchange earnings, the diversification of their exports, the acceleration of the rate of growth of their trade... and a better balance between developing and developed countries in the sharing of the advantages resulting from this expansion.[28]

That was in 1973, at the outset of the Tokyo Round, and yet, it strikes eerily close to the premise of the Doha "Development" Round some three decades later. In the Tokyo Round, developing countries, by opting out of agreements, also forwent many potential benefits from trade liberalization. By contrast, the single

Settlement System in the WTO," ICSID Resource Paper No 5 (March 2003) <http://ictsd.org/downloads/2008/06/dsu_2003.pdf>.

[26] *Negotiations on Improvements and Clarifications of the Dispute Settlement Understanding: Proposal by Mexico*, TN/DS/W/23 (4 November 2002); K. Bagwell, P.C. Mavroidis and R.W. Staiger, "The Case for Auctioning Countermeasures in the WTO," National Bureau of Economic Research Working Paper No 9920 (July 2003) <http://www.ssc.wisc.edu/econ/archive/wp2003-14.pdf>; see also J. Pauwelyn, "Enforcement and Countermeasures in the WTO: Rules are Rules   Toward a More Collective Approach" 2000 *American Journal of International Law* 94(2) 335.

[27] *Negotiations on the Dispute Settlement Understanding: Proposal by the LDC Group*, TN/DS/W/17 (9 October 2002) (proposing monetary damages equal to injury suffered); see also *Negotiations on the Dispute Settlement Understanding: Proposal by the African Group*, TN/DS/W/15 (25 September 2002) (proposing monetary compensation to be continually paid pending and until the withdrawal of the measures in breach of WTO obligations); M. Bronckers and N. van den Broek, "Financial Compensation in the WTO" 2005 *Journal of International Economic Law* 8(1) 101; C. Carmody, "Remedies and Conformity Under the WTO Agreement" 2002 *Journal of International Economic Law* 5(2) 307; J.P. Trachtman, "Building the WTO Cathedral" 2007 *Stanford Journal of International Law* 43(1) 127, at 128–9.

[28] *Declaration of Ministers Approved at Tokyo on 14 Sept 1973*, BISD 20S/19 (1974), at 19–20, para 1.

undertaking approach now operates as the glue that holds multi-faceted negotiations together: Members find it beneficial to bargain for a balance of commitments not only within a specific agreement but also across agreements. The continued use of the single undertaking as an engine for reaching a broader deal is, however, questionable. For instance, many technical proposals submitted in the Doha Round could have been agreed upon independently from the rest of the negotiations, and holding off on these issues has not helped foster a broader deal on the more contentious negotiations on services and agriculture.

The single undertaking in its traditional form really comprises two elements: *All members* must agree, and they must agree to common rules on *everything*. Based on discussions with some developing country negotiators in Geneva, it appears that those countries are willing to forgo gaining more advantages in one agreement in order to keep leverage and an effective veto power over other agreements by virtue of the single undertaking system. As discussed in Chapter 9 (dealing with voting, decision-making, and modalities for negotiation), this leverage and veto power is, for many countries, a fairly illusory one.

How would allowing developing countries to opt out of certain agreements that are too onerous for them to implement or not calibrated to their level and style of development affect the modalities for negotiation? Two situations may be envisioned: First, the single undertaking could be maintained but modified by *ad hoc* variances; second the single undertaking approach could be eliminated altogether. Each is explored in turn, leading to the conclusion that a modified single undertaking may be the best compromise between the need for coherence and cohesion in the multilateral trading system and the need to cater to individual members' needs and capabilities.

4.1 Single undertaking with *ad hoc* variances

While there is evidence in the past (and to some extent, in the present as well) that the single undertaking operated to the detriment of developing countries, current shifts in the balance of power amongst WTO members may explain why some middle-income members are in favor of that framework: The single undertaking now gives them political leverage as it gives them the power to block negotiations. Here again, interests of developing countries are increasingly divergent, but modified single-undertaking approaches, particularly critical mass negotiation design with opting out for marginal players may provide benefits to all. It would allow emerging developing countries to keep their leverage power if they are part of the required critical mass to go forward with a package, while protecting the interests of weaker members by allowing them to opt out. Embedding development as a core normative co-constituent with trade liberalization would further ensure that a package of negotiations presented to members would be more adapted to the situation of the bulk of the members. More generally, the "normative co-constituent" paradigm has a powerful role to play, both legally and politically, in the various negotiation designs proposed here.

How can the benefits of the single undertaking be combined with a more flexible approach to balance the need for going forward in the negotiations with the recognition that not all members may be interested in committing on all issues at the same time? This section argues that a modified single undertaking would allow developing countries to reap the benefits of a more flexible system while preserving the coherence of the multilateral trade system. Two variances are explored below: A package of measures could be adopted even in the absence of unanimity, or a package of measures could be adopted in respect to some, but not all, agreements.

Less than unanimity

The emphasis here is to preserve the single undertaking approach enough to allow cross-sectoral bargaining amongst a critical mass of participants, while letting some individual members opt out from making concessions under some agreements. The basic insight is that if countries with a negligible part of world trade opt out of certain agreements, it will not have a heavy impact on the overall balance of concessions and the cost of letting them opt out will be small for other players. Members that opt out would still benefit from whatever MFN concessions accrue under the agreement among the rest of the members. This limited free-riding by the opting-out countries should remain fairly negligible for other players, in economic terms, but the benefit would be quite significant for the beneficiary members. Given the mixed evidence on trade diversion and the limitation of the opting out to economically negligible actors, the distortive effect should also be fairly minimal.

Several proposals have been put forward regarding agreement-by-agreement opt-out for developing countries and the conditions for opting in and out.[29] Some thresholds could be set, either by agreement or overall, to determine which countries can opt out. For instance, LDCs could be allowed to opt out of any agreement. Because some LDCs or other vulnerable economies may still be important players in particular sectors, the opt-out option could exclude these key sectors. Alternatively, qualifying factors for opting out could be defined as objective benchmarks allowing a dynamic evolution as countries' economic circumstances change over time.

When a country no longer qualifies for opting out, the member could fully reintegrate the agreement:

- automatically (with an appropriate transitional time-period), or
- subject to negotiations with other members (a mini accession negotiation), or
- as part of the next general round of negotiations.

Another advantage of this mechanism is to provide an opportunity for small economies with limited negotiation capacity to focus on the aspects and sectors that are

[29] Z.K. Wang and L.A. Winters, "Putting 'Humpty' Together Again: Including Developing Countries in a Consensus for the WTO," CEPR Policy Paper No 4 (6 April 2000); A. Keck and P. Low, "Special and Differential Treatment in the WTO: Why, When and How?" WTO Staff Working Paper ERSD-2004-03 (May 2004); B. Hoekman, "Operationalizing the Concept of Policy Space in the WTO: Beyond Special and Differential Treatment," above Ch 6, fn 2, at 412.

most important to them without having to accept problematic commitments in other areas where they had no genuine opportunity to bargain.

This approach is mindful of the two core issues that developing countries are facing at the WTO: domestic economic and regulatory difficulties, and limited capacity to participate in negotiations.

In practice, members could proceed on a single undertaking basis much as they currently do, but when the proposed package is submitted for approval to the full membership, a reasonable period of time would allow qualifying countries to opt out of specific agreements. Key players could get a sense of the level of interest from the potential opt-outs while the package is still being negotiated. This approach maintains the single undertaking feature with respect to the critical mass of members who cannot opt out, but it makes some exceptions for a limited number of members. Such a system would not be as radically different from the current practice as it seems: Many members currently are only concerned with parts of the package of negotiations and have little or no stake in other parts of it. The proposal would make members' actual assent to the package—or lack thereof—more transparent, which in turn may increase the legitimacy of the package. Most importantly, it would reverse the presumption of participation (and commitments) by the weakest members: If the default rule is that they can opt out, it will be more difficult for more powerful members to extract unsustainable concessions from them.

One drawback is that members that opted out of an agreement and later seek to join it will still not have an opportunity to negotiate its design and disciplines.

Less than all agreements: Towards partial linkage

Another approach to increase flexibility consists in modifying the "package" format for the negotiations. While some linkage may be productive, inasmuch as it allows for cross-sectoral bargaining, it may be suboptimal to link all topics at all times. The expansion and diversification of WTO regulation to very technical matters and the focus on technical harmonization is quite distinct from substantive trade concessions on goods or services. Indeed, why should a review and amendment of the DSU be contingent on the conclusion of negotiations on agriculture, as is currently the case? While import licensing procedures certainly affect the actual trade in goods, should harmonization of these customs procedures hinge on a possible agreement on competition or telecommunications? More crucially for developing countries, should their lagging administrative capabilities in some areas be such a hindrance to their market access negotiations? A partial de-linking of agreements up for negotiation would provide significant advantages for developed and developing members alike.

Developing members would be able to deal with the linked and the de-linked negotiations separately, and if some need to be sacrificed for lack of human resources, they can make a more strategic choice as to which negotiations to withdraw from. If they are negotiating in groups with a type of proxy system described in Section 5 below, de-linking certain agreements may simplify the mandate and feedback procedures within the group.

If some technical and rules-oriented negotiations are de-linked from the single undertaking, developing countries will be less penalized for their lack of capacity in those areas because they would not be prevented from participating in negotiations and obtaining concessions in the cross-sectoral bargaining. At the same time, members willing to advance negotiations on technical rules would be able to move forward without being held back by members unable to make commitments on that front.

The Doha negotiations confirm the theoretical value of this approach. Some insular technical negotiations as well as a number of the SDT proposals affecting rules-based agreements were reportedly essentially agreed upon early on in the Round but have since been in limbo because of the deadlocks on NAMA and agriculture. Discussions on the DSU, as well as proposals on the TBT and SPS Agreements could probably have been concluded and implemented years ago. Instead, not only have they been put on stand-by, but it is now assumed that they will not even make it to the final package. This seems like an unnecessarily wasteful and inefficient process. The Doha Work Programme itself appears to have anticipated this scenario by allowing members to provisionally implement certain areas up for negotiations pending a full package. Members failed to avail themselves of the facility.

The question then is how to determine which segments of the negotiations would be de-linked from the central package. First, an overall clause, perhaps in the Marrakesh Agreement, could state that if an agreement's central object is not trade liberalization in a particular economic sector, that agreement *may* be negotiated, submitted to members for approval, signature, and ratification, and implemented independently from general rounds of negotiations. Alternatively, for an even stronger mandate, the clause could stipulate that such agreements *shall* be negotiated independently from other agreements. Second, the launch of a round of negotiation could, at the agenda-setting stage, determine which parts of the negotiations are to be conducted independently from the main package. This *ad hoc* approach would add an additional step at the beginning of the negotiations, but would provide more flexibility than an overall mandate that may not cover all future subjects or types of negotiations.

Ultimately, some individual member opting out combined with some de-linking from the central negotiation package would maintain the spirit and process of the single undertaking. At the same time, it would provide valuable flexibilities for developing members that do not wish—or are unable—to attend to all aspects of the negotiations and to implement all agreements resulting from a given round. Yet, those members would not be marginalized from the negotiations and its trade liberalization benefits as they were during the Tokyo Round. Additionally, developing members could also retain greater control over their domestic agenda for development by opting in when the regulated subject matter becomes ripe domestically.[30] Meanwhile, other members (developed and developing) wishing a deeper

---

[30] Ibid. See also S. Prowse, "The Role of International and National Agencies in Trade-Related Capacity Building" 2002 *World Economy* 25(9) 1235 (describing the possible role of international organizations as monitors of this process).

level of commitments and faster pace of liberalization would not be held back. Overall, the multilateral trading system would maintain a core regulatory coherence and still provide a flexible platform for bargaining, which are the main benefits of the single undertaking.

4.2 Doing away with the single undertaking altogether?

This approach would resemble more closely the Tokyo Round resulting in a series of plurilateral agreements. Members would have no obligation to subscribe to any agreement, and the conclusion of one agreement would be de-linked from that of others so that cross-sectoral bargaining would be virtually eliminated.

Such a structure would likely reinforce bilateral and mini-lateral bargaining, since the only way to engage in cross-sectoral trade-offs would be to secure a promise from trade partners that they will subscribe to other sectoral agreements involved in the trade-off. Game theory suggests that such promises will be harder to keep except if members see the negotiations as a repeat game with identical players and no foreseeable last round.

Members wishing to liberalize at a faster pace could conclude agreements without having to water down their commitments in order to satisfy other members. Conversely, members with a more modest trade liberalization agenda could either not subscribe to an agreement or subscribe to a more limited agreement.

Whereas the "single undertaking with *ad hoc* variances" framework is essentially an opting-out model, this framework would operate on a full opt-in basis. The WTO would play its primary role as a negotiation forum, with an overall mandate that would include the balancing of development and trade liberalization, but it would not create a unified set of agreements binding on all members. Given the already complex network of agreements, such a system would make WTO commitments difficult to read and to value. This would be the price to pay for a trading system that could be fully tailored to individual members' needs and capabilities. Arguably, it would be the end of the fairly integrated WTO system as we know it, and it may even be the death of the broad multilateralism that the GATT and WTO have nurtured over the past sixty years.

Yet, considering that multilateral negotiations have been mostly unproductive for the past decade and that trade liberalization now is effectively conducted on a bilateral or small group basis with RTAs, some have argued that we may in fact already be past the heyday of multilateralism. The somewhat bold suggestion is that the current trade system is *de facto*, if not *de jure*, already operating on a segmented opt-in basis, with the multilateral WTO agreements forming an increasingly remote backdrop to negotiations taking place in alternative fora. The saga of the so-called "TRIPS-Plus" provisions inserted in bilateral and RTAs, and the ACTA negotiations , discussed in Chapter 11, are examples of the multilateral baseline being overtaken by extraneous agreements.

What would be the effect of such a system on negotiations for developing countries? As suggested, the present situation offers some insights as developing members already find themselves in the position of negotiating RTAs and bilateral agreements in lieu of multilateral agreements. While a full opt-in system should ensure in theory that members are not forced to make commitments they cannot sustain, in practice, bilateral or regional negotiations present two major hurdles for developing countries: They are a drain on human resources and they may put the weaker countries at a significant disadvantage in case of asymmetric bargaining power. The asymmetric bargaining issue may not have played out in practice to the disadvantage of developing countries as much as could have been expected. As discussed in Chapter 9, the US record of bilateral and regional FTAs since the beginning of the Doha Round is actually quite modest, though it has gained momentum more recently. Still, these RTAs follow relatively strictly the template developed by the United States, with little margin of maneuver for developing country counterparts. Moreover, the exclusion of topics of paramount interest to developing countries, agriculture in particular, also suggests that bilateral and regional deals might not provide to developing countries the market access opportunities they most want. The EU's Economic Partnership Agreements follow similar trends.

The insistence on maintaining a single undertaking in the Doha Round led in part to the failure to secure some early agreements on the less controversial technical matters and even to turn the cotton negotiations into a firm agreement in 2005, which could have been a good faith voucher for the United States and the EU to counter some developing countries' more extreme positions in subsequent agriculture talks. Similarly, the 97 percent of duty-free, quota-free access for LDCs offered in 2005 could have been implemented by now, leading to economic benefits for all parties and political goodwill for developed members. Instead, all these elements are now drowned in the miasma of the failed NAMA and agriculture talks. Cotton has even reverted to being an irksome subject, as the agreement in principle of the Hong Kong Ministerial is now put into question and essentially subject to renegotiations.

In sum, the single undertaking that has shaped the WTO system since its inception may now have become part of the problem, rather than a productive feature of the negotiations. Its benefits, however, may be preserved by modified approaches that would offer some developing members the flexibility they need. More radically, it is also possible to envision a multilateral trading system that is no longer governed by the single undertaking, and the current proliferation of regional negotiations gives a preview of what that would entail.

5. Systemic Issues: Empowering Groups of Developing Countries at the Institutional Level[31]

Another approach to enabling a development dimension in the WTO is to consider that substantive outcomes hinge on the institutional power of the actors. Indeed, the WTO is a platform for political bargaining, but it is also an institution

---

[31] Parts of this section are taken from S.E. Rolland, above Ch 5, fn 5.

governed by rules and that produces law for its members. The position of developing countries in this institutional framework is therefore crucial to the outcome of the negotiations. Having a development norm built into the WTO's mandate will mean little if the institutional structure does not also reflect it and support development-oriented regulatory outcomes.

The fundamental insight is that by modifying developing countries' institutional place (individually and collectively), the outcome of negotiations, and, more specifically, the likelihood that their demands will be part of the final package, will also be affected. Additionally, it is likely that under a modified institutional setting, proposals that would not even see the light of day at present will emerge, thereby expanding the range of possible regulatory outcomes. In political science terms, the outcomes are currently limited by the institutional constraints put on developing members' participation and by decision-making rules.[32]

Developing members' ability to form and sustain effective coalitions in the WTO could be of paramount importance to regulatory and negotiations outcomes, as well as for their day-to-day participation in the organization. Yet, their capacity to act through groups depends not only on the coalitions' inherent characteristics and the political environment, but also on the institutional and legal framework. In the domestic context, the right of association, standing in court afforded to groups representing collective interests, the ability to defend individual and collective rights as a group (the Civil Rights movement in the United States and collective bargaining in the labor context everywhere are salient examples), and the ability of a community to choose representatives constitute some rights and institutions that empower groups. They facilitate the participation of a large number of individuals in the legal and political process through indirect representation. They are also used to make the political process accessible to groups that would otherwise be excluded. Ultimately, these representative processes also account for a legal system's legitimacy. Although domestic law and international law have different underpinnings and dynamics, the political rationales for the legal recognition of groups and coalitions are similar.

With 153 members in the WTO, coalitions are crucial not only to strengthen the position of countries lacking the political and economic capacity to negotiate single-handedly, but also, some have suggested, to facilitate negotiations by reducing the number of principals[33] (although the current high number and complex

---

[32] W.H. Riker, "Implications from the Disequilibrium of Majority Rule for the Study of Institutions" 1980 *American Political Science Review* 74(2) 432, at 443; see also K.A. Shepsle and B.R. Weingast, "Structure-Induced Equilibrium and Legislative Choice" 1981 *Public Choice* 37(3) 503.

[33] B. Hoekman, "Cancún: Crisis or Catharsis," Paper Presented to the Brookings-George Washington Trade Roundtable on Trade and Investment Policy (20 September 2003) <http:// siteresources.worldbank.org/INTRANETTRADE/Resources/Hoekman-CancunCatharsis-092003.pdf>, at 5. However, the author also notes that coalitions may lead to the entrenchment of positions and, thus, a higher risk of breakdown in negotiations if groups are less flexible about their positions than individual members would be.

mapping of coalitions may ultimately rebut the latter claim).[34] Groupings also reinforce the weight and credibility of some medium-income countries, which are now established as key players in negotiations.

Developing country coalitions may be divided broadly into two types for the purposes of this analysis: discussion and research groups, and negotiation-oriented groups. Each raises separate legal and institutional issues and calls for different legal tools to pursue their participants' objectives.

5.1 Supporting discussion and research groups

Coalitions focusing on sharing information and pooling research resources help develop common platforms and negotiating positions for their members. They may also act as liaisons between the WTO and coalitions' members. Keohane and Nye have recognized the importance of these interconnections.[35] The WTO, and particularly the Secretariat, have been increasingly active in giving institutional support to these groups even though the groups are informal and have no legal status within the organization.

The WTO's technical assistance and training activities support research and discussion groups and foster connections between the organization and groups of members. A number of programs are regionally focused and aim at building capacity, synergies, and networking within regional groups. Some activities are specifically offered to particular coalitions. LDCs are also identified as a group and given particular consideration as such. The 2010–2011 Technical Assistance Plan underlines the continued commitment to:

using regional configurations, to take advantage of existing structures already developed by regional economic organizations, as well as to use the familiarity of these regional bodies with regional dimensions of the WTO issues. A key objective of this programme is to ensure that . . . particular national and regional dynamics are incorporated to ensure relevance and consistency with emerging priorities. This regional approach will also enable the WTO to fully utilize regional experts on various subjects to complement WTO resource persons.[36]

Indeed, the activities offered are designed to reflect existing patterns of collaboration between members, as well as to strengthen these groupings in a two-way flow of information and institution building. The 2010–2011 Plan offers a range of

---

[34] Draper and Sally note that the proliferation of smaller developing country coalitions focused on specific issues has made negotiations more complex. P. Draper and R. Sally, "Developing-Country Coalitions in Multilateral Trade Negotiations, Workshop on Trade Policy Making in Developing Countries," London School of Economics and Political Science Trade Policy Unit (2005) <http://www.ppl.nl/bibliographies/wto/files/3071.pdf>, at 11–12.

[35] R.O. Keohane and J.S. Nye, Jr., "Transgovernmental Relations and International Organizations" 1974 World Politics 27(1) 39, at 50–5. See also A.-M. Slaughter, "Global Government Networks, Global Information Agencies, and Disaggregated Democracy" 2003 *Michigan Journal of International Law* 24(4) 1041, at 1045 (on governmental and intra-governmental transnational networks).

[36] Committee on Trade and Development, *Biennial Technical Assistance and Training Plan 2010–2011*, WT/COMTD/W/170/Rev.1 (21 October 2009), at para 82.

capacity-building strategies specifically tailored to regional needs. In recent years, regional coordinator internships have been offered for the following groups: ACP Group, African Group, CARICOM, Group of Latin American and Caribbean Countries, South Asian Association for Regional Cooperation, WTO LDCs Consultative Group, Informal Group of Developing Countries, Arab Group, and Pacific Islands Forum. Other internships are aimed at LDCs and Small and Vulnerable Economies.

The WTO Secretariat has also undertaken a role in servicing regional groups by "provid[ing] assistance to regional groupings in support of their meetings and organiz[ing] briefings on specific WTO-related topics in light of negotiations."[37] Members are free to request support for groups that they have formed independently. The process is bottom-up rather than top-down. The Secretariat's support was particularly germane to the African Group's increased participation in the Doha Round. The assistance enabled the Group to meet on a regular basis in the run-up to the Round to formulate a coordinated negotiation plan and to continue its activities throughout the Round. In that case, the Secretariat's training and capacity-building activities were instrumental in bridging the gap between a discussion group and the group's participation in negotiations as a coalition. It is unclear in the 2010–2011 Plan whether such activities are ongoing.

Thus, the WTO as an institution (primarily the Secretariat) have taken heed of the existence of discussion and research groups. More importantly, from a legal perspective, the WTO has found it within its mandate to support developing members not only individually but also as groups. It has created tools and devoted resources on an ongoing basis to support and even foster the creation, sustainability, and activism of these groups. Trade Policy Reviews, another activity undertaken by the Secretariat, may also be conducted on a group basis, rather than as individual reviews. For instance, East African Community members (Kenya, Tanzania, and Uganda) requested a joint review (2006), as did the Southern African Customs Union (Botswana, Lesotho, Namibia, South Africa, and Swaziland).[38]

5.2 Formalizing group representation in negotiations and in the decision-making process

By contrast with research and discussion groups, the WTO has afforded virtually no legal recognition to groups formed for the purpose of negotiations. Decision-making also works strictly on a basis of individual participation and formal equality that disenfranchises weaker members. Two sets of issues are considered here: enhancing weak members' representation in WTO bodies, and including group representation in the negotiation process.

---

[37] Committee on Trade and Development, *Technical Assistance and Training Plan 2007*, WT/COMTD/W/151 (17 October 2006), at para 138.

[38] WTO Secretariat, *Trade Policy Review: East African Community*, WT/TPR/S/171 (20 September 2006); WTO Secretariat, *Trade Policy Review: Southern Africa Customs Union*, WT/TPR/S/114 (24 March 2003).

Enhancing weak members' representation in WTO bodies

Defining a set of members as a group at the institutional level is an explicit acknowledgment of these members' shared circumstances and interests. Giving them a platform allows the identification of common negotiation objectives and concerns, and creates incentives for collective action. For instance, while many LDCs likely would not have much or any individual voice, making it difficult to organize and sustain a coalition without any institutional support, the anchor that the WTO agreements gave them as a group (the Subcommittee on LDCs in the Committee on Trade and Development) has raised their profile and influence, as demonstrated by ostensible initiatives in their favor at the Hong Kong Ministerial Meeting in 2005.[39] A more consistent approach and enhanced support could further empower them in negotiations, making up for their structural limitations with respect to institutional capacity. Such institutional support could also be extended to other groups.

LDCs could be specifically represented as a group in virtually all committees and councils, in addition to the existing Sub-Committee of the Committee on Development. Because all aspects of trade regulation in the WTO affect LDCs in a particular way, it would be logical that the group be consistently represented throughout the organization's activities, not just in an isolated committee cut off from sectoral negotiations.[40] The effect would be two-fold. First, the group representation would ensure that the interests of LDCs are better and more systematically represented in the various WTO organs. Second, it would help build capacity for the group's members as they would gain access to a more central and streamlined channel of information (through the group representation) and in turn be able to better formulate their own policy positions.

[39] Hong Kong Ministerial Declaration, at para 8; see also para 47 ("Building upon the commitment in the Doha Ministerial Declaration, developed-country Members, and developing-country Members declaring themselves in a position to do so, agree to implement duty-free and quota-free market access for products originating from LDCs as provided for in Annex F to this document."). Annex F specifies that duty-free, quota-free access will cover "at least 97 per cent of products originating from LDCs, defined at the tariff line level, by 2008 or no later than the start of the implementation period," but this leaves a number of crucial issues unresolved. In particular, there is no actual timetable for implementation, and the tariff line level is ambiguous, which can lead to very different results depending on how many tariff line digits (four, six, or eight) are taken into account. Basing the percentage of products on tariff lines means that an importing country could exclude a single tariff line that constitutes the bulk of imports from a particular LDC and still meet the 97 percent obligation.

[40] In the Doha Round, a number of proposals have been tabled by developing countries, particularly LDCs. These proposals were initially tabled and discussed in a Special Session of the Committee on Trade and Development, not in the sub-committee on LDCs. Many of these proposals were considered again at the Cancun Ministerial Meeting. See, eg, Committee on Trade and Development, *Special Session: Report to the General Council*, TN/CTD/7 (10 February 2003); General Council, *Draft Cancun Ministerial Text*, JOB(03)/150/Rev.2 (13 September 2003). However, a number of these proposals were then dispatched to various committees dealing more specifically with negotiations on the substantive issues at stake. That dissemination made the process much harder for LDCs to monitor and participate in the discussions, since they were not necessarily able to simultaneously follow the activities of all committees and often had no particular representation on the committees.

Other groups of countries suffering from structural insufficiencies due to their domestic political and economic circumstances would benefit from a similar institutional representation to ensure a minimal threshold of participation. Small Island Developing States[41] also are active in the WTO as a coalition to raise awareness on the particular trade issues that they face. Much like LDCs, they have limited institutional capacity and little bargaining power to push forward their demands, keep them on the negotiation agenda, or obtain concessions. Having an institutional umbrella could allow their needs to better be served, subject to the same drawbacks as have been identified for the Subcommittee on LDCs.

Subject-specific committees and councils may also find that official and systematic presence of relevant groups would help elaborate proposals that better take into account the interests of various segments of the membership. For example, the Committee on Agriculture could include a formal permanent representative of the group of Net Food-Importing Countries. Given that many members of that coalition are amongst the poorest in the WTO (and therefore have little capacity to participate next to powerful developing and developed members) but have a vital interest in agriculture negotiations, a permanent representative would ensure that their interests are represented even if all individual members cannot be present at all times. At the same time it would ensure from the outset that agriculture negotiations balance the interests of food exporters and less vocal and poorer food importers.[42] Even though such a process may already exist to some extent in practice, a greater formalization would improve transparency and the participation of members with limited institutional and financial capacity, increasing the WTO's legitimacy and improving the quality of regulatory outcomes.

Both the organization as a whole and individual members would benefit directly from this type of institutionalized group representation. It may be argued that, in practice, informal mechanisms already provide for the presence of LDC members in the various committees and that these members act as channels of information

---

[41] The United Nations maintains a list of Small Island Developing States and has recognized the need for special measures in favor of these countries since 1994, calling particular attention to their vulnerabilities in the context of the Uruguay Round (UN General Assembly Resolution 49/100, A/RES/49/100 (24 February 1995)). The United Nations also has defined a list of Landlocked Developing Countries. For a survey of UN undertakings for LDCs, Small Island Developing States, and Landlocked Developing States, see generally, Office of the High Representative for the Least Developed Countries, *Landlocked Developing Countries, and Small Island Developing States* <http://www.un.org/ohrlls>. A number of countries belonging to these three groups have joined the coalition of Small and Vulnerable Economies at the WTO, even though the issues of each group are quite different.

[42] The EU has an incentive to bring attention to the issue of Net Food Importing Countries to support its own position on the continuing subsidization of agriculture. See, eg, *Report of the Inter-Agency Panel to the General Council on the Marrakesh Ministerial Decision on Measures Concerning the Possible Negative Effects of the Reform Programme on Least-Developed and Net Food-Importing Developing Countries*, WT/GC/62 (28 June 2003). As such, Net Food Importing Countries have found support among much more powerful members of the WTO, but there are important political risks attached to this type of proxy representation by an interested third party. Some rich members also are food importers, such as Japan. However, rich members are not under the same type of economic pressure as poor food importers, as the latter lack a significant source of currency income that would decrease their sensitivity to rising world prices.

for other LDCs. Such informal group representation, however, will not always achieve the results that an institutionalized representation mechanism can provide because informal processes do not afford automatic, systematic, transparent, and coherent representation throughout the WTO's activities.

The existence of external composite criteria for defining membership in groups would likely make the identification of groups more politically acceptable to WTO members. In recent years the self-defining mechanism for consideration as a developing country in the WTO has generated controversy as some members felt that certain countries should not benefit from that status even though they still have a low income. By contrast, the definition of LDCs is perceived as objective and less open to manipulation.

Objective definitions of groups also allows for a fluid membership dependent on members' economic, social, and political evolution. This is important in light of the continued pressure to strengthen graduation policies, a process often open to political interpretation. The recognition of specific subgroups of developing countries based on transparent and uniform criteria would support a shift in graduation policy toward predetermined, objective criteria, in line with the AB's recent insistence on the nondiscriminatory character of the Enabling Clause's provisions. Linking differentiation and graduation to objective and transparent criteria would also improve weak states' bargaining position as they would no longer need to waste political capital on negotiating graduation.

Including group representation in the negotiation process

Chapter 9 considered the WTO's decision-making rules and concluded that despite superficially guaranteeing equal treatment of members, they do not in fact provide many developing countries with effective access to the decision-making process. This is particularly problematic in the rounds of negotiation where rules and disciplines are formulated and eventually put up for approval by the members. This section proposes a mechanism for improved participation by developing members building on their current coalitions practice.

One caveat must first be mentioned. Trade negotiations are a political as well as a law-making exercise. Procedural rules need to maintain a balance between the two: Political plays are a healthy part of the negotiation process, but the legal framework must strive to ensure a fair participation by all segments of the constituency if the WTO is to maintain its legitimacy as a global organization. Formalizing representation and participation of otherwise disenfranchised members through groups should not obliterate the important role of some groups as purely political platforms. In particular, many developing country coalitions focus on certain products (such as fisheries and cotton) or specific sectors. For example, should the Friends of Fish, the Cairns Group, and the G-20, to name a few, have designated seats on the Committee on Agriculture? What of nominally regional groups that really address only one specific sector, such as the South Pacific Forum, which primarily coordinates positions between its members on fisheries and marine products trade? Membership in issue-based coalitions generally represents a broad spectrum of country sizes, economic and political power, weight in world trade, etc. Institutionalization of these types of groups would be extremely difficult, particularly given the concurrent membership of many countries in several groups. Fluid membership and the lack of objective criteria for determining membership is another difficulty. For such groups, political dynamics is better suited than legal enabling.

Although it may be neither politically desirable nor feasible to formalize the participation of issue-based coalitions in the negotiation process, some aspects of the negotiations may lend themselves to the institutionalization of some groups of developing countries. The objective would be to provide a stronger procedural framework, rather than to constrain the substance of the negotiations directly.

Since a major bottleneck is members' insufficient capacity to participate directly and even to remain apprised of ongoing negotiations, one avenue for improvement would be to develop quasi proxy mechanisms whereby individual countries could participate as part of a group in addition to their own individual participation. This obviously is an imperfect, second-best approximation, but it could at least ensure that members with little capacity gain a better knowledge and understanding of negotiations. Groups could be defined, and proposed packages would need to be approved by the groups before being submitted to the full membership for approval. Such a procedure would allow small or weak countries to negotiate within their group, where they would be relatively more powerful.

Some members already participate in negotiations through submissions in groups. Representatives from individual members regularly speak on behalf of groups such as the Paradisus Group, the African Group, and the ASEAN in working groups, committees, and even at the General Council. Members, including developing countries, recognize that consultations among individual members or among groups of members are part of the negotiation process and should not be eliminated. At the same time, they insist that decision-making belongs to the membership as a whole through the consensus procedure, and that the latter must take its full effect, instead of becoming a last-stop rubber-stamp for decisions already made by a limited number of members. The question is how to bridge the gap between discussions in open-ended, fluid, issue-based working groups that are indeed valuable to the process, and the finalization of a legitimate package of proposals for approval by the full membership. In constitutional terms, could participation by members with limited resources be enhanced by combining individual representation (ie, direct representation) at the working group level with some form of legitimate formal group representation (ie, indirect representation) at the stage of putting together a package?

One way to achieve this would be to create an advisory body that adequately represents the membership, but is small enough to function efficiently as an active synthesizer of proposals emerging from the working groups and could suggest ways to achieve a consensus in a similar way to the role of Chairpersons at the committee levels. Its position would give it a comprehensive view of all aspects of negotiations, which in turn would allow it to propose some trade-offs to lift potential deadlocks. It would act as a liaison between working groups and members acting as a decision-making body (General Council). In line with the position of many developing countries that ultimate decision-making should remain with the full membership, it would be advisory because this body would not have any decision-making power. The composition of such a body could be geographically based, with a periodic rotation of elected members, as are many other bodies designed to equitably represent members of large international organizations. This body would have a duty to disseminate its work-product uniformly and systematically to all members, which would increase transparency and perhaps even contribute to capacity building for some members.

While such a structure would not eliminate power plays by the WTO's most influential members, it would alleviate most of the problems related to the Green Room. Its functioning would be more transparent, it would constitute a more legitimate representation of the membership, and it would have a more specific mandate. At the same time, it would preserve a large amount of flexibility, which is a necessary ingredient to successful negotiations, and it would allow members with limited institutional resources to gain a better perspective on the negotiations as a whole.

The crucial question then would be how to define the groups. While imperfect, geographical bloc representation has proved successful in other organizations. For instance, the UN uses geographical allocation to ensure an equitable representation of member states on the bench at the ICJ,[43] the International Law Commission, the Economic and Social Council, and even, to some extent, amongst the non-permanent members of the Security Council. Equitable geographical distribution is also a guiding principle for representation in many international organizations and treaties.[44]

Modified continental mapping could be a starting point. Africa forms the basis for several existing coalitions. Latin American countries also seem to find common positions on a regular basis. Asia presents a more difficult case, with members as diverse as India and Japan. The same issue would arise for North America, where Mexico would find itself alongside the United States and Canada. Although NAFTA has contributed to bringing the trade policies of these countries closer, important divergences remain. The formation of two Asian groups, one comprising

---

[43] The International Court of Justice, *The International Court of Justice: Handbook* (5th edn, The Hague: International Court of Justice, 2004), at 24 (for the informal geographic breakdown of judges at the International Court of Justice); see also UN General Assembly Resolution 60/251, A/RES/60/251 (3 April 2006), at para 7 (for the formal allocation of seats on the Human Rights Council of the United Nations); see also the World Health Organization geographic representation on the Executive Board.

[44] The Convention on the Elimination of All Forms of Discrimination against Women refers to equitable geographical distribution (Art 17); "equitable geographical distribution" is also a criterion for elections to the Security Council under Art 23(1) of the UN Charter. See also H. Kelsen, "Organization and Procedure of the Security Council of the United Nations" 1946 *Harvard Law Review* 59(7) 1087, at 1088–9. R. Thakur (ed), *What is Equitable Geographic Representation in the Twenty-first Century?* (Tokyo: United Nations University, 1999), at 55; World Health Organization, *Equitable Geographical Distribution of the Membership of the Executive Board*, SEA/RC61/20 (29 August 2008); F. Bouayad-Agha and H.L. Hernández, *Comparison of Methods of Calculating Equitable Geographical Distribution Within the United Nations Common System*, JIU/REP/96/7 (21 August 1997).

China and Far Eastern Asian countries, and the other including South and Central Asia, would allow for greater coherence and would also limit the size of the group by disaggregating the Asian giants India and China. If economic disparities within blocs are perceived to be an obstacle to reaching a consensus within the groups, or if groups comprising both developed and developing countries are not politically acceptable, separate groups could be formed for industrialized, developed members on the one hand and LDCs on the other hand. Forming a separate group of industrialized members worldwide (using, for example, a high threshold of GDP per capita as a benchmark) would eliminate some of these disparities. At the other end of the economic spectrum, LDCs are specifically identified as a group in many provisions of WTO agreements, and they also form an active coalition; as such, they could form another group.

A problem arises for countries that would qualify for several groups (African LDCs, for example, or countries at the border of two regions). If membership is based on self-designation, members could choose to participate in either group. Modified geographically based groups could include the following blocs: a bloc including South and Central America, an African bloc, two Asian groups (one including China and Eastern Asian countries and the other one comprising South Asian and Central Asian countries), a Middle Eastern bloc, a European bloc (EU and possibly Southern European countries and other Western European countries with close ties to the EU); a Central European bloc; a Pacific group; and possibly a bloc of industrialized members and an LDC bloc.

Membership in specific blocs would have some measure of fluidity, as members crossing the GDP per capita threshold set for members of the industrialized group would join that group, and, similarly, members no longer designated as LDCs by the UN would join the relevant geographical group. If each group carries equal weight in the formal decision-making, less powerful members would gain a comparatively greater weight, but the quality of the consensus may be improved and the decision perceived as more legitimate and equitable.

Such a mechanism would give each group a quasi-veto power (but the advisory body would not make binding decisions), which may cause opposition from the traditionally more influential members. However, because the procedure is aimed at cementing a stronger and more legitimate consensus, it ultimately seeks to strengthen the organization. In the current context of stalled negotiations, a common realization that interests of all segments of the membership must be taken into account before any global deal can be reached may provide a helpful way forward.

6. Conclusion

Factual evidence, the literature, and interviews with trade negotiators from developing countries and other WTO participants all converge to suggest that the shortcomings of the WTO, when it comes to making trade liberalization workable for its developing members, is not just an economic or a political problem, but also one stemming from the legal framework itself.

Taking stock of the research and analysis developed throughout this book, this chapter has proposed several avenues for managing a development dimension at the WTO. The proposals call for a fundamental reexamination of the normative place of development within the organization. They account for the fact that the WTO's regulatory output and its institutional organization have a synergetic relationship. If development is to be considered on an idiosyncratic basis, the dispute settlement system should assume a pivotal role in ensuring consistency, transparency, and non-discrimination in the application of waivers and exceptions. That is only possible if the dispute settlement system is empowered legally, politically, and operationally to undertake that role. If, by contrast, development becomes a normative benchmark informing trade liberalization then developing members must, individually and collectively, be empowered at the institutional level in a way that formal legal equality cannot deliver. Building on the existing coalition practice may provide a starting point.

A normative embedding of development at the WTO also requires the reconsideration of the modalities for negotiations, and in particular the role of the single undertaking. This chapter proposed a number of novel approaches in that respect, ranging from valuing members' concessions relative to their own economies, rather than in absolute terms, to variances on the single undertaking to better tailor the agenda for trade liberalization and its pace to WTO members. While the abandonment of the single undertaking altogether may radically reconfigure trade relations, more limited implementation of the single undertaking that would allow some opting out by some qualified members, and some partial de-linking of certain trade topics may provide a more optimal balance.

Conclusion

More than ten years into the Doha "Development" Round, WTO members are all but resigned to the fact that the broad overhaul of the WTO system envisioned in the Doha Work Programme will likely not come to fruition. As a result of the combined pressure of stalled negotiations and a global financial and economic crisis that has spurred protectionist responses, some commentators even go so far as to proclaim the decline of the WTO as a relevant regulatory forum.

Yet, WTO trade disciplines remain in force; the dispute settlement system is still active and supported by a unique, if imperfect, enforcement mechanism. Moreover, the success of large emerging developing economies, such as Brazil, in leveraging the system against more economically powerful countries suggests that the WTO is still not to be dismissed as a forum or as a source of law. The increased frequency of references to the WTO as a rule-making body in corporate annual reports also signals that the private sector is aware of the relevance of multilateral trade disciplines. The last major economic player to join, Russia, gained membership in August 2013, after a protracted accession bid. A number of developing countries also continue to work on their accession, including several LDCs.

The Doha Round also reveals major transformations in the place and role played by many developing countries in the multilateral trading system, both politically and economically. China's economic power and the reach of its interests are causing major realignments throughout the Asian region and as far as Africa, which have not yet been fully evaluated. Evolving trade flows between large developing countries are reflected in changing patterns in trade law enforcement, to wit the increased use of trade remedies by these members. The WTO is a major component of these transformations.

In the face of this dynamic environment, the development debate seems largely frozen in time. Many of the demands of large segments of the WTO's developing membership are eerily similar to what they were three or four decades ago if not more: a realignment of agricultural support policies in developed countries, better access for "tropical products" from developing countries, a roll back on tariff escalation clauses, and other similar schemes that have stifled developing country exports of manufactures. New issues dating to the Uruguay Round also remain unresolved and continue to be raised: capacity building, technical assistance, aid for trade, a revision of the dispute settlement process, and particularly the available enforcement remedies, which are not effective for small developing countries. Last, the call for policy space often translates into proposals for increased waivers to implement industrial development tools very much reminiscent of the 1960s and 1970s (infant industry protection in particular).

The continuity of these concerns, in the face of the many changes in the economics of international trade, raises several fundamental questions. Are the issues really still the same? Have the stakeholders failed to update their positions in light of the more recent developments? Or is the WTO as an institution impeding a forward-looking debate? The answer is likely a mix of all three aspects.

First, older concerns have still not been addressed and continue to be relevant to many developing countries, as shown in the first three chapters of this book. Critical studies literature has demonstrated the continued impact of colonialism and neocolonial dynamics affecting a number of developing countries. Economists highlight continued difficulties for market access for semi-processed goods from developing countries due to tariff escalation clauses. Agricultural subsidies in rich, industrialized countries show no sign of receding, their effect on the competitiveness of developing country producers unabated.

Second, as discussed in Chapter 10, the proposals submitted in the first four years of the Doha Round used similar legal instruments and drafting techniques to existing SDT provisions that have already shown their limits during the sixty years of practice of the GATT and WTO. Indeed, members' practice and the case law, as discussed in Chapters 6 and 7, have amply demonstrated the shortcomings of current approaches: Their usage is very low, members themselves are hesitant to claim the provisions in adjudication, and panels and the Appellate Body have often refused to substantiate provisions that did not include clear criteria for implementation. Altogether, this suggests that the current strategy for improving the trade and development relationship is perhaps more reactionary than forward-looking.

Third, regarding institutional aspects, Chapter 5 showed that developing members have achieved a remarkable improvement in their participation in negotiations since the Uruguay Round. While they have acquired a defensive power, they have yet to leverage this blocking power into the ability to deliver positive outcomes in support of their agendas. Chapter 9 argued that the WTO's institutional framework was not neutral in that respect, and that a number of features, including decision-making processes, modalities for negotiations (including the single undertaking), emerging "secondary legislation" activity within WTO bodies, and the inability to institutionalize group participation are hurdles to many developing members' ability to represent their interests. Other dynamics discussed in Chapter 11 also raise strategic challenges to building a development dimension at the core of the WTO regime.

The ultimate balance of the trade and development relationship at the WTO is subject to political dynamics, yet these dynamics are also influenced by the WTO legal framework. As such, even the most progressive political consensus amongst members would likely fail to achieve a substantial transformation of the WTO regime because of the institutional hurdles that have been discussed in this book. Moving the trade and development relationship forward, then, is more likely to be achieved by an iterative process, rather than by a single complex round. Tiered negotiations that tackle institutional and participation issues as a priority may be a necessary starting point.

This book, then, seeks to open some paths for reconsidering the trade and development relationship at the WTO, taking into account both the heritage of the trade regime and present dynamics. To assist in mapping how the relationship may be evaluated, it posits two paradigms. One is based on an *ad hoc*, idiosyncratic relationship between trade and development, where tensions between the two are managed on a case-by-case basis, when required, without any overarching normative principle. The other is grounded in a co-equal consideration of trade liberalization and development objectives as normative co-constituents that would underpin both the law and the institutions of the WTO. Neither of these theoretical constructs is meant, in themselves, as models for reforming the trade regime. Rather, they are presented solely as conceptual benchmarks that help situate legal instruments, assess their purpose, what they are meant to deliver, and determine whether they can produce the intended result. As a prescriptive matter, the two paradigms help to frame a menu of options that members could draw from to develop legal tools better tailored to their stated needs and objectives.

The normative co-constituent paradigm is helpful to reconsider institutional processes, such as decision-making, negotiation design, and dispute settlement. It underpins reforms discussed in Chapter 12 to mitigate the capacity constraints of many members and to increase their participation and representation. In particular, a move beyond fictional juridical equality in favor of formalizing indirect representation of members through proxies and other forms of group representation, with adequate accountability safeguards, would be key. It also translates into a move away from an overly restrictive textual reading of the WTO agreements and outdated interpretation of language in the agreements. In practice, much of these transformations could be achieved without cumbersome amendments. For example, shifts in members' and the organizations' practices, interpretative decisions by the General Council, a reexamination of the valuation of concessions in negotiations are all tools that can help build development at the core of the WTO system.

The idiosyncratic paradigm is useful to inform the drafting of development-oriented provisions in cases where there is value to tailoring commitments to members' individual priorities and resources. It promotes instruments that are flexible and potentially well adaptive. In practice, instruments such as legal standards, criteria, trigger mechanisms, and benchmarks in SDT provisions can assist in differentiating commitments while increasing transparency and enforcement through adjudication.

In an era of difficult political dynamics, the *ad hoc* model may also help to look for incremental, achievable aims to better account for developmental discrepancies, starting with discreet, technical regulatory issues. Yet, its limits are both substantive and conceptual. Substantively, the *ad hoc* paradigm is unlikely to generate the more fundamental realignments of the trade liberalization regime that could help overcome the current deadlocks and ensure the continued relevance of the WTO. It can only help modulate trade commitments at the margins; it can only buy temporary peace with the promise of derogations and exceptions. Conceptually, it lacks an overall direction, precisely because it is devoid of a strong normative embedding. How can it assist in a reconsideration of the trade and development relationship if it does not require members to come together with a mandate in that respect? Put simply, the idiosyncratic model is an agreement to disagree.

By contrast, the normative co-constitutive model is grounded in an affirmative understanding of the balancing between trade liberalization objectives and development priorities. In itself, it does not seek to prescribe what that balance should be: Indeed, both development theory and economics, and the examination of regional trade agreements show that there are many possibilities for meshing the two. Ultimately, it is for WTO members to define the normative ethos for this relationship. The normative constituent model then advocates the creation of an institutional framework that will in turn foster regulatory tools in line with the overall mandate. It allows the measurement of progress and the consideration of the impact of particular trade measures for a trade and development objective because it presupposes a normative framework for assessing the WTO's activities. While the normative co-constituent paradigm has a transformative ambition, it can be realized progressively, through a combination of pragmatic and formal changes in the law and practice of the WTO, as shown by many of the proposals offered in this book. While it is a long-term enterprise, it may help members to reshape their approach to trade negotiation and regulation now.

Bibliography

UNITED NATIONS AND UN AGENCIES DOCUMENTS

Committee on Economic, Social and Cultural Rights, General Comment 3, *The Nature of States Parties' Obligations*, UN Doc E/1991/23 (5th Sess 1991).

Commission on Human Rights, "Report of the UN Secretary-General on the International Dimensions of the Right to Development as a Human Right," Res 4 (XXXIII), UN Doc E/CN.4/1334 (1979).

Comparison of Methods of Calculating Equitable Geographical Distribution within the United Nations Common System (UNESCO), JIU/REP/96/7 (21 August 1997).

International Court of Justice, *The International Court of Justice: Handbook* (5th edn, The Hague: International Court of Justice, 2004).

Office of the High Representative for the Least Developed Countries, *Landlocked Developing Countries, and Small Island Developing States* <http://www.un.org/ohrlls>.

United Nations Conference on Environment and Development, *Rio Declaration on Environment and Development*, A/CONF.I51/Rev. 1 (14 June 1992).

United Nations Conference on Trade and Development, *Developing Countries in International Trade 2007: Trade and Development Index,* UNCTAD/DITC/TAB/2007/2 (10 January 2007).

United Nations Conference on Trade and Development, *Generalized System of Preferences Handbook on the Scheme of the European Community 2008,* UNCTAD/ITCD/TSB/Misc.25/Rev.3 (3 January 2009).

United Nations Conference on Trade and Development, *Global System of Trade Preferences among Developing Countries* (1985) <http://www.unctadxi.org/templates/News____1723.aspx>.

United Nations Conference on Trade and Development, *Handbook on the Scheme of Australia 2000*, UNCTAD/ITCD/TSB/Misc.56 (6 January 2000).

United Nations Conference on Trade and Development, *Handbook on the Scheme of Canada 2002*, UNCTAD/ITCD/TSB/Misc.66 (12 January 2002).

United Nations Conference on Trade and Development, *Handbook on the Scheme of Japan 2006,* UNCTAD/ITCD/TSB/Misc.42/Rev.3 (8 January 2006).

United Nations Conference on Trade and Development, *Handbook on the Scheme of New Zealand 1999*, UNCTAD/ITCD/TSB/Misc.48 (4 January 1999).

United Nations Conference on Trade and Development, *Handbook on the Scheme of the United States of America 2003*, UNCTAD/ITCD/TSB/Misc.58/Rev.1 (8 October 2003).

United Nations Conference on Trade and DevelopmentSecretariat, *Quantifying the Benefits Obtained by Developing Countries From The Generalized System of Preferences*, UNCTAD/ITCD/TSB/Misc.52 (7 October 1999).

United Nations Conference on Trade and Development, *Trade Preferences for LDCs: An Early Assessment of Benefits and Possible Improvements*, UNCTAD/ITCD/TSB/2003/8 (30 January 2004).

United Nations Conference on Trade and Development, *WTO Accessions and Development Policies* (Geneva: UNCTAD, 2001).

United Nations Conference on Trade and Employment, *Final Acts and Related Documents,* UN Doc E/Conf. 2/78 (21 November 1947).

United Nations Department of Economic Affairs, *National and International Measures for Full Employment* (New York, 1950).

United Nations Development Programme, 2005 Human Development Report.

United Nations Development Programme, 2004 Human Development Report.

United Nations Development Programme, 2009 Human Development Report <http://hdr.undp.org/en/media/HDR_2009_EN_Complete.pdf>.

United Nations Economic and Social Commission for Asia and the Pacific, *Towards Coherent Policy Frameworks: Understanding Trade and Investment Linkages—A Study by the Asia-Pacific Research and Training Network on Trade* (New York: United Nations, 2007).

United Nations General Assembly Resolution 626(VII), A/RES/626(VII) (21 December 1952).

United Nations General Assembly Resolution 1707(XVI), A/RES/1707(XVI) (19 December 1961).

United Nations General Assembly Resolution 1710(XVI), A/RES/1710(XVI) (19 December 1961).

United Nations General Assembly Resolution 1711(XVI), A/RES/1711(XVI) (19 December 1961).

United Nations General Assembly Resolution 1712(XVI), A/RES/1712(XVI) (19 December 1961).

United Nations General Assembly Resolution 1713(XVI), A/RES/1713(XVI) (19 December 1961).

United Nations General Assembly Resolution 1715(XVI), A/RES/1715(XVI) (19 December 1961).

United Nations General Assembly Resolution 1718(XVI), A/RES/1718(XVI) (19 December 1961).

United Nations General Assembly Resolution 1720(XVI), A/RES/1720(XVI) (19 December 1961).

United Nations General Assembly Resolution 1785(XVII), A/RES/1785(XVII) (8 December 1962).

United Nations General Assembly Resolution 2571(XXIV), A/RES/2571(XXIV) (13 December 1969).

United Nations General Assembly Resolution 2626(XXV), A/RES/2626(XXV) (24 October 1970).

United Nations General Assembly Resolution 2692(XXV), A/RES/2692(XXV) (11 December 1970).

United Nations General Assembly Resolution 3201(S-VI), A/RES/3201(S-VI) (1 May 1974).

United Nations General Assembly Resolution 3202(S-VI), A/RES/3202(S-VI) (1 May 1974).

United Nations General Assembly Resolution 3281(XXIX), A/RES/3281(XXIV) (12 December 1974).

United Nations General Assembly Resolution 34/46, A/RES/34/46 (23 November 1979).

United Nations General Assembly Resolution 35/174, A/RES/35/174 (15 December 1980).

United Nations General Assembly Resolution 36/133, A/RES/36/133 (14 December 1981).

United Nations General Assembly Resolution 37/199, A/RES/37/199 (18 December 1982).

United Nations General Assembly Resolution 37/200, A/RES/37/200 (18 December 1982).

United Nations General Assembly Resolution 41/128, A/RES/41/128 (4 December 1986).

United Nations General Assembly Resolution 49/100, A/RES/49/100 (24 February 1995).

United Nations General Assembly Resolution 60/251, A/RES/60/251 (3 April 2006).

United Nations Millennium Project, *Investing in Development: A Practical Plan to Achieve the Millennium Development Goals* (New York: Earthscan, 2005).

IMF and World Bank, *Market Access for Developing Countries' Exports* (27 April 2001) <http://www.imf.org/external/np/madc/eng/042701.pdf>, at 18.

World Bank, *World Development Indicators* (Washington, 2001).

World Bank, *World Bank Support for Developing Countries on International Trade Issues*, DC/99-19 (14 September 1999).

World Health Organization, *Equitable Geographical Distribution of the Membership of the Executive Board*, SEA/RC61/20 (29 August 2008).

GATT DOCUMENTS

Committee on Tariff Concessions, *Minutes of Meeting held on 19 July 1985*, TAR/M/16 (4 October 1985).

Committee on Trade and Development, Note by the Secretariat, *Objectives of the Kennedy Round Negotiations for Less-Developed Countries*, COM.TD/W/69, BISD 14S/19 (24 October 1967).

Decision on Anti-circumvention, LT/UR/D-3/1 (15 April 1994).

Decision on Measures in Favour of Least-developed Countries, LT/UR/D-1/3 (15 April 1994).

Decision on Review of Article 17.6 of the Agreement on Implementation of Article VI of the General Agreement on Tariffs and Trade 1994, LT/UR/D-3/2 (15 April 1994).

Declaration of Ministers Approved at Tokyo on 14 September 1973, MIN(73), BISD 20S/19 (14 September 1973).

Ministerial Declaration Adopted on 29 November 1982, L/5424, BISD 29S/9 (29 November 1982).

Ministerial Declaration on the Uruguay Round, GATT Doc MIN.DEC, BISD 33S/19 (20 September 1986).

Programme for the Expansion of International Trade—Trade in Tropical Products, GATT Doc MIN (63)7 (21 May 1963).

GATT Contracting Parties, *Decision on Safeguard for Development*, L/4897 (28 November 1979).

GATT Contracting Parties, *Waiver Decision on the Generalized System of Preferences*, L/3545 (25 June 1971), BISD 18S/24.

GATT Contracting Parties, *Decision on Differential and More Favourable Treatment, Reciprocity and Fuller Participation of Developing Countries*, GATT Doc L/4903 (28 November 1979).

GATT Secretariat, *GATT Activities 1992—An Annual Review of the World of the GATT* (Geneva: June 1993).

GATT Working Party Report, *Report of the Working Party on the Australian Request to Grant Tariff Preferences to Less-Developed Countries*, GATT Doc L/2527 (23 December 1965).

Interpretative Note ad Article XXVIII (30 October 1947).

Protocol amending the General Agreement on Tariffs and Trade to introduce a Part IV on Trade and Development and to amend Annex I (Geneva, 8 February 1965; 572 UNTS 320).

Understanding on the Interpretation of Article XXVIII GATT, LT/UR/A-1A/1/GATT/ U/6 (14 April 1994).

WTO DOCUMENTS

Accession of Ecuador, WT/ACC/ECU/5 (16 August 1995).

Committee on Agriculture, Special Session, *Revised Draft Modalities for Agriculture*, TN/ AG/W/4/Rev.1 (8 February 2008); TN/AG/W/4/Rev.2 (19 May 2008); TN/AG/W/4/ Rev.3 (10 July 2008); TN/AG/W/4/Rev.4 (6 December 2008).

Committee on Budget, Finance and Administration, *Report on Diversity in the WTO Secretariat*, WT/BFA/W/195 (1 March 2010).

Committee on Market Access, *Minutes of the Meeting of 23 March 2000*, G/MA/M/23 (12 May 2000).

Committee on Trade and Development, *Biennial Technical Assistance and Training Plan 2010–2011*, WT/COMTD/W/170/Rev.1 (21 October 2009).

Committee on Trade and Development, *Communication from India*, TN/CTD/W/6 (17 June 2002).

Committee on Trade and Development, *Communications from Egypt*, WT/GC/W/109 (5 November 1998).

Committee on Trade and Development, *Implementation of Special and Differential Treatment Provisions in WTO Agreements and Decisions*, WT/COMTD/W/77 (25 October 2000).

Committee on Trade and Development, *Participation of Developing Economies in the Global Trading System*, WT/COMTD/W/172/Rev.1 (21 January 2010).

Committee on Trade and Development, *Special Session: Report to the General Council*, TN/ CTD/7 (10 February 2003).

Committee on Trade and Development, *Technical Assistance and Training Plan 2006*, WT/ COMTD/W/142 (16 September 2005).

Committee on Trade and Development, *Technical Assistance and Training Plan 2007*, WT/ COMTD/W/151 (17 October 2006).

Communication from the Chairman of the Committee on Agriculture, Special Session (25 May 2007) <http://www.wto.org/english/tratop_e/agric_e/agchairtxt_25may07_e.pdf>.

Council for Trade in Goods, *Waiver Concerning Kimberley Process Certification Scheme for Rough Diamonds: Communication*, G/C/W/432/Rev.1 (24 February 2003).

Council for TRIPS, *Notification Under Paragraph 2(a) of the Decision of 30 August 2003 on the Implementation of Paragraph 6 of the Doha Declaration on the TRIPS Agreement and Public Health*, IP/N/9/RWA/1 (19 July 2007).

Council for TRIPS, *Notification Under Paragraph 2(c) of the Decision of 30 August 2003 on the Implementation of Paragraph 6 of the Doha Declaration on the TRIPS Agreement and Public Health*, IP/N/10/CAN/1 (8 October 2007).

Decision Adopted by the General Council on 1 August 2004, WT/L/579 (2 August 2004).

Decision of 16 August 1995—Accession of Ecuador, WT/ACC/ECU/5 (22 August 1995).

Decision on Implementation-related Issues and Concerns, WT/MIN(01)/17 (14 November 2001).

Dispute Settlement Body, *Minutes of the Meeting held on 20 May 2008*, WT/DSB/M/250 (1 July 2008).

Draft General Council Decision of July 2004, JOB(04)/96 (16 July 2004).

Formula approaches to tariff negotiations, TN/MA/S/3/Rev.2. (11 April 2003).

General Council, *Article 27.4 of the Agreement on Subsidies and Countervailing Measures—Decision of 27 July 2007*, WT/L/691 (31 July 2007).

General Council, *Decision on Amendment of the TRIPS Agreement*, WT/L/641 (8 December 2005).

General Council, *Decision on Implementation of Paragraph 6 of the Doha Declaration on the TRIPS Agreement and Public Health*, WT/L/540 and Corr.1 (1 September 2003).

General Council, *Decision on Least-Developed Country Members—Obligations Under Article 70.9 of the TRIPS Agreement with Respect to Pharmaceutical Products*, WT/L/478 (8 July 2002).

General Council, *Draft Cancun Ministerial Text*, JOB(03)/150/Rev.2 (13 September 2003).

General Council, *General Council Chairman's Proposal for an Approach for Special and Differential Treatment*, JOB(03)/68 (7 April 2003).

General Council, *Minutes of the Meeting Held in the Centre William Rappard on 17 and 19 July 2000*, WT/GC/M/57 (14 September 2000).

General Council, *Proposed Agenda*, WT/GC/W/498 (13 May 2003).

Fifth Protocol on the General Agreement on Trade in Services, S/L/45 (3 December 1997).

Fourth Protocol on the General Agreement on Trade in Services, S/L/20 (30 April 1996).

Kenya, *Proposal for an Agreement on Trade and Economic Development* (non-public WTO document).

Ministerial Conference, *Declaration on the TRIPS Agreement and Public Health*, WT/MIN(01)/DEC/2 (20 November 2001).

Ministerial Declaration Adopted on 14 November 2001 (Doha Ministerial Declaration), WT/MIN(01)/DEC/1 (14 November 2001).

Ministerial Declaration Adopted on 18 December 2005 (Hong Kong Ministerial Declaration), WT/MIN(05)/DEC (22 December 2005).

Ministerial Declaration on Trade in Information Technology Products, WT/MIN(96)/16 (13 December 1996).

Negotiating Group on Market Access, *Draft Modalities for Non-Agricultural Market Access*, TN/MA/W/103 (8 February 2008); TN/MA/W/103/Rev.1 (19 May 2008); TN/MA/W/103/Rev.2 (10 July 2008); TN/MA/W/103/Rev.3 (6 December 2008).

Negotiating Group on Rules, *New Draft Consolidated Chair Texts of the AD and SCM Agreements*, TN/RL/W/236, (19 December 2008).

Negotiations on the Dispute Settlement Understanding: Proposal by the African Group, TN/DS/W/15 (25 September 2002).

Negotiations on the Dispute Settlement Understanding: Proposal by the LDC Group, TN/DS/W/17 (9 October 2002).

Negotiations on Improvements and Clarifications of the Dispute Settlement Understanding: Proposal by Mexico, TN/DS/W/23 (4 November 2002).

Notification under paragraph 2(a) of the Decision of 30 August 2003 on the Implementation of Paragraph 6 of the Doha Declaration on the TRIPS Agreement and Public Health—Rwanda, IP/N/9/RWA/1 (19 July 2007).

Notification under Paragraph 2(c) of the Decision of 30 August 2003 on the Implementation of Paragraph 6 of the Doha Declaration on the TRIPS Agreement and Public Health—Canada, IP/N/10/CAN/1 (8 October 2007).

Papua New Guinea—Statement by Minister for Foreign Affairs and Trade, WT/MIN(96)/ST/112/Rev.1 (13 December 1996).

Preferential Tariff Treatment for Least-Developed Countries, Decision on Waiver, WT/L/304 (17 June 1999).

Proposal by Cuba, the Dominican Republic, Honduras, India, Indonesia, Kenya, Pakistan, Sri Lanka, Tanzania and Zimbabwe, TN/CTD/W/1 (14 May 2002).

Proposal by Mexico, Negotiations on Improvements and Clarifications of the Dispute Settlement Understanding, TN/DS/W/23 (4 November 2002).

Proposal for a Framework Agreement on Special and Differential Treatment: Communication from Cuba, Dominican Republic, Honduras, India, Indonesia, Kenya, Malaysia, Pakistan, Sri Lanka, Tanzania, Uganda and Zimbabwe, WT/GC/W/442 (19 September 2001).

Report (1995) of the Committee on Balance-of-Payments Restrictions, WT/BOP/R/10 (4 December 1995).

Report (2007) of the Committee on Balance-of-Payments Restrictions, WT/BOP/R/88 (16 November 2007).

Rules of Procedures for Meetings of the Ministerial Conference and the General Council, Rules of Procedure for Sessions of the Ministerial Conference, WT/L/161 (25 July 1996).

Report of the Inter-Agency Panel to the General Council on the Marrakesh Ministerial Decision on Measures Concerning the Possible Negative Effects of the Reform Programme on Least-Developed and Net Food-Importing Developing Countries, WT/GC/62 (28 June 2003).

Report to the Trade Negotiations Committee, by the Chairman of the Special session of the Committee on Agriculture, Ambassador Crawford Falconer, JOB(08)/95 (11 August 2008).

Saint Lucia—Special and Differential Treatment Provisions, TN/CTD/W/8 (24 June 2002).

Secretariat, *Rules of Procedure for Meetings of WTO Bodies* (Geneva: WTO, 1997).

Second Protocol on the General Agreement on Trade in Services, S/L/11 (24 July 1995).

Special and Differential Treatment Provisions: Communication from Thailand, TN/CTD/W/7 (20 June 2002).

Special and Differential Treatment Provisions: Joint Communication from the African Group in the WTO, Revision, TN/CTD/W/3/Rev.2 (24 June 2002).

Special and Differential Treatment Provisions: Joint Communication from Cuba, Dominican Republic, Egypt, Honduras, India, Indonesia, Kenya, Mauritius, Pakistan, Sri Lanka, Tanzania and Zimbabwe, TN/CTD/W/2 (14 May 2002).

Special and Differential Treatment Provisions: Joint Declaration by the Least Developed Countries, TN/CTD/W/4 (24 May 2002); *Special and Differential Treatment Provisions: Joint Declaration by the Least Developed Countries, Addendum*, TN/CTD/W/4/Add.1 (1 July 2002).

Statement by H.E. Mr. Kamal Nath, Minister of Commerce and Industry, WT/MIN(05)/ST/17 (14 December 2005).

Statement by the Chairman, Decision-Making Procedures under Articles IX and XII of the WTO Agreement—As Agreed by the General Council, WT/L/93 (15 November 1995).

Sub-Committee on Cotton, *Sectoral Initiative in Favour of Cotton—Proposed Modalities for Cotton*, TN/AG/SCC/GEN/4 (1 March 2006).

Subsidies and Countervailing Measures Committee 2007 Report, G/L/840 (12 November 2007).

Third Protocol on the General Agreement on Trade in Services, S/L/12 (24 July 1995).

Trade Policy Review Body, *Trade Policy Review: East African Community*, WT/TPR/S/171 (20 September 2006).

Trade Policy Review Body, *Trade Policy Review: Israel*, WT/TPR/S/58 (13 August 1999).

Trade Policy Review Body, *Trade Policy Review: Southern Africa Customs Union*, WT/TPR/S/114 (24 March 2003).

OTHER INTERGOVERNMENTAL DECLARATIONS AND DOMESTIC LAW

19 USC § 2411.

19 USC § 2462–7.

Association of Southeast Asian Nations (ASEAN), Terms of Reference and Guidelines for the Organization of ASEAN Committees in Third Countries (Adopted by the 2nd Meeting of the 13th ASEAN Standing Committee) (Kuala Lumpur, 17 October 1979) <http://www.asean.org/14814.htm>.

Charter of Algiers (Algiers, 10–25 October 1967).

Islamic Conference of Foreign Ministers, *Cairo Declaration on Human Rights in Islam*.

Rio Declaration on Environment and Development, 31 ILM 874, 13 June 1992.

Section 301 of the US Trade Act of 1974, 19 USC § 2411.

SCHOLARLY WORKS

Task Force on Amiable Composition and ex æquo et bono, Interim Report, ICC Doc 420/555 (2008).

"Towards a Development-Supportive Dispute Settlement System in the WTO," ITCSD Resource Paper No 5 (March 2003) <http://ictsd.org/downloads/2008/06/dsu_2003.pdf>.

Aaronson, S., *Trade and the American Dream: A Social History of Postwar Trade Policy* (Lexington: University Press of Kentucky, 1996).

Abbott, F.M., "The WTO Medicines Decision: World Pharmaceutical Trade and the Protection of Public Health" 2005 *American Journal of International Law* 99(2) 317.

Ackerman, F., "The Shrinking Gains from Trade: A Critical Assessment of Doha Round Projections," Global Development and Environment Institute Working Paper No 05-01 (2005).

Alavi, A., "On the (Non-)Effectiveness of the World Trade Organization Special and Differential Treatments in the Dispute Settlement Process" 2007 *Journal of World Trade* 41(2) 319.

Alavi, R., *Industrialization in Malaysia: Import Substitution and Infant Industry Performance* (London: Routledge, 1993).

Alston, P. and Quinn, G., "The Nature and Scope of States Parties' Obligations Under the International Covenant on Economic, Social and Cultural Rights" 1987 *Human Rights Quarterly* 9(2) 156.

Alston P. and Robinson, M., (eds) *Human Rights and Development Towards Mutual Reinforcement* (Oxford: Oxford University Press, 2005).

Amorim, C.L.N., "The WTO from the Perspective of a Developing Country" 2000 *Fordham International Law Journal* 24(1–2) 95.

Andersen, S.D. and Taylor, M.A., "Brazil's WTO Challenge to U.S. Cotton Subsidies" 2000 *Richmond Journal of Global Law and Business* 9(1) 135.

Anderson, K. and Norheim, H., "From Imperial to Regional Trade Preferences: Its Effect on Europe's Intra- and Extra-Regional Trade" 1993 *Review of World Economics* 129(1) 78.

Andreassen B. and Marks, S. (eds), "Development As a Human Right: Legal, Political, and Economic Dimensions," in *Harvard Series on Health and Human Rights* (London: Harvard University Press, 2006).

Anghie, A., "Colonialism and the Birth of International Institutions: Sovereignty, Economy, and the Mandate System of the League of Nations" 2002 *New York University Journal of International Law and Politics* 34(3) 513.

Anghie, A., *Imperialism, Sovereignty and the Making of International Law* (Cambridge: Cambridge University Press, 2004).

Apter, D., *Rethinking Development: Modernization, Dependency and Post-Modern Politics* (Thousand Oaks, CA: Sage Publications, Inc., 1987).

Arnold, H., "Africa and the New International Economic Order" 1980 *Third World Quarterly* 2(2) 295.

Atapattu, S., "Sustainable Development, Myth or Reality?: A Survey of Sustainable Development Under International Law and Sri Lankan Law" 2001 *Georgetown International Environmental Law Review* 14(2) 265.

Avramovic, D., *Economic Growth and External Debt* (Washington: Johns Hopkins University Press, 1965).

Bacchetta, M. and Drabek, Z., "Effects of WTO Accession on Policy-Making in Sovereign States: Preliminary Lessons From the Recent Experience of Transition Countries," WTO Development and Economic Research Division, Paper No DERD-2002-02 (April 2002).

Bagwell, K., Mavroidis, P.C., and Staiger, R.W., "The Case for Auctioning Countermeasures in the WTO," National Bureau of Economic Research Working Paper No 9920 (July 2003) <http://www.ssc.wisc.edu/econ/archive/wp2003-14.pdf>.

Baldwin, R., "The Case against Infant-Industry Tariff Protection" 1969 *The Journal of Political Economy* 77(3) 295.

Barro, R.J. and Lee, J., "IMF Programs: Who Is Chosen and What Are the Effects?" 2005 *Journal of Monetary Economics* 52(7) 1245.

Basra, H., "Caribbean States and the Politics of WTO Accession", 2008 Thesis, University of Manchester.

Bedjaoui, M., *Towards a New International Economic Order* (New York: Holmes & Meier, 1979).

Benvenisti, E. and Downs, G.W., "Distributive Politics and International Institutions: The Case of Drugs" 2004 *Case Western Reserve Journal of International Law* 36(1) 21.

Bethlehem, D., McRae, D., Neufeld, R. and Van Damme, I. (eds), *The Oxford Handbook of International Trade Law* (Oxford: Oxford University Press, 2003).

Bhagwati, J.N., *Development and Interdependence* (Cambridge: MIT Press, 1985).

Bhagwati, J.N. (ed), *Economics and World Order* (New York: Macmillan, 1972).

Bhagwati, J.N. and Srinivasan, T.N., *Foreign Trade Regimes and Economic Development: India* (New York: Columbia University Press, 1975).

Bhagwati, J.N. and Srinivasan, T.N., "The General Equilibrium Theory of Effective Protection and Resource Allocation" 1973 *Journal of International Economics* 3(3) 259.

Bhala, R., "Enter the Dragon: An Essay on China's WTO Accession Saga" 2000 *American University International Law Review* 15(6) 1469.

Bhala, R., "The Myth About Stare Decisis and International Trade Law" 1999 *American University International Law Review* 14(4) 846.

Bhala, R., "Theological Categories for Special and Differential Treatment" 2002 *Kansas Law Review* 50(4) 635.

Bjørnskov, C. and Lind, K.M., "Where do Developing Countries Go After Doha? An Analysis of WTO Positions and Potential Alliances" 2002 *Journal of World Trade* 36(3) 543.

Blake, R.C., "The World Bank's Draft Comprehensive Development Framework and the Micro Paradigm of Law and Development" 2000 *Yale Human Rights and Development Law Journal* 3(1) 158.

Blustein, P., *The Chastening: Inside the Crisis that Rocked the Global Financial System and Humbled the IMF* (New York: Public Affairs, 2001).

Bordo, M. and James, H., "The International Monetary Fund: Its Present Role in Historical Perspective," NBER Working Paper 7724, National Bureau of Economics, 2000.

Bouayad-Agha, F. and Hernández, H.L., *Comparison of Methods of Calculating Equitable Geographical Distribution Within the United Nations Common System*, JIU/REP/96/7 (21 August 1997).

Boutillon, S., "The Precautionary Principle: Development of an International Standard" 2002 *Michigan Journal of International Law* 23(2) 429.

Bown, C.P., "The World Trade Organization and Antidumping in Developing Countries," World Bank Policy Research Working Paper 4014 (September 2006).

Bown, C.P. and Hoekman, B.M., "Developing Countries and Enforcement of Trade Agreements: Why Dispute Settlement is Not Enough" 2008 *Journal of World Trade* 42(1) 177.

Bown, C.P. and Hoekman, B.M., "WTO Dispute Settlement and the Missing Developing Country Cases: Engaging the Private Sector" 2005 *Journal of International Economic Law* 8(4) 861.

Boyle, A., "Human Rights or Environmental Rights? A Reassessment" 2007 *Fordham Environmental Law Review* 18(3) 471.

Bradlow, D.D., "The World Bank, the IMF, and Human Rights" 1996 *Transnational Law & Contemporary Problems* 6(1) 47.

Braithwaite, J., "Methods of Power for Development: Weapons of the Weak, Weapons of the Strong" 2004 *Michigan Journal of International Law* 26(1) 297.

Bronckers, M. and van den Broek, N., "Financial Compensation in the WTO" 2005 *Journal of International Economic Law* 8(1) 101.

Broude, T., "Essays on the World Trade Organization: The Rule(s) of Trade and the Rhetos of Development: Reflections on the Functional and Aspirational Legitimacy of the WTO" 2006 *Columbia Journal of Transnational Law* 45(1) 221.

Brown, D.K., "Trade Preferences for Developing Countries: A Survey of Results" 1988 *Journal of Development Studies* 24(3) 335.

Bunn, I.D., "The Right to Development: Implications for International Economic Law" 2000 *American University International Law Review* 15(6) 1425.

Busch, M.L. and Reinhardt, E., "Developing Countries and General Agreement on Tariffs and Trade—World Trade Organization Dispute Settlement" 2003 *Journal of World Trade* 37(4) 719.

Carmody, C., "Remedies and Conformity Under the WTO Agreement" 2002 *Journal of International Economic Law* 5(2) 307.

Carrasco, E.R. and Kose, M.A., "Income Distribution and the Bretton Woods Institutions: Promoting an Enabling Environment for Social Development" 1996 *Transnational Law and Contemporary Problems* 6(1) 1.

Cazala, J., "L'invocation de l'estoppel dans le cadre de la procédure de règlement des différends de l'OMC" 2003 *Revue Générale de Droit International Public* 107(4) 885.

Chang, H.-J., *Kicking Away the Ladder—Development Strategy in Historical Perspective* (London: Anthem Press, 2002).

Charlton, A., "A Proposal for Special and Differential Treatment in the Doha Round," Working Paper for WTO SDT Working Group (2005) (on file with the author).

Charnovitz, S., "Triangulating the WTO" 2002 *American Journal of International Law* 96(1) 28.

Chimni, B.S., "Alternative Visions of Just World Order: Six Tales from India" 2005 *Harvard International Law Journal* 46(2) 389.

Chimni, B.S., "A Just World under Law: A View from the South" 2006 *American Society of International Law Proceedings* 100(1) 17.

Chimni, B.S., "Co-option and Resistance: Two faces of Global Administrative Law" 2005 *New York University Journal of International Law and Politics* 37(4) 799.

Chimni, B.S., *International Law and World Order: A Critique of Contemporary Approaches* (New Delhi: Sage Publications, 1993).

Chimni, B.S., "The World Trade Organization, Democracy and Development: A View from the South" 2006 *Journal of World Trade* 40(1) 5.

Cho, S., "Linkage of Free Trade and Social Regulation: Moving Beyond the Entropic Dilemma" 2005 *Chicago Journal of International Law* 5(2) 625.

Chua, A., "Markets, Democracy, and Ethnicity: Toward a New Paradigm for Law and Development" 1998 *Yale Law Journal* 108(1) 1.

CIA, *CIA World Factbook* <https://www.cia.gov/library/publications/the-world-factbook>.

Clark, D.L., "The World Bank and Human Rights: The Need for Greater Accountability" 2002 *Harvard Human Rights Journal* 15(1) 205.

Clark, J.M., *National and International Measures for Full Employment* (New York: United Nations Department of Economic Affairs, 1950).

Cogan, J.K., "Representation and Power in International Organizations: The Operational Constitution and its Critics" 2009 *American Journal of International Law* 103(1) 209.

Correa, C.M., "Bilateralism in Intellectual Property: Defeating the WTO System for Access to Medicines" 2004 *Case Western Reserve Journal of International Law* 36(1) 79.

Coutinho, D.R. and Mattos, P., *LANDS—Law and the New Developmental State (Brazilian pilot project)* (Madison, University of Wisconsin Law School, 2008) at <http://www.law.wisc.edu/gls/lands.html>.

Cox, R.W. and Jacobson, H.K., *The Anatomy of Influence: Decision Making in International Organizations* (New Haven: Yale University Press, 1973).

Crawford, J. and Espiell, H.G. (eds), *The Rights of Peoples* (Oxford, Oxford University Press, 1988).

Croome, J., *Reshaping the World Trading System: A History of the Uruguay Round* (Geneva: Kluwer Law International, 1995).

Crozier, A.J., *The Causes of the Second World War* (Oxford: Blackwell Publishers Ltd, 1997).

Della Valle, M., *Das Decisões por Eqüidade na Arbitragem Comercial Internacional* (São Paulo: Mimeo, 2008).

Demas, W., "The Caribbean and the New International Economic Order" 1978 *Journal of Interamerican Studies and World Affairs* 20(3) 229.

Denis, G., "Un régime de préférences tarifaires généralisées pour le tiers monde" 1971 *Etudes Internationales* 2(2) 231.

Dinwoodie, G.B., "The International Intellectual Property System: New Actors, New Institutions, New Sources" 2004 *American Society of International Law Proceedings* 98(1) 213.

Dollar, D. and Svensson, J., "What Explains the Success or Failure of Structural Adjustment Programmes?" 2000 *The Economic Journal* 110(446) 894.

Drahos, P., "Developing Countries and International Intellectual Property Standards-Setting" 2002 *Journal of World Intellectual Property* 5(5) 765.

Draper, P. and Sally, R., "Developing-Country Coalitions in Multilateral Trade Negotiations," Paper, Jawaharlal Nehru University (2004) <http://www.ppl.nl/bibliographies/wto/files/3071.pdf>.

Dunoff, J.L., "Is the World Trade Organization Fair to Developing States?" 2003 *American Society of International Law Proceedings* 97 153.

Dyal-Chand, R., "Reflection in a Distant Mirror: Why the West has Misperceived the Grameen Bank's Vision of Microcredit" 2005 *Stanford Journal of International Law* 41(2) 217.

Eglin, M., "China's Entry into the WTO with a Little Help from the EU" 1997 *International Affairs* 73(3) 489.

Eisen, J.B., "China's Renewable Energy Law: a platform for green leadership?" 2010 *William and Mary Law and Policy Review* 35(1) 1.

Elkins, Z., Guzman, A. and Simmons, B., "Competing for Capital: The Diffusion of Bilateral Investment Treaties, 1960–2000" 2008 *University of Illinois Law Review* 2008(1) 265.

Elsig, M., "Agency Theory and the WTO: Complex Agency and the 'Missing Delegation'?" (submitted to The Political Economy of International Organization Conference held 2 February 2008 through 8 February 2008, on file with the Center for Comparative and International Studies at <http://www.cis.ethz.ch/events/past_events/PEIO2008/Elsig_PAWTO>).

Emmerij, L. (ed), *Economic and Social Development into the XXI Century* (Washington: Johns Hopkins University Press, 1997).

Endres, A.M. and Fleming, G.A., *International Organizations and the Analysis of Economic Policy, 1919–1950* (Cambridge: Cambridge University Press, 2002).

Epstein, S.B., "GATT: The Uruguay Round Agreement and Developing Countries," Congressional Research Service Report <http://www.natlaw.com/pubs/gatt.htm>.

Espiell, H.G., "The Right of Development as a Human Right" 1981 *Texas International Law Journal* 16(2) 189.

Everett, S.J., "Preparing for WTO Accessions: Insights from Developing Countries," IRDC Research Project (22 January 2005).

Ewart, A.M., "Small Developing States in the WTO: A Procedural Approach to Special and Differential Treatment Through Reforms to Dispute Settlement" 2007 *Syracuse Journal of International Law and Commerce* 35(1) 27.

Ewelukwa, U., "Special and Differential Treatment in International Trade Law: A Concept in Search of Content" 2003 *North Dakota Law Review* 79(4) 831.

Ezeani, E.C., *The WTO and its Development Obligation* (London, New York: Anthem Press, 2010).

Faculté de droit de l'Université de Genève (ed), *Recueil d'études de droit international en hommage à Paul Guggenheim* (Geneva: Institut universitaire des hautes études internationales, 1968).

Fawcett, J.E.S., "The Legal Character of International Agreements" 1953 *British Yearbook of International Law* 30(1) 381.

Feuer, G., "Libéralisme, mondialisation et développement: à propos de quelques réalités ambiguës" 1999 *Annuaire Français du Droit International* 99 148.

Fiorentino, R.V., Verdeja, L. and Toqueboeuf, C., "The Changing Landscape of Regional Trade Agreements: 2006 Update," WTO Discussion Paper No 12 (Geneva: WTO, 2006) <http://www.wto.org/english/res_e/booksp_e/discussion_papers12a_e.pdf>.

Food and Agriculture Organization (FAO), "State of Agricultural Commodity Markets," (2004), <ftp://ftp.fao.org/docrep/fao/007/y5419e/y5419e00.pdf>.

Footer, M.E., *An Institutional and Normative Analysis of the World Trade Organization* (Leiden: Martinus Nijhoff, 2006).

Francois, J.F., McDonald, B., and Nordström, H., "The Uruguay Round: A Global General Equilibrium Assessment," CEPR Discussion Paper No 1067 (November 1994).

Frank, A., *Capitalism and Underdevelopment in Latin America: Historical Studies of Chile and Brazil* (New York: Monthly Review Press, 1967).

Gallego F. and Loayza, N., "Financial Structure in Chile: Macroeconomic Developments and Microeconomic Effects," *Econometric Society* (December 1999) <http://www.econometricsociety.org/meetings/wc00/pdf/1115.pdf>.

Garcia, F.J., "Beyond Special and Differential Treatment" 2004 *Boston College International and Comparative Law Review* 27(2) 291.

Garcia, F.J., "Is Free Trade 'Free?' Is it Even 'Trade?' Oppression and Consent in Hemispheric Trade Agreements" 2007 *Seattle Journal for Social Justice* 5(2) 505.

Garcia, F.J., *Trade, Inequality, and Justice: Toward a Liberal Theory of Just Trade* (Ardsley: Transnational Publishers, 2003).

Gathii, J., "Alternative and Critical: the Contribution of Research and Scholarship on Developing Countries to International Legal Theory" 2000 *Harvard International Law Journal* 41(2) 263.

Gathii, J., "Institutional Concerns of an Expanded Trade Regime: Where Should Global Social and Regulatory Policy Be Made? Re-characterizing the Social in the Constitutionalization of the WTO: A Preliminary Analysis" 2001 *Widener Law Symposium Journal* 7 137.

Gathii, J., "Patents, Markets and the Global Aids Pandemic" 2002 *Florida Journal of International Law* 14(2) 261.

Gerhart, P.M. and Kella, A.S., "Power and Preferences: Developing Countries and the Role of the WTO Appellate Body" 2005 *North Carolina Journal of International Law & Commercial Regulation* 30(3) 515.

Goldman Sachs Global Economics Group, *BRICs and Beyond* (2007), <http://www.goldmansachs.com/ideas/brics/BRICs-and-Beyond.html>.

Gosovic, B., *UNCTAD Conflict and Compromise—The Third World's Quest for an Equitable Economic Order through the United Nations*, (Leiden: A.W. Sijthoff, 1972).

Halverson, K., "China's WTO Accession: Economic, Legal, and Political Implications" 2004 *Boston College International and Comparative Law Review* 27(2) 319.

Harris, D.P., "The Honeymoon is Over: The US-China WTO Intellectual Property Complaint" 2008 *Fordham International Law Journal* 32(1) 96.

Harriss, J., Hunter, J., and Lewis, C.M. (eds), *The New Institutional Economics and Third World Development* (London: Routledge, 1995).

Hauserman, B., "Review Essay—Exploring the New Frontiers of Law & Development: Reflections on Trubek/Santos (eds), The New Law and Economic Development (2006)" 2007 *German Law Journal* 8(6) 533, at 547.

Hoda, A., *Tariff Negotiation and Renegotiation Under the GATT and the WTO: Procedures and Practices* (Cambridge: Cambridge University Press, 2001).

Hoda, A., and Verma, M., "Market Access Negotiations on Non-Agricultural Products: India and the Choice of Modalities," Working Paper 132, Indian Council for Research on International Economic Relations, 2004.

Hoekman, B.M., "Cancún: Crisis or Catharsis," Revised version of paper presented at Brookings-George Washington Roundtable on Trade and Investment Policy, Washington, DC, 23 September 2003 <http://siteresources.worldbank.org/INTRANETTRADE/Resources/Hoekman-CancunCatharsis-092003.pdf>.

Hoekman, B.M., "Operationalizing the Concept of Policy Space in the WTO: Beyond Special and Differential Treatment" 2005 *Journal of International Economic Law* 8(2) 405.

Hoekman, B.M. and Kostecki, M., *The Political Economy of the World Trading System: The WTO and Beyond* (2nd edn, New York: Oxford University Press, 2001).

Hoekman, B.M., Martin, W., and Braga, C. (eds), *Trade Preference Erosion: Measurement and Policy Response* (United Kingdom: Palgrave Macmillan, 2009).

Hoekman, B.M., Mattoo, A. and English, P. (eds), *Development, Trade and the WTO: A Handbook* (Washington, DC: The World Bank, 2002).

Horlick, G.N. and Mizulin, N., "Developing Countries and WTO Dispute Settlement" 2005 *Integration and Trade Journal* 23(1) 125.

Horn, H. and Mavroidis, P.M., "The WTO Dispute Settlement System 1995–2006: Some Descriptive Statistics" (14 March 2008) <http://siteresources.worldbank.org/INTRES/Resources/469232-1107449512766/DescriptiveStatistics_031408.pdf>.

Horowitz, D., *The Horowitz Proposal: A Plan for Financing the Economic Development of Developing Countries* (Washington: IBRD, 1965).

Hudec, R.E., "GATT and the Developing Countries" 1992 *Columbia Business Law Review* 67(1) 74.

Ierley, D., "Defining the Factors that Influence Developing Country Compliance with and Participation in the WTO Dispute Settlement System: Another Look at the Dispute Over Bananas" 2002 *Law and Policy in International Business* 33(2) 615.

Ikonicoff, M., "Sous-développement, tiers monde ou capitalisme périphérique" 1972 *Revue Tiers-Monde* 13(52) 691.

IMF and World Bank, *Market Access for Developing Countries' Exports* (27 April 2001) <http://www.imf.org/external/np/madc/eng/042701.pdf>.

Inama, S., "Trade Preferences and the World Trade Organization Negotiations on Market Access: Battling for Compensation of Erosion of GSP, ACP and other Trade Preferences or Assessing and Improving Their Utilization and Value by Addressing Rules of Origin and Graduation?" 2003 *Journal of World Trade* 37(5) 959.

Irwin, D.A., Mavroidis, P.C., and Sykes, A.O., *The Genesis of the GATT* (Cambridge: Cambridge University Press, 2008).

Ismail, F., "Mainstreaming Development in the World Trade Organization" 2005 *Journal of World Trade* 39(1) 11.

Ismail, F., "Rediscovering the Role of Developing Countries in GATT before the Doha Round" 2008 *Law and Development Review* 1(1) 13.

Jackson, J.H., "Process and Procedure in WTO Dispute Settlement" 2009 *Cornell International Law Journal* 42(2) 233.

Jackson, J.H., *Restructuring the GATT System* (New York: Council on Foreign Relations Press, 1990).

Jackson, J.H., *Sovereignty, The WTO, and Changing Fundamentals of International Law* (Cambridge: Cambridge University Press, 2006).

Jackson, J.H., *The World Trading System* (2nd edn, Cambridge: MIT Press, 1997).

Jones, K., *The Doha Blues* (Oxford: Oxford University Press, 2010).

Kaneko, Y., "Symposium: The Future of Law and Development, Part III—An Asian Perspective on Law and Development" 2009 *Northwestern University Law Review Colloquy* 104(November) 186.

Keck, A. and Low, P., "Special and Differential Treatment in the WTO: Why, When and How?" WTO Staff Working Paper ERSD-2004-03 (May 2004).

Kelsen, H., "Organization and Procedure of the Security Council of the United Nations" 1946 *Harvard Law Review* 59(7) 1087.

Kelsen, H., "The Principle of Sovereign Equality of States as a Basis for International Organization" 1944 *Yale Law Journal* 53(2) 207.

Kennedy, D.L.M. and Southwick, J.D. (eds), *The Political Economy of International Trade Law: Essays in Honor of Robert E. Hudec* (Cambridge: Cambridge University Press, 2002).

Keohane, R.O. and Nye, Jr., J.S., "Transgovernmental Relations and International Organizations" 1974 *World Politics* 27(1) 39.

Kingsbury, B., Krisch, N., and Stewart, R.B., "The Emergence of Global Administrative Law" 2005 *Law and Contemporary Problems* 68(1) 15.

Kiwanuka, R.N., "Developing Rights: The UN Declaration on the Right to Development" 1988 *Netherlands International Law Review* 35(3) 257.

Koehler, G., "The Future of STABEX," Issues Paper Prepared for the Summit of ACP Heads of State and Government (November 1997) <http://www.acpsec.org/summits/gabon/koehler.htm>.

Krasner, S.D. (ed), *International Regimes* (Ithaca: Cornell University Press, 1983).

Krueger, A.O., "Whither the World Bank and the IMF?" 1998 *Journal of Economic Literature* 36(4) 1983.

Krugman, P., "The Myth of Asia's Miracle" 1994 *Foreign Affairs* 73(6) 62.

Lang, A. and Scott, J., "The Hidden World of WTO Governance" 2009 *European Journal of International Law* 20(3) 575.

Langhammer, R.J. and Lücke, M., "WTO Accession Issues," Institut für Weltwirtschaft an der Universität Kiel, Kiel Working Paper No 905 (February 1999).

Lanoszka, A., "The Promises of Multilateralism and the Hazards of 'Single Undertaking': The Breakdown of Decision-Making within the WTO" 2007–2008 *Michigan State Journal of International Law* 16(3) 655.

Lauterpacht, E. (ed), *International Law: Being The Collected Papers of Hersch Lauterpacht, Vol 4: The Law of Peace* (Cambridge: Cambridge University Press, 2004).

Lee, Y.S., "Facilitating Development in the World Trading System—A Proposal for Development Facilitation Tariff and Development Facilitating Subsidy" 2004 *Journal of World Trade* 38(2) 935.

Lee, Y.S., *Reclaiming Development in the World Trading System* (Cambridge: Cambridge University Press, 2006).

Leebron, D.W., "Linkages" 2002 *American Journal of International Law* 96(1) 5.

Lewis, W.A., "The State of Development Theory" 1984 *American Economic Review* 74(1) 1.

Lewis, W.A., "World Trade Since the War" 1968 *Proceedings of the American Philosophical Society* 112(6) 363.

Lichtenbaum, P., "Procedural Issues in WTO Dispute Resolution" 1998 *Michigan Journal of International Law* 19(4) 1195.

Lothian, T., "The Democratized Market Economy in Latin America (and Elsewhere): An Exercise in Institutional Thinking within Law and Political Economy" 1995 *Cornell International Law Journal* 28(169) 176.

Low, P., "Developing Countries in the Multilateral Trading System: the Insights of Robert E. Hudec" 2003 *Journal of World Trade* 37(4) 719.

Low, P., *Trading Free: The GATT and the U.S. Trade Policy* (New York: Twentieth Century Foundation, 1993).

Low, P., Piermartini, R., and Richtering, J., "Non-Reciprocal Preference Erosion Arising From MFN Liberalization in Agriculture: What Are The Risks?" WTO Staff Working Paper, ERDS-2006-02 (March 2006).

Macrory, P. and Suchman, P. (eds), *Current Legal Aspects of International Trade Law* (Chicago: American Bar Association, 1982).

Maizels, A., "The Continuing Commodity Crisis of Developing Countries" 1994 *World Development* 22(11) 1685.

Marceau, G., "Conflicts of Norms and Conflicts of Jurisdiction—The Relationship Between the WTO Agreement and MEAs and Other Treaties" 2001 *Journal of World Trade* 35(6) 1081.

Marceau, G., "WTO Dispute Settlement and Human Rights" 2002 *European Journal of International Law* 13(4) 753.

Martin, W. and Winters, L.A., "The Uruguay Round and Developing Countries," World Bank Discussion Paper No 307 (1995).

Matsushita, M., Schoenbaum, T.J., and Mavroidis, P.C., *The World Trade Organization: Law, Practice, and Policy* (New York: Oxford University Press, 2003).

Mavroidis, P.C., *The General Agreement on Tariffs and Trade—A Commentary* (Oxford: Oxford University Press 2005).

Mavroidis, P.C., "No Outsourcing of Law? WTO Law as Practiced by WTO Courts" 2008 *American Journal of International Law* 102(3) 421.

M'Baye, K., "Le Droit au Développement comme un Droit de L'Homme" 1972 *Revue Des Droits de L'Homme* 5 503–4.

M'Bow, M.-A., "The Practice of Consensus in International Organizations" 1978 *International Social Science Journal* 30(4) 893.

Mercurio, B., "The WTO and its Institutional Impediments" 2007 *Melbourne Journal of International Law* 8(1) 198.

Merillat, C.L., "Law and Developing Countries" 1966 *American Journal of International Law* 60(1) 71.

Michalopoulos, C., *Developing Countries in the WTO* (New York: Palgrave, 2001).

Mitchell, A.D. and Wallis, J., "Pacific Pause: The Rhetoric of Special & Differential Treatment, The Reality of WTO Accession" 2010 *Wisconsin International Law Journal* 27(4) 663.

Narlikar, A., *International Trade and Developing Countries: Coalitions in the GATT and WTO* (New York: Routledge, 2003).

Njinkeu, D. and Cameron, H. (eds), *Aid for Trade and Development* (Cambridge: Cambridge University Press, 2008).

Nottage, H. and Sebastian, T., "Giving Legal Effect to the Results of WTO Trade Negotiations: An Analysis of the Methods of Changing WTO Law" 2006 *Journal of International Economic Law* 9(4) 989.

Nussbaum, M.C., *Women and Human Development: The Capabilities Approach* (Cambridge: Cambridge University Press, 2000).

Nwobike, J.C., "The WTO Compatible ACP-EU Trade Partnership: Interpreting Reciprocity to Further Development" 2008 *Asper Review of International Business and Trade Law* 8(1)87.

Ohnesorge, J.K.M., "Developing Development Theory: Law and Development Orthodoxies and the Northeast Asian Experience" 2007 *University of Pennsylvania Journal of International Economic Law* 28(2) 219.

Okediji, R.L., "Public Welfare and the Role of the WTO: Reconsidering the TRIPS Agreement" 2003 *Emory International Law Review* 17(2) 819.

Oloka-Onyango, J., "Beyond the Rhetoric: Reinvigorating the Struggle for Economic and Social Rights in Africa" 1995 *California Western International Law Journal* 26(1) 1.

O'Neal Taylor, C., "The U.S. Approach to Regionalism: Recent Past and Future" 2009 *ILSA Journal of International and Comparative Law* 15(2) 411.

Osieke, E., "Majority Voting Systems in the International Labour Organisation and the International Monetary Fund" 1984 *International and Comparative Law Quarterly* 33(2) 381.

Ostry, S., "Looking Back to Look Forward: The Multilateral Trading System after 50 Years," in WTO Secretariat (ed), *From GATT to the WTO: The Multilateral Trading System in the New Millennium* (The Hague: Kluwer Law International, 2000), at 101.

Pauwelyn, J., *Conflicts of Norms in Public International Law—How WTO Law Relates to Other Rules of International Law* (New York: Cambridge University Press, 2003).

Pauwelyn, J., "Enforcement and Countermeasures in the WTO: Rules are Rules—Toward a More Collective Approach" 2000 *American Journal of International Law* 94(2) 335.

Pauwelyn, J., "The Role of Public International Law in the WTO: How Far Can we Go" 2001 *American Journal of International Law* 95(3) 535.

Picker, C.B., "Neither Here Nor There—Countries That Are Neither Developing Nor Developed in the WTO: Geographic Differentiation as applied to Russia and the WTO" (2004) *George Washington International Law Review* 36(1) 147.

Prebisch, R., *Towards a New Trade Policy for Development: Report by the Secretary General of the United Nations Conference on Trade and Development,* E/CONF.4613 (1964).

Prowse, S., "The Role of International and National Agencies in Trade-Related Capacity Building" 2002 *World Economy* 25(9) 1235.

Qureshi, A.H., "Interpreting World Trade Organization Agreements for the Development Objective" 2003 *Journal of World Trade* 37(5) 847.

Rajagopal, B., *International Law from Below: Development, Social Movements and Third World Resistance* (Cambridge: Cambridge University Press, 2003).

Reitz, J.C., "Symposium: Export of the Rule of Law" 2003 *Transnational Law & Contemporary Problems* 13(2) 429.

Ricardo, D., "Ricardo on Population" 1988 *Population and Development Review* 14(2) 339.

Rich, R., "The Right to Development as an Emerging Human Right" 1983 *Virginia Journal of International Law* 23(2) 287.

Riker, W.H., "Implications from the Disequilibrium of Majority Rule for the Study of Institutions" 1980 *American Political Science Review* 74(2) 432.

Rittich, K., "The Future of Law and Development: Second Generation Reforms and the Incorporation of the Social" 2004 *Michigan Journal of International Law* 26(1) 199.

Robiquet, P. (ed), *Discours et Opinions de Jules Ferry* (Paris: Armand Colin & Cie, 1897). Trans. by Ruth Kleinman in Brooklyn College Core Four Sourcebook.

Rodrik, D., "How Should Structural Adjustment Programs Be Designed?" 1990 *World Development,* 18(7) 933.

Rodrik, D., "Rethinking Growth Policies in the Developing World," Luca d'Agliano Lecture in Development Economics, Torino, Italy (2004).

Rolland, S.E., "Developing Country Coalitions at the WTO: In Search of Legal Support" 2007 *Harvard International Law Journal* 48(2) 483.

Rolland, S.E., "Redesigning the Negotiation Process at the WTO" 2010 *Journal of International Economic Law* 13(1) 65.

Rosen, J.B., "China, Emerging Economies, and the World Trade Order" 1997 *Duke Law Journal* 46(6) 1519.

Rothstein, R.L., *Global Bargaining: UNCTAD and the Quest for a New International Economic Order* (Princeton: Princeton University Press, 1979).

Sacerdoti, G., Yanovich, A., and Bohanes, J. (eds), *The WTO at Ten: The Contribution of the Dispute Settlement System* (Cambridge: Cambridge University Press, 2006).

Sachs, J., "International Economics: Unlocking the Mysteries of Globalization" 1998 *Foreign Policy* 110 (spring) 97.

Sachs, J., "The Global Innovation Divide" in *Innovation Policy and the Economy, Vol 3* (Chicago: University of Chicago Press, 2003).

Salazar-Xirinachs, J.M., "The Trade-Labor Nexus: Developing Countries' Perspectives" 2000 *Journal of International Economic Law* 3(2) 377.

Sauvé, P., "Economic Impact and Social Adjustment Costs of Accession to the World Trade Organization: Cambodia and Nepal" 2005 *Asia-Pacific Trade & Investment* 1(1) 27.

Savoie, B., "Thailand's Test: Compulsory Licensing in an Era of Epidemiologic Transition" 2007 *Virginia Journal of International Law* 48(1) 211.

Schachter, O., *International Law in Theory and Practice* (The Hague, Netherlands: Kluwer Academic Publishers, 1991).

Schachter, O., and Joyner, C. (eds), *United Nations Legal Order* (Cambridge: Cambridge University Press, 1995).

Schnepf, R., "Brazil's WTO Case Against the U.S. Cotton Program: A Brief Overview," Congressional Research Service Report for Congress No RS22187 (17 March 2009) <http://www.nationalaglawcenter.org/assets/crs/RS22187.pdf>.

Seidman, A. and Seidman, R.B., *State and Law in the Development Process* (New York: St. Martin's Press, 1994).

Sen, A.K., *Development as Freedom* (New York: First Anchor Books Edition, 2000).

Serrano, K., "The Trade-Development Nexus in EU-Pacific Relations: Realism, Dependence or Interdependence?" 2011 *Global Change, Peace & Security* 23(1) 89.

Shaffer, G., "How to Make the WTO Dispute Settlement System Work for Developing Countries: Some Proactive Developing Country Strategies" ICTSD Resource Paper No 5 (March 2003), at 1 <http://ictsd.org/downloads/2008/06/dsu_2003.pdf>.

Shaffer, G. and Meléndez-Ortiz, R. (eds), *Dispute Settlement at the WTO—The Developing Country Experience* (Cambridge: Cambridge University Press, 2010).

Shaffer, G., Mosoti, V., and Qureshi, A. (eds), *Toward a Development-Supportive Dispute Settlement System in the WTO* (ICTSD Resource Paper No 5, 2003).

Shepsle, K.A. and Weingast, B.R., "Structure-Induced Equilibrium and Legislative Choice" 1981 *Public Choice* 37(3) 503.

Shihata, I.F.I., "Human Rights, Development, and International Financial Institutions" 1992 *American University Journal of International Law and Policy* 8(1) 27.

Shoyer, A.W. and Solovy, E.M., "Operation of the Appellate Process and Functions, Including the Appellate Body: The Process and Procedure of Litigating at the World Trade Organization: A Review of the Work of the Appellate Body" 2000 *Law and Policy International Business* 31(3) 677.

Singer, H.W., "The New International Economic Order: An Overview" 1978 *The Journal of Modern African Studies* 16(4) 539.

Slaughter, A.-M., "Global Government Networks, Global Information Agencies, and Disaggregated Democracy" 2003 *Michigan Journal of International Law* 24(4) 1041.

Sohn, L.B., "The New International Law: Protection of the Rights of Individuals Rather than States" 1982 *American University Law Review* 32(1) 1.

Sornarajah, M., "Power and Justice in Foreign Investment Arbitration" 1997 *Journal of International Arbitration* 14(3) 103.

Srinivasan, T.N., *Developing Countries and the Multilateral Trading System—From the GATT to the Uruguay Round and the Future* (Boulder: Westview Press, 1998).

Stein, J.G. (ed), *Getting to the Table* (Baltimore: Johns Hopkins University Press, 1989).

Steinberg, J. and Mazarr, M., *Developing Country Participation in Transnational Decision-making: Lessons for IT Governance* (2003) unpublished manuscript.

Steinberg, R.H., "In the Shadow of Law or Power? Consensus-Based Bargaining and Outcomes in the GATT/WTO" 2002 *International Organization* 56(2) 339.

Stiglitz, J., "Capital Market Liberalization and Exchange Rate Regimes: Risk without Reward" 2002 *Annals of the American Academy of Political and Social Science* 579 219.

Stiglitz, J. and Charlton, A., *Fair Trade For All: How Trade Can Promote Development* (Oxford: Oxford University Press, 2005).

Stokke H. and Toslensen A. (eds), *Human Rights in Development Yearbook 1998: Global Perspectives and Local Issues* (The Hague, Netherlands: Kluwer Law International, 1998).

Sutherland, P., Bhagwati, J., Botchwey, K., FitzGerald, N., Hamada, K., Jackson, J.H., Lafer, C., and de Montbrial, T., "The Future of the WTO" <http://www.wto.org/english/res_e/publications_e/future_wto_e.htm>.

Swineheart, N. and Swineheart T. (eds), *Human Rights in Developing Countries: Yearbook 1989* (The Hague: Kluwer Law International, 1990).

Tamanaha, B.Z., "Review: The Lessons of Law-and-Development Studies" 1995 *American Journal of International Law* 89(2) 470.

Taxil, B., *L'OMC et les pays en developpement* (Paris: Montchrestien, 1998).

Thakur, R. (ed), *What is Equitable Geographic Representation in the Twenty-first Century* (Tokyo: United Nations University, 1999).

Thelen, C., "Carrots and Sticks: Evaluating the Tools for Securing Successful TRIPs Implementation" 2005 *Temple Journal of Science, Technology and Environmental Law* 24(2) 519.

Third World Foundation Selection Committee, "Third World Prize 1980" 1981 *Third World Quarterly* 3(1).

Tobin, J. and Rose-Ackerman, S., "Foreign Direct Investment and the Business Environment in Developing Countries: The Impact of Bilateral Investment Treaties," Research Paper No 293, Yale Law School, Center for Law, Economics and Public Policy, 2005.

Tortora, M., "Special and Differential Treatment and Development Issues in the Multilateral Trade Negotiations: The Skeleton in the Closet," UNCTAD WEB/CDP/BKGD/16 (January 2003).

Trachtman, J.P., "Building the WTO Cathedral" 2007 *Stanford Journal of International Law* 43(1) 127.

Trachtman, J.P., "Legal Aspects of a Poverty Agenda at the WTO: Trade Law and 'Global Apartheid'" 2003 *Journal of International Economic Law* 6(1) 3.

Trubek, D.M., "Developmental States and the Legal Order: Towards a New Political Economy of Development and Law," Legal Studies Research Paper No 1075, University of Wisconsin Law School, Madison, 2009.

Trubek, D.M., "The Political Economy of the Rule of Law: The Challenge of the New Developmental State" 2009 *Hague Journal on the Rule of Law* 1(1) 28.

Trubek, D.M., "Toward a Social Theory of Law: An Essay on the Study of Law and Development" 1972 *Yale Law Journal* 82(1) 1.

Trubek, D.M. and Galanter, M., "Scholars in Self-Estrangement: Some Reflections on the Crisis in Law and Development Studies" 1974 *Wisconsin Law Review* 1974(4) 1062.

Tumbarello, P., "Are Regional Trade Agreements in Asia Stumbling or Building Blocks? Implications for the Mekong-3 Countries," IMF Working Paper No WP/07/53 (March 2007), at 15 <http://www.imf.org/external/pubs/ft/wp/2007/wp0753.pdf>.

United Nations Economic and Social Commission for Asia and the Pacific, *Accession to the WTO: Issues and Recommendations for Central Asian and Caucasian Economies in Transition*, Studies in Trade and Investment No 48, ST/ESCAP/2160 (2001).

United Nations Economic and Social Commission for Asia and the Pacific, *Facilitating the Accession of ESCAP Countries to the WTO Through Regional Cooperation*, Studies in Trade and Investment No 49, ST/ESCAP/2215 (2002).

Verdirame, G., "The Definition of Developing Countries under GATT and Other International Law" 1996 *German Yearbook of International Law* 39 164.

Viner, J., *The Customs Union Issue* (New York: The Carnegie Endowment for International Peace, 1950).

Wallerstein, I., "Dependence in an Interdependent World: The Limited Possibilities of Transformation within the Capitalist World Economy" 1974 *African Studies Review* 17(1) 1.

Wang, Z.K. and Winters, L.A., "Putting 'Humpty' Together Again: Including Developing Countries in a Consensus for the WTO," CEPR Policy Paper No 4 (6 April 2000).

Warwick Commission, "The Multilateral Trade Regime: Which Way Forward?" <http://www2.warwick.ac.uk/research/warwickcommission/worldtrade/report/uw_warcomm_tradereport_07.pdf>.

Whalley, J., "Non-Discriminatory Discrimination: Special and Differential Treatment under the GATT for Developing Countries" 1990 *Economic Journal* 100(403) 1318.

Williamson, J., "What Washington Means by Policy Reform," in J Williamson (ed), *Latin American Adjustment: How Much Has Happened?* (Washington: Institute for International Economics, 1990), at 445.

Winham, G.R., *An Institutional Theory of WTO Decision-Making: Why Negotiation in the WTO Resembles Law-Making in the U.S. Congress* (Toronto: Munk Centre for International Studies, 2006).

Wolfe, R., "Arguing and Bargaining in the WTO: Does the Single Undertaking Make a Difference?" (Prepared for the Canadian Political Science Association held 4–6 June 2008, on file at <http://www.cpsa-acsp.ca/papers-2008/Wolfe.pdf>).

World Bank, *The East Asian Miracle: Economic Growth and Public Policy* (New York: Oxford University Press, 1993).

World Bank, *World Bank Support for Developing Countries on International Trade Issues*, DC/99-19 (14 September 1999).

World Trade Organization, *A Handbook on Accession to the WTO* (Cambridge: Cambridge University Press, 2008).

Zamora, S., "Voting in International Economic Organizations" 1980 *American Journal of International Law* 74 (3) 566.

Zang, D., "From Environment to Energy: China's Reconceptualization of Climate Change" 2009 *Wisconsin International Law Journal* 27(3) 543.

Zartman, I.W. (ed), *International Multilateral Negotiation: Approaches to the Management of Complexity* (San Francisco: Jossey-Bass, 1994).

Zeiler, T.W., *Free Trade, Free World—The Advent of GATT* (Raleigh: University of North Carolina Press, 1999).

PRESS ARTICLES

"African Countries Complained Friday," *Xinhua General News Service* (4 December 1999).

"EU Offers Out of WTO Settlement on Drug Seizure Row" (published online 1 December 2010) <http://www.business-standard.com/india/news/eu-offers-outwto-settlementdrug-seizure-row/117841/on>.

"In the Twilight of Doha," *The Economist* (29 July 2006), at 63–4.

"OMC: le Brésil et l'Inde rompent les négociations avec les Etats-Unis et l'UE," *Le Monde* (with AFP and Reuters) (21 June 2007).

"WTO Powers Fail to Revive Trade Talks," *Associated Press* (27 January 2007).

ASEAN, "Joint Media Statement of the Sixth AEM-India Consultations Singapore" (28 August 2008) <http://www.asean.org/21895.htm>.

ASEAN Secretariat, "ASEAN Secretariat Enters into Cooperation Agreement with Guangdong Province, China" (5 September 2008) <http://www.asean.org/21942.htm>.

BBC News, "Timeline—World Trade Organization" <http://news.bbc.co.uk/2/hi/europe/country_profiles/2430089.stm>.

Beattie, A., "Lamy snubs Mandelson on call to rescue parts of agenda," *Financial Times* (27 July 2006).

Burgess, J., "Green Room's Closed Doors Couldn't Hide Disagreements," *Washington Post* (5 December 1999).

Dowd, M., "The 1992 Campaign: Campaign Memo; Voters Want Candidates To Take a Reality Check," *The New York Times* (17 February 1992).

Khor, M., "WTO Services Talks Caught in Webs of 'Horizontal Process' and Blame Game" (10 March 2008) Third World Network <http://www.twnside.org.sg/title2/wto.info/twninfo20080309.htm>.

Lamy, P., "Time Out Needed to Review Options and Positions" (Speech delivered on 24 July 2007) <http://www.wto.org>.

Mitchell, R., "Intellectual Property: Japan Trade Official Suggests ACTA Should Serve as Model for WTO Rules" 2011 *International Trade Reporter* 28 575.

Morrison, A.V., "GATT's Seven Rounds of Trade Talks Span More Than Thirty Years—General Agreement on Tariffs and Trade," *Business America* (7 July 1986).

Osnos, E., "Green Giant: Beijing's Crash Program for Green Energy," *The New Yorker* (21 December 2009), 54.

Pani, N., "Seattle Fails to Find Common Ground for Fresh Talks," *Economic Times of India* (5 December 1999).

Third World Network, "Concerns Voiced at TRIPS Council Over Seizure of Drugs," (published online 11 June 2009) <http://www.twnside.org.sg/title2/wto.info/2009/twninfo20090611.htm>.

Williams, F., "US backs new approach to Doha negotiations," *Financial Times* (13 May 2009) at <http://www.ft.com>.

WTO Press Release "Statement by P. Lamy to the Trade Negotiations Committee" (24 July 2008) <http://www.wto.org/english/news_e/news09_e/tnc_dg_stat_24jul09_e.htm>.

WTO Press Release, "Supachai: Sluggish Trade Growth Calls for Urgent Pick Up of Stalled Trade Talks" Press/363 (5 November 2003).

Yongtu, L., Vice Minister and Head of the Chinese Delegation, Address at the Eleventh Session of the Working Party on China (27 July 2000) <http://www.fmprc.gov.cn/ce/cegv/eng/gjhyfy/hy2000/t85629.htm>.

Index